And the Devil Shivered…

A Year In My Life

Dustin J. Pari

Cover Design by Jeff Ouimette

ISBN 978-1519217080

DEDICATION

This one is for my Uncle Bub. He was the first person to ever inspire me to put pen to paper and chronicle my thoughts and dreams. He also told me life was simpler when there were only three kinds of beer. Here's to you.

CONTENTS

A NOTE FROM THE EDITOR

Full disclosure time. I didn't think we'd be here again so quickly but this is a perfect example of the way Dustin's mind works. He's never satisfied with mediocre or doing just enough to skirt by like other people do. The second he finishes one project, he's on to the next one. If he's not busy trying to touch a life or encourage a lost soul, then he believes he's not doing enough. For that reason, Dustin has been my only author client for more than a year because he works so fast.

There's a lesson to be drawn from a strong work ethic. Dustin isn't one to churn out book after book for the sake of seeing his name in print. Anyone who has written a book knows it's a lot of work for a few months of glory before readers move on to the next big thing. On the contrary, people like Dustin write these motivational books because their lives have led them to the point of needing to pass on life lessons or burst.

As an editor, it can be difficult to keep up with a mind built that way, especially when the book in question is done in the style of a journal. That's exactly what you'll find in these pages. Dustin kept a journal almost every day for a year, allowing his audience to see the man behind the curtain, as he likes to say. Parts of it might surprise you. He was transparent in ways that he hasn't been before, which sometimes led to long phone calls between author and editor about whether such honesty was wise. A man willing to expose his struggles and insecurities, I'd tell him, will touch more lives in the end. People want to feel like they're not alone.

When you read this book, my hope as Dustin's editor is that you feel motivated by the universal truth that struggling strengthens the soul. Dustin is, in fact, one of the strongest souls I know. He'll show you the way.

Jessica Jewett
October 20, 2015

FOREWORD

I've always been a comic book kid. Strange throwaway tomes of startling powered beings and haunted locations were my entrance into the world of the supernatural. More than 25 years ago I stood in front of a crowd of strangers and gave my first "weird lecture". There were perhaps fourteen people in attendance and due to the lecture occurring during the winter, in Detroit, I'm pretty sure ten of those people were just trying to get inside and get out of the cold. I told my stories, gesticulated wildly, and expounded ideas and theories which, I thought, were little insights to the wider and weirder reality which we seem to share with one another. When I was done I listened as others told me their stories. That was where I truly began to understand that listening and learning about my earthly extended family was going to teach me unending lessons about my infinitely larger ethereal other-worldly family. Yes, I love a good ghost story and I do indeed still have bookshelves filled with comic books and science fiction, but those works are vastly outnumbered by non-fiction, biographies, and poetry. People and their lives teach us not just about what they have experienced but who we are; and they provide us with unending insights into our own involvement with the world.

Years ago when I met Dustin, we sat and chatted like old friends. We didn't talk about ghosts or haunted locations. We talked about our lives and the paths that led us to a hotel bar in Chicago where people asked us to sign our names on photos of ourselves because we explored the world of ghosts. Also, let me tell you as honestly as possible, signing your name on a photo of yourself is stranger than investigating ghosts. We chatted and laughed, exchanged stories and toasted each other and before I knew it I had found a long lost brother. When we parted we knew it was not the "sweet sorrow" people speak of but it was more of the "happy nonsense" that the universe will often throw at you.

As predicted by the two of us that night, we continued to be friends.

As a person who questions the nature of life and death, as someone who has spent my adult life reaching out to some questionable, untouchable netherworld, I find a certain amount of comfort in knowing that there are others out there who don't get caught up in the darkness which can surround such mental quests. Dustin is an example of the fortitude and persistence of positivity in a world which many times seems surrounded by purveyors of fright and negativity. We are who we are with all our seemingly endless faults and flaws. The knowledge that those stumbling blocks which appear in our lives are actually stepping stones is that which Dustin repeatedly shows to us.

Reading the following book exposes the world we all share; a world of weirdness, love, music, nostalgia, questioning, and perseverance. It reveals a world weirder than the one allegedly populated by ghosts and spirits. A world where a man's family and friends can be a team of superheroes, where music can be his magic castle, where this seemingly normal man can change people's lives for the better while flying through the skies above us. The world of paranormal phenomena is never-endingly interesting. Science fiction is fun and transports us to imagined worlds of high-strangeness. The reality of our situation is that we have superheroes all around us ... and this is a small part of the story of one of them.

His name is Dustin and I'm overwhelmed with pride and love to call him my friend.

Look, up in the sky
It's a bird.
It's a plane....

John E.L. Tenney

AUTUMN
SEPTEMBER - NOVEMBER

Wednesday, September 3, 2014

Well, isn't this a splendid little undertaking? I'm going to write every day for an entire year. Yikes. Talk about commitment. Hopefully between now and the time I finish this little literary misadventure, I'll still be above the dirt, looking to the heavens and not committed to an institution somewhere looking out of the narrow windows at the clouds and thinking about yesterday. But, then again, there are worse fates. I think they provide pudding in those institutions.

Just so I'm being honest, this book has no direct purpose but I bet it has a lesson in here somewhere, so keep on reading. My plan is to write something every day, like a journal. Some days I fancy I shall write more than others. There will neither be rhyme nor reason, but there may be some rhymes and the good Lord knows I have my reasons. The bad guy downstairs does, too.

You see, I'm a philosopher and a dreamer. I'm a cloud artist and a master of many things but none of which matter much in the current ways of the world. In another time, I might have been well regarded, but then again, probably not.

"Shotgun Willie sits around in his underwear, biting on a bullet, and pulling out all of his hair." That soulful lyric was penned by one of the most beautiful gypsy bastards who ever traversed this great land, Mr. Willie Nelson. He's currently playing his guitar in my mind as I fly the friendly skies from Lexington, Kentucky, to the city of brotherly love, Philadelphia. Many lyrics will be referenced in this literary effort, as in all of my misadventures. I communicate best through music. For the full experience, I strongly suggest doing a quick internet search for whichever song may be referenced at the time and play those songs while you read. It'll make for a nice backdrop to the story at hand and it'll be like we're listening together.

At the moment, I'm aboard U.S. Airways flight 3877 in seat 3D, an aisle seat, albeit a narrow one that hugs my buttocks like a lover in the throes of passion, or at least one who used to do such things. The young lady in 3F next to me (yes, 3F there is no 3E. I don't know why)—she's fast asleep with her own blanket, pillow, and teddy bear. She looks like she's about 33—the same age Christ was when they hung him on the tree and made him a star, yet Christ had no pillow, blanket, or teddy bear for comfort. He only had a crown of thorns as thanks all the horrible things we'd do for years to come. Thank you, Jesus. When I get up to heaven, I'd like to buy you a sarsaparilla and toast to unconditional love, grace, and forgiveness. I love you.

I'm flying home via Philadelphia to Rhode Island after filming for two days at the Wild Turkey distillery for that ole ghost show, *Ghost Hunters*. We're currently filming season ten. I haven't been on all ten seasons, though. I come and I go but not as much as I like to, if you get my meaning. Yes, I'm a dirty sinful bastard sometimes but it's all in fun. I like to joke and I'm sucker for puns, especially bad ones.

I've been travelling a lot again lately. I haven't filmed for television in about four or five years after quitting the *Ghost Hunters International* program. I can't commit to television projects. I do a year or two here and there. I quit. I resurface. I quit again. I come back to dance one last time.

Andy Kaufman, genius or madman—there's really little difference—kept his job as a busboy when he was filming *Taxi*. In many ways, I feel like Mr. Kaufman. I'm also a little mad and often performing for the amusement for the live studio audience in my mind. They are there. I know they are. They sit just off to the side, behind the cameras, behind the eggnog river, the dancing elves, the peppermint dam and Jolly Good Times, the pirate-themed bar we just built last year. It's a great place to hang out and I picnic there often. It's loads of fun, especially when the elves start skinny-dipping in the eggnog river. Join me there sometime. Tell the gorilla at the door that D. Pari sent you.

So, whilst filming, I've always held down a day job, originally as an EMT and Operations Director for an ambulance company and later an anesthesia technician for an oral and facial surgery clinic. At the moment, I serve as the practice manager for that surgical gig, on top of *Ghost Hunters*, and I do motivational lectures, college lectures on the paranormal, as well as events, conventions, and Christian lectures of faith and salvation. Yes sir, or madam, or both, I'm one beautiful bastard out here on the front lines, fighting misery with my own special blend of happy nonsense and defiance.

The days to come should prove interesting. I don't have much time off, as you will see. We're booked pretty much through Thanksgiving shooting one place or another and sometimes two places in one day. Who says you can't be in two places at once?! Charlatans, fools, liars, and lazy asses who only put down the cheese balls and get off the couch to go to Wal-Mart to get more cheese balls. Don't believe the naysayers. You're capable of much more than you give yourself credit for! Few of us know exactly what we can do because we're afraid to push our limits. No one drives their truck until it runs out of fuel because we get nervous when that little light on the dashboard illuminates our dark and scary world. I've disconnected that light in my mind and I'm driving to the ends of the earth and back. Try and stop me, bitches!

"It's so damn easy to say that life's so hard. Everybody's got their share of battle scars...." These are the words Willie Nelson is whispering to the gypsy in my soul right now, and he is so right. I'm alive and well and that's good enough for me.

You'll notice I jump around a lot. There's nothing wrong with that unless you can't keep up—in which case, there's something wrong with you, not me. I'm alive and well. We just covered that. Pay attention.

Music is interlaced with my very essence. Since I was a wee lad kicking my feet in the brown vinyl car seat in the back of my mom's Chevy Nova, music and I have been a notorious tag team. I swear to this day Mom tied a bagel to a string and tacked it to the ceiling of the car, but she insists she tied it to the bar of my car seat so I could fish it back up if I dropped it. But Mom is getting older and thus her memory is subject to the things age does to memories, so I win. Why she made me reach and perform for those bagels like a trained seal, I'll never know. But I do remember listening to two songs and screaming along like a happy little moron to them both. Barry Manilow's "Copa Cabana" and John Lennon's "Days Like These" were the first songs entered into the ever-expanding jukebox in my mind. It's been a very eclectic mix since then. Currently I'm adding to my classic country catalogue with additions offered by Willie, Waylon, and David Allan Coe. I love outlaws. I fancy myself a regular Billy the Kid without any of the killing.

Anyhow, as I mentioned somewhere few paragraphs back, in recent weeks I have been working the day job and filming for that ole ghost show by night.

A normal day goes a little something like this. Are you ready?

- 6am—Get up. Thank the Lord. Curse the devil. Brush my teeth- Go to the gym.
- 7:45am—Shower at the gym, and no, I don't care if the other guy in the showers is usually a gay gentleman. I have love and respect for all of God's creations equally. Plus, I have nothing to hide—go ahead and take a long, hard gander. Not that I think gay men are always out and on the prowl. Nor do I think I'm so remarkably attractive. I simply fancy myself to be a legend in my own pants... err ... mind.

- 8:00am—Drive to the medical practice. Sit in traffic. Listen to James Brown. Make pictures out of the clouds. Smile.
- 8:30am—Work.
- 12pm—Picnic in my mind.
- 12:30pm—Work.
- 4:30pm—Leave work and drive to wherever we are filming. Lately it's been Vermont, Massachusetts, and Connecticut.
- 6:30/7:00pm—Start filming with that ole ghost show.
- 3:30am—Finish filming. Travel to the hotel.
- 4am—Pass out form exhaustion face-first into the forgiving pillow of the hotel bed.
- 5:30/6am—Get up and do it again.

If I'm lying I'm buying. And I've only promised Jesus a sarsaparilla, so the rest of you beautiful bastards are on your own.

Last weekend I did a motivational event in Pittsburgh, Pennsylvania. Then I flew to Kentucky, and now I'm here with you—and the flight attendant is making me shut off my computer as we are landing in Philly. Be right back.

And we now resume our regularly scheduled program.

Here I'm in Philadelphia once again, fresh from a visit to the restroom. Don't judge me. It was a quick flight and they never shut off the seatbelt sign. Like my animated friend Sally Brown from *Peanuts*, I wouldn't want to be accused of taking part in a rumble, so I stayed in my seat.

Speaking of staying in my seat, the damned automatic flusher wouldn't allow me due time to process what needed processing in the men's room. I was sitting peacefully upon my toilet paper nest and *bawoosh*! It flushed not once, not twice, but three times! How is a fellow supposed to make bears in peace with such robotic nonsense? This artificial intelligence thing is going too far. They should have stopped just before automatic toilets. I'll flush when I'm done, thank you kindly. No wonder people have become so lazy. Soon there will be a model that wipes your bucket for you. Won't that be an unpleasant surprise when you are halfway through your dirty business and that cold, unfeeling robot claw presents itself in your hindquarters? No thank you.

Now most people, upon arriving in Philadelphia for a stopover, rush over to see where their next flight is boarding. Not me. I go right to Chick-fil-A. There will be plenty of planes, and if I miss this one, there will be another, but mama's baby boy needs his Chick-fil-A.

So here I sit, eating my delicious treat and writing for you. Aren't you special?

The world needs more smiling. I'm watching the people shuffle by whilst listening to Leon Redbone sing sweetly into my ears through my Jack Skellington earbuds because I'm a fancy boy. I'm smiling. People probably think I'm a little bit off. They might be right but let's keep that between us. I don't want to confirm any suspicions. I smile a lot. I like it. I like to see how others respond, too. Some really don't know what to do. Others eke out a grin of sorts that makes them look a bit gassy, like a constipated baby. Few will return with a full set of pearly whites. But no matter, I smile anyhow.

Oh wait … a scene is developing here.

It appears a gent has been shorted some noodles by the Far East Restaurant here at the airport's food court. He should have gone to Chick-fil-A. Lesson learned.

Well, methinks it's good time for a wander. This airport offers much in the way of sport and entertainment if one knows where to look. There are exercise bikes scattered throughout the place, for example. Ride them all. There's a shuttle tram of sorts that can take you to Terminal F. I suggest riding it. It's akin to a ride at a really bad town fair. Then you might finish off your day with a mojito at the sushi bar.

Hmm … good idea. Don't mind if I do.

I fully defend this decision as I do all my decisions. A mojito is a manly drink if had by a manly man. It's made with rum, you know. Rum is the drink of pirates. I'll have you know we serve mojitos with little jolly roger flags in them at Jolly Good Times (the pirate-themed bar in my mind) just on the shore of the mighty Eggnog River. We should get a paddleboat like they had on the mighty Mississip'. I'll have the elves look into it.

To the sushi bar!

Well kids, here we are again, back in the air. I find I write best up here. It's also the only place I enjoy drinking tomato juice for some odd reason. I'm like an in-flight vampire streaking across the skies of the world. Well, not really streaking, I'm wearing pants … but I wish I wasn't. I'm not a nudist but I feel bad that parts of me don't get to see daylight very often. 'Tis good to let the sun shine upon your naughty bits from time to time.

Now I'm aboard U.S. Airways flight 3316 headed from Philadelphia to Providence. The airplane actually lands in Warwick, Rhode Island, but no one seems to pay it any mind. We land, the passengers clap, get off of the plane, and bitch about their baggage anyway.

I never understood why some people clap for the pilots when the airplane lands. Don't get me wrong. I appreciate the safe passage and all, but no one claps for the bus or the taxi driver and those guys don't have autopilot; they have to drive the whole way with lots of traffic! You normally don't even see another plane when you're navigating through the air—at least the passengers don't. Nor do you see aliens, but here I sit in 11F looking out the window for them anyway. I'm not expecting to see the mother ship, but I would like to see something. Some *thing*.

"There's something on the wing! Some! *Thing*!" Wasn't William Shatner in *The Twilight Zone* the greatest?

Funny enough, I asked Mr. Shatner to breakfast just yesterday. He couldn't make it due to travel commitments, but he was kind enough to pop over a reply. We aren't really that close but we did meet at DragonCon in Atlanta a few years ago and we have since communicated via Twitter fairly often. Perhaps I didn't get to have breakfast with the legend, but how many other people can truly say they asked him and garnered a response? It would be a feather in my cap, if I chose to wear one.

We'll be on the ground shortly. It's not a long flight to Rhode Island, nor is it a big state. I'm looking forward to seeing my wife and our daughter when I land. Today was the little one's first day of second grade. She wore a cute little outfit that had matching fingerless gloves. My wife sent me pictures this morning. Our little girl gets her style from me and she strikes her poses like me but she looks just like Mama Bear, which is a good thing for her. I like to think I make a handsome man but I fear my looks would not be so charming if I had lady parts.

Play us out Leon Redbone! The theme from *Mr. Belvedere*? Good choice ole boy! Cheerio!

"Streaks on the china never mattered before. Who cares? When you dropkicked your jacket as you came through the door, no one glared."

Thursday, September 4, 2014

"Some days are diamonds. Some days are stones. But all of them rock."

That was my own twist on a phrase in an old song made popular by John Denver. I wrote it back after I graduated high school, give or take a few years, back when I thought I was cleverer than I am. Or when I was cleverer than I thought. I still need to think about it. There is truth in it.

I returned to work today after what seemed like a week on the road. I actually left the gym this morning around 7am thinking it was Monday but it's actually Thursday. That is a good thing as the week's almost over. I have to fly out to Michigan for an event on Saturday though, so I suppose my weeks never end.

Work was good. Things were done. I couldn't quite find my flow today, though. That may be a common thing for some people but it only happens about once a year. I'm glad it's behind me.

I'm lying here in bed next to my little wife. I call her that, not to be demeaning, but because she stands 4'10". She's my little wife in the most literal way.

Lying in bed gets me thinking about random things, like how I hung around with a kid named Michael Connelly when I was a child. He was a few years younger than I. Michael had an older brother named Bobby who looked like a white Mike Tyson. No one messed with him. He told me what I felt were wise words for a boy of eleven-years-old to hear: "Short girls do it better." And thus, my pursuit of ladies 5'2" and under began. I can't say he was wrong, and so I married the shortest one I could find.

Mama Bear, as I call her, is watching *Pawn Stars* as I type away here. We enjoy the show together every week. There aren't too many shows we enjoy together, mostly because she watches crap. That's not true. I like cartoons, historical documentaries and well … crap. But as comedian George Carlin said, "The only difference between my stuff and your shit is perspective." Wise words. Maybe not as helpful as those of the white Mike Tyson but still wise words.

I started my "Celebrate Life Challenge" today. The story behind that has to do with a friend of mine named Clay Smith, a beautiful modern day pirate of a man from Virginia, who dumped a bucket of confetti on me last weekend when I was in Pittsburgh doing a motivational lecture. We filmed it. I said a few words about the recent passing of Robin Williams and how I wanted to celebrate life and bring awareness to suicide prevention. I'm hoping to raise five thousand dollars for the American Foundation for Suicide Prevention. We raised $100 on our first day. Oh, and I was wearing a clown nose. I was hoping it would tie people's memories to Robin Williams' role in *Patch Adams*. I'm happy with it no matter how much we raise because I'm trying to change the world and I'll continue to do so until I leave this world. It's the least I can do. It's my home, after all.

Unfortunately, my little celebration of life meant I ended up with confetti in my pants right before I had to do my lecture. When Clay dumped the bucket upon me, it went mostly down the back of my shirt, slid down my spine, over the small of my back, and right between the elastic band of my underwear and my skin. It wouldn't have been so bad if I'd bought paper confetti, but I wanted the whole thing to sparkle and shine so it would look good on camera, so I bought the hard foil variety. I ended up with glitter stuck to my ass and other various parts that are encased within my jockey shorts. I remember peeing in the urinal at the hotel just before going on with the show. I stepped up to the porcelain receptacle, undid my belt, and I looked down. Upon seeing my manhood covered in confetti I thought, "It's about time you threw yourself a party, old friend. Well deserved."

Well deserved, indeed.

Tomorrow is Friday so that's good. Then again, all days are good.

"Some days are diamonds. Some days are stones. But all of them rock." – Dustin Pari

Yup.

Friday, September 5, 2014

It's barely still September 5th, being a little after 11pm. I just finished packing my bag to head to Michigan in the morning. I don't bother putting my luggage downstairs this time of year since I'm packing and unpacking at least once a week.

It's been a long day in a series of long days. When all is said and done, I think I'll have had four days off for myself between August 1st and Thanksgiving this year. But I'm thankful for my opportunities and that I'm healthy enough to take advantage of them. I do recall it was only three years ago that I was putting air in my front tires every three days to prevent getting a flat. It took most of the money we had to move into our home, and things were tight. I didn't have a lot of extra cash floating around for new sneakers for ole Angelina, but I made sure my wife, daughter, and my step-sons never went without.

Angelina is my 1999 Mazda B3000 pickup truck I bought when she was brand new. She's still shiny, majestic, and black with orange flames stretching down both sides of her bed. Angelina is a true beauty. Right now, we have over 263,000 miles and still on the road; still together. I bought her from the brother of the girl who stole my virginity. She was 25; I was much, much younger. I always did fancy the older ones. Shorter than me, brunette, full figured, and older. That's what I like. Always have. Always will.

Funny, I'm still driving that ole truck, many years and many dance partners later. And for the last seven years, Angelina has sported a little pink car seat sitting shotgun next to me, for now there is only one woman in my life. Well, her and Mama Bear, but Angelina only seats two, so Mama Bear has to sit on the hump. (Sorry, wife.)

Work was good today. I was able to meet with my employees, do their yearly evaluations, and inform them of their raises. I like that part. Who doesn't like making others happy? I have good people that work for me, and good people that I work for. That's one of the reasons I could never fully commit to television. I sincerely like my day job.

My daughter, little Beans, is at a friend's house for a sleepover, breaking my heart. I keep walking by her room and wanting to check in on her. She's such a daddy's girl and nothing will ever change that. My little girl's had me wrapped around her finger since they took her out of Mama and she reached out with her tiny hand for mine. If there was one thing I did right in my life, it was in being her father. (You are my world, Beans.)

Aside from being with my daughter, one of the things I like doing most is going to the gym, even when my workouts are a little tough. My chest is pretty sore right now, I'm guessing from today's workout, but feeling the burn the *right way* means you're making healthy progress.

I was in the shower at the gym today and thinking, because that's where I get most of my good thoughts, while enjoying a good, rich lather. I was thinking if I was wealthy and didn't have to work today, I would go downtown, wear a mayoral sash, and hand out mini pies, hugs, and balloons to those who crossed my path. Dustin Pari—Mayor of Happytown. I may never be a wealthy man but I would like to do that someday anyway because I like to see how people react to unexpected happy nonsense. Those surprises make people stop thinking about the dark drudgery in the world for a few minutes.

This whole life thing slips by fast. You don't notice as much when you're young, not that I'm old now. But at 37, I see my little girl growing up way too fast. I see my parents aging. I don't know what the hell I'm doing most of the time but I'm doing the best I can with trying to help others and not let anyone down too much. A little happy nonsense seems more and more necessary the older I get.

Big Fish is on the television, just beyond my laptop screen. I remember seeing it before. A magical little film, if you ask me. I liked this movie because there is a bit of a lesson in there. We should live as large as we want to live. We should leave a legacy.

I enjoy a good story. We all need stories. We need something to listen to, to believe, a place to escape. I'll need to escape the usual chatter of the folks on my flight tomorrow because I don't like yakety-yak and a lot of talk about nothing.

I also like books. I like being quiet and thoughtful. I like music. In fact, I downloaded some new music tonight. Well, technically it's old music, but new to my collection, though not to my life. Willie Nelson, David Allan Coe, Harry Belafonte—not exactly modern day pop hits. I'll be flying through the clouds tomorrow morning listening to that Banana Boat song and smiling out the window like a happy idiot patiently waiting for the flight attendant to bring him a drink and a snack.

Where's my bag of salty nuts?

Oh, right where it always is. I think I may put confetti on it again.

Day-o! Me say day, me say day, me say dayyyyy-o!

Saturday, September 6, 2014

Delta flight 4968 is humming along quite noisily over the clouds as she makes her way to Detroit. I'm snuggled in window seat marked 14D. I say snuggled to comfort myself but it's more like pressed into sausage casing or a sardine can. There's barely any room to open the laptop to even write. I have you fine folks in my laptop balanced on sort of a half angle upon my tray table, the other corner of which is holding my pumpkin iced latte from Dunkin Donuts.

My airline roommate in 14C is a tiny Asian gentleman that looks and dresses like a grandfather, and smells like the Marlboro Man. I detest cigarettes. I hate the smell of them. I hate the look of them. I hate them for the people they have taken from me in the past and are still taking from me today. But the Chinese Cowboy next to me seems to like them. I'm just glad airlines no longer allow smoking on planes.

Mr. Willie Nelson is singing "Bloody Mary Morning" sweetly into my ears. God bless that redheaded gypsy bastard. He has provided the background music for more moments in my life than he could ever know.

God, this plane is tight. I've flown all over the world—20-something countries, I think. I like the little prop planes best. They make me feel like I'm really up there in the air. These bigger planes with their jet engines make me feel like we're cheating gravity and that kind of arrogance leads to moments like the Titanic. I don't mind flying. My family minds it very much but they watch the news a lot more than I do. Me? I worked in news for CBS and Fox for too many years, so I know it's better not to watch.

I walk in faith, not fear. Whatever the Good Lord has in store for me will unfold as He intends it. I get to make some little choices, but He has the master plan. If He had put it in my care I probably would have misplaced it. I can't even keep track of my keys.

I do keep an eye on things whilst in flight, though. I like to board the plane last so that I can walk back to my seat and give everybody the once over. If anyone looks shifty, I make note of it. I also look to see who might be useful if we crashed on an island somewhere, as well as who would need looking after.

I try to get exit row seating, or at least an aisle seat, whenever possible. I bet heavily on myself in this life. I know no matter what the odds are, and who else is around me, I'm my best bet when it comes to my own survival. But I'm a true humanitarian and would sacrifice myself for a stranger without even thinking. At least, that's what I think. Thankfully I haven't been in that situation yet but I always think it's going to be my fate in the end. We shall see. I'm in no rush to find out how it all ends but I do hope I garner an invite to the after party upstairs with John Lennon, Elvis, Robin Williams, my old dog Cassidy, and the many loved ones I've lost over these long years.

I'm no angel, but I try. I like to think I still have my halo; it's just a little bent and rests slightly askew atop the tiny horns that sometimes have reared through my head in darker times.

It's not that hard to imagine occasional horns on my head. I can be your best friend. I have been so to many, though a lot of them have been strangers to me. I'll do anything for anybody, as long as I'm available and able but there was a time when I was also known to be relentless when I was crossed. There was a time when I knew how to cripple someone emotionally with the right words alone. The sharpest sword is the tongue, you know. Plus, I was never one for violence, yet as clearly as I can remember, I never lost a fair fight.

Nowadays I'm a mellow fellow. I'm protective of my family and my friends but I always operate in love and kindness. I'm thankful for having been blessed with the ability to see trouble coming a mile away, so I simply keep my eyes on the horizon and steer clear of any darkness coming my way. Stay vigilant in all that you do. Know your surroundings. Know what other people are capable of. Don't underestimate anybody. And never bet against yourself. Walk in faith, not fear. I say it again because it needs to be said. Not enough people have the courage to really follow those words, and not just say them because they sound good.

Life is a game of give and take and I prefer to give. You'll find more comes back to you than you could ever put out there as long as you're sincere in all that you do and help others as much as you can. I try to impart as many of my life lessons as I can to anyone who wants to listen, and I try to show even more by example, as it should be.

Tonight I'll do the same. I'll be in Manistee, Michigan, working a paranormal event on two ships—a former Navy vessel and a U.S. Coast Guard boat. My old friend Mr. John Zaffis is joining me, with whom I have done everything from college lectures to private events and even television. John has been a mentor and a friend throughout the years. His name and family lineage are like royalty in the paranormal field. His aunt and uncle, Ed and Loraine Warren, investigated such places as the Amityville house and various other locations of great notoriety.

John is a kind, yet cantankerous old man, and it's always good sport to watch him get riled up because he's definitely not afraid to tell it like it is. Sadly, much of the world doesn't want to hear it like it is, but that doesn't dissuade John from being honest. He's also the only person I know who may be spotted driving down the highway with a trunk full of Ouija boards that were used in occult rituals, along with various other crazy objects. He picked me up once and just threw my luggage back there with all that stuff. Crazy bastard. We need more people like that old man in the world.

I'll also be working with Miss Kris Williams, with whom I've been fortunate enough to travel with doing paranormal television and events alike. She's a bit of a spitfire if ever there was one. Kitty has claws, that's for sure. Luckily, through charm, wit, honesty, and kindness, I have always stayed on her good side and I intend to keep it that way.

Well, it appears they're about to put this metal bird on the ground. I'm more than glad because the guy in front of me thinks he's lounging in a recliner and keeps stretching back onto my laptop. Some people really do think they're the only people in the world. I feel bad for them. So unaware. I adjusted my air vents forward to give him a little chill and friendly reminder that this isn't a private jet.

I have another flight coming up. I'm not sure when. I should look into that.

Woohoo! Found my gate and made it on time. I stopped by The Irish Pub for a pint of Octoberfest. Sure, it made me almost miss my flight but some things are worth enjoying even if they potentially derail the rest of your day. I think we live by incredible structure and regimen but I like to spice things up and create excitement. I worry not about travel details and such. I'll get where I need to go, when I need to get there. And this time it looks like I'm going to … where is this plane going to again? Ah! There's my boarding pass. Traverse City. All right, then. Let's get this bird in the air shall we? Surely. Don't call me Shirley.

Back again, safely snuggled into a hotel. I just had a two-hour nap. Sleep is at a premium these days … make that months … so I have to squeeze in some quick winks whenever and wherever I'm able. I arose with the urge for pizza. Well, an urge for something else too, but I'm on the road so I could only order the pizza.

There was a menu for a place called "Big Al's" on the hotel room desk. I had a principal in elementary school that my friend Darren Valedofsky and I refer to as Big Al, so I took it as a good sign and ordered a cheese and pepperoni before I hit the showers to make myself pretty for tonight's investigation event. Soon afterward, the pizza man knocked on the door. I grabbed my pants and answered.

"Holy shit! You're Dustin Pari," said the pizza man.

I chuckled and said, "Yes, and you're my hero."

I truly thought this was a funny exchange as I have not been on television for four or five years, with the exception of my appearance in a Dunkin Donuts commercial. The fact that anyone recognizes me or remembers me, or brings me a pizza in some hotel in Michigan, is pretty amazing and I'm thankful for it.

He explained that his wife was a big fan. I explained that I was a big fan of pizza. I gave him an autographed photo for his wife. It was a really good pizza.

Sunday, September 7, 2014

Here I am, back in Detroit. Last night's event went very well. I told some jokes and some people laughed. My wife says I'm not funny. I think my act has just worn thin on her over the years.

I'm running on two hours of sleep, four if you count the nap from yesterday. I told you sleep was at a premium. Two orange cupcakes are filling my belly from a gas station I stumbled across on the way to Traverse City this morning. Orange cupcakes are the best.

My flight here was something else, as in, I can't remember it, and so it could have been something else. Who knows? I like mystery. I prefer to not have all the answers. People are too obsessed with control. I say, "Let go and let God." This is His show anyway; I'm just a glorified extra.

Gate A33 is where I'm writing now, awaiting my flight home to Rhode Island. A woman in her early 50s or so sitting across from me is making me thirsty for pink lemonade with her pink yoga pants, a neon yellow running jacket, and pink and yellow sneakers. That's a serious commitment to two colors right there. I haven't had pink lemonade in ages. Maybe I'll look into it when I get home.

I've said it before and I'll say it again: I truly believe we are all God's sons and daughters. But there are times when He makes me feel like He has my picture hanging up pretty highly on the fridge. I'm aboard Delta flight 5596 from Detroit to Providence, and instead of being mired back in 16B, I was able to canoodle myself up to 13C, the exit row. Lots of legroom for this 6'1" tall glass of water and with no one sitting in 13D, so soon I'll sleep in heavenly peace like the little baby Jesus did so many lonely manger nights ago.

Mr. David Allan Coe is singing "Another Pretty Country Song" softly in my ears. It's a beautiful song with lyrics I can relate to about traveling, drifting, but overall feeling lonely and overworked.

"Well, I've got to take a drink to keep from shakin'. Motel rooms ain't nothing like a home. Money can't make love grow any stronger. When you leave your woman home alone. "

That is pure beauty right there. Brings a tear to my soul.

Luckily my travel schedule isn't as bad as it once was. Back in my *Ghost*

Hunters International days, I was gone a month to a month and a half, easy. I hated it. I appreciated the opportunities, of course, and I saw some great places but the only things I wanted to see were the inside my home and my wife and child's faces. But these are the things that parents need to do sometimes. The balance between sacrificing to provide and being home to be a parent is a tough balancing act indeed.

I'm just glad my little one was young enough that she couldn't have any recollection of my time away. I remember it though, and it still hurts me. As I do in everything else, I did my best. I think I did well enough. To this day, my time at home is focused on our little girl first and foremost. Everything else can wait.

I come from a long line of hustlers and hard workers. My mother's father, Papa Cheech, consistently worked at least two jobs all the time. He drove trucks from Rhode Island to New York and then back again, only to walk home as they didn't have a car. Then he worked for the city doing things like patching roads, painting guardrails, and the like. He was a gas station attendant, and in the winter, he cut ice from the reservoir and delivered it to local homes for their iceboxes. Always working two or three jobs to provide for his family was normal to him. Finally, he retired as a night watchman at a spinning mill but he still pumped gas on the side.

My father was an over-the-road truck driver who spent time away when I was little before settling in driving an asphalt truck for Cardi Corporation in Warwick, Rhode Island. He would then work nights and/or weekends hauling the U.S. Mail to New York or taking longer trips down to the steel yards in Bethlehem, Pennsylvania, or hauling produce, clothes, stone, or chemicals down to every state between home and Florida. In the winter, he worked for the city plowing streets during the snowstorms. I'm thankful to him for all he did to keep our family going all those years.

Here is a short list of the jobs I remember having, starting from when I was 13 years old:

- Dishwasher at the Jefferson Diner in Warwick, RI
- Dishwasher/Busboy/Host/Bar Back at the Ground Round in Warwick, RI
- Sales/Stock/Cashier at Bliss Marine Supply in Warwick, RI
- Bagger/Cashier/Grocery/Frozen Clerk at Stop and Shop in Greenville, RI
- Morning Stocker at Barnes and Noble bookstore in Warwick, RI
- Weekend and Overnight Board Operator for WPRO AM and WSKO AM in East Providence, Rhode Island. A talk and sports station respectively.
- Pizza delivery guy for Nino's Pizza in Cranston, RI (Still one of my

favorite jobs)

- Field Producer for Traffic Net in Providence, RI
- Show Editor/Field Camera Operator/Live Truck/Satellite Truck Operator for WPRI/WNAC CBS/FOX News in East Providence, RI (I worked here twice. Once for about six years, and then another one year stint when I needed money to buy Mama Bear an engagement ring.)
- Cardiac Level EMT/Operations Director for MedCare Ambulance in Warwick, RI
- Anesthesia Assistant/Practice Manager for MSL Facial & Oral Surgery in Warwick, RI
- On camera talent for Ghost Hunters/Ghost Hunters International
- Author
- Christian Lecturer
- College Lecturer
- Motivational/Inspirational Speaker

I might be missing one or two things but those are the main jobs. Oh, I once worked for UPS for two nights unloading trucks on humid summer evenings. That wasn't for me.

It should be noted that most of these jobs were done in addition to the one, and sometimes one or two, listed previously. Right now I'm still doing the last six.

And so, I sleep when I can, which is what I'm about to do now. I have to stop at the hardware store when I land since they're painting my house tomorrow and I have to replace the dryer vent and a piece of wood on the shed door frame before they prep. There's no time to rest, especially since I just agreed to film two more cases for that ole ghost show tomorrow night and Tuesday. I'll hit the gym in the morning, and then work all day, followed by travel to New York and an all-night investigation.

Lather, rinse and repeat.

Oh well. It looks like 13C will be my bed for the next hour. Good thing I can sleep anywhere. I once fell asleep at an aquarium surrounded by the soothing soft hues created by lights reflecting and refracting through the water. It reminds me of being in utero, I suppose. Suspended in water and a little bit of my own pee. Comfortable. Happy. When I dozed off at the aquarium, I was watching the penguins. Magnificent birds those penguins are. Those African Penguins on display are supposed to mate for life. I remember watching them and penning a little poem that included the line, "I'm alone with the sadness of the seventh penguin," since seven is an odd number, and if they mate for life, it meant one poor fellow was shit out of luck for life. Not only do those little wings not allow them to fly but they look too stubby to reach their naughty parts, so masturbation is out too. Poor bastard. A whole existence upon display surrounded by three couples that were getting what they wanted for Christmas and he can't even reach his own candy cane.

Mama Bear, the Beanie Baby, and I recently did a penguin experience at the aquarium in Mystic, Connecticut. We were able to pet one, take pictures with it, and listen to its breath sounds and heart. And our bird, Red Blue, almost projectile pooped on Mama Bear's sneakers. Ha! Good times.

Monday, September 8, 2014

"Well, I'm up and gone at the break of dawn. I've been working like a regular dog. To keep my woman and the lights and the water and the phone turned on." – David Allan Coe

It's 6am. I'm up and feeling fine. I finally crashed last night around 9pm after putting some new wood on our shed as it was starting to rot. Then I put away the patio furniture, trimmed back some hedges, put away the grill, fixed a broken gate, changed the cat litter (damn cats), and played with my daughter. That last part was my favorite. There wasn't much time for Mama Bear and me, as I had to pack before bed, and Beans crawled in to sleep in our bed before I was even in it. That's okay though. I like to hold my little lady as she sleeps with her head on my chest. My heart beats for her.

Today I'll work my day job at the surgeons' office, and then I'm off to New York to film for that ole ghost show at some culinary school.

I keep saying I'm done and I will not film any more episodes but apparently I keep saying a lot of things.

Maybe there will be pie at the school. That'd be a sweet reward indeed.

Tuesday, September 9, 2014

It's 5:02 in the morning and I just got back to the hotel, unpacked and took a shower. Filming went easily tonight. I didn't witness much in the way of paranormal activity but I did meet a very nice fan on the culinary institute campus and KJ and I finished the night by ringing the bells in the bell tower at around 3 o'clock in the morning. It's always good to get up to a bit of mischief and I like working with him a lot. Mr. KJ McCormick and I have only worked together for a short time, but our energies mesh well, and that's half the battle.

Well, the ole eggnog river in my mind is about to overflow. I best get to sleep before those naughty little ladies from the Lullaby League track me down and knock me over the head. The two tall ladies aren't the problem; it's that little one I worry about. She's a biter!

Now I lay me down to sleep....

I've just awoken in my hotel room a little bit dazed and confused at just after 11am. This has happened before. Traveling to different places every couple of days makes a person wake up fuzzyheaded a lot, which makes me wish for my bed at home even more.

This morning, what is left of it, will be spent doing some things for my day job back home, and reviewing audio from last night's investigation. No matter what I do, I'll be eating a box of Sno Caps. They're amongst my favorite types of candy and a must for trips to the movie theater, which I sneak in after buying elsewhere. Yes, I'm a rebel. I still feel a little thrill when I get my candy contraband into the show. In my head, there's a SWAT team just waiting to descend from the rafters of the cinema to tackle me, pat me down, and confiscate my confectionary wonders. The bastards.

I was just sitting in the shower and doing some thinking. Well, technically it was the tub. All this travel and minimal sleep in strange beds leaves my muscles aching, so sitting in a tub full of hot water with the shower beating on my neck and shoulders seems to help. I'm only 37 and even younger in my mind, but time does take its toll.

I'm trying to figure out what I have to do today. I know I have another investigation tonight, and then I drive directly from the case in New York back to Rhode Island. I'll probably get back to Rhode Island about five in the morning if I'm lucky. I think I'll sleep in ole Angelina tonight. No sense in driving home and chance waking up Mama Bear and the Beanie Baby only to get an hour of sleep and drive back to my office.

I've spent many a night sleeping in my truck or a rental car. It doesn't bother me much. My family worries for me because that's what families should do. I'm not personally prone to worry about anything but my family.

Often during the last few weeks of October, I can be found in restaurant parking lots along the highways and byways, squeezing in a couple of hours sleep before getting back on the road again. I do a lot of college lectures about the paranormal every year around Halloween. Naturally, it's my most popular time. I'm like a paranormal Santa Claus. All hail the Pumpkin King! Ha! I do love that Jack Skellington from Tim Burton's *The Nightmare Before Christmas*. It's a great movie with enchanting music. Anyhow, I usually rent a car and drive from college to college, night after night, to hustle a couple of extra dollars. It's rather pleasant for me, more so than others could understand.

I enjoy the fall weather and the crisp air. I love flying down the highway as the orange, yellow, and burnt red leaves blow by the window of the rental car. It reminds me of being a kid and going on the road with my dad. We once took a trip together on a run to Georgia (he was a truck driver, you know). I loved listening to the truckers talk on the CB radio. I liked the squelch, the static, as they would key their mics, tell dirty jokes, and warn each other about where the cops were hiding. Country music and rainy nights mixed with flashes of lighting and flashes of brilliance. Truckers are the modern day cowboys. I greatly enjoyed being there with my father and I have many fond memories that I carry with me today. I also carry affection for truck stop restaurants and all night diners.

So, every October when I saddle up the rental car and go out on the road, I make my own memories. There are nights when it gets colder than expected and I put on two sweatshirts, recline the driver's seat, grab my pillow, and pull my blanket up over my head, the cold air permeating every crack in my cotton armor like light breaking through horizon after a long dark night.

I like to drive all night and sleep in the early hours of the morning, usually from four till nine. You can make better time when no one else is cluttering up the highway. This is a good lesson not just for driving, but also for life. If you really want to get ahead, you have to work hard even when no one is working. That's one of my little gems of knowledge right there. You may want to take note of it.

So far this year, it appears that my lectures are very centralized and will take me from Maine to New Jersey with almost a night in every state in between. One of the nice things about doing lectures at the colleges in New England is the locations are only about two to three hours apart, which allows for much adventuring.

"Life moves pretty fast. If you don't stop to look around once in a while, you could miss it." – Ferris Bueller

I'm looking forward to this year's college lectures. Crisscrossing New England will allow me to see beautiful places at the peak of foliage season. The hillsides, tightly packed with the tones of the treetops, look like crayons sticking up out of God's crayon box.

My travels will also allow me to stop at home as I go here and there, so I can check in on Mama Bear and the Beanie Baby when I need a little taste of home.

Speaking of taste—syrup! Ah, yes! Last year when I did a lecture up in Vermont I stopped by one of these little shops that allowed you to taste test samples of pure maple syrup. And since you could serve yourself, with no one there to chaperone or give you a disapproving glare, I did shot after shot of pure maple flavored happiness. The ride out of that place was like none I had ever seen. I blasted Bob Dylan and shot down the highway like an elf that fell into the sugar bowl. Sweet Christmas ... I have to do that again this year.

Another hot shower in the logbook and I'm off to investigate another place out here in New York. I'm not even sure what or where it is. The production company sent me some literature about it but I didn't read it. I like to be surprised. If spirits want to show themselves in some way, they will. Spirit is all around us anyway, all the time.

Hotels can sometime be a welcomed respite from the trials and tribulations of life. And they can often feel like a prison cell. This stay was a quick turnaround, so I didn't mind it that much but I'm looking forward to getting back home to the ones I love the most.

"This ol' highway's getting longer. Seems there ain't no end in sight. To sleep would be best, but I just can't afford to rest. I've got to ride in Denver tomorrow night." – Garth Brooks

Wednesday, September 10, 2014

Well, here I sit at 11:43 wondering what in the hell happened to me? This day is almost over and yet I cannot rest. I only slept two hours last night ... err, make that this morning. I arrived home from New York at 5am and slept till 7am before going to my day job.

I made it through the day without issue and I had a wonderful evening with my wife and our daughter at a Disney On Ice production at the Dunkin Donuts Center in Providence. We had front row seats to watch the Disney cast act out the story of *Frozen*. It was a fantastic performance. I started to get a little teary eyed when they sang "Do You Want To Build a Snowman" and "Let It Go". I attributed it to being on only two hours sleep but the truth is I cried when we saw it in the movie theater, too. I'm not sure what it is about animation and music but it gets me every time. Anything to do with love, sacrifice, and struggle just chokes me up. Luckily my wife and daughter were so into the show that no one noticed.

My daughter had brought a friend over to the house for the first time late last year. I was sitting on the couch watching NASCAR and she brought this young girl of six-years-old over to me and said, "This is my dad. He cried when we saw *Wreck-It Ralph*." Then they just walked away. I didn't even know what to say. I had no excuses.

We came home from the show around nine and found one of our four cats was missing. My wife said she hadn't seen Ella, our cat, all day. She's black with a little white bowtie mustache and the oldest of our feline brood. We have no idea how she was able to get out but she definitely wasn't in the house, and so Daddy, despite two hours of sleep, had to do what Daddy had to do.

There I was, walking around the neighborhood under a low hanging moon, shaking and rattling a package of cat treats, and making that kissy-kissy sound you only make when calling a cat even though it's not a sound I've ever heard a cat make.

I wandered through the neighborhood and made my way along the forest tree line. Two coyotes showed themselves in the moonlight. Thankfully they looked hungry, which is better than seeing them looking full when you're looking for your cat.

Ella has pulled this escape act before, only to show up under the porch three days later. So there's still hope.

Well, now I've done it. Cinderella time is approaching. I must get some rest. I look forward to what tomorrow holds. You never know what could happen. Plus, there is dreamtime between now and then. I love dreaming.

Thursday, September 11, 2014

Fall is unofficially here! This time of year has always been my favorite. I love the cool crisp breezes, the change of the leaves, and fall fashion. I'm most comfortable in ripped jeans, sneakers, a t-shirt, and a zip-up hoodie.

Since I was a kid I was in love with Halloween. It wasn't even about the candy, but the candy didn't hurt either. I was truly enamored with the feel of it. I was taken with the intangible haunting mystery of the unknown and the almost tangible possibility of knowing it. I loved the ghost stories. I adored the pageantry. I found graveyards to have a certain romantic quality to them.

And the food! Oh, the food! Everyone knows I love pie. You'd be crazy not to love a good pie. My personal favorite flavor is pumpkin and I love all the other pumpkin flavored treats, too. The coffees, the donuts, the beers, the crème liquors—they are all so wonderfully delicious. Drink responsibly and deliciously.

When I was a child, my godmother, Aunt Elaine, would delight in telling me ghost stories. My grandfather, Papa Cheech, once took me to a pumpkin patch on a farm where he bought me several pumpkins and gourds. It's one of my favorite memories from my childhood. I hope to make the same memories with my daughter. Mama Bear and I take Beans to the pumpkin patch every year to pick out our candidates for jack-o-lanterns. Sure, you can get them cheaper at the supermarket or at the evil empire of Wal-Mart, yet I prefer to support my local small farmer and go have a truly pleasant autumnal experience with my family. We drink cider, go on hayrides, and shuffle our feet through crisp and colorful fall leaves as we wander through corn mazes. That's the way it should be. One should never buy a Halloween pumpkin between the avocados and the family planning section.

The history of Halloween is intriguing to me. There are layers of stories and mysteries layered upon each other like a giant candy corn. Even trick-or-treating came about almost as if by accident. Go research how the poor and desolate would go door-to-door begging for "soul cakes". I love that term. Maybe I should try and bring that back. On one of my Mayor of Happytown days, if I ever get to do them, I shall wear the sash and go downtown to offer people soul cakes in exchange for prayer.

Ah, Halloween will be here soon. Till then, I'll eat my Boo Berry cereal and keep an eye on the pumpkin patch in the backyard. My daughter and I planted it late this summer and it has since taken over a corner of our yard, much like the one my mother and I planted when I was a child.

I believe in doing things that made you happy as a child and that's why I do most of the things I do. I remember being a kid starting to decorate my bedroom for Halloween around this time each year, and in an effort to pass along the tradition, I sneaked into my daughter's bedroom before she came home from dance class and strung up Halloween garland featuring pumpkins, cats, and bats inside the canopy top of her princess bed. She was quite happy to see it. I hope that the tradition will live on.

Speaking of living on, Ella the cat is alive and well! The treats I left on the front and back porch were still there this morning when I was leaving for work, which worried me. I gave one more look through the house but found nothing. The little one was crying thinking one of her cats was dead somewhere out there. Sadly, I couldn't stay and console her for long as I had to get to work again.

A few hours into my day, I received a text message from Mama Bear saying Ella was found. Turns out she was stuck in the couch. Damn cats. There are two reclining segments of the couch that create little pockets of fabric underneath them when their legs are extended. She had crawled into one of them at some point the day before and was trapped there when my wife got up from the couch. I had opened up the recliners last night and even lifted up the couches. She never made a sound but when Mama Bear sat down today, out popped a cat.

I called our daughter's school to ask the secretary to send a note to the teacher with the request to tell Beans that her cat was okay and safe at home. The secretary thought it was so sweet that I called with the request that she had my daughter brought to the office to take my call. When I heard her sweet little voice come to the phone, my heart melted as it always does. She must have wondered why she had a phone call at school and I'd imagined most second graders don't receive calls in the office. I'm making it a habit for her to expect the unexpected when it comes to her father. When I told her that Ella was found in the couch, she laughed and squealed with joy. The secretaries in the office cheered with her.

I needed a win today. I have been running on faith and vapors for some time now. But today … today Daddy was triumphant. Even if I needed the assist of a crazy cat trapped in the cozy catacombs of the couch … today I was a winner.

And tomorrow, I'm in Kentucky. My flight pulls away from the gate in five hours.

Friday, September 12, 2012

I just walked off of US Airways flight 1981 and into the Philadelphia airport again. For those of you paying attention, when we started this book, I was flying from Kentucky to Philadelphia. I'm now flying from Philadelphia to Kentucky. Last time it was for filming and this time it's for a convention. Potato. Potato. Oh, that doesn't work in print does it? Oh well. Lots of things in this life don't work out in other mediums, but as long as I'm working out, I can wear a medium.

I have been up since 4am Eastern Standard Time. At least my body has. My mind has been up for a few weeks now but it doesn't seem to mind much. (Did you get that one? Thank you.) It's going to be a pun filled day. "Better living through puns," I always say. Well, I say it most the time anyway. I often say other things, too. A lot of them can be a bit dirty but done solely for comedic effect and for the entertainment of the LIVE studio audience in my mind.

Mr. Willie Nelson was telling me it would be a Bloody Mary Morning, and that beautiful, redheaded, gypsy bastard was right. He usually is.

As I saunter through this airport, I see where I was sitting the other day eating Chick-fil-A. And over there is where I was a fancy boy and had my mojito at the sushi place. And there is the Rocky store where I bought my "Italian Stallion" shirt. I feel like old Ebenezer Scrooge when the Ghost of Christmas Past transports him back to places he knew as a child. I know this place, Spirit. I know it all too well. I've had an elongated layover here many a time.

"Stop, look, and listen, baby. That's my philosophy." It isn't really *my* philosophy but apparently Mr. Elvis Presley was fond of it since he's singing it on the plane with me as we fly US Airways flight 3877 across the friendly skies to Lexington, Kentucky. The King may have left the building but he is still on the plane with me and we are Rubberneckin'.

Mr. Presley and I have had a long life together. My father introduced me to his music when I was just a wee lad. He also introduced me to this huge oil painting of the King that he proudly hung upon the wall of our apartment when I was a child. It's a striking piece. A heavy frame hangs around Elvis in his white Hawaiian concert jumpsuit against a background of black with lighting affects painted in the composition. There's also a bit of sparkle on his ring. Fantastic. Simply fantastic.

Of course, beauty is in the eye of the beholder and when my mother beholds it, she hates it. Thus, there has been a feud going on for as long as I can remember between my parents because of this painting. My father had it beautifully displayed out toward the living room in our apartment when I was a child until my mother redecorated and moved Elvis to the hallway at the top of the stairs. Then my father moved it into the bedroom. And then, my mother moved it back above the stairwell.

When I was seven, my mother, father, the King and I, all moved to a new house. My mother made the front door entryway the permanent resting place of the Elvis portrait, and she only used the back door. She was trying to get the King to leave the building.

Ten years later we moved once more, and the King proudly hangs once again in my parents' bedroom, just opposite my mother's wedding portrait. Given the choice between the two, I know my father would choose the one his heart truly adores and sell my mother's wedding painting at a yard sale next to his collection of broken things that may still have some use to someone.

Recently my friend Mr. Clay Smith, made famous for being an accomplice in the aforementioned great confetti video of 2014, gave me an autographed photo of the King that he acquired at a concert just before Jesus rang the triangle and called Mr. Presley home for supper. It's a great picture. The King is there with his rich dark hair, smiling confidently in a golden jumpsuit. And so now, Mama Bear and I are dancing the same dance with Elvis that my parents did. I'm not sure why both my father and I were cursed with women whom have poor taste in music and art, but thankfully they have other favorable traits.

I'm headed to The Scarefest. It's a three-day convention of various horror and paranormal celebrities from all over the country, or even the world. They are expecting over 10,000 guests to come through the doors between now and Sunday. It's my first time doing this particular convention, so we'll see how it goes. I hear good things.

I like doing conventions because I get to meet so many of the people who have been kind enough to watch me on various programs and interact with me on social media over the years. A few friends of mine come to almost all of my conventions and they usually bring me confectionary treats. To have friends is a good thing. To have ones that bring you Sno Caps and pumpkin fudge is a *really* good thing.

My eyes are blanking out sporadically; a sure sign that I must rest. Looks like it's time for an in-flight nap. I think I shall ask Mr. Frank Sinatra to sing me out today. That old crooner still has the world on a string and he is sitting on a rainbow.

Saturday, September 13, 2014

Yesterday proved to be a fantastic day at The Scarefest and today was even better. Thousands of people came to the convention and I did a great little lecture yesterday. I felt great up there on the stage alone telling my stories, making jokes, trying to motivate people, and entertain them all at the same time. Sure it was a paranormal lecture, or at least it was supposed to be, but I can't help but be who I am, and thus the motivation shines through.

I just came up to bed after seeing a few good friends of mine for a nightcap. Although I don't drink much alcohol normally, I drink even less at these events. I normally wouldn't have a drink at all, as I find it inappropriate to be seen drinking at a public event with friends and fans, but at the same time, some of these people I'm truly friends with and I don't get to see them very often. I felt it was warranted to spend a few moments with them over a Captain and Coke. The pirate in me was happy.

My left ankle is killing me. I'm not really sure what I did to make it so but I think I might have injured it recently on an investigation. Walking around in the dark leads to these types of potential injuries. I felt a little twinge of pain earlier this week, and then two days of standing on concrete for 8-12 hours per day has left it slightly swollen and sore as hell.

They do provide you with chairs at your table for these events but I never use them. I believe I should always be standing at attention and on display for everyone to see—and with a friendly smile on my face. People pay a lot of money to come to these conventions and such, and if they are paying to see me, see me they will.

Conventions during the day are fine since I'm so very busy signing autographs, taking pictures, and giving all of my energy away. But when I return to my room I feel quite alone and I look forward to being home with my family.

I was able to get ten hours of sleep yesterday, which has been unheard of as of late. I awoke confused today. I wasn't sure where I was. I thought I was still living with my parents. I was also very concerned that I didn't know who my girlfriend was. As strange as this sounds, it happens more and more often lately. The same thing happened when I was on the road filming with *Ghost Hunters International.* I couldn't keep track of what country I was in and I'd wake up at home and wonder why my wife was with me on the road. I was a complete mess. I never experienced jet lag, but I did experience confusion as to time and place.

Looks like I'll get eight hours of sleep tonight. That sounds good.

When I awake I'll work the convention floor for six hours, and then head to the airport to fly back home. I like that part the best.

Sunday, September 14, 2014

Did you know horses could fly? A few hours ago I was in the Lexington, Kentucky, airport again and this time whilst I sipped on a beer and watched some NFL games at the bar, I looked out the window and saw a plane they refer to as "Air Horse One". Apparently they crate up horses, load them on this massive plane and fly them wherever horses need to go. Amazing. I would have never thought horses traveled by airplane. I like how there are still plenty of things out there that I don't know. It must blow their little horsey minds to suddenly hear the roar of the engines and feel the thrust of the throttle as they go down the runway and up into the clouds. I engaged in a little flight of fancy of my own, imagining what it must be like to have a plane full of horses and what the stewardesses provide on the beverage cart. Mostly water, carrots, and oats I would imagine.

US Airways flight 4560 just delivered me from Kentucky and dropped me off in Charlotte, North Carolina. I have a few minutes before US Airways flight 1996 brings me home to Rhode Island.

I was so tired on that last flight that I slept from takeoff until landing. Those two hours of sleep were precious and will serve me well going in to tomorrow. I take my rest where I can get it.

I slept well last night, about eight hours, so I'm not sure why I'm this tired. I think it's probably because of my demeanor at conventions, as I try and give away every ounce of energy I have and ensure everyone has a good time. Judging by the comments on my Twitter feed, it looks like everyone did. There's a picture of me smiling with a guest, and another, and another. I take great pride in my choice of t-shirts in these things. They are always a topic of conversation and also a good way to get a person to come to your booth and engage you, which then gives you an opportunity to peddle your wares and make a sale. As much as I enjoy doing these things and meeting thousands of people at a time, at the end of the day. I have to bring home some money to take care of Mama Bear and Beans.

This weekend was a success for several reasons, one of which being financial, but the one most important to me is how I know I reached a few people—truly making connections and helping them. Despite it being a paranormal event, there were so many people that heard my lecture, stopped by my table, and thanked me for something I had said that resonated with them. As I read through Twitter I see my name and the word "kind" mentioned next to it time and time again, that's a big victory for me. I must be doing something right. If nothing else, I'm leaving this world a little better than I found it.

I'm seriously looking forward in getting back to Rhode Island, saddling up my truck, ole Angelina, and pointing her towards home. I'm looking forward to seeing my wife and our daughter, and kissing them on their peaceful heads as they sleep. And waffles. I'm looking forward to buttermilk waffles with lots of butter and maple syrup. I think I'll make waffles in the morning before I go to the gym.

I just boarded the flight to Providence. Seat 23D. Exit Row. Everything is coming up Milhouse! That's a little saying I borrowed from *The Simpsons*. Whenever things come up surprisingly right, I often exclaim it, much to the curiosity of passersby.

This flight is like a flying infirmary. We haven't taken off yet and so far all I'm hearing is multiple sneezes and coughs. I'll do my best to keep my mouth closed and breathe as shallowly as possible. At least I'm rested and I can take my vitamins when I get home before bedtime. I'm a big believer in vitamins. I take a regular mix of them daily and I'm hardly ever sick; maybe once a year if that.

Professional wrestler Hulk Hogan said to take my vitamins, say my prayers, and drink my milk. And who am I to question the Hulkster?

On this flight I'll have to listen to some audio evidence from the recorder I used whilst filming for that ole ghost show earlier in the week. Mr. David Allan Coe and my all-star lineup of country heroes will have to wait until I'm done listening to whispering messages from spirits who have left their human shells years before. After all these years, I actually still find it enjoyable when I find such a recording but not as enjoyable as listening to my music.

This upcoming week will be a good one. I don't have to film for anything, so that is a nice change of pace. I do have a local library lecture to do on Tuesday evening, a paranormal-themed type thing. And next weekend I'm off completely! It's my first weekend off in what feels like forever, and in reality may be about a month. I'm taking my dad up to the NASCAR race in Loudon, New Hampshire, this Sunday. I bought tickets early in the season and I presented them to him recently as a birthday present. He doesn't know it yet but I also have arranged for us to be able to go and hang out in the garage area before the race thanks to a pair of "Cold Passes" given to me by a large gasman named Tiny who is currently with the number 13 Geico car. He was a fan of that ole ghost show and kind enough to get my father and me the same passes when we visited Charlotte Motor Speedway last year.

That was a good race, too. I'll never forget, as we were walking back towards our seats and leaving the garage area, my father told me thank you and how being there was one of the best days of his life. I felt so proud to be able to give back and do something for him after all he had done for me.

My father James Pari with me at New Hampshire Motor Speedway

Well, it's time to put my tray table up and place my seat in its upright and locked position. Pretty soon this oversized metal bird will be touching down and I'll go and saddle up Angelina. I love that truck. Together we will fire up our James Brown music and hustle down the highway that leads us back home.

Another weekend in the books and another gig done. I'm tired but thankful, always thankful. I wonder what magic and mysteries this week will unfold before me. And if nothing else, I get to have a week of my life where I'm not living in airplane mode.

Thanks for flying D. Pari airlines. I know you have a choice in your happy nonsense and I'm happy you chose me.

Monday, September 15, 2014

The Colts are beating the Eagles at halftime. I'm a Dolphins fan but I have Andrew Luck as my fantasy quarterback and he needs 13 points for me to beat my adversary for the week.

It was a splendid first day home. I got up early, went to the gym, went to work, came home, watered the pumpkin patch, and then spent time with my wife and our daughter. We had dinner and played Scrabble together afterwards. Then I sat with Beans as she read me a book and wrote a report on it for school tomorrow.

I finished up with a relaxing walk along the tree line whilst drinking a Woodchuck Private Reserve Pumpkin Cider. It was delicious and complimented the cool fall breezes that were blowing down the moonless street. It was the first night of the season that I was able to wear my trusty old red hooded sweatshirt with happiness in the pockets.

Life was good today. Life is always good. You are either dreaming to live, or living the dream. I tend to dance on the side of the latter.

Good night, my friends. May all of your dreams be wet ones.

Tuesday, September 16, 2014

It's Tuesday? Hell. I thought it was Monday until just now. Hooray! I'm one day ahead of the game.

It's just after 10pm and I'm saddled up in bed next to a sleeping Mama Bear. I had to do a lecture tonight up in Amesbury, Massachusetts, for a teenage audience. It was a good night. The teen crowd is usually pretty open to the paranormal and will thus be very interactive. There will always be one or two kids whom are interested but are too cool to participate, but once in a while you'll see them looking on with great curiosity.

I'm thankful for the opportunities to educate anyone I can about the spirit world. Plus, I always weave in a bit about faith, positivity, and love. I feed it all to them with a spoonful of sugar just like Miss Mary Poppins had instructed me so many moons ago when I was but a young chimney sweep flying a kite up in the atmosphere, up where the air is clear.

This is truly my favorite time of year. As I sidestepped it out of the library tonight my lungs were filled with the cool, crisp air of an early autumn. Magic filled the darkness of the night sky. Anything was possible.

For two hours ole Angelina and I flew down the highway with Hank Williams blaring on the radio. She lost her dashboard lights some time earlier in the year. Last year she lost the left side of them, and this year, the right side gave out, too. The only thing that lights up inside the cab is the radio and I. But that is okay; Angelina and I do our best work in the dark.

"The best part of hillsides is there must be a valley, for nothing goes upwards forever, my son." – That was written in a song by my uncle, Mr. Frank Smith, also known as Uncle Bub since his son, my cousin, is also named Frank Smith. He's a gray haired guru somewhat like Willie Nelson who has inspired me much over the years.

One of the best summers of my life happened at Uncle Frank's house—Uncle Bub to you and me—back in 1995 after I had just graduated high school. My parents were having work done to the home they had just purchased, which left me without a bedroom for some time. So I went to live a few minutes away with my uncle. My girlfriend at the time lived nearby with her aunt, as her parents were doing the same thing with a home they had purchased. Serendipity and young love. What a summer.

My uncle lived life in shades of gray, not quite rebelling but not quite conforming at the same time; just dancing happily in the middle. He often listened to Mr. Leon Redbone while washing dishes in the nude around one in the morning. My then-girlfriend even saw the woodpecker tattoo on his hindquarters when we sneaked in late one night. Good times.

My uncle has written a lot of great poems and songs that many have never gotten to hear. One plays in my head a lot and it goes something like this:

"The best part of hillsides, is there must be a valley, for nothing goes upwards forever, my son. And the sad part of this life is there must be a parting. And the best part of heartaches is when they are done. So pick up your pack and turn your face towards the wind, for you'll never be younger and stronger again."

Or something like that … at least that's how it plays in my mind from time to time.

It played in my mind tonight when I was downstairs getting my vitamins and my water with lemon juice. I looked over on the counter and there was my daughter's paperwork from her school's open house tonight. Second grade. I can't believe it. I really wanted to go but I had contracted to do this library lecture about three or four months ago. Even though it was for short money, we needed it, and so I did it. And in doing so, I couldn't go to the open house. Fortunately, Mama Bear went, and she brought back the Beanie Baby's crafts and writings.

There was a picture of our family in there. I was the tallest member. Her two brothers from my wife's previous marriage were in it along with Mama Bear, our four cats, and her brother Jake's girlfriend Kayla, who isn't part of the family yet, but we all hope she will be.

Beans wrote that she likes to play video games, which is something only she and I do together. She also wrote that her favorite place is New York. That struck me as funny as she has never been there other than when we are driving through on our annual pilgrimage to Hershey Park. Then I looked at the picture she drew next to the text, and it was of a balloon being held by several people in the Macy's Thanksgiving Day Parade.

That made me smile. One of the things I have always wanted to do since I was a kid, was go to that Macy's Thanksgiving Day Parade and ride the turkey float.

A few months ago I was asked to film a particular episode of that ole ghost show that required me to drive from my office in Rhode Island to Vermont right after quitting time at my day job, arrive in time to film, sleep for an hour and a half, and then drive back to work. I'd have to do it all again for one more day. Three days of work, six hours of driving—all on three hours of sleep. And I did it. I told myself that if I did it, I would book a hotel room in New York for my family and I so that we could sit in comfort and watch the parade.

Apparently my little lady is as excited as I am about seeing it. I don't think they'll let us ride that turkey float, though. Maybe, as a family, we can press our little white butt cheeks against the hotel room's cold glass window and moon the damn thing. That would be equally as unique of a memory.

I like making unique memories. I once urinated on Dracula's Castle. But that is another story.

Lately, life has been all hillsides but that valley is on the horizon. Though it broke my heart that I couldn't go to that open house tonight and show the teacher I'm not an absentee father, I know that the best part of heartaches is when they are done.

Wednesday, September 17, 2014

I was writing back and forth with my reverend at church. She's a charming woman with a heart full of love, a spirited delivery of the message of God, and a smile that could light up the darkest soul. She was interested in speaking with me at some time about where Christianity and the paranormal meet. I told her it's somewhere down by the crossroads of Spirit Street and Essenes Way. I like to be cryptic. There is truth in my riddles. I'm like the mighty sphinx but less sandy. The answer is in the Dead Sea Scrolls. I asked her to remind me to speak with her about my desire to do more within our faith. I'm often so strongly guided to do more. To speak. To teach. To listen.

I feel like I should do youth ministry or something. I don't know where He is guiding me or when He wants me to get there. God's riddles are better than mine, and tougher to crack. All will be revealed in His time, not mine.

I was once told by a cardinal—the kind with the red beanie hat, not the feathers, (I'm crazy but not talk-to-animals-crazy)—anyhow, a cardinal rested his hands upon my head when I was a child and said I was to do great things for God. I thought he was talking to animals kind of crazy at the time and many times afterward. But now ... well, now I wonder.

I'm no angel. I've said it before, and I'll say it once more—I'm no angel—but I do my best. My wings may be a bit tattered and busted. My halo is bent and slightly askew. But I do the best I can for everyone, especially for those closest to me.

Lately my life is like the directions on a shampoo bottle: Lather. Rinse. Repeat. Even so, this is my time of year. As I stated a few days ago, I'm like a paranormal Santa Claus. I'm very popular for two months out of the year, those months being September through October. I do well the rest of the year, too. I'm always able to hustle an event a month, if not more, and I'm thankful to do so. These two months, though, are action packed with events, lectures, and yard work. It's hard to keep it all straight, plus juggle the day job, answer emails, respond to tweets, guide those looking for motivational direction, and spend time with my family. This year has been especially crazy since I have been filming and such.

Listen up kids! Break out your highlighters. Here is one of those little nuggets of wisdom.

The secret of it all is I don't think too far ahead. A journey of such magnitude is daunting. I know in my heart that I only have six days off in three months' time but I don't let myself think about it. I get through one day at a time. Forget about that nonsense that employers like to throw at you at job interviews about five year plans. Life is a game of inches. You just need to take life moment by moment. Sure, you should have goals. Of course, you need direction. But don't look so far ahead that you become jaded, scared or worse.

Walking down your path and staring into the distance, some obstacles may appear to be insurmountable. Usually the closer you draw to some type of impasse, you will see it for what it really is. You will find your way around it, over it, under it or through it. You will overcome it because you need to. Just focus on the here and now and be alive in it. Taking life one day at a time is even too much. Moments are precious. Each one is fleeting. And each one is about all you can honestly control, if that.

So live in each moment. Truly be alive in it. Use all of your five senses and then some. What does the air taste like? What color is your mood? Combine and contrast your senses to make new experiences for yourself. Enjoy each moment, even the mundane. As a matter of fact, especially enjoy the mundane.

If you were to lose your sight tomorrow, you would like to see even the darkest and cloudiest day just one more time. If you were to lose your legs tomorrow, even carrying out the trash one more time would seem like a pleasure instead of a chore. Whatever it is you have, whatever it is you can do, do it with all that you can while you can. Be thankful in these moments.

Change your attitude to one of gratitude.

Okay, you beautiful bastards. The muse must rest, and so must I. Till the morning comes, here's mud in your eye.

Thursday, September 18, 2014

There has been much debate regarding when I'll buy a new truck and give up ole Angelina. My wife and various other family members are pushing for me to sell it sooner than I want to. Angelina and I have a date with 300,000 miles and I won't stand her up. So, I fired the first shot in the battle of Angelina. I bought Mama Bear a new 2014 Dodge Durango Citadel. Boom! Confetti. Battle over. I won the war.

The plan was this: If I traded in my wife's car, a 2008 Rogue, and put some money down, I could finance the new Durango. The Rogue still has resale value, which will depreciate over time. Angelina only has sentimental value that is appreciating over time. It makes financial sense and makes me feel warm inside.

The Durango is a safer vehicle for Mama Bear and the Beanie Baby. Since they are the core of my family, I have to keep them safe. And, by purchasing the Durango, I lock up our finances, so now we cannot afford a new truck, so it looks like I have to keep Angelina!

I'm one clever son of a bitch … and a bit generous, too.

Friday, September 19, 2014

We picked up Mama Bear's new ride after work today. Beans had a tough time parting with the old Nissan Rogue which she calls "Pumpkin". Our little lady doesn't like change or letting things go. Neither do I, hence why I still drive Angelina. I also still have a striped t-shirt I bought freshman year of high school. I wear it to bed or around the house on Saturday mornings. Wife and Beans hate it. Ha! It only makes me love it more.

The weekend starts tomorrow and I'm not working! I believe it's my first weekend off in about six or more weeks. I'm looking forward to it.

I'm so tired. All these nights filming, doing event appearances, holding lectures and traveling have really worn me down. I can see it in my eyes. I must rest. All work and no play make … zzz … zzz … zzz….

Saturday, September 20, 2014

Lots of fun today! I was able to sleep for about nine hours and so I started my day with energy to spare. I also started my day with waffles smothered in extra butter and extra syrup, so I was a very happy little elf.

Mama Bear, Beans, and I all piled into the new Griswold family vehicle and headed up to Bridgewater, Massachusetts. We went on a hayride and picked our own pumpkins right out of the patch. That's the best way to do it. As I mentioned, my grandfather had taken me to a pumpkin patch as a child just one time, and I never forgot how magical an experience it was. Since I was about sixteen or so, I have gone to a pumpkin patch every year to pick out a few pumpkins for myself. I always bring a pumpkin to my grandparents' grave every year as well, re-affirming the bond between us.

The past seven years my wife and I have gone to the pumpkin patch with Beans. She seems to enjoy it as much as I do. We always take pictures, go through corn mazes, have cider, or do whatever is offered. We picked out some beauties today. Beans picked out the biggest pumpkin, mine was the fattest, and Mama Bear picked out the littlest one.

After returning our bright orange pumpkins back to our home, we headed out to pick up one of our daughter's friends from school and brought her with us up to Canobie Lake Park in New Hampshire. We had a splendid day with lots of laughs and good old-fashioned family fun. Both of the girls won a stuffed animal at various games. The little ones and I were soaked to the bone on one of the flume like rides. Mama Bear had a good laugh at us from outside the splash zone.

I was quite proud of our little girl. Not only does she have no fear of roller coasters or the haunted house attractions, but she's also so kind and thoughtful. I witnessed her getting off a ride, and then staying there to hold the exit gate open for everyone else that was on the ride. Much different from most children who dash off of each ride, running to the next, the spring loaded exit door slamming back behind them. I was very proud of her at that moment. I'm always very proud of her.

We stopped off for pizza on the way home and I won my daughter and her friend a stuffed animal each on the old claw game. That made my daughter proud of me.

The day has turned to night now. It seems that they go quickly. The girls are having a sleepover in the next room, and the pumpkins are sleeping outside our front door.

Life is good. God is great. Always.

Sunday, September 21, 2014

What kind of bees don't bite?

Boobies!

Ha! That was the first joke I ever learned. I was in kindergarten but that joke wasn't told to me by some kid. I heard it from my mother. It kind of explains why I have such a twisted little sense of humor. I was a dirty old man before my pee-pee even worked for the purpose God intended. For some reason, that joke was in my head when I awoke today.

Today was race day! Sweet Christmas! Glorious, wonderful, NASCAR race day! I took my dad up to Loudon, New Hampshire, to watch the Sylvania 300. We usually catch one race a year. My father's birthday is coming up later this week, so I thought it made for a good gift.

I called in some favors to some awesome people that I know, Nick Catanese who is a true rock n' roll star, a good friend, and former guitarist for Black Label Society. As much as I was a fan of BLS for many years, when he left the group, my allegiance went with him. Nick hooked me up with his friend Tiny, a misnomer of course. Tiny is a great guy and a mountain of a man. He has made a living traveling on the NASCAR circuit working in the pits. Tiny hooked us up with passes to go on the track and hang out in the garage before the race started.

I also met my favorite NASCAR driver, Mr. Kurt Busch. My dad and I went to Kurt's merchandise trailer and were allowed to hang out inside whilst he was signing autographs for his fans. This meeting between us was set up by the guy that handles all of the creative advertising for Kurt, Mr. Jonathon Helfman, whom I started to chat with on Twitter recently after being hooked up with him by another Kurt Busch fan.

Kurt gave me a hat, which he autographed, and then took pictures with my dad and me. He hung around and talked with us for about ten minutes or more.

I was as giddy as a schoolgirl inside, but I tried to play it cool the whole time. It looked like rain all day, but luckily it stayed away from the track. Sadly Kurt wrecked late in the race, so I didn't get to see him and the #41 car take the checkered flag, but my father and I had an incredible, unforgettable day.

I wonder what magical mystery tomorrow holds….

Monday September 22, 2014

I came home from work tonight and there was a freshly baked pumpkin pie in the kitchen. Mama Bear had left it for me before she went to take the Beanie Baby to dance class. There are few things as wonderful as a warm pumpkin pie. I celebrate all types of pies—don't get me wrong—but pumpkin is my absolute favorite. If you see me eating pumpkin pie, you probably can't tell what flavor it is due to the mountain of whipped cream towering atop it. I believe the amount of whipped cream one places upon their pie should be in direct correlation to the amount of joy that they have in their heart.

Now Mama Bear is a sweet little woman and I do my best to dote upon her as well. This morning I got up earlier than usual and made breakfast for her before I left for work. That woman loves her bacon almost as much as I do. But that is what makes a relationship work. Feeding each other.

It's getting tougher and tougher to watch television these days when my daughter is around. She's fine and causes me no trouble but all those damned advertisements do. Inappropriate shows, though growing in number, are avoided easily enough but the barrage of medication commercials for low testosterone and erectile dysfunction are tougher to navigate. I don't even want my daughter hearing about such things yet. She's only seven-years-old and I personally believe in extending the innocence of youth for a decent amount of time—not until it gets creepy but just until they naturally mature.

The death of Santa Claus is your own. I wrote that last phrase back when I was in high school and I stand by it still today. The moment someone tells you Santa Claus isn't real, and you believe them, you start to die. Your innocence slips away. The world loses some magic and it continues to darken around you but only if you let it.

Too often the harsh reality of our world and its problems are thrust upon these young kids and that's one of the reasons they're so messed up as they age. They barely have time to be kids before ideas such as sex and depression are thrust upon them.

I've worked in the medical field for the better part of twenty years now, and I can tell you from looking over countless medical histories that some of these diseases and syndromes that are heavily medicated, though hard to diagnose, are running rampant. If a kid doesn't pay attention, we medicate them. Sad? Medicate them. Too happy? Medicate them.

I hate to have to pander to the lowest common denominator, but at risk of coming off as some uncaring selfish bastard, I will. I understand some kids go through some traumatic things and need help and I believe those kids should get help, but sadly a lot of kids are born to parents who just don't make time for them and want a quick fix for their child. Some kids are born to parents who trust doctors too much. Top of the class and bottom of the class get the same diploma out of medical school. Do you know which doctor you are seeing?

Anyhow, I think we should make sure we know what we are pumping into our children, be it media, medicine, or macaroni.

As I was in the kitchen fixing up a snack, a commercial came on for Viagra. I heard it and tried to make my way into the living room before they start talking about asking your doctor if your heart is healthy enough for sex because I don't want my child to ask what sex is yet. I know some parents have that discussion very early on with their kids, and I plan to have it when the time is right, but not while we are still playing with Legos and making our Christmas list for jolly ole Saint Nicholas.

I walked in and my daughter reported to me that maybe Mommy should be on this medication because the commercial mentioned something about headaches. Ha! I quickly flipped the channel with a good chuckle and reported to my wife her need for the little blue pill.

Funny thing happened a few weeks back on a related note. Despite being on the national do not call registry, from time to time I get a telemarketing call, as many of us do. I don't yell and cuss at the poor schlep trying to earn a living. I leave that to my wife. I normally just explain that I'm on the do not call list and to kindly remove my name and number. Then I go online and report the number and the time called. It only takes a minute and it doesn't get me frustrated.

This gentleman sounded like he was from India, yet the caller ID read Indianapolis, Indiana. That alone seemed highly ironic to me so I decided to let the man do his little pitch before telling him about my do not call super-duper elite status.

As it would turn out the young man was offering me pills for male enhancement. I kindly explained to him about removing me from the list and so on and so forth. However, he persisted with the pitch and told me it was not a solicitation call but a great offer for male enhancement pills. I thought for a very brief moment and then with a laugh I informed him that I'm 37 years of age, the captain still gets up before I do in the morning, and the only way to enhance him would be to hang a frame around him for he is truly a masterpiece. Ha! Humble, I know. It's a curse.

If you can't laugh in this life you might as well be letting the worms deliver your mail, if you get my meaning. Lighten up. Smile, damn it. It's only life, after all.

Mama Bear went out for the night with some of her friends, which made it a Daddy-Daughter night! I love these nights since I get special time with my little girl. She means everything to me and time alone is very rare these days. I'm so busy with work, travel, lectures, filming and such; I don't get nearly enough time with Beans, never mind time alone.

I made her dinner—macaroni and cheese, a toasted bagel with butter, and some of the cake I made the other day. We played video games and read books together. I watched her do her homework to make sure everything was right. She's very smart and they estimate she reads about two grades ahead of her current grade. Mama Bear and I are very proud. We spent a great amount of time reading to her when she was young and she took a liking to books early on.

I always fancied books myself. I remember reading quite a bit as a kid and I still enjoy it today. Most of my reading is done on planes lately because I have little other free time but Beans and I had time tonight to read together for a little while.

I just watched her brush her teeth and helped her clean up. I tucked her into bed and turned the country music on low, as that is what she likes to listen to at bedtime. A little kiss on the head, the covers pulled up tight and she is good to go.

Here I am, alone, writing. It reminds me of old times back when I was single. I did a lot of reading and writing back then. I have a whole book of poetry that I started back when I was in high school. Then I started with social commentaries and short stories. I mostly enjoyed sitting in parks or down by the water and writing in my notebooks. Back when you could go to the airport and walk right up to the gates without security, I would sit and watch couples say goodbye and other couples reunite. I found the pure human emotion to be inspiring. Passionate. Beautiful. Honest.

Many moons after they put up security details at the airports, I went on to write two paranormal books with my good friend Mr. Barry Fitzgerald. The first was called *The Complete Approach*, and the second was *My Home Is Haunted, Now What?*

We wrote both of them completely by ourselves. They contain some of the most honest information in the field to date and I'm quite proud of them. I don't consider myself the expert in the paranormal realm but I'm an honest man and put out things as I see them, in collaboration with Barry, who is also a man of integrity. Sadly, the first book also contained a lot of editing errors as the publisher, not a man of integrity, rushed it and put out the version with the editor's notes rather than the final version. He then disappeared with the money and the initial rights to the book. Such is life. Lesson learned.

I then penned an autobiographical self-help book called *What's Next* that is currently being edited by my friend Jessica Jewett down in Georgia. (If you are reading this, then *What's Next* has already been published and you should go pick that book up soon!) I wrote it a few years ago but I waited on putting it out. It sat in my nightstand for some time until I decided that I found the right person to edit the damned thing. I'm not very particular about my punctuation but I'm particular about my voice in my works. Jessica knows me. We talk almost daily. She has a penchant for dirty jokes. Ha! Not really. No … really.

I think I shall go wash up and watch a little television before my wife returns. She doesn't like a lot of things that I watch. I like historical documentaries and cartoons. She fancies reality shows and competitions. We watch sitcoms and ghost shows together; the recreation ghost shows—not the reality ones—those are crap! Ha!

Good night, Seattle! We love you!

Tuesday, September 23, 2014

"Busy! Busy! Busy!" – Professor Hinkle

Professor Hinkle was the magician in the animated Christmas classic *Frosty The Snowman.* Why a magician called himself a professor I'll never know. Perhaps he was a professor of magic. And why he was so busy, is also a mystery. But, he often stops by the stage in my mind and utters his trademark catch phrase much to the amusement of the live studio audience sitting there just beyond the eggnog river.

Either God or Satan must have been listening to me closely today, maybe both. On my way to the gym this morning, I was speaking with my long time booking agent turned very close personal friend, Marc Tetlow. We speak almost daily, although I barely can hear him throughout most of the conversation. Marc mumbles, he often utilizes speakerphone, and is most likely also ordering coffee at a drive-thru each time we speak. Luckily for me this morning, it was I that was doing most of the speaking.

We were discussing events planned for next year. What locations we were doing and on what dates and such. I was asking him if I had done enough episodes of that ole ghost show again this season to set us up good for 2015. He said three or four would have been enough and that I shouldn't be killing myself doing all I have done, sacrificing sleep, driving all night, and working all day. I told him that I think in all I have filmed for six or seven episodes and that I'm hoping that will be enough to refresh my name in the paranormal community, and also help us to book more motivational lectures for years to come.

I didn't mind doing all those episodes because I really do enjoy doing investigations, and since my spiritual awakening a few years back, it appears my ability to interact with the spirit world has grown exponentially. I have been so grateful for my spiritual connection that I attribute to God and specifically the Holy Spirit. It works on greater levels than mere spirit communication on investigations, but I don't like to talk too much about it.

I'm also grateful for the opportunities filming the show have brought me. Thanks to the notoriety derived from it, I've been able to provide for my family, travel the world, lecture at colleges and libraries across the country, received numerous free clothing and food items, and met so many interesting and amazing people, not to mention NASCAR Champion Kurt Busch. By returning to film with the show again this season, I've been able to pave my driveway, get our home painted, purchase the new Durango for my wife (with many payments still to come, of course), and we all will be going to the Macy's Day Thanksgiving Parade this year.

With all that in mind, I still told Marc that I'm growing more and more tired with each passing day and I'm not sure I'll do any more episodes. He reiterated that I had done more than enough and I should relax. As I said, Marc is more of a friend than a manager or promoter. He gets me events and bookings, but he never pushes me to do anything that he thinks is too much. If anything, he tries to talk me out of most the things I do.

I don't know my limits. He looks out for me. Not that I listen much.

And so tonight, when I came home from work and was on the phone with a co-worker, that ole 818 area code popped up on the other line. It seemed the good people in Los Angeles wanted to speak with me again about filming for the rest of the season. I told them that although I appreciated the offer, I didn't think it was for me. They said they would like me to be on every episode going forward, but as of now, could I at least commit to filming one more case next Tuesday in Newport, Rhode Island? I said yes—once again, without giving it much thought. It's in my home state after all, so it isn't like I need to travel far.

The case is at Fort Adams, which I'm very familiar with. Newport is an old Navy town and Fort Adams was just one of its many strong holds. My family shared a mooring just off the floating dock in the Fort Adams harbor from when I was about ten until I was sixteen. Many of my summers were spent on our 23-foot Sportcraft boat, driving my Achilles raft throughout the harbor, and walking around Fort Adams. I couldn't deny the ole gal now.

Oh well, so much for my conversation with Marc and my declaration that I made this morning. Like I said, someone was listening, devil or angel.

Frosty, cue the good Professor Hinkle for me would you? I think it's time for him to say his familiar "Busy! Busy! Busy!" phrase once again.

When will I learn?

Wednesday, September 24, 2014

THE TURKEYS ARE BACK!

Hot damn! They're back! They're back! They're back! The turkeys of the Belwing Turkey Farm are back!

The Belwing Turkey Farm on route 44 somewhere between Seekonk and Rehoboth, Massachusetts, has been a staple for procuring a fresh turkey for Thanksgiving and Christmas for local area families for many moons.

Now I'm not someone who cares much for turkey meat. I have never eaten a slice of turkey on any other day except Thanksgiving, and I have never purchased a turkey from the Belwing Turkey farm, but every year, when the turkeys return to the farm it brings me great joy! I know technically the turkeys are not returning, as each year brings new birds, but I like to phrase it that way anyway so that the upcoming holiday massacre isn't so macabre. Trust me, I prefer pizza. Not just for Thanksgiving either—pretty much for every meal.

When I drive by the turkey farm in the morning on my way to work I roll down the driver's side window in ole Angelina, I beep my horn, lean out the window and bellow "Good morning, turkeys!" with amazing gusto in the early light of day. At first they seem startled by it, but as the season rolls on, they become accustomed to it, and I like to think that they look forward to it.

Last year there was one turkey that would jump every time I beeped and yelled. The live studio audience in my mind was quite amused and really thought that one particular turkey had made a connection with me.

On the way home from work, I crank down the passenger side window of ole Angelina, beep my horn, lean over and yell out, "Good night, turkeys!" into the setting sun.

Last year there was a great batch of birds. In the morning there was often one standing on the little coop roof. There were several days when one or two of them would be just outside the fence, standing there watching the traffic go by.

I like when I have to work late and I drive by and see them all huddled in the coop with their little heat lamps on. God bless those turkeys.

Each year I take my daughter there and we take pictures with them outside of the fence. What? You can go take pictures with the Easter Bunny and Santa Claus, but you can't take pictures with turkeys?

I often tell myself I'm going to buy one and release it back into the wild. I'm not sure it would be a great idea, though. I mean, I see the way the escapees just stand there and stare at the traffic.

Tonight I did a paranormal lecture at the Seekonk Public Library in Massachusetts. It was phenomenal, if I do say so myself, and I do.

The place was packed to the gills. Standing room only. They added as many chairs as possible, and there were still people leaning up against the walls. It was very humbling and made me feel quite good. To have a crowd like that for one of my paranormal lectures so early in the season is a good sign—and I believe in signs. I don't always obey them but I at least glance at the ones that the elves in my head hold up. Those little fellows seem to offer good guidance.

Except on skinny-dipping Sundays. Then all bets are off, as are their tiny knickers. I weep for the purity of the eggnog river in my mind on those days.

Thursday, September 25, 2014

"The stars at night are big and bright deep in the heart of Texas!"

Tomorrow morning I fly out to Texas for Fantomfest. It's a fun event held in San Antonio running through the weekend. The promoter actually booked me two years ago to do the show and I had a great time. I met some great people and so I'm looking forward to returning.

The only issue is the flight out of here in the morning is at 6am, which means I have to get up and out of my house at 4am in order to check in by 5am. Tick tock clock. But I'll fly there tomorrow. Do the gig. Pass out from sheer exhaustion. Then give all of my energy away again on Saturday.

Lather. Rinse. Repeat.

Sunday I'm flying back home, only to hop in Angelina and drive about three hours north to an event near the New Hampshire/Massachusetts border. That one is a fundraiser for cleaning up a river, or at least I think that's what Marc told me it was.

Two events. Two States. One weekend. One man.

I should have my head examined. Nah! It would only piss off the elves.

Now I'm cuddled up in my new Jack Skellington pajama pants and I'm signing off for the night. If I can say my prayers and get to sleep in the next ten minutes or so, I can get almost four-and-a-half hours of sleep. Yee-ha!

Friday, September 26, 2014

"Livin on the road my friend is gonna keep you free and clean. Now you wear your skin like iron. Your breath as hard as kerosene." – "Pancho and Lefty" by Willie Nelson.

I'm back on the road, and I hope, at least for the sake of the well-to-do woman sitting next to me, that my breath is not as hard as kerosene. I'm on Southwest Airlines flight 562 flying from Baltimore/DC airport to San Antonio, Texas. The seat is 13D and the time is too damn early. It's actually closer to 10am, but I've been up since before 4am and the day has been an hour-long drive, a 20-minute walk, and a flight from Rhode Island to the

Baltimore/DC airport. Needless to say, I'm a bit tired at the moment but the moment is almost past, which is why, tired or not, we must seize and enjoy each of them.

It was pitch black when I awoke this morning and something was askew with my left leg because my hip and shin were hurting when I slid out of bed and stood up to greet the dark morning. Not sure what all that was about but I'll keep it in mind. I know I didn't hurt it at the gym as I only did a vanity pump yesterday so I'd look nice for this weekend's events and also so I could eat a pizza in my hotel room without feeling too bad about myself for it.

Ole Angelina was in great form this morning. Her engine roared to life and purred all the way to TF Green airport. I changed her oil yesterday and she likes when I do that. I gave her a little scratch beneath her steering wheel. She likes that, too. I've been changing the fluids under that ole gal's skirt for over fifteen years now. Once I get my tools out and slide underneath that engine, I can get everything done in ten minutes or so. I know my lady and she knows me. It's a splendid union of love and lubrication.

I left her parked in my spot at my office on Jefferson Boulevard in Warwick about a mile or so from the airport. I told everyone I was having someone pick me up and drive me to the airport but in truth, I had always planned to walk it. There's something romantic about an early morning walk whilst the sun is still finishing up her beauty sleep. Plus, I was toting my luggage behind me, so there was a bit of a hobo vibe to it that the gypsy in my soul enjoyed.

The opportunity has never presented itself in this life but there have been many times in my mind when I've hopped a box car and played the harmonica whilst the wheat fields of America drifted by the open train door; just me, Bob Dylan, and the passing breezes of freedom and heartache. Good times. Good times.

I met up with Mr. Jeff Belanger at the airport this morning. Jeff is a great guy; a truly good family man with a heart full of love. I met Jeff many moons back at some convention or another. He has done writing and field research for more shows than I can think of and you have probably enjoyed at least two or three of them on a regular basis. He's also a talented author and orator. Jeff is an enigmatic storyteller in a time that needs good storytellers.

I think we resonated with each other right off the bat, as we both like to write, to speak, and to entertain. Neither of us has ever been caught up with the "celebrity" nonsense of television despite our involvement with various programs over the years. We are both doing it all because it's fun and because it helps to provide for our families. He recently has had me be a part of one of his Legend Trip events on my birthday this past year. He and his crew even had a cake there for me. I instinctually trust and like anyone that offers me dessert.

We decided upon our first flight that we shall go visit the Alamo later today when we get to San Antonio. Neither of us has ever seen it and we've heard good things about the basement there. If all works out, I'll be riding Pee-Wee Herman's bicycle back home.

I'm forever entertaining my inner-child and the live studio audience in my mind. Speaking of which, I think it's about time that I recline my seat back, close my eyelids, and visit the pirate-themed bar on the coast of the eggnog river. Here's to Jolly Good Times! (That's how the elves and I named the bar when it finished construction last fall.)

"Away in a Menger, no crib for his bed. Little D. Pari just raised up his head." I just awoke from a brief nap in The Menger hotel in downtown San Antonio, Texas. I have to go to a VIP dinner with some of the attendees of Fantomfest in about an hour.

This is a historic hotel, which means it's classically beautiful with quaint rooms. They also have a great bar that reminds me of the old west, as much as I can recollect it with never having lived it. I bellied up to the bar and had a Lobo Octoberfest after touring the Alamo, which is right across the street.

I knew, thanks to Mr. Herman's big adventure, there was not a basement in the Alamo but I didn't know there wasn't a cover charge. In New England, we charge for access to almost anything historical and most things of no true significance. Yet here in Texas, you're just asked to remove your hat out of respect. Classy. I like that.

I took the Alamo tour and admired the artifacts before returning to the hotel for my nap. Oh, I also stopped to get ice cream, because the name "Alamo" reminded me of "a la' mode", and although there was no pie to be had, there was an ice cream shop on the corner, so I figured God wanted me to indulge. Perhaps He will provide pie later. Till next I write, I urge you all to join me, living life a la' mode.

Not only was there pie tonight, but it was German apple pie! I've never had it before but it was delicious. My friends Carol Jean and her husband Curt brought it to the hotel for me. They're a charming couple and as sweet as pie themselves. Curt is a regular cowboy with his grizzled look and white whiskers but underneath his hat are warm eyes and a heart of gold. His wife has been kind enough to run online fan clubs for me for many moons now. She's too kind and often dotes upon my family and me with unique homemade gifts, and tonight, a pie. Good people with hearts as big as Texas itself.

I returned to my room to eat in peace. I spent the last few hours taking pictures with people, calling their family members who couldn't make it to the event, and otherwise just making myself accessible to all these nice people who are kind enough to come out to these events and spend their hard earned money to meet me and the rest of the misfit toys on this island.

It's never lost upon me that all of this is a blessing of which I'm unworthy. All of it. The fans, the friends, the finances, and the pie—I don't deserve any of it. Yet all these things make it possible for me to continue on and provide for Mama Bear and our sweet little Beans.

I may work hard to keep all of this going—the day job, the events, the lectures, the books, and the shows. Lord knows I barely sleep and constant travel isn't easy, but I'm thankful that even though I haven't been on television in five years, I'm still relevant in the paranormal field and beyond.

I was blessed with being given the foresight of knowing that I had to embrace what was next in my life and continue to push myself outside of what was comfortable. Not simply doing paranormal events and lectures—getting by on my name from seasons of television appearances—but working on my motivational desires and my faith based work in Christian ministry. These are things I'm so very passionate about doing. This recent return to paranormal television is just a fun bonus. I can't imagine what my schedule next year will be like when people see me back on television again. I'm sure the paranormal events will spike, which is great, but I'm hoping it allows me to help more people with my motivational lectures. And if God sees it fit for this broken little angel to limp out there and hold up the mirror to reflect His love and teachings for more to see, I would be elated.

I found out the bar here at The Menger Hotel, where I enjoyed a beer earlier today with Jeff, is actually where President Teddy Roosevelt recruited the Rough Riders, the 1st United States Volunteer Calvary, back when the West was still a bit wild and the Spanish-American war raged. I left the comfort of my hotel room and my pie to have a spirit in honor of the Rough Riders and drifting cowboys throughout time.

Whilst at the bar sipping on a little Captain Morgan rum, as yes, I'm a pirate (even when I'm a cowboy), I ran into Mr. Christopher Quaratino, also known as Christopher Lutz, of The Amityville Horror notoriety. Chris is a splendid guy to talk with. We spoke a few years back when doing an event in the upper peninsula of Michigan. He aims to set the story straight about what happened at his former home in Amityville, and more importantly, why it happened.

Tonight Chris and I were moved to speak with each other at length about spirituality, Christianity, and the deeper questions of the realm that few people discuss openly these days. As he leaned in to mention various Bible passages to me and ask certain questions, I couldn't help but think of President Theodore Roosevelt as he must have been doing the same over a hundred years ago, whispering in the ears of cowboys and forming the Rough Riders. We chatted for a bit and I felt good to have had the opportunity to speak with him about such things. Talking about religion with those whom you don't know well is always dicey at best, but it's comforting when I find someone whom is like-minded and not afraid to speak up.

However, sleep is at a premium once again, so I slipped away after finishing my rum and I'm back up here in my room finishing off one more piece of pie before taking up residence at the Jolly Good Times pirate bar in my mind for the rest of the night.

The elves don't like to talk about religion much; they are more concerned with labor laws and governmental issues at the North Pole.

Time to shut my eyes and close the drapes because, as they say, "The stars at night are big and bright deep in the heart of Texas!"

Saturday, September 27, 2014

I just finished up today's events here at Fantomfest. I was on the floor from eight o'clock this morning until just about seven this evening. I did a lecture for just about an hour and really felt like I connected with some people. We had lots of laughs and I was able to get a good number of my motivational points in there, along with some thoughts upon the necessity for spiritual understanding.

I'm heading out for dinner with Carol Jean and Curt. I'm looking forward to having a delicious steak and some good conversation.

Well, after dinner I wanted to simply go have one drink with the event organizer and a few of the VIPs, but Jeff Belanger made my Hurricane multiply, the bastard. I don't like to hang out and drink at these events, nor do I drink much anywhere else. I enjoy a simple beer or hard cider and that's good enough for me but once in a while, I think it's good to enjoy oneself in a responsible way. And so, I finished the additional beverage and headed off to bed. I know I'll feel bad about it in the morning, even though there is nothing wrong with having more than one adult beverage.

The issue is I hold myself to impossible standards and I shouldn't. I've been like this since I was a child. I feel guilty for taking pleasure in the things of this world. My spiritual side is much stronger and more important than my physical side. Those times when I cater to my humanity I often feel bad about it but this human experience is a training ground. It's a schoolroom for the soul. We are all here to live and to learn. Are you writing this down?

I've learned a lot early on. Call me an old soul or whatever you will. These lessons often make it hard for me to just let go, to relax, and to live. But I'm doing my best.

Sadly, there are only about four hours until I have to get up and head to the airport again. I have to do another event tomorrow night just north of Boston, Massachusetts, so I best go get some shuteye. Did I mention I have been struggling with a kidney stone since Thursday? Well, I am still struggling with it.

Sunday, September 28, 2014

Southwest flight 794 is streaking across the sky taking me home from Baltimore, Maryland. I didn't write on the early flight today, as I was able to catch a few hours of sleep flying from San Antonio to Baltimore. I needed every one of those forty winks.

I'm trying to figure out how to make the rest of this day work. Thankfully I didn't have any flight delays today, so I'll be able to make it up to tonight's event on time. I should have just enough time to stop home for a quick shower, and then head up to Methuen, Massachusetts, to appear at a fundraiser for the Clean River Project.

I like to do charity events and fundraisers because they give me an opportunity to help give back to the communities and help others. Plus, I'll be working with my old friends Mr. Joe Chin and Mr. Bruce Tango. The three of us have worked together at many events over the years. Joe and I traveled the world together filming for *Ghost Hunters International.* Tonight we simply have to do a little lecture, sign some autographs, and take some photos.

Oh good, the stewardess is bringing me pretzels. I do enjoy pretzels. I like to dip my finger in the bottom of the bag and lick all the salt up. I should be more concerned about my arteries but I let my arteries worry for themselves. I really like salt.

I have to be honest; I don't like Southwest. I know the fares are cheap and your bags fly free, but this nonsense of picking your own seat is a pain in the ass. When I book the flight, let me pick my seat then. If not, then when I check in I'll choose where to sit. Enough with this whole nonsense of paying extra to board first to pick the best seat—are we children picking out what color car we want to drive at the amusement park? Seriously, it's all so ridiculous. Someone get me more salt. You can keep the pretzels.

Tonight's event was a pleasant one and I was able to get home in time to see my little one before she went to sleep. I love going in to her room and seeing her laying there under the convers, listening to her country music with her little eyelids closed over her radiant eyes.

Beans has my eyes. They change from green to blue depending on her clothes and her mood. Mine seem to have settled on green permanently. I haven't seen them blue in many moons.

I carried up my suitcase and emptied it out whilst catching up with my wife. Mama Bear wasn't feeling well and didn't have much to say. She usually doesn't have much to say anyway. I'm not sure what she thinks about all the time but it must be fascinating.

I have one hell of a week ahead of me. It looks something like this:

- Monday: Day job at MSL Facial & Oral Surgery. Working late to facilitate updates on x-ray imaging software in both of our offices.
- Tuesday: Day job at MSL followed by filming for that ole ghost show down in Newport. I imagine we'll film till about 4am.
- Wednesday: Day job at MSL followed by an evening event we are putting on for our referring dentists. This is something I have been putting together for a few months, so I'll have to be there to ensure it goes off without a hitch.
- Speaking of "hitch", this Wednesday is also October 1st, which is our wedding anniversary. Mama Bear and I'll have been hitched for eight years, and together for ten. I feel bad that I have to work day and night on our anniversary, but my wife doesn't mind. I just purchased the new Durango for her so we aren't doing any gifts, and we will go out for dinner some other night. These things happen.
- Thursday: After the day job I'm doing a paranormal lecture at the Dighton, Massachusetts, library.
- Friday I'll be meeting up with my manager Mr. Marc Tetlow and driving down to Winchester, Virginia, for a weekend event.

You see why I choose to just take things moment by moment don't you? Overwhelming if I think of it as a whole. But I'm here and now in the here and now. My gym bag is packed for the morning and I'm resting in bed watching today's NASCAR race in Dover on DVR. Mama Bear is snoring lightly beside me and our Beanie Baby is sleeping sweetly in her room across the stairwell.

I'm home safely after a crazy travel weekend. I brought others laughter and joy, and I pray I gave them a little bit of hope.

As for me, I'm alive and well.

"And today you know that's good enough for me. Breathing in and out's a blessing, can't you see? Today is the first day of the rest of my life. And I'm alive and well." – Mr. Kenny Chesney (Though I prefer the version done by Mr. Willie Nelson.)

Good night, Willie, wherever you are.

Monday, September 29, 2014

It's 11pm and I'm still at my office. I had to do some software upgrades for the imaging equipment at both offices, so I have been getting some work done and helping the IT guy with the x-ray equipment.

This day started at 6am and I've been here since 8am but soon I'll be in sweet ole Angelina, listening to Bob Dylan, windows cranked down and the cool fall breeze blowing through my hair. It's the simple things in life that are the sweetest, and you cannot fully enjoy the sweet unless you have experienced the sour.

I personally believe that Mr. Bob Dylan's album *Blood On The Tracks* is the perfect soundtrack for the fall season. It's just so damn beautiful it almost hurts. Bob's imagery is as colorful as the treetops; his lyrics are as poetic as the falling leaves. Sing it to me Mr. Zimmerman, you curly haired bastard!

I have Uncle Bub to thank for my love of Dylan. That same summer when I stayed with him and he unknowingly flaunted his woodpecker tattoo in front of my high school sweetheart was when he also introduced me to the musical styling of one Mr. Bob Dylan. (When he had his pants on, of course. My uncle, that is. Not Bob. Who knows when Dylan is ever wearing pants?)

I'm excited to hear that there will be a photo shoot tomorrow when I arrive on set at Fort Adams in Newport. SyFy has requested some more photos of me and my friend the Spaceman, Mr. KJ McCormick. I started calling him the Spaceman recently. We were doing an investigation for that ole ghost show and he told the spirits we were from the future, which struck me as funny mostly because he was so serious in his delivery of it, and also because he was against the backdrop of a bright greed laser grid that gave a spooky space like effect. Hence the Spaceman was born!

Hanging with KJ McCormick at a photo shoot for the show

We've been working together a lot on camera lately and getting some great evidence of the spirit world. Prior to filming this season, we had only worked one event together and never investigated on or off camera with each other. So our pairing has been a very splendid happy accident.

I do fancy a photo shoot. It has nothing to do with vanity, but it doesn't hurt any either. Ha! It's just fun to do. Look this way and that. Stare down the lens of the camera. Now you're a tiger! Work it, baby! Work it! Well, okay, maybe isn't really like that but in my head it is and by now you must have realized that what goes on within my head is all that really matters to me anyhow.

Tuesday, September 30, 2014

Just finishing up at the office and I'll be heading out to film for that ole ghost show down at Fort Adams. The office closed early, which worked out perfectly for my newly scheduled photo shoot with the Spaceman. Looks like I'll get down to Newport for just after 3pm. If I was a betting man, and I'm not, I would wager I would be filming to sometime after 3am. The smart money is on me always as I would also never bet against myself.

Not much time to write today, just hi and bye because I've got to fly!

Wednesday, October 1, 2014

Wow! What an investigation. Fort Adams made for a great case. Lots of personal experiences and such, but as I'm prone to say in a canned manner, we won't know what we have until we do evidence review. But since I just collapsed in my hotel room and it's 4am (see, I told you we would film past 3am)—and so evidence review will have to wait. Sleep cannot wait as I have to get back in ole Angelina and drive to work in … two-and-a-half hours?

That can't be right?

Are you sure?

Son of a -!

It's last call at Jolly Good Times! Ring the bell! All elves out of the eggnog river!

Good night to our in-house studio audience. We love you!

And I now begin my broadcast day. Cue the National Anthem and the patriotic montage. Those were the days. Back when television signed on and off. There were no late night infomercials or countless reruns of reality shows. Stations started and stopped every day, yielding way to bars and tone. I would love to watch channels sign on and off again. I remember in high school getting up early, making my breakfast, turning on the television just a minute or two before they would start broadcasting and then "Beeeeeeeeeep. We now begin our broadcast day."

Ahh, memories. I can almost taste the waffles.

Today is the first of October. Whilst growing up this was one of the days I always looked forward to. Regardless of our calendar year, space in the cosmos, and all that other time related jazz, I look to the first of October with great anticipation because in my mind, it signifies the beginning of my favorite time of year, the fall.

Sure it may have started a few days back or whatever, but when it's October, it's on like Donkey Kong! The leaves have already started changing. Pumpkins are everywhere. There are many fancy hard ciders in my special fridge and regular cider in the family fridge. Boo Berry cereal is haunting my cupboards.

I enjoy my evening walks the most at this time of year. I crank up Mr. Bob Dylan when I walk through the cemetery at dusk. I play some Led Zeppelin when I wander through the woods. Life is good and God is great, but in the fall, everything is awesome!

Another reason I look forward to October 1st is because it's my wedding anniversary. Mama Bear and I celebrate eight years married, and ten years together today.

We met in a parking lot, and no, it was nothing like what you're thinking, but not due to my lack of trying.

We actually first saw each other across the floor at a multiplex club named Mardi Gras, in a little country bar called The Diamond Rodeo, and all of it just around the Cranston/Warwick border in Rhode Island.

She was sweet in her little red jeans and black shirt sitting on a stool near the disc jockey area, talking with her friend at a table. I was there with my buddy and his girlfriend at the time, but they were in the rock n' roll club. I like all types of music, so it was when I was feeling my country music side that I first locked a gaze with the sweet little lady that would come to be known as Mama Bear.

I was instantly intrigued as I love short brunettes with dark eyes and shapely womanly curves—and she was all that and then some. I was so sure of my abilities at that time that I went to find my friend and his girl and tell them that I saw a girl I would probably go home with for the night, and not to worry about me. I did this without even speaking to my future wife. Talk about confidence! However, when I went back into the Diamond Rodeo, the target of my affection had disappeared. I looked over every barstool in that place at least twice but she was nowhere to be found. They had an outside patio. She wasn't there either.

I went to the disco club but found nothing. Upstairs to the hip hop club—stumped again. I ran into the rock club and still came up empty-handed. I hung my head low and went back into the country bar just to look one more time. I didn't see her or her friend anywhere.

I ordered a Corona and stepped out onto the patio to drink away my cares and tell my troubles to the moon and the stars. The moon and the stars make for great listeners. I also enjoy looking up to them and feeling so small and non-permanent.

"All we are is dust in the wind." – Kansas.

My second grade teacher sang that one to me on a regular basis. She had good taste in music. I still love that song, but not as much as I enjoy "Carry On Wayward Son" from Kansas, too. It's going to be one of my funeral songs if everything goes right. Not much worried about it, though, for when I go, I go, and I'll be eating pie in Heaven with Jesus and John Lennon. But I would like three songs played at my funeral and they are: "Carry On Wayward Son" by Kansas. "Hallelujah" by John Cale. "Simple Man" by Lynyrd Skynyrd.

Some people think me odd for having a funeral playlist. Others think I'm odd for a variety of reasons in addition to having a funeral playlist. I think if you die, and you haven't had any input as to the music played when they lower you down into the underground all you can eat worm buffet, well then, my friend, you deserve it if they are playing "I've Got a Lovely Bunch of Coconuts". You should have had a playlist.

I only named the main three songs but there are many others for the after party. And I want it to be a party. Have fun, damn it! It's only death, after all. I want it to be a celebration of my life, who I was, what I did for others, and all that happy nonsense. No gloom and doom. Blow bubbles. Tell stories. Have fun whilst you are still alive, because you are still alive.

I've mentioned this to my daughter many times. We have a very special relationship. I know lots of parents think they have special relationships with their children but there are some relationships in this life that just click beyond words and measures, and that is Beans and I. So when I die I told her that it's okay to be sad, it's okay to cry, and it's okay to miss me. But it's not okay to not move on. Think of me often and fondly, but know you'll see me again—perhaps a couple of pounds heavier due to all the pie I'll be eating in Heaven with Christ and John Lennon. So I told her that when she misses me, she could always close her eyes and think of me. She can come and visit my gravesite and blow bubbles there. I would like that. I also like to think it'd remind her of all the fun and joyous times we had together.

Anyhow, back to the lecture at hand—how I met Mama Bear. Be honest, you forgot what we were talking about. That's okay. I did, too. I had to scroll back up to check and see.

So there I was under the moon and stars drinking my Corona and wondering where Little Miss Red Pants and her friend had gone and wondering if I'd ever find the one. And then, in one of those moments that only happen in one of those moments, I looked across the parking lot and I see a little brunette with red pants walking to the next parking lot over. I took a swig of the Corona, gave a quick thank you to the Big Man upstairs, hopped the patio railing and was making my way to my future.

I was approaching her when she and her friend looked back. She exclaimed, "Well, thank God!" or, "There is a God!" She and I debate this still, and she paused for me to catch up.

I walked her and her friend to her car. She gave me a fake name of Desiree. I asked her out to a late night breakfast, she said no. I insisted. She persisted. I got her real name and phone number. Two years later we were married. Three years later we had our daughter. Ten years later I'm writing this on our eighth wedding anniversary.

"Ain't it funny how time slips away?" – Mr. Willie Nelson.

Sadly, I won't see my wife until later tonight as I have to work all day and I'm running an event for the surgeons' office this evening.

What's that? When will I sleep you say?

When I'm dead. Until then, I have too much living to do to slow down.

Time for work!

The dental implant lecture and dinner event that I put together for my office and our referral base was a success. I'm good at facilitating these types of things. It went till just after 8:30 this evening, which made for a twelve-hour workday on top of yesterday's two-job marathon.

"More weight," as my friend Giles Corey said.

In truth Mr. Corey and I were not friends. But that is in part due to the fact that he was killed in Salem, Massachusetts, on September 19, 1692. Giles was accused of witchcraft along with his wife Martha during the famed Salem Witch Trials. He would not confess to being involved with witchcraft, so they pressed him to death. They put a board on him and placed stones upon it, pausing to ask him to confess. When they did so, Mr. Corey would simply reply, "More weight." He did so until he expired beneath the weight of the stones.

I love this true story because it's a testament to many things I care about. Amongst them, not giving in to the pressure of others. Standing up for what's right, even when what's right isn't what's easy. Take what life is giving you and ask for more. I've said it before and I'll say it again. Most of us don't know our own limits. We tap out and give up long before we are truly done. We don't know how much we can take or what we are really capable of because we give up as soon as things get difficult.

As soon as that light on the dashboard pops up indicating we're running low on fuel, we pull into the next gas station. I press on. I want to know how much is truly in the tank. What am I capable of overcoming? How far can I truly go? I'm still learning the answers to some of these questions. I'm not giving up. I'm pushing the limits. I'm getting the most out of my human experience and each tank of gas.

Work for days on minimal sleep, travel to several different locations, work multiple long hour shifts at multiple jobs—sure, I can do that. More weight.

"Carry on my wayward son. There'll be peace when you are done. Lay your weary head to rest. Don't you cry no more." - Kansas

This concludes my broadcast day.

Beeeeeeeeeeep.

Thursday, October 2, 2014

Well, well, well! Tonight's lecture was a great one! I knew it was going to be busy as they moved the location from the town library to the town hall but I didn't think that the town hall would be packed! It's always great to do a lecture. If there were only one person that showed up, I would still go through with it. But when you walk into a venue and it's packed from wall to wall and there isn't an empty seat in the house, well, it's humbling to say the least.

I really enjoyed speaking to everyone tonight. They were very receptive and interactive. There were even two small children that came with their mother. Kids are the best. I always make sure to keep my lectures positive, as I feel there is too much gloom and doom in the paranormal world anyway, but when kids are there, I make sure to tell them that the spirit world is a wonderful place full of love and light, and that they need not be afraid. There is no reason to scare anyone, especially children.

After the lecture, I had dinner with my young friend Cody Ray DesBiens. He's a mere twenty-years-old but wise beyond his time. He has already fought cancer and won. A feat few people can state, never mind doing so at such a young age.

Whilst eating my first ever club sandwich--yes, the first one ever in 37 years. Nope, I've never had anything in club sandwich form. To be honest, I found it cumbersome. Just give me a sandwich, don't put in extra bread and try to cut it up all cute and fancy. I have big man hands with calluses and such. That's why I normally just eat steak.

Anyhow, while I was eating this thing, I received a phone call from that ole 818 area code. Before I even answered I knew I had to decide if I was going to do another episode of the show. Don't get me wrong, great opportunity, thankful, yada, yada, yada.... But at some point, I must rest.

Apparently I'll rest when I'm dead because the ole 818 call informed me that I'm going to Kentucky (again) in two weeks' time. I've been to Kentucky more in the last few weeks than I have ever been in my life. Good thing I rather fancy it there.

I live in the moment and right now I'm home sweet home. I have packed up my bags for tomorrow's trip to Virginia. Mama Bear and Beans are here in bed with me, sleeping soundly already. I'll get up with the sun and pack up the rental car. Then I'll spend a little time with them before getting behind the wheel and heading south.

I can hear the naughty little ladies from the Lullaby League creeping down the staircase in my mind. Soon they'll carry me off to sleep. I don't mind them much, except for the littlest one; she is a bit of a biter.

Friday, October 3, 2014

I just arrived at my hotel in Winchester, Virginia. Greeting me at the front desk was a bag with a Southern Tier Pumking Ale—one of my favorites—and a bottle of Sweet Baby Jesus, a peanut butter flavored beer. My good friend, Mr. Clay Smith, dropped off these delectable beverages for me earlier today. He is the same gentleman that helped me in my suicide awareness video, and the gent who gave me the picture of Elvis. Speaking of which, I haven't seen the King around lately. I better see where the wife hid him this time. Elvis better not have left the building!

I had a splendid ride down here. It took a mere seven and a half hours from my door to my hotel, and that was with stopping twice to eat. Once was at Dunkin Donuts, and the other at some place called Yocco's the Hot Dog King. Dunkin is a regular stop and I simply couldn't pass by the "Hot Dog King" without saying hello to processed meat royalty.

Speaking of Dunkin, my good wife called me on my way down here and said we received a residual check from the commercial I did for Dunkin Donuts last year. We hadn't seen one of those in a while. I thought they had stopped running the commercial completely. It's been over a year, after all, but apparently it played somewhere, and thus a check showed up in the mailbox. I hung up the phone and thanked God for these continued blessings for which I'm still undeserving.

I'm looking forward to this evening at the hotel. I'll do my ritual of watching the History Channel and ordering a pizza. And then I'm hoping to explore a little thing called "sleep" that I have been hearing good things about.

Saturday, October 4, 2014

It happened again. Jamais vu.

Everybody knows about déjà vu, the term used for when something unfamiliar feels remarkably familiar without any explainable reason. Jamais vu is when you are unfamiliar with something that you have already encountered and are familiar with.

When I woke just moments ago, I had no idea where I was. I knew it was a hotel but the room seemed completely unfamiliar. I didn't know what state I was in and I had no idea why I was here. I actually thought I flew in yesterday, when now, I realize I drove seven-and-a-half hours to get here.

I'll have to keep an eye on this or at least ask Mama Bear to write my name in my underwear in case I get really confused someday. Then again, knowing me, I may think "D. Pari" is the official name of my penis. That would be odd. Having a penis with a name but not knowing who you are.

I just emerged from my hotel room after eleven hours of hibernation. I'm a new creation. Fresh, clean, and beautiful—that's me.

In the hallway I came across my old friend Mr. John Zaffis. Now John has been doing this gig since Fred Flintstone was working at the Bedrock quarry. I'm pretty sure John has dinosaur EVP's around his museum somewhere. John is a dear friend of mine and well-respected in the paranormal community. I admire his honesty and his dedication. Every year John says he's going to retire, but he never does. Just like I keep saying I'm only going to film just one more episode of that ole ghost show.

Johnny greeted me with, "Dude! What have you been doing? I've seen your schedule. You're an animal!"

The fact that John, who has made a career out of lectures and shows and events is telling me that I've been doing a lot and cautioning me to slow down is actually quite an honor. At least that's the way I look at it.

I left the old man, which I say with the utmost love and respect, and headed down to the lobby where they have some of that fancy water in the large glass decanter, complete with fresh slices of citrus.

I drank nine glasses. I was parched. I think bears fill up on that stuff before they hibernate but I didn't. I also think bears plug their hindquarters with something to prevent defecating upon themselves whilst they hibernate. I don't do that either, so although I did wake up thirsty today, it's a fair trade.

I went over to the Harvest Moon, a health foods and supplement store that my friend Mr. Clay Smith owns. We met with his wife Joy and their friend Mike in the back room there and had some pizza. My friend Ms. Rosalyn Bown came down from New Jersey to see us and attend the event as well. Ros greeted me with a loving hug before telling me I looked like hell. But that's Ros. She's from Jersey. She will remind you of that many times as that somehow allows for her unapologetic commentary. Some of us have social grace. The rest of you are from Jersey. (Kidding Ros! Much love to you and the Garden State.)

Personally, I think I look rather dashing today. At least the best I've looked in some time. It does take me a few hours to shift gears in the morning with waking up my sleepy eyes, so I'll attribute it to early morning roughness, even though it was well after noon.

It's just about time for a quick costume change once again. Thanks to the cell phones in everyone's pockets there aren't many phone booths around to change in these days so I do my best to keep my cape clean and easily accessible. I must head off to tonight's event at historic Jordan Springs in Winchester, Virginia, where I'll do a meet and greet, a little Q&A, and an event investigation with a hundred-and-some-odd people, trying to give away every ounce of energy that I have to ensure everyone has a good time.

"Here I am, on the road again. There I am, up on the stage." – Bob Seger, "Turn The Page".

Sunday October 5th, 2014

It's just after 1am and I just finished up tonight's event. I'm alone in the Waffle House. That sounds like lyrics to a sad old country song. I ordered a grilled cheese with bacon along with a tall glass of chocolate milk. I love chocolate milk. And grilled cheese with bacon reminds me of eating at truck stops with my dad when I was a kid. It's still one of my favorite dishes. It's a simple sandwich, not a pretentious club sandwich that is difficult to eat. Snooty bastards.

The event went well tonight. I had a good time interacting with the crowd; lots of laughs, lots of fun, and a good bit of spirit interaction. I'm always thankful for that.

Something happened to me tonight that has never occurred before, and I still don't have a reasonable explanation for it. During the second run of attendees at Jordan Springs, we were standing in a small salon in the old house on the side of the property. I was in the middle of a circle of guests and was going through my little soliloquy about respecting the spirit world and being aware of what is around us, and all the sudden, the K2 meters of those standing close to me started lighting up. These meters are supposed to light up if a spirit moves close to them or grabs onto them according to the theory. There are many other natural things that can trigger these sensors so I don't put too much stock in them but I'll use them as a secondary piece of equipment to help gather evidence for a stronger case.

As these meters started to light up, I turned and walked toward the other side of the crowd when their meters began to light up as well. I walked away and they shut off. I walked closer and they went on. I was sure to have my cell phone powered off and I had nothing else in my pockets. Strangely, as I extended my hand towards the meters, they would light up once again. I have never seen anything like it before. The only thought I have now is that we are indeed all spiritual beings, not just in the next life, but also in this one. We are spiritual beings going through a human experience.

On my drive down here two days ago, I had the radio cranked up in the rental, singing along to Mr. Willie Nelson, Mr. James Brown and They Might Be Giants. I was so happy in that moment, just pure innocent joy; it felt as if my body could not contain my soul. It was like I was bursting with light, seeping through my pores, fully alive in the moment.

Perhaps that was what happened there in that moment. I was very much enjoying myself whilst talking to people. Everyone was receptive and interactive in the run just before I was able to get some great spirit communication with my old Radio Shack AM/FM radio. Nothing fancy, but it gets the job done. It was a wonderful moment, and I can't help but to wonder if my interaction with the meters was a bleed over of my own spirit.

I can't say for sure that this is what happened but I can't offer any other explanation for it that makes any more sense.

It's almost 3am now and I must get myself off to sleep. The hotel is quiet and lonely, but I can get rest, which I'll need to get through the ride home and the week ahead.

I cannot wait to get home and tackle my little Beans and give her kisses in her beautiful face. I do miss her and Mama Bear so very much when I'm away.

The ride home should be a good one. The rental has satellite radio, which means I can listen to the NASCAR race on my way home. I love my NASCAR. Vroom! Vroom!

The elves are locking up at Jolly Good Times. It looks like the little pirate-themed bar in my mind did a hell of a business tonight.

Last call!

I got some sleep and I needed it
Not a lot, just a little bit
Someone's always tryin' to keep me from it

It's a cryin' shame
It's a royal pain in the neck
I'm just tryin' to get by
With my pride a little bit intact

—"Royal Pain" by The Eels

It's 10am and I just woke with that song in my head. Waking up with a song in my head is not uncommon. The DJ in there plays me something every day. Some days the song is foreshadowing for my life. Others it's a throwback to an earlier part of my life, a distant musical memory. And then there are days like this where it fits perfectly to what I'm doing.

That song was featured in *Shrek The Third.* That movie resonated with me quite a bit. Shrek is just trying to keep his family together and at the same time he is being pulled apart, as he needs to be everything to everyone. I could relate to my big green animated brother. I'm a son, a father, a husband, a step-father, a son-in-law, a manager, a TV personality, a good little Christian soldier, a close friend to many, and a closer friend to a few more.

I'm thankful for all these important roles, but there are days where I just want to connect with me. There are days when I just want to do some of the old things I want to do, and days when I just want to be alone with my wife and daughter. But there is always so much going on that I feel stretched a bit thin, and I'm just trying to get by with my pride, just a little bit intact.

But today I have slept in a bit late, and I needed it, for everyone is always trying to keep me from it.

Time to saddle up the rental and ride home to Mama Bear and Beans.

"Yah mule! Yah! Yah!" – Yosemite Sam, The World's Roughest Toughest Bad Man.

Sitting in the parking lot at the Hertz rental car office waiting for wife and Beans to come and pick me up. I'm listening to Bob Dylan sing "Shooting Star", one of my favorite songs that Mr. Zimmerman performs. For some reason, it always reminds me of my grandmother on my mother's side. Nana passed many moons ago but she remains a part of my memories and my life still today. And though I like to think I have made her and all my ancestors proud, I often wonder if I really have.

Ah, well. I'm doing my best. I never give up. I can hold my head high knowing that I am not out here just going through the motions. I just drove back and forth to Virginia on my weekend just to help provide for my family. That has to count for something.

The stars are twinkling up above. The man in the moon is looking right at me. Life is good. Soon I'll be home sweet home. It doesn't get much better than that.

> Seen a shooting star tonight
> And I thought of me
> If I was still the same
> If I ever became what you wanted me to be
> Did I miss the mark or overstep the line
> That only you could see?
> Seen a shooting star tonight
> And I thought of me

—"Shooting Star" by Bob Dylan

Monday, October 6, 2014

I hit the gym first thing this morning and it felt fantastic! Being able to exercise is one of the things I enjoy the most in this human experience. It felt great to get back into my routine. Starting my morning with my headphones on and the world blocked out really helps me to recharge.

Exercise is so important. It isn't about looking like a model or winning a fitness competition. It's about staying healthy and energized. It sounds crazy to those who will not leave the couch, but I'm telling you, the more energy you use, the more you end up having. How else could I be doing all this happy nonsense? You have been reading right? This isn't your average nine to five life.

After work I went over to another of my favorite places, the cemetery. I enjoy the peaceful solace it offers. This time of year is the best for walks through the old bone yard. The paths are covered with bright red, orange and yellow leaves. The crisp smell of the season hangs heavy on the breeze. I wandered for over an hour in the graveyard; washing off stones, straightening up flags, fixing up statues, raising toppled grave markers, and listening to Mr. Bob Dylan sing songs from *Blood On The Tracks*. It was truly a magical evening. I took some photos. I pondered life. I felt like I did back when I was in high school.

There was a wonderful pile of crunchy orange leaves on the ground and I couldn't resist laying in them for a bit. I looked up at the clouds moving by the moon, which was out a bit early. Mr. Bob Dylan sang "Simple Twist of Fate" softly in my ears. It was a near perfect moment. There was just one thing missing. I got up from the leaf pile, dusted myself off, and made my way over to sweet Angelina. From inside her cab, I removed a can of blueberry ale, responsibly, and placed it in an unmarked container. Okay, so it was just a can of blueberry ale hidden in a Styrofoam Dunkin Donuts cup, but I still enjoyed it responsibly.

This life is full of beautiful fleeting moments. When you are alive in the moment, you must cherish it. Don't worry about the things that you cannot control. Pretty much anything that exceeds your grasp you cannot control and more than likely you will mishandle what you can get your hands on anyway. So screw it.

Forget about your troubles and just smile.

Smile, damn it! It's just life, after all.

Tuesday, October 7, 2014

This doesn't happen often, which is a good thing. Today was one of those days where I mentally eject the 8-bit Nintendo game, blow in the cartridge, and press reset.

The first four hours of work were spent on my cell phone with the IT company that services our x-ray machine. Need I say more? I didn't think so.

Here is the difference between how I handle bad days and how others handle them. When things go pear shaped, as they often do, many of us stop and say, "Why me?" I get frustrated and such as well but I stop and think, "Why not me?" These things are going to happen. Not one of us is an exception to the rule. We all go through tough days, rough times, and truly horrible moments but in those absolute truths are also beauty. There is a great commonality there. No one gets by without a few bumps, scrapes, and scars, and that's wonderful. Life will throw me lemons. I choose to throw them right the hell back!

In these moments, I take the Etch A Sketch in my mind, flip it over, and start again. Things will be okay. All is as it should be. Some days are diamonds. Some days are stones. All of them rock.

The highlight of the day was doing a radio interview with my friend Mr. Clay Smith for his Spirit Watch radio show on LiveParanormal.com. Of course there were some technical difficulties in getting the show started, which made it stumble out of the gate. I blame myself, though it had nothing to do with me. It was just that kind of day. But Clay was able to right the ship, and he and his golden tones navigated a journey for all to hear. I like to think it was a pleasant interview with lots of high points regarding spirituality, religion, and understanding. Clay knows me well. His questions were like Nana's homemade meatballs being lobbed over the plate for me to hit out of the park.

But today, well, today was a stone … and that's okay.

I'll get the bastards tomorrow. I never let them keep me down.

Wednesday, October 8, 2014

I awoke early and was about to go to the gym, but then a cool breeze that smelled like rain wafted in playfully through the window. These moments are special to me. My senses come to life. I can taste the fall. I can feel the emotion of the rain. As much as I love the gym, moments like this must be savored. I simply laid there for the better part of an hour, breathing in all that the world was placing before me, the gym would have to wait.

Work was work as work often is. I really enjoy my job, but there isn't enough to write about it every day. We did have pizza for lunch, so, you know, pizza.

After I left the office I drove south to the North Kingstown Library and did my paranormal lecture. A packed house again. There had to be around eighty people in a public library on a Wednesday night. I must be doing something right but not sure what, though. I'm so glad that they all came out and enjoyed the night as much as I enjoyed being there with them.

Lecturing to me, whether it is motivational, paranormal, or faith-based, is a blessing. I so enjoy speaking to people. I love looking into the crowd and locking eyes with a few people throughout the night as I tell my tales. Our souls connect, if even for an instant, and there is a sparkle of magic, happiness and life in their eyes that I helped to put there. Amazing. I wonder if they know that I have to go home from here, do a radio interview, pack my gym bag, and go to work in the morning in hopes of paying all my monthly bills again? Probably not, and who am I to pull back the curtain on the Wizard of Oz.

The truth is, though, if you have ever been to see me at a conference, at a lecture, at an appearance, please know while it may appear that I'm up there entertaining you, educating you, or inspiring you, you are actually saving me. The feeling I get, the raw emotion of it all, the rush of endorphins when I'm up there on that stage, pacing back and forth like a caged tiger, or sitting uncomfortably forced into that chair, I'm ALIVE. I'm more alive there than I am almost anywhere else, with the exception of being with my loved ones. They get the best of me. The world gets the rest of me, but when I'm on stage, that's as good as I get.

"But Oz never did give nothing to the Tin Man that he didn't, didn't already have." – America's song "Tin Man".

The DJ in my mind keeps playing that song lately. I'm not sure what he's trying to tell me. Maybe I should be worried about my heart? I don't know.

I came home from my lecture, Angelina's windows down, eating a pumpkin donut from Dunkin' and beeping good night to the turkeys.

I checked in on sleeping Beans, stroked her hair, and gently kissed her head. Seeing her there, sleeping peacefully, her face warm with the reflected glow of the night-light, it made me feel good. All that I'm doing allows for her to have this safe, warm home and bed. I'm doing well as a provider and a father, no matter what I have to do.

Mama Bear was half-asleep. I gave her a kiss on her head and she grunted a good night. I then made it back downstairs to light some candles, pour a drink, and heat up some cheesy garlic biscuits of the Red Lobster variety (from the box not the restaurant).

Here I sit, waiting to do an interview for Darkness Radio with your host, Mr. Dave Schrader. Dave and I have known each other for a few years. We've shared tight little plane rides together to a yearly convention in northern Michigan and we have also shared company whilst enjoying an adult beverage after an event or two. I really do enjoy doing the radio programs, and Dave's a great host. Smooth and polished, (and that's just his head!). He's a professional's professional.

He gave me an honest and wonderful introduction about how he enjoys seeing me interact with fans at the events, and said I was sincerely one of the nicest and kindest guys. That simple statement made me feel really good. To know that my name is often up there with adjectives like nice and kind means a lot to me. In a world with lots of darkness, misery and strife, I try to be a happy little dancing flicker of light and love. But don't get too close or I'll burn your ass! Ha! (I don't really know what that means. I think I just like the imagery. I'm a bottom man. I mean, I do love a great pair of breasts, but without a curvaceous derrière, I'll simply bid you good day.)

It's a few minutes after midnight and I just ate a pile of whipped cream atop a sliver of pie, and then I headed up to bed. Mama Bear is lying beside me singing in her sleep. Well, actually she is snoring, but we will call it singing as it sounds more pleasant a description, whilst also painting her with a bit of a brush that could cause you to think she was possibly a sort of mad woman, which she is. You would have to be to get along with my mental elves and me.

Speaking of the little beautiful bastards, they are really getting down at Jolly Good Times tonight. The elves are hitting up the karaoke songbook with such spirit. There's so much frolicking and merry making that I fear the ole eggnog river may overflow her banks and bust the peppermint dam. For the life of me, I don't know what they're all so happy about. Personally, I'm exhausted. Maybe I should have had more for dinner besides donuts, biscuits, and pie with extra whipped… oh, now I see why they're so excited. Damn tiny sugar vampires.

There they are. Those naughty little ladies of the Lullaby League are shimmying their way down the chimney in my mind. Soon they will carry me off to the enchanted land of nod.

I wonder what glorious misadventures we will have tonight.

This is D. Pari signing off. Till next time—keep your head up, keep your eyes on the horizon, keep moving forward, and don't let anyone steal your sunshine. And smile, damn it! It's only life, after all.

I now end my broadcast day.

Beeeeeeeeeeeeeeeeeep.

Thursday, October 9, 2014

"Heeeeeey, kidsssss! Get your lazy bottoms out of bed, and do jumping jacks with Binky the Clown!" – *Garfield's Halloween*

That segment from the old Garfield Halloween special plays in my mind so very often. The image of a strangely twisted, red-nosed clown, screaming at you to do calisthenics first things in the morning is just pure genius to me. There are many mornings when I wake thinking of that exact scene.

There was also a great song in that cartoon called "What Should I Be" in which Garfield sings about what Halloween costume he should wear. That little ditty gets a lot of airplay by the DJ in my mind as well.

Today should be great. I got up early and did some exercise, without the help of an animated clown. I think it should be an easy day at the office and I'm leaving early to watch my daughter perform in reading theater at school. They take turns reading their assigned parts of a book and act it out as if it were a play. She has been practicing and I'm very excited to go see her in her first performance of this kind.

There have been many dance recitals these past few years but this is her first bit of theater. Beans is a very expressive child and a fantastic reader so I cannot wait to see how she does.

We shall finish up the night with a paranormal lecture. What else? Ha!

I told you, I am the Pumpkin King. Sorry Jack Skellington, but the people have spoken. This time every year I'm a regular paranormal Santa Claus except, instead of appearing at plaza malls with candy canes, I show up at quiet little libraries with exorcism recordings. So tell me, have you been a good little girl?

Gosh, that sounded creepy….

Well, I couldn't be prouder of our little Beanie Baby. She was one of the narrators in the first reading theater performance this afternoon and she was the lead character in the second one. Her projection and inflection were both spot on. My favorite part, however, was watching her bow. She has always loved performing and makes a big show of bowing and throwing kisses to the crowd. There were no kisses today but the bowing after each performance was really spectacular.

I remember at her first dance recital when she was about four-years-old, she was the last one on stage and had stepped forward to bow to the crowd. She's amazing. I have never loved someone so much as I love my little girl.

And there we have it. I just returned home from my last local paranormal lecture for the season. This one was a bit smaller than the last few but it was a nice chance to connect on a personal level with everyone who came.

Next week I'm filming for that ole ghost show, and then my college lectures start. That reminds me, I need to reserve my rental car for those trips. Angelina won't be up to it, though I would like to take her with me up through New Hampshire and Vermont again. Neither my truck nor I have been to Maine before, but alas, I guess it's not meant to be. I hate driving rentals on such occasions as I feel like I'm cheating on my truck but Angelina is getting up there and I don't want to risk her on a trip that spans the better part of a week.

Oh! I just remembered. A certain tradition must be continued out on my collegiate lecturing misadventures.

Every previous year I've picked up a pumpkin at a roadside stand and taken it with me on the journey. We stop and take pictures together. We get into trouble. Good times are had all around. And of course the pumpkin gets a clever name like Lieutenant Gourdsmith. I find giving them a military title lends to the credibility of their being.

I wonder whom I shall take with me this year.

I do like to entertain myself.

Friday, October 10, 2014

My whole day was spent anticipating the moment I would be able to come home and cuddle up with my daughter and watch a movie. I was thinking *Corpse Bride* or *The Nightmare Before Christmas*, to celebrate the Halloween season. I even picked up a pumpkin pie on my way home from work for us to share.

Sadly, I have been home for about two hours, and she is still out with Mama Bear and some friends. I knew they were going bowling but I thought they would have been back by now. So I caught up on some shows on DVR like *Sleepy Hollow* and *Pawn Stars*, and now I'm catching up on some writing whilst enjoying my favorite fall beverage for adults, Southern Tier's Pumking Ale. It's a delight for the senses, especially when you pour it in a glass and coat the rim with cinnamon and brown sugar.

The day was busy but good. I didn't have to work too late, at least for my standards. I have to pack for tomorrow's trip to Charlotte Motor Speedway down in North Carolina. Thanks to some connections I made on Twitter, I'll be able to stay on the track in the pits for the entire race!

The passes I have obtained previously are called Cold Passes and they allow you on the track up to an hour before the race starts. Tomorrow I'll get a Hot Pass, which allows me to stay on the track the entire time. I'm so excited. I'll get to see the cars come down pit road for service. I'll hear the sounds of the air guns. I'll smell the beautiful mixture of racing fuel and burning rubber.

Tomorrow will be a good day for sure. It's a nighttime race and one in the new playoff format in NASCAR's Chase For The Cup. I'm really looking forward to it but at the same time I feel bad because I won't be home with my family. I'm flying in tomorrow morning and returning Sunday morning, but still, it could have been a much needed day at home. I hate being away from my family but an offer like this doesn't come up too often and it'll be nice to do a little something to reward myself. Still, I have difficulty taking time for me. I always feel like I could be doing more for them if I wasn't doing things like this for me.

Ah! I hear the garage door! Wife and Beans are home. Perhaps I'll write later.

Saturday, October 11, 2014

Well, it looks like I did not write later.

I'm now on US Airways flight 821 in seat 23A. It's one of those exit row seats with no seat in front of it. I've learned seat configuration for various types of planes and where the best seats are to park yourself in my many years of traveling. The best seats to survive a crash are the ones in the back. It's where I normally sit because it's also where less people go, it's adjacent to the bathroom, and the place where they hide the snacks. When I was on those long international flights a few years back, it was not uncommon for me to go back into their little galley area and sneak some snacks out for my friends and me.

I stretched out and slept for the first hour and a half of this flight. My head was nuzzled in the fuzzy lining of my hooded sweatshirt, pressed up against the plastic window covering.

I had an issue waking up just moments ago in seat 23A. I simply could not lift my head and open my eyes. Damn sleep paralysis. I have dealt with it in the past. Terrifying little problem. Your mind if wide-awake but you cannot manipulate your body. There's this whole scientific reason about why it occurs but it basically boils down to a safety mechanism that kicks in when we hit REM sleep to stop us from thrashing about in reaction to our dreams. Or at least that's how I understand it.

I've had an issue with it about nine years ago, back when I was dating Mama Bear and the Beanie Baby was still a cute little ovum nestled in an aisle seat adjacent to Mama Bear's fallopian airlines. There were nights when I'd lie there screaming in my brain for my now-wife to grab my body and shake me back to life like a dormant snow globe. But in your head, no one can hear you scream. Well, in my head, the elves can but there's little they can do to help from inside anyway.

I've found my sleeping position makes a big difference. I'm a side sleeper. I like to curl up in the fetal position and say my prayers before the naughty little ladies of the Lullaby League sneak in to carry me to the Sleepy-Time Express, an enchanted old hobo train that carries me, Mr. Bob Dylan, and Mr. John Lennon to the Land of Nod. I expand when I sleep and usually end up on my belly, legs akimbo, and one arm hanging off the side. But that is okay, as it causes me no issue when I wake up. If I'm flat on my back with my hands behind my head, which I do find terribly comfortable, I sadly often stay in that position and slip into sleep paralysis, the Sleepy-Time Express derailed in a fiery heap of frustration.

Thankfully, now it only occurs to me whilst sleeping on planes. With the way I travel, I usually don't sleep much in the air, or on the ground. Though this last week has been a pleasant respite from the rigors of extensive travel. I can't complain about this one as this is a joyous journey and a little reward for me. It's race day!

I just finished feeding my in-flight vampire his customary beverage of tomato juice without any ice. Why I only drink it on planes I'll never know.

The lady sitting in the row in front of me, but to the right, as I have no seat in front of me—just sweet, sweet leg room—anyhow, the old bird in front of me is wearing a yellow scarf with zebras on it. Very bizarre. You don't see a lot of zebra fashion. She looks to be in her mid-to-late sixties. She also has big dangling golden earrings and perfume just about as brazen and flashy as the rest of her outfit accessories.

She's reading some type of old softcover romance novel, one of those dime-store trashy things that used to get the ladies all buttery. The pages of the book are yellowed and brown around the edges and the print is very small. She is making notes in the back cover with a fine tipped blue marker. She's intriguing in her strangeness. I wonder what her life is like. It probably involves a lot of cats. A disturbingly large amount of cats. And Tupperware parties, that are really code for an intimate sampling of exotic oils, motion lotions, and sex toys.

Tawdry dime-store romance novels, cats, and gently used sex toys... all wrapped up here in front of me in a zebra scarf. Well played my lady, you mile-high sex freak. Ain't no shame in it. You do your thing. This is your life. You do you like no one else can. I respect that.

"Not bad for a LaQuinta." – Stewie Griffin, *Family Guy*.

I just checked in to the LaQuinta and, as is customary every time I check into one, I think of little lemon-headed Stewie Griffin saying, "Not bad for a LaQuinta." When I checked in I couldn't help but notice everyone I encountered was of some sort of Hispanic descent. I'm curious if there's just a large Hispanic population here, or if they purposely employ Hispanic people to put the "La" in LaQuinta. I just feel it wouldn't really be a LaQuinta if it was staffed by a bunch of vanilla-looking, pasty-faced, middle-aged white guys complaining about their lackluster lives, ungrateful wives, and soft erections.

Either way, not bad for a LaQuinta.

I'm off to the races!

Sunday, October 12, 2014

I'm currently at Charlotte International Airport in North Carolina. I'm seated at gate C5, waiting on a twice-delayed flight. But I have no worries as my wife and daughter have plans for the morning that don't include me, and I have no connecting flights. As Mr. Willie Nelson once sang, "It's my lazy day." I could use a lazy day too. I was at the race track for just over twelve hours yesterday!

This is what I choose to do with my one weekend off in three weeks. Walk around a speedway for hours on end until the race begins, at which time I stand around and watch cars go in a circle for more hours on end.

"Classify these as good times. Good times." – Also a song by Mr. Willie Nelson.

I arrived at the track yesterday shortly after noontime and after stopping at Chick-fil-A for a snack. I met up with a few people that I had come to know through Twitter and I obtained my Hot Pass credentials from the NASCAR trailer.

As I was walking through the garage area I saw Miss Danica Patrick. To date, she has been the most successful female driver in NASCAR history and she is also rather easy on the eyes. I approached her and asked if we could take a quick selfie pic together and she kindly obliged. I said, "Thanks, babe," before I could catch myself but she gave a quiet giggle and politely gave me a smile before going back to her trailer. I quickly sent the picture over to my cousin, Frank Smith, an avid Danica fan. He calls her "The Princess". I told him she was very sweet and smelled like warm vanilla cookies. I know my cousin well enough to tell you that he is probably at the store today stocking up on vanilla cookies.

I was invited to a promotional event for Mr. Kurt Busch by my advertising genius friend, Mr. Jonathon Helfman, the same gent who hooked me up with the meet and greet in New Hampshire a few weeks back for my father's birthday. One of Kurt's sponsors is a water heater company and they decided to play off of his love/hate relationship with the media and place him in a dunk tank where the media could then throw balls at him, thus landing him once again, in hot water. He was a great sport about it and was quite funny. I was surprised to be called up to throw a few balls and dunk my NASCAR hero in the tank. I apologized to him in advance as I do have such respect for the guy. In hindsight, I should have apologized for being such a bad shot.

He antagonized me from his seat in the tank, saying that I had one foot over the throwing line and still couldn't hit it. On my final shot, the ball nicked the corner of the target but did not activate the dumping mechanism. He laughed. I smiled and then walked up to manually press the target and dunk him. He got up out of the water and splashed me a good bit, then gave me a high five and said it was good to see me again. He's a good guy, that Kurt Busch.

It then proceeded to downpour for over an hour. I took refuge under an overhang at the concession stand in the garage area. I ate pizza and french fries whilst many drivers drove by in canvas covered golf carts or strolled by under umbrellas.

The access that fans can have in NASCAR is unlike any other sport of which I'm a fan. With the right passes you can walk in and out of the garages and see all the cars, see the drivers walking around, visit the pit crews, take pictures on pit road, it's amazing. Before the race started I was standing on pit road watching the driver introductions. I saw Kurt, Danica, Clint Bowyer, Jimmie Johnson, and everyone who is anyone on the NASCAR Sprint Cup level. I had to make sure to get a picture of Dale Earnhardt Jr. for my father, as that is his favorite driver. I quickly snapped one and emailed it over to my mother to share with him.

When it was time for the National Anthem I went and stood behind Kurt's car along with Jonathan and a few other guys that had joined our motley crew throughout the day. After the anthem had finished and the planes flew over our heads, Kurt slipped into the window of the #41 car and the rest of us went behind the wall of the pits as the cars roared to life and the race began.

I have been to many races over the years but it sounds a lot different when the cars are racing around you! It was really amazing. I didn't think it could get any better than that, and then Helfman took out tickets to the suite located in turn four at the top of Charlotte Motor Speedway.

Son of a bitch. It just got better.

We walked out of the pits and through the now ghost town of a garage area whilst the cars continued to echo around us like the roaring of the most angry ocean. We stopped at the #78 hauler and were given a tour of where the cars are loaded up and where the team meetings are and such. Then we hopped on the golf cart and headed through the infield and down through one of the tunnels that would lead us outside of the track and to the suite elevators.

It was at this very moment when one of those things happened; one of those things that seems to slow down time ever so briefly and yet forever.

As Helfman was driving up front, I was sitting on the back bench, staring out as the haulers, the garages and at the few stragglers wandering around who were passing me by. Directly in front of me was the backstretch heading into turn three. Cars were fender to fender battling for position in a thunderous roar. My senses were alive with burnt rubber and racing fuel, and above me—a peaceful starry sky, and the lower half of a red moon.

Life is good. God is good. Always.

Never let the excitement of a moment allow you to take it for granted. We're only alive in the moment, so enjoy it, but be thankful. We only get so many. This was one of my moments. I'll never forget it.

The next thing I knew, we were in the elite suite. The whole track stretched out before me just beyond this glass box, and Lady Charlotte is shining like a diamond with her lights shimmering against the darkened night sky, the cars reflecting the stars of the heavens as they continue to outmaneuver each other across the blacktop.

Food was plenty, as was the beer. This is how the emperor and his squeeze enjoyed the Coliseum. I indulged in cheesecake—three pieces. I had some cookies—about four. I ate some brownies—three, to be precise. And I had a few cherry tomatoes; only a child eats just desserts. I drank mostly water but I did have a Blue Moon ale to commemorate the occasion.

The race ended with Kevin Harvick the winner. Kurt finished 11th, despite running in the top ten all night. Then a fight broke out amongst a few of the drivers due to some post-race shenanigans, which, as we know, are the best type of shenanigans.

Helfman was kind enough to drive us all back to our cars on the golf cart. He gave me a bunch of hats, one of which Kurt had autographed for him in his home this morning. I bid adieu to my new friends and hopped back in the rental, turned on the 40's music channel and headed for the hotel.

Another flight awaited me in the morning.

Flight 5798 is landing in twenty minutes. I have been seated in 8C, just in front of a small child whose parents saw fit to disrobe him and allow him to fly in merely his underwear. I'd wager that it would not be permissible for me to board the plane and then strip down to my undies. I'm wearing red jockey shorts that hug my body and my manhood just right. I like to think they make me look like a superhero. Others may have other opinions, but this is my book, so I only offer mine. If you would like to offer your opinions, go write your own book. Ha!

Monday, October 13, 2014

You never know where you may find yourself on some mornings. Currently I'm sitting on the floor at TF Green Airport in Rhode Island, waiting on a plane. I'm on my way to Kentucky, once again, to film for that ole ghost show. I'm not sure why we keep doing cases in Kentucky. There must be a tax credit or something going into someone's pocket. Not my pocket of course, but someone's.

Funnily enough, I have to change planes in Charlotte, North Carolina, where I flew into on Saturday and home from yesterday. In three days, I'll have been in the Charlotte airport three times. Three is the magic number.

Three, oh, it's the magic number,
Yeah it is, it's the magic number

Somewhere in that ancient mystic trinity
You get three
It's the magic number

With the past and the present and the future
And faith and hope and charity
And the heart and the brain and the body
It'll give you three; it's a magic number

-*Three Is a Magic Number* - School House Rock –
(Best as covered by Blind Melon)

I love that song. I dug it as a kid and I still dig it. It was originally a part of these little public service announcement learning initiatives for kids called *School House Rock*. They put times tables, historical tidbits, and the like all to music to help teach us little nose pickers by tricking us into thinking we were just watching cartoons. Clever bastards.

When I was in high school they made an album of the best songs from *School House Rock*, and Blind Melon, whom is still one of my favorite bands, covered "Three is the Magic Number".

If you have some time on your hands, go listen to *Soup* by Blind Melon. It will change your life. Such a soulful album filled with incredible lyrics scrawled across soul resonating melodies. Amazing stuff. Check out "Mouth Full of Cavities", and it will haunt you on quiet nights at random points in your life, long after you think you have forgotten it.

Speaking of long since forgotten. The reason I'm sitting here on the floor of the airport is it seems the good people at US Airways have forgotten to book a crew for flight 604. I'm sure it has something to do with turnaround time and crew sleep requirements and such. Which is all good as it gives me time to sit here and write and listen to music, so I'm perfectly pleasant.

Remember how much fun I had at the races on Saturday? I met all kinds of cool people and really enjoyed the day. I mentioned that I had one of those moments that I'll always remember.

Well, as life would have it, I had one yesterday that topped it.

After I arrived home and covered the pool with Mama Bear, we picked up Beans from a friend's house and went to the movies to see *Boxtrolls*. It was a terribly clever movie with great artistic merit. There was a great underlying tone about the haves and the have-nots, our place in society, our perception of value, and what makes you who you are.

But what I really loved was when our daughter climbed up to sit in my lap about halfway through and said simply and softly in my ear, "Snuggle." She remained there throughout the last half of the movie, occasionally stretching her arms back and wrapping them around my neck. It was a win for Daddy when he needed one the most.

I often struggle with being at work, traveling, and being on the road in order to be a provider, and being at home to be the father I want to be. But as God had intended it, I'm sure, in the movie there is the great little dialogue betwixt the characters about who a father is. He is someone that looks out for you, and listens to you and loves you. And as this scene was playing out, my daughter stretched out on my lap with her legs upon mine, my feet resting on the empty row of seats in front of us, I gave her a kiss and she told me she loved me. I told her I loved her and that, out of everything I have done in life, I'm most proud of being her father.

That was one of those moments. Time slowed down and allowed me to be alive in it on so many levels. It was amazing. And I was thankful.

I'm currently aboard US Airways flight 5435 and trying to catch my breath in seat 16A. I fell asleep right after nestling into my middle seat on that last flight. We were an hour delayed to start with, but I guess we must have also been delayed in taking off, as I awoke when the wheels touched the ground only to look at the time and see that my connecting flight to Louisville started boarding 17 minutes before. That left me with just about another 13 minutes to catch this flight.

I quickly made a sticky note in my mind of things in my favor, and things against me. You should always know the odds and think of alternate scenarios in every situation. I don't worry about much. If I miss a flight, I miss a flight. But if I had missed this flight, I'd really screw the film crew for tonight. As it is, I have an hour after I land to get to the hotel, shower up, get what I like to call "TV Pretty" and make call time in the hotel lobby. I don't want to put the production schedule behind.

Things against me:

- Time. I have 13 minutes.
- Terminal distance. We landed in terminal B and I have to get to Terminal E.
- Gate distance. E36 is literally the furthest terminal and gate combination possible from my current location. I know this because I fly way too often.
- Bags. I hate checking bags so I have my laptop and my suitcase with me to carry as I make this journey. The weight isn't much for me as I'm "big and strong like bull" but it's cumbersome.
- Boots! Whilst filming a case at the Wild Turkey distillery a few weeks back (also in Kentucky), Mr. KJ McCormick smashed his foot on a pipe whilst walking in the dark. I found this particularly funny, and then did the same damn thing when I was laughing at his misstep. So my left ankle has been specifically been bothering me quite a bit lately. Standing up at all these conventions for hours on end, and then walking the racetrack for twelve hours hasn't helped either. So, instead of sneakers, I wore my hiking books for extra support. Great for support, not for speed.
- People. There is a sea of humanity betwixt E36 and me. Many of them are in a rush going their own way but there's also a bunch of slack-jawed mouth-breathers just window shopping on their layover. Human hurdles. Hard to jump in boots.

Things in my favor:

- I'm only in the fifth row of the plane. This is huge and cannot be underappreciated. Normally I switch to a seat in the back of the plane, but since I was already flying yesterday during check-in time for this flight, I was unable to pick my seat. A blessing in disguise.
- I know the layout of the airport well. I know what gate I have to get

to and can run there without having to stop and look at a single sign.

- I'm Dustin Pari and I never bet against myself. And neither should you. Always believe in yourself. Even when the stewardess tells you that you won't make it and to talk to the gate agent to see about getting on the next flight. Always bet on yourself, and bet heavy. No one knows you like you do.

With that all in mind, I sent out a tweet to entertain my friends, fans, and fellow freaks, and then I put on my headphones.

Each moment in your life should have a proper background track. My whole day does, each and every day. It helps cement you in the moment and it provides for an enhanced experience. Trust me. I knew exactly what a moment like this needed. A hard run through three terminals and 36 gates with two bags in tow whilst wearing hiking boots requires one group and one group only: Public Enemy. Sorry Chuck D, right now you and Flava Flav are my hype men in the story of my life.

See? It isn't always old country, rock n' roll, and 40's jazz in my head. It depends on the scenario. Most of the time it's actually Christmas music.

"Bass! How low can you go? Death row. What a brother know." – This was blaring through my headphones as I stepped off of the plane and began my run against time and humanity. I made it to the gate just as the door was closing. I smiled politely, handed the nice gate agent lady my ticket, and then stepped out onto the walkway to the tiny plane to Louisville.

Mission accomplished.

So here I'm seated up against the window, drinking my warm tomato juice to keep my in-flight vampire satiated. My heart is beating out a rhythmic tune echoing against the boney walls of my rib cage like a tribal drum deep in the heart of the African jungle. Public Enemy for the win. As a note, Hanson's "*MMM Bop*" also works.

Soon we will be landing. I'll find a taxi and head to the hotel, get "TV Pretty", and meet up with the production crew for tonight's investigation.

Never bet against yourself kids. You have more at stake than anyone.

Made it to the hotel with exactly 21 minutes to shower and get down to the lobby and head out for tonight's filmed investigation for that ole ghost show. These are the moments that no one knows about when they are sitting comfortably at home watching episodes with their hands in the popcorn. These crazy, rushing, running, barely having time to breathe moments.

Here we go!

Tuesday, October 14, 2014

It's 3:17am. I'm in room 317. I just got back to my room after tonight's investigation. I'm exhausted. Zzz … zzz … zzz….

Yawn … good morning. Last night took a lot of my energy. Flying in and going right to an investigation is never easy but when the investigation goes late, it makes it worse.

The case was at Fort Harrod, and in truth, it wasn't much of a case. I didn't get much of a chance to investigate, as we had to cut the night short due to tornado warnings. We also had a new person in training, which left us with an odd number of people and so I was seated in the van watching the ole DVR for most of the night. But I made the most of it.

I had a camera and two stools, so I did what any reasonable person would do; I hosted an imaginary late night talk show, complete with an imaginary guest, and imaginary late night band. It was splendid. I was a hit in my own mind, as per usual. When the credits rolled on my new late night venture, it was just after 2am and time to head back to the hotel. The ride home was fun with the wind swept rain and flashes of distant lightning. As Mr. Eddie Rabbit once sang, "I love a rainy night."

And now here I'm in my snuggly little hotel bed and it's time to scrub up, grab a snack, and head out to film once again.

Tonight I'll be wandering around in the dark at the Conrad-Caldwell House just outside of Louisville, Kentucky. The area is said to be one of the most haunted neighborhoods in America. I wonder what their property taxes are like. Hauntingly low I would guess. Ha! Oh, how I do amuse me.

I'm off to see the wizard!

Wednesday, October 15, 2014

I'm on US Airways flight 5445 from Louisville to Philadelphia, on my way home. It's a very cold flight and I'm huddled in my brown fuzzy zip-up hoody in exit row window seat 13A.

Last night was a great case and I was back to the hotel and in bed for just after 2am. I slept for almost two-and-a-half hours before washing up and catching a taxi to the airport.

I'm not sure I'll be making my connecting flight in Philadelphia. They didn't board this flight until five minutes after our regularly scheduled departure time due to some nonsense about trying to rebook passengers from another flight that was cancelled this morning. In an effort to correct one mistake, the good folks at the airline continue to cause a chain reaction of chaos. Good times.

Speaking of which, I did take a peek inside of Jolly Good Times this morning. As you know, that is the pirate-themed bar that the elves run in my mind. They really tore up the place last night. One patron was still face down on the bamboo bar, his empty glass stained with eggnog down the side of it sat next to his head.

Apparently there's a new fellow in town named Jasper P. Jinglebottom. Former head of PR for Santa back at the North Pole, he recently took up residence in my mind, but he keeps an address is Jackson Hole, Wyoming.

I'm not fully sure as to what he is up to, but he has had a Twitter account and a Facebook page for a few weeks now. Mr. Jinglebottom is a rather established little fellow. I'll have to give him that.

Gosh, this plane is cold. I suppose we are halfway through October, so it will only be getting colder.

"Seasons change, so do we. It's nothing new." – Tripping Daisy's "Trip Along".

If I make my connecting flight in Philly, I should be able to get back to Angelina just shortly after 11am today. Then I can head home, exchange pleasantries with Mama Bear, and get a little shuteye before Beans returns from school.

The reason for taking the early flight home was so they could get the best of me and not just the rest of me. A few hours of sleep would recharge my batteries just enough to ensure a good evening. But if this flight delay causes further delay … well, let's just say my plans will have gone astray.

Looks like we will be landing soon. And it looks like I'll be running to catch yet another flight. I felt like I was doing the same thing just the other day. "Ain't it funny how time slips away?" – Willie Nelson.

Well, as the saying goes, "the best laid plans" and so on and so forth.

It appears that although I never bet against myself, the good people at US Airways don't know me very well, or their guy in Vegas gave them great odds to be otherwise. I dashed from the plane. I was the first to get my bag from the gate check valet. I was the first on the tram shuttle from Terminal F over to Terminal C. As I approached the gate agent at C26, she looked up at me from her cell phone and said. "We didn't think you were going to make it, so the plane pushed back early." Say what?

I know the rules. I play this game all the time. Ten minutes before departure time the plane closes the door and that's that. But it was twelve minutes before departure time and I had ran the gauntlet and emerged victorious. I pointed this out to the not-so-pleasant woman who didn't want to be distracted from her iPhone but, as they say, "No dice."

So I made my way down to customer service and stood in a line of forty-odd people for the better part of an hour since they only had two people working the six-person desk. When I was about to approach, a third representative had appeared. I kindly explained my situation to her and I reported upon the not so nice woman at gate C26. I never take out frustration upon people working customer service for the situation they are trying to help me with is not of their doing. I find it best to be respectful and calm. She actually commented upon my demeanor and I explained my philosophy.

Sadly there was apparently no room on the next flight but she gave me a place on the standby list, and as I thanked her and was walking away, she asked for my original ticket and told me that she would follow up on it for me and that I would in fact have a seat on the next flight, US 5925, to Providence, Rhode Island.

Feeling satisfied, and a bit hungry, I decided to make the most of the situation. I have been in the Philadelphia International Airport many times and I know where the Chick-fil-A is, and I know where the fancy sushi bar is that makes delicious mojitos, and there is a Dunkin Donuts, too.

Listen up chipmunks to my advice. Layovers are what you make it. Life is what you make it. You may have been served from the well of anger, disappointment, and depression, but you don't have to keep drinking out of it. Flip that Etch A Sketch over in your mind. It's time to start anew.

First stop was Chick-fil-a where I had a delicious bacon, egg, and cheese biscuit for three dollars. At the last airport, they were almost ten dollars. I was hungry at the last airport but I wasn't foolish. Next up was the fancy sushi bar for a mojito. That put a smile on my face.

And then it was my turn to put a smile on someone else's face. I went to the Dunkin Donuts to purchase myself a large pumpkin mocha iced latte, with extra flavor, extra sugar, and skim milk. I do have to watch my girlish figure you know.

I then turned and saw a kind looking old man of tiny stature who was ordering a coffee of the same size. I stepped in and paid for it whilst he was reaching for his wallet. The old man looked up with a wondrous smile and insisted upon shaking my hand for doing something to kind. I don't think it even cost me two dollars but the look upon the old man's face was priceless. It filled my heart with joy and charged my soul. No thanks are needed for things given of a kind heart for the rewards make themselves known internally.

I shook the man's hand and merrily walked to gate C23, only to find the plane had been delayed. No worries. though. They weren't going to ruin my Christmas spirit! The elves in my head, including newcomer Mr. Jasper P. Jinglebottom, rejoiced and then ran naked into the eggnog river. I'll have to get it sanitized again.

I went over to one of the little stationary bikes to work off the little bit of food that I had consumed. It's always good to stay fit, and the Philadelphia International Airport is the only one I know that has these little stationary bikes set up throughout the terminal. I would bet dollars to donuts, and you know how much I love donuts, that I was the only person in the airport using the exercise bike and listening to The Carpenter's sing "I Won't Last a Day Without You".

After my brief workout, I returned to the gate for my flight. On my walk, I could not help but notice all the passengers wearing surgical masks. There is an Ebola thing going on right now in the country. The CDC seems unsure as to exactly how it may be spreading, and now they are asking people that shared flights with those diagnosed to come in for testing. I remember during the SARS outbreak and the Bird Flu, I would see lots of people wearing masks in the airport. I never did though. If it gets to the point where I have to wear a mask I'm going to draw a big smile on the outside of it so that strangers know I'm friendly.

D'oh! Stumped again. It appears there was yet another delay due to rain and a low ceiling.

Since I had time to kill, and I was on very little sleep mind you, I decided to start a sing along at gate C23. Sadly no one else sang. One woman did ask what song I was singing, but she didn't join in. It was Mr. Barry Manilow's "I Can't Smile Without You"—a true classic.

Finally we boarded the plane, and now, here I sit, living my life in airplane mode. Which, by the way, I was pondering the idea that setting my phone to airplane mode would be a lot more fun if it then allowed me to control said airplane by my phone. There must be an app for that in development somewhere.

I'm in the last row; seat 21D, an aisle seat. Luck of the draw I guess. I wasn't even supposed to be on this flight as it were, and yet I get my favorite seat. Buying that little man a coffee paid off.

That's how we are going to change the world, you know. One cup of coffee, one little old man, one sing along, and one act of kindness at a time.

My apologies to the very nice lady next to me in 21F. There's no E seat on this type of plane. She was kind enough not to be bothered by my constant air guitar, air drums, and otherwise thrashing about which I was doing whilst listening to Green Day's *21st Century Breakdown* album.

Just about ready to land. Soon I'll be back in the driver's seat of sweet Angelina and headed home.

Rhode Island, your favorite wayward son hath returned!

Angelina and I returned home safely. Mama Bear was on the couch watching soaps and the Beanie Baby was on her way home from school. I barely saw them for twenty minutes before they went on with their after school activities and such. So it looks like Daddy's going to crack open a much deserved Southern Tier Pumking Ale and cut the lawn. I urge you all to drink and mow the lawn responsibly. When I'm done, I shall shower and then crawl to bed, for it has been a long day to have only had just over two hours of sleep.

Thursday, October 16, 2014

There was a great overnight rainstorm that made waking up in the cool breeze the stuff that dreams are made of. I stayed in bed for a little bit this morning and just breathed in the world. It was refreshing and it made me feel alive. I decided to take the morning off of work and ask Mama Bear out for breakfast. It was a rare treat having time alone with my wife and a sit-down breakfast. Usually it's protein shakes, protein bars, and life on the run.

I realized that life has been going by really fast these last few weeks and I need to slow down a bit. Luckily I have this weekend off, which has also been a rarity as of late. I'm declaring this weekend my own personal holiday! The elves and I are in the early stages of putting together a tickertape parade. It should be a great time.

Saturday morning will start with the customary cartoons and cereal, as all Saturday mornings should start. Then I'm getting my haircut at 9:30am with Cheryl from NBC Hair Studios in Cranston, Rhode Island. She has been cutting my hair for 19 years now. She is the only one I trust. At 10am I'll go to McShawn's Pub for hot dogs and beer. I know what you are thinking, and trust me, it tastes even better than it sounds!

McShawn's has been a tradition for me since I turned 21. I started going there on Saturday mornings with my Uncle Bub and my dad. I then started inviting my friends. My cousins stop by there regularly. And it's just one of those places that are comforting in a way that you feel like anything can happen.

On Saturday mornings, they offer free hot dogs cooked up in a big pot with sauerkraut and beer. The bar doors open at ten, but I'm a regular so I can walk in the back door any time after nine. I haven't been in over a month—maybe two—but there was a time when I never missed a Saturday morning. I could always be found there in the corner stool next to the hotdog pot. I'd play a little Willie Nelson on the juke box and then settle in for two hot dogs with just a touch of ketchup and a Miller High Life.

The bartender's name is Moe, a tall fellow with a bright shock of gray hair and two different colored eyes. He has a friendly face and big shoulders like an aging football player. Moe is always there with a kind word and an open ear. He is everything that a bartender should be.

When I arrive up in Heaven (assuming they let me in), I do hope Moe will be there to pour a little rum for Jesus, John Lennon, and me.

Friday, October 17, 2014

Today isn't quite the day the music died but Angelina did drop her exhaust system from the manifold back whilst I was driving on route 37. This resulted in a precarious situation because when the pipes drop from the back, you're dragging them and that isn't great, but it's okay. When the pipes drop from the front—well, now you're pushing them. Good luck if you hit a pothole or take a turn to sharply. You're going to be in a messy situation no matter what when it breaks like this.

Luckily for me, I wasn't far from my office and I knew how to dance with my ole gal better than anyone. I waltzed her back to the office parking lot and let her cool down whilst I finished my day. Once the whistle blew and I slid down the back of the dinosaur ala Mr. Fred Flintstone, I slid up under her skirt to see what I could see. It appeared the flange of the pipe that slides up onto the manifold simply rusted off just before the bracket. My options were to try and hang it up under the body with some wire or an old coat hanger or remove the entire exhaust system. Neither option was an easy one at work with no tools.

After searching around the office I found a hammer and a screwdriver-they would have to do. Rust fell everywhere, I managed to cut my forehead in my haste as my phone was chirping at me thanks to my wife. Tonight was the Fall Hoe Down Dance at my daughter's school and Angelina with her broken, dangling exhaust was putting the squeeze on me regarding how much time I had to get home and get ready for the dance, hence the numerous text messages from Mama Bear.

I got the exhaust dismounted from its various hangars, brackets, and mounts in relatively short order. I threw it in the back of Angelina's truck bed and headed home.

Wife and Beans looked adorable. Mama Bear had bought a cute pair of cowboy boots for the Beanie Baby; light brown with a sky blue inlay. It matched her shirt that tied just above her belly button. Beans also wore one of my wife's cowboy hats that she used to wear back in the day around the time we met at the Diamond Rodeo Bar.

The dance was as most school dances go. The children ran all over the place and the parents stood or sat along the wall, some staring intently at their phones, others having small talk with whomever they were standing near. I had my wife there to talk with, but she was more involved with some of the other moms, so I turned to the snack table for comfort. Apparently I needed lots of comfort as I think I ate more brownies, cookie pie, cupcakes, and pizza than anyone else there.

"Ziggy piggy! Ziggy piggy!" – *Bill and Ted's Excellent Adventure.*

There were a few moments that made me very proud to be there, even if my daughter wouldn't dance with me, and Mama Bear was conversing with other members of the ladies club.

They had a limbo stick set up and all the children were in a line to take their chances going underneath. My daughter had taken a small boy by the hand (a younger brother of one of her friends) and made it her charge to stay with him through each loop of the limbo line until he tired of it and ran off. She continued on until the stick was at its lowest notch, crawling underneath it, but making it through nonetheless.

Beans played games—bowling with a foam bowling pin set, and a neon ring toss with scarecrow targets. She did well at both, getting a strike and looping the smallest scarecrow with a ring.

She loves country music, mostly the top 40 pop country Mama Bear listens to, but I sneak in some of the classics like Johnny Cash, David Allan Coe, and Willie Nelson. Being at a dance where they mostly played country was right up our little girl's alley. I watched as she strutted up to the center of the gymnasium floor, walking heel-toe, heel-toe all the way whilst kids were running by her. She then placed one hand upon the brim of her hat and shook her hips to the music whilst she sang along to a Brad Paisley song. That's my girl.

Saturday, October 18, 2014

It's National Dustin Pari Day! Yeaaaahhh!

Well, I'm celebrating myself today, anyhow. This is my first weekend completely off and home since I can't remember when. I just finished off a bowl of Boo Berry cereal and I watched some cartoons with my daughter. Mama Bear is upstairs sleeping but will be up soon.

I'm going to get my haircut and then off to McShawn's for a tasty adult beverage. I'm planning on stopping betwixt the two errands to bring a small pumpkin to my grandparents' gravesite—Papa Cheech and Nana on my mother's side. Then I'll walk across the lot and place a gourd upon my Aunt Elaine's gravesite, too. She was my "Gourd-Mother", after all, and a great woman with an eternally optimistic point of view. She was also one of the earliest influences in my life, cultivating my interest in the paranormal.

Angelina still needs work but the store where I get exhaust pipes closes early today and my ole gal's still functional. Let her sound and feel like a racecar for a few days. This is a weekend off.

Tonight I'm planning on watching Disney's *Tower of Terror* movie with Wife and Beans. I envision three bowls of popcorn with us all snuggled behind them in bed to close the day.

Happy National Dustin Pari Day, you beautiful bastards!

Sunday, October 19, 2014

National Dustin Pari Day came and went. Jinglebottom and the elves are cleaning up Jolly Good Times from last night's festivities. That damn tickertape parade made a mess upon the floors of my mind.

I'm thankful to have Jinglebottom. He has really taken on a leadership role, considering he is the newest figment of my imagination. He's doing well on social media also. Jingelbottom's Twitter account is up to almost thirty followers as of today. Not bad for a fictitious elf with a fictitious position and a fictitious backstory. Not bad at all.

I overslept this morning and so I missed church. I have to be honest. I didn't sleep through my alarm because I never set my alarm. I know my body has been beaten down lately with all of this travel, sleepless nights, and hectic work schedule. I figured it was best to rest this morning. I think The Late Great JC and the Trinity would allow me this day to rest up.

Beans and I snuck downstairs whilst Mama Bear was still sleeping. We watched *It's The Great Pumpkin Charlie Brown* on DVR whilst eating Boo Berry cereal. Then we adjourned to the playroom in the basement to play Disney Infinity's Incredibles on the Wii U system.

Mama Bear and I had lunch together whilst Beans went to the movies with her friend and her family. I stopped afterwards and picked up some things to prep the yard and the homestead for winter.

Fall is my favorite season by far, but it never lasts nearly long enough. This fall started early but then was interrupted by a string of warm days reminiscent of summer. I know Old Man Winter will be hobbling up the path soon enough, and then it'll be cold, wet, and windy until sometime in late April. Alas, I remain hopeful that we will have a long fall.

I don't mind the winter. I love watching the snowfall; dropping a thick white blanket over the land, the trees empty branches traced in snowflakes. October through December is my favorite three months of the year. The holidays are awesome. Halloween with all of its dark surprises and spookiness; Thanksgiving with its colorful bounty and parades; then Christmas comes with feelings of good will and Christmas music.

And the food! Oh, the food. I emptied out the egg holder in the fridge and replaced the chicken eggs with chocolate Cadbury "Screme Eggs". I must have already eaten a baker's dozen worth of pumpkin pies. Eggnog found its way into my home yesterday and I have already drunk a half-gallon. Good thing I work out a lot.

There is a certain mix of Halloween music I like. Songs that sound spooky or those that were mentioned in various Halloween cartoons and movies make my list. But come November 1st, I'll have switched to Christmas music, which is my absolute favorite. Most Christmas music harkens back to the 40's era with its melodic harmonies and whimsical arrangements. I do fancy music from that time period the most. I actually listen to Christmas music ten months out of the year. I don't listen to it in January or in October. In January it just seems a bit too played out, and in October I have my Halloween playlist. But the rest of the year, it's in my regular rotation.

Not too long ago, I was on a flight and had my laptop open as I listened to my Christmas tunes. What I didn't know was that my headphones were not plugged in, and the whole plane was treated to Mr. Chuck Berry's "Run Run Rudolph", for about two verses before the stewardess came to ask me to plug in my headset. I was surprised the people next to me didn't say anything. Perhaps they needed a shot of happy nonsense in their lives. Most people do but would never admit it, not even to themselves.

Happy nonsense is a large part of my life. Listening to Christmas music in the springtime, keeping a jar of cake frosting in the fridge at all times, rewarding myself with donuts when I overcome an obstacle—these are all fine examples of happy nonsense. It keeps me moving forward and brings me joy. I suggest you try it.

I just finished watching the NASCAR race in Talladega on ESPN. It's always a great race but with the new Chase Championship format, it made for a crazier race than usual. Kurt Busch finished 7th whilst Brad Keselowski took home the checkered flag.

My Miami Dolphins defeated the Chicago Bears today 27-14, so that's good.

It looks like I should get my firm little apple of a hiney outside and tend to some raking and seeding before twilight time is upon us. The cycle of life continues as another year prepares to close up shop.

Have yourself a merry little evening!

Monday, October 20, 2014

"What a day for a daydream. I've been dreaming since I woke up today." – Lovin' Spoonful

This time of year lends to a certain amount of whimsy and wanderlust that only occurs on crisp fall mornings such as this. Good times.

I'm just getting ready to head out to the gym before I start my workday. But first, I must do the un-fanciful things like changing the cat litter, carrying out some boxes to the recycling bin, blah, blah, blah.

But these small moments in life are the glue that holds together the larger than life moments. You need them. Be alive in them. Hum happy little songs whilst you do your mundane tasks, for all moments are miracles; some just shine brighter than others.

I brought Angelina over to my parents at lunch today to see what Dad thought of the exhaust situation. After looking at it, he shared my sentiment. Sadly we'll be unable to repair her ourselves. Between the two of us, we can fix just about anything but metal cutting and welding are not our specialties, so I'll be dropping her off at a friend's backyard garage over the weekend, which actually works out pretty well. For you see, though this week is a hectic one, working the day job every day and such, but on Wednesday I have to leave early, hop in a rental car, and drive up to New Hampshire for my first college lecture of the season. Then on Friday I have to do the same in New Hampshire again. After that, it's Vermont on Saturday and Maine on Sunday. So Angelina can relax over the weekend and get her undercarriage fixed. I don't allow just anyone under my girl's skirt but I know whom I can trust.

Time to pack up the ole suitcase.

Here we go again.

Tuesday, October 21, 2014

We have a bizarre little family tradition taking root: silly string.

Last year I came home from work and Mama Bear and Beans attacked me with silly string. I was able to grab a can and we then went around the house making a mess and having a jolly good time. This summer I came home and parked Angelina in the driveway, locked her up, and made my way up the path. Halfway up my walk I see a lonely can of silly string. As I bent down to pick it up my wife stepped out from the porch and my daughter jumped out from behind a tree—it was on!

Outside seemed to make a better place for our silly string game, and so it continued today after dinner. This one wasn't spontaneous, though. My wife picked up the cans earlier in the day. My daughter put one at each place setting on the dinner table. As soon as we were done clearing our plates we stepped outside onto the battleground … our driveway. It really is good fun. I don't think I see Mama Bear laugh and smile as heartedly as she does when shooting silly string at me. The battle raged on and when we were done, the driveway was a smooth sheet of asphalt with bright splashes of neon string strewn about. Fantastic.

Life is made of these moments, these oh so very important moments. I keep telling you this because it's important.

Wednesday, October 22, 2014

Well, the midnight headlight
Find you on a rainy night
Steep grade up ahead
Slow me down makin' no time
I gotta keep rollin'
Those windshield wipers
Slappin' out a tempo
Keepin' perfect rhythm
With the song on the radio
Gotta keep rolling

– "Drivin' My Life Away" by Eddie Rabbit

That song was playing loudly at Jolly Good Times, the pirate-themed bar in my mind, whilst I was driving home in a terrible rainstorm after lecturing at Rivier University in Nashua, New Hampshire. It was my first college lecture of the season. Rivier is a private Catholic liberal arts university. I was surprised they were having me there for a paranormal lecture because a lot of Catholic establishments keep the paranormal at vestment's length. However, having me there was a nice little stroke of luck considering my Catholic upbringing and Christian/Episcopalian faith.

The crowd wasn't huge, but considering the storm coming over the Massachusetts state line and beating on the windows of the lecture hall, I understood.

Colleges are hit or miss. All lectures are unless you're at a convention or special event. College kids are out doing college things. Even when they plan on doing something like attending a phenomenal lecture, they sometimes forget or find something else to do. And when the weather outside is frightful, staying in your dorm is so delightful.

Regardless, the show must go on, and so it did. And it went off without a hitch … until the end. As is customary at most of my college lectures, I end with a brief little investigation to give everyone a taste of spirit world interaction. We couldn't go out and about across the campus due to the rain, and so I allotted some extra time for questions and answers, I showed everyone some of the equipment I like to utilize in investigations, and then I plugged my little AM/FM radio into the lecture hall speaker system.

Static was rolling on in the background as I explained to those in attendance how I conduct my investigations. I never want to mislead anyone. I know how easily people can manipulate various devices to make it look like spirit activity is occurring and I respect the spirit world too much to do that.

At all of my events and my investigations, and in everything I do, if things happen, they happen. If they don't happen, they don't happen. Life goes on. I'm not in control, nor do I pretend to be. I'm just living and that's glorious in and of itself.

However, on this night at a Catholic university after I finished explaining how I use the box to ask the spirits to come forth and only repeat the words I say—as to not ask leading, open-ended questions involving numbers and names—I asked any spirits that were listening to come forward out of respect and let us hear their voice, and for the first time since I turned the radio on, the static was broken, and a voice said "F---".

Son of a!

I tried to talk over the end of it as I didn't want the kids or the people running the event to hear it. I asked it to specifically say the name of the university, and the same voice came back with, "River." I correctly said the name of the university, Rivier, and asked it to focus and try again, and this time it came back with, "Damn it." Some of the girls in the front row giggled this time, as girls in the front row often do. I explained that sometimes you will get a spirit that says curse words and uses crass language.

I tried to right the ship and simply ask it to say good night but it would not comply. I closed the lecture and started to wrap up my gear as people were asking questions and coming up to take photographs. One of the young ladies running the event told me she heard the box say the F-word. I laughed and apologized. These things only happen to me.

The storm raged on as I tossed my laptop and bag of equipment into the trunk of the rental. I went to the hotel but they didn't have my reservation that the university was supposed to have set up. These things happen. Considering the late hour, I decided to not bother anyone from the university and simply hopped back in the rental and headed for home. As I crossed the line from New Hampshire into Massachusetts the sky cracked open and it really started to come down. The wind swept rain made travel very difficult. Puddles quickly turned into small flood zones and thus hydroplaning was becoming an issue. I tried to keep the little rental on the road and in between the lines. Lighting streaked across the sky whilst the thunder roared through the clouds. I really do love such weather.

An unfortunate thing I had to admit to myself is that I'm starting to get night blindness. Not so much on crisp nights when the moon shines brightly above but on the dark moonless nights when the roads are shiny and slick with rain, the oncoming headlights of cars, and the headlights of cars in my rearview mirrors cause my eyes to shut down quite a bit. Oh well. As they said in *Fight Club*, "Even the Mona Lisa is falling apart."

Thankfully, with Mr. Eddie Rabbit and Jinglebottom singing a duet version of "Driving My Life Away" at Jolly Good Times in my head, the rental and I made it safely back home.

So here I sit, Mama Bear snoring her own little tune next to me, and the storm in high gear outside my bedroom window, writing this down for you.

It's time to say my prayers and turn out the light. I'll then listen to the winds, the rain, and the thunder, because, as Mr. Eddie Rabbit also wrote, "I love a rainy night."

Thursday, October 23, 2014

Tonight I drove ole Angelina to my friend's house so he could pull her in the garage over the weekend and repair her exhaust system. I then picked up my 1990 Dodge Daytona ES that recently got a new radiator. I usually enjoy doing a lot of this type of work myself, but with my work, filming, events, and lecture schedule lately, there's only so much I can do. A cold winter is closing in fast.

The Daytona's name is Angel and I've had her for about six years but our history stretches back to when I was in high school twenty years ago. My first Daytona was blue and beautiful. Her name was Babe after Babe the Mighty Blue Ox, fabled companion of Paul Bunyan. Her license plate was OX-820, so that fit. I purchased that car back in 1994, early in my senior year when my Toyota pickup truck was stolen from the Warwick Mall parking lot when I was working as a busboy for The Ground Round Restaurant the day after I dropped my theft insurance because I couldn't afford it. You can't make these things up. I was heartbroken, but when Babe and I met, she mended me and taught me to love again.

However, three short years after that, her valve seals were going, her rear main seal was leaking and her head gasket was suspect. It was time to say goodbye. I sold it to a young girl and her father from Massachusetts. When they came to pick it up, I went in the house and up to my room. I couldn't stand to see her go.

I then bought a Mitsubishi Eclipse that I named Mitsy. She was quick and steady, and together we delivered pizza for Nino's Pizza just over the Johnston/Cranston line in Rhode Island. Mitsy was a good car and we had good times but she was a rebound. We never really connected. Two years later in 1999, it was time to let her go when I met sweet Angelina, my ole pickup that I still have and love dearly.

Sadly, tonight Angelina was left in the rain outside of an old, wooden, backyard garage but I know she's in good hands and we will be reunited on Monday if all goes well.

However something struck me whilst driving Angel home tonight that I wasn't expecting. Nostalgia. This 1990 Dodge Daytona ES has the same interior, same stock radio, and even the same Miami Dolphin floor mats that my old Daytona had. The floor mats were for my old Daytona, Babe. And when I sold her, I went outside and brought the Miami Dolphin floor mats into the house before the young girl and her father came to take her away. Tonight I drove through the woods, the rain pouring down and the radio up high. The new radiator was working well and she was staying cool despite the speed I was doing with her on the highway. Good times. I knew this would probably be our last ride together. I had the radiator dropped in her so I could sell her. It's time.

Last year around this time, I sold Daisy, my 1973 Dodge Charger with a matching number 340 Magnum engine. She was a beauty too and I hated to see her go. Big as a boat, fast as a bullet, and she danced through the turns on the highway like a ballerina. I sold Daisy for the same reason I'm going to sell Angel. I don't have time for them and they need further restoration. They deserve better than I can give them and I'll use the money to prepare for Angelina's eventual replacement, though it pains me to think about it.

So there I was, driving Angel, sunk down low in her black bucket seat with the multicolor pattern inserts, the radio's tape deck emitting a soft and warm green glow. My hands were gripping the wheel and my mind was gripping the past. Queen came on the radio singing "You're My Best Friend" and I cranked it up loud. Angel still has a great sound system.

I started thinking about the first time I saw her. She was on a car lot that I passed every day when I was dating my wife about ten years ago, back in in 2004. I was working back at WPRI/WNAC News Channel 12 and Fox 64 full time in the evenings and working at the doctors' office part time in the mornings. I had been out of the news game for a couple of years at least, but I needed some extra money, and it was something I knew I was good at it and could slip right back into doing. I did it to get enough money for a nice engagement ring and a wedding. The hours were killing me, though. I was at the doctors' office in the morning from 8 to 12 and then filming for the news from 2 to 11 with built-in overtime till 11:30 or midnight depending on where the live on-scene shot was for the 11:00 show. I should have seen the foreshadowing. The irony of my consistently ridiculous work schedule is not wasted upon me now. Trust me.

One of the roads on my route to and from work took me by one of those shady stand-alone corner car lots you should never buy anything from. As fate would have it on one of my trips into work, I saw Angel sitting there looking like a shiny white diamond in the rough. Truth be told, I'd been looking for a 90 Daytona ES since Babe left my side years ago.

I couldn't believe my luck. The body was in great shape. The engine needed some work and the tranny shifted a little rough but I could handle it. I was psyched. I talked figures with the slimy salesman and had it down to a reasonable price fairly easy as I knew more about the car than he did. I told him I would get back to him and I went to work, dreaming of her all day long. I went from job one to job two, full of anticipation. I couldn't wait to get home and tell Mama Bear, my then-girlfriend, of my find. She was very supportive and urged me to buy it, as she knew I was looking for one for some time. I didn't need much coaxing. I decided I'd go back in the morning and purchase Angel for my own.

The next day came and as I was driving to the lot, I thought about it more and more. I was working like crazy to purchase an engagement ring and to save some money for a wedding. I shouldn't be buying a car. And so, I drove past Angel that day, and many days after, until one day she wasn't there anymore and it hurt me.

I bought the engagement ring. I took my girl out for a nice dinner at Prime Steakhouse on historic Federal Hill in Providence. I then asked her to marry me, down on one knee, underneath the Mount Hope Bridge in Bristol, Rhode Island, on a dark and rainy night.

It rains on most of the important days of my life. My birthday, the day we were engaged and our wedding day. It was sunny when my daughter was born, which was fitting as I would put the headphones on Mama Bear's belly and play "Here Comes The Sun" by The Beatles during pregnancy. It's our song, Beans and me. But, back to the weather, well, I would wager that it would probably rain when I die, which will also be fitting.

So we did get married, and Beans was born, and life was good. And then one day, my wife told me someone she knew back from high school was selling a 90 Daytona ES. You could imagine my surprise when I pulled up and saw Angel sitting there. It was an easy sell. The current owner already did the transmission work on it and they were selling it because it was too fast for their son who had gotten into some trouble with it.

I drove her home that night. She needed some work. The fuel tank now had a hole near the top so you could only fill her up three quarters of the way. My father and I replaced it with ease. I drove her around regularly and was happy, but then her engine started showing the same wear that Babe did years before. Luckily this time around, I had more money to fix up what was ailing my dear Angel. I sent her to Ocean State Performance to have her engine completely taken out and overhauled. It took several months but they bored out the engine, put in bigger pistons, and a hairy cam that made her sound like an animal. Angel finally had wings.

I was driving her tonight, giving her a little juice, listening to Freddie Mercury sing, "I've been with you such a long time. You're my sunshine and I want you to know that my feelings are true. I really love you. You're my best friend." Oh, I knew I was going to miss this car when the time comes. Angel is great in her own right, but the fact that she reminds me of my youth, of my innocence, well, there is some magic in there.

I live in the now. I don't worry about the future. I look back on fond moments but I don't stay too long because life is made up of fleeting magical moments that you have to be present in if you want to enjoy them. This—me, Angel, and Freddie Mercury—this was a moment.

I remembered being in high school and driving my buddies around in Babe. I thought about my high school sweetheart, Miss Jennifer Santanello, and the time we were making out over the center console of Babe for what seemed like forever. She wore a blue scrunchie in her dark hair that smelled like vanilla and wore a soft white sweater that I was excited to run my hands over. In hindsight it was so innocent. Just kissing and some over-the-sweater stuff, but man, was it amazing at the time. That was a moment. Good times.

Funny too. I remember we had steamed up the windows quite a bit and when we finally released from our embrace, we noticed kids from the little league team in the park came over and with cupped hands against the glass, were peering in the windows at us. Ha!

She left for college and I stayed in Rhode Island. Last I heard she was married with children, living in Chicago, and working at a theater. Theater was always her passion. As Harry Chapin once sang in a great tune named Taxi, "She took off to find the footlights and I took off to find the sky." She wanted to be an actress. I ended up on TV. Go figure. Funny how these things happen.

But as I have had loved and lost with my various vehicles before finding my sweet Angelina, I did the same with the ladies until I found Mama Bear, and I never leave her in the rain outside of an old, wooden, backyard garage.

I'll tell you this—when Freddie Mercury finished singing "You're My Best Friend" I shut down the radio for good. It was a fitting send off for such a lady.

I came inside and checked on Mama Bear who was already drifting off to sleep in our bed. Then I went to look in our daughter who was sleeping like a modern day princess in her own bed. Flat on her back, arms up by her head, eyes closed, mouth open, and county music playing on Pandora in the background. She is my best friend. She also has been sleeping like that since we first brought her home from the hospital. She likes what she likes I suppose.

Oh, look at the time. It's just about Cinderella hour and I still have to pack for three colleges and four days of travel.

Enjoy each moment my friends; the ones in the past and the ones in the present—but especially the ones in the present.

Friday, October 24, 2014

I'm in the Colby Farm House on the corner of the Colby-Sawyer College in New London, New Hampshire. It's a nice old farmhouse with wide wooden plank floors and lots of character. I just finished up my paranormal lecture and the investigations, so I can now rest.

It was a great night. Good people. A great set up. And the young ladies running it had their act together and then some. It's nice when things run smoothly like this.

Earlier today I worked my day job, and then I stopped at the market to pick up my co-pilot, as is customary. I have been doing College lectures for the past five or six years, I think. And for the last three years I have been stopping to pick up a pumpkin to take with me as my co-pilot on the trip. This year I picked up Admiral Gourdington. He was in the United States Navy in World War II. He has a ton of tales about adventures on the high seas, and he can be a bit salty at times. He also has a penchant for a well-made mint julep.

Every pumpkin has an individual name and personality. I like to have ones that have military or teaching backgrounds, with names like Lieutenant Gourdsmith, or simply "The Professor". I always let the pumpkins ride shotgun in the rental (which by the way, happened to be the same Kia Soul that I had rented a few weekends prior for the gig in Winchester, Virginia). I seatbelt them in and together we have misadventures on the open road.

I had a little fun with the Admiral when I came back to the old farmhouse tonight. There was a fancy little pumpkin that was on the front steps, so I brought it in and placed it in the bed with the Admiral and took a photo of them for social media promotional purposes along with the caption, "Really Admiral?! I'm out working and I come back to this?! Get that li'l hussy out of my bed!"

The elves in my head thought it was funny at least.

I may need to seek psychiatric help.

Nah.

The Admiral (right) with his lady friend.

Saturday, October 25, 2104

I woke up late in the morning, which was nice for a change. The old farmhouse was large, lonely, and quiet. There wasn't even a television in the place, which was great. Quiet is often good for the soul. Our world is so terribly noisy.

I took a shower and so did the Admiral. We took a photo of him in there that was eerily similar to a scene from the movie *Psycho.* Then he and I sat quietly in the living room and I took a picture of him regaling tales of the high seas. We staged an investigation photo of the two of us on the stairwell. Then we took a goodbye photo of the old farmhouse with him and last night's strumpet saying goodbye on the front steps.

The rental then took us on a charmingly magical journey from New Hampshire into Quechee, Vermont. Our first stop was Everything Dog & Hot Dogs Too. A wonderful little roadside store with dog toys, dog treats, and unbelievably delicious hot dogs on homemade rolls. Delicious!

It just about a two-hour ride to the hotel in Rutland, Vermont, for tonight's gig at the College of St. Joseph, and so the Admiral and I decided we'd take it easy and stop at the little places along the way that make life worth living.

I pulled the rental over at the Quechee Gorge, a breathtaking view of a rocky waterway making its way through the foliage covered mountainsides. It was amazing. I took the obligatory photo, and then stood there peacefully for a few minutes to absorb the beauty stretched out before me and to breathe in the fresh air. It's quite possible I may never pass this way again, so I felt it important to submerge myself in the moment.

I made my way back to the rental to find the Admiral gone. He was off in the woods, urinating behind a tree. Looks like someone had one too many mint juleps. I photographed him to shame him for his small pumpkin bladder.

Back on the road and what do I see but a little sign that said "Fool On The Hill" and underneath it in small letters "Wonderful Things". I quickly pulled the little red rental up the drive. It was an abandoned shop. The building had a real estate agency sign on it. That was okay, though. I was more interested in the sign itself.

I started listening to The Beatles in eighth grade. My mother introduced me to them at an earlier age, back when I was in my car seat. I remember sitting in that little brown car seat in her brown Chevy Nova listening to John Lennon sing, "Nobody told me there would be days like these." But I would sing, "Nobody told me I had to wear black beads." It must be a tough lyric to hear. My daughter, just about two years ago when she was five, sang, "Nobody told me I had to eat these leggies." I don't know what *leggies* are but neither did she. I'd venture to guess it would be a mystery to Mr. John Lennon as well.

When I was in junior high, though, I heard the lyrics better and they meant something to me. I bought all the albums and compellations on tape. I sat in my room pining for the love of some girl I had yet to meet and let the lyrics of the mop-topped lads carry my soul to whimsical places of magical mystery. I remember the first time I heard "Fool On The Hill". My mother told me the song reminded her of me. I wasn't really sure how to take it at the time but now I feel like it describes me quite a bit.

I've always been rather unique. Thankfully I come off as charming and imaginative instead of, what is the term, oh yes, bat-shit crazy. I think it's because I have a kind face, a warm smile, and soulful eyes. You can say crazy things when people don't find you off-putting, which isn't a compliment to me, nor is it a boast. It's just science.

So as I stood there on the sloped hillside looking at the sign, the Admiral sitting in the idling rental in the distance, I knew my mother was right. I'm the fool on the hill, living my life with a foolish grin as the eyes in my head see the world spinning round.

I get life more than most people. I understand it. At least I think so. Regardless, I'm unhurried, unworried, and otherwise unaffected by most things that give people fits. You may have noticed here and there in this literary misadventure that I keep trying to impart a little insight the best I can. There's a reason. This book is more than a collection of daily happenings, tales of mind elves, and journeys with pumpkins. No, there is some real substance in here … somewhere. Read it again.

Oh, the wheels are off the bus at Jolly Good Times tonight!

One of the elves is swinging from the wicker ceiling fan. The girl elf in the midnight blue hat with the white trim just took off her top, thus cementing her position on the naughty list, or the nice list depending on whom you ask.

The Admiral and I have been drinking Woodchuck Cider and singing loudly to Barry Manilow videos here in the hotel room. My apologies to my neighbors, if there are any. The hotel is rather empty.

We just came back from my lecture tonight. The students really seemed to enjoy it. We started late due to an issue with their AV department but it all went well anyhow, especially the investigation part. The spirits were eager to answer tonight.

I stopped at Denny's on the way back to the hotel. Nothing like a little late night breakfast, except maybe a little late night greasy pizza but I couldn't find any. Strange, actually. How is there not a greasy pizza place next to a college?

I have some maple sugar candy and a stuffed animal kitty cat to bring home to my daughter. I'm going to do my best not to open the maple sugar candy until I bring it home to her.

Sunday, October 26, 2014

I opened the damned maple sugar candy for breakfast. I'm so weak. I blame the elves.

Time to get on the road. St. Joseph's College in Maine awaits.

Monday, October 27, 2014

I left right after the lecture yesterday evening and drove through the night to get back home. Just me, the Admiral, the rental, and Elvis. Well, Elvis was there in spirit. We were listening to him on Elvis satellite radio. They played the Live Elvis Presley Aloha from Hawaii concert in 1973. The King was in great form tonight. The white lines on the highway ticked past as did the minutes on the clock. In between songs I thought about my recent journey. Three lectures in three States in three days. Good times.

I have to say, my first time in Maine, though a bit rushed, was pleasant. I toured a little bit of Portland and Brunswick. I stopped by the Joshua Lawrence Chamberlain home and museum. It was closed but I took a photo there. Then I went to the old Brunswick Diner for a grilled cheese and bacon. I like my diners old. This one was from 1946. I like my grilled cheese and bacon dusted in salt and dipped in ketchup.

When I came home I placed the little stuffed kitty cat in the corner of my daughter's bed so it would be the first thing she saw when she woke up. I then crawled into bed and grabbed a quick four hours of sleep.

This morning started with my daughter crawling into bed and laying on top of me with the little gray stuffed kitty cat under her arm. She was glad to have me back home, and as I had hoped, she found the little stuffed cat as soon as she woke up. That's how she knew I was home. It was the perfect way to start the day.

Unfortunately the rest of the day had yet to unfold. To say it was a day and a half is not saying nearly enough. It could be simply because I'm exhausted from travel and lectures this weekend. It could be simply because some days are diamonds and some days are stones, but all of them rock. It was hard to remember that last part today. Nothing was going right. All the surgeries went fine but there were a bunch of other things that went astray.

Amongst them, Angelina was not repaired. The lift was busy at my buddy's garage, so Angelina sat outside all weekend, with her exhaust in the back of her pickup bed. That left me with an issue as I needed her for work tomorrow since Mama Bear needs the Durango and the Daytona needs an inspection sticker.

Speaking of the Durango, as predicted, it took just about a month before my wife scraped it up. I had texted to her to see how her day was and she didn't respond for a while, which is not unfamiliar. But when she did respond, she said she was having an awful day and I would hate her. I knew what it was right away. I called her to find she had the Durango in the garage with the rear hatch open when she pressed the button to close the garage door … right on the hatch. Scrape number one.

Truth be told, I was disappointed but I told her I could never hate her. The Durango is a material thing. Material things can be fixed. Not that I was thrilled about it but what can you do? She already feels bad about it. No sense in making her feel worse. Making others feel better when they expect us to make them feel worse is an act of kindness; an act of kindness that most people don't do enough. Keep that in mind when an opportunity like this presents itself.

Anyhow, knowing I have to get a rental again on Wednesday night for a lecture Thursday evening in New Jersey, I decided to simply keep the little red Kia Soul for the week. This way Mama Bear can use the Durango, I can use the rental, Angelina can get the parts under her skirt fixed, and the Daytona can sit in the yard until I get the nerve to sell her.

Days like this are Etch A Sketch days. It's time to pack up my gym bag, take a hot shower, eat a chocolate bar, and go to bed and rest. In my sleep the angels will knit up the holes in my heart. The Etch A Sketch will be flipped over and I'll start tomorrow with a new canvas to create a bright new day. A frame around an empty canvas, my portrait of the future.

Never give up.

Tuesday, October 28, 2014

Sleep! Glorious sleep!

Last night was a blessing. I was able to get all the sleep I needed and then some. I actually woke up around 11pm and I was wide awake. I contemplated going to the kitchen to have a glass of eggnog and some cookies but I then thought against it.

I was feeling empty, but not due to lack of food. I had been away for some time—not just this weekend but over the last few months. I needed some time with my family, specifically my little girl. I went over to her bedroom and saw her sleeping there, her face illuminated by the soft glow of her iPod set on Pandora playing her Brad Paisley country station. So peaceful. So sweet. So innocent. Oh, how I love that Beans of mine. I crawled up the slide into her bed. It's one of those fancy princess beds with two levels, a ladder and a slide. I put it together for her last Christmas Eve as a surprise for Christmas morning. A set of stairs can take you up to the canopy-covered bed, and the slide can take you down to the play area underneath. She sleeps with her head near the stairs, so I had to climb up the slide as to not wake her.

She just started sleeping in it on a nightly basis this year. Although she started out most nights there in her own bed, she always ended up snuggled betwixt Mama Bear and I, usually on my left arm with her head on my chest. I honestly didn't mind but she's getting older and the time has come. However, I had been away for a while and wanted to be close to her so I snuggled up next to her and watched her sleep for a long while. I looked at her little nose. I admired how beautiful she looked laying there a million miles away in the Land of Nod. I counted her eyelashes and I prayed to God to continue to watch over her, to keep her safe, happy and healthy, and to protect her from the evils of this world and the next. My daily and nightly prayers are always very focused, especially when my prayers are for her and her well-being.

After prayer I apparently dozed off for about an hour and some odd minutes. I awoke with a stiff neck and realized it was time to get back into my own bed, so down the slide I went.

I awoke to a wonderful day full of wonderful things.

It was just a flip of an Etch A Sketch away.

Wednesday, October 29, 2014

Angelina is back! My friend Cody DesBiens brought me to pick her up tonight. The exhaust system was welded back on and now she's as good as new. The bond between a man and his truck cannot be overstated. I drove her home with the same joy that I had when I first picked her up at the dealership back in 1999.

Thursday, October 30, 2014

Today is a marathon day. I'm scheduled to leave work a bit early as I need to hop in the rental and head to New Jersey for tonight's lecture at Rowland University. The lecture is scheduled to start at 10pm, followed by the investigation portion an hour later. If I can stick to the schedule, I should be able to get back in the rental and home for 5am.

I would have liked to get a hotel room for the night and just head back to the office in the morning, but due to logistics, driving through New Jersey, New York, and Connecticut traffic in the morning is a bit out of the question. Just to be on the safe side I'm bringing my pillow and a down blanket in case I can't make it all the way home. Driving in the wee small hours of the morning is one thing but I know my limits and sometimes I have to pull over and get some rest.

Time to head off to work. Oh, I almost forgot. The Admiral will be coming along for the ride as well.

It's just before 2pm. I was supposed to leave an hour ago. Looks like we'll be a little behind schedule getting down there but that's okay. I have a two-hour window to do sound check and be interviewed by the local newspaper and school television network before doing tonight's lecture.

Friday, October 31, 2014

Happy Halloween!

It's just before 5:30 in the morning. I'm at a tiny little truck stop and all night diner just off of exit 93 in Connecticut, the last exit before Rhode Island.

The lecture went long and the investigation went longer. I couldn't help it. The audience was really good tonight and I was having a great time.

I was hoping to make a little better time coming back home but literally all of the roadways I had to travel in New York were down to one lane due to construction, and Connecticut was more of the same. There wasn't much traffic but you can only go so fast through construction zones.

The Admiral is in the back seat of the rental cuddled up with my hooded sweatshirt trying to keep his seeds warm. I have the driver's seat reclined all the way back and I have my pillow and blanket. Looks like I have time for two hours of sleep before I drive back to my office. There is no time to go home, so I'll just shower at work and get on with the day.

"I don't like Halloween the way you like Halloween." That's what Mama Bear told me when I called her on my way home from work to see if I could coerce her into trick-or-treating tonight with Beans and me. No dice.

I'm on two hours of sleep. I made it through work. I had a sharp pain in the center of my chest right at the end of the workday that rocked me for a moment but it passed. I just need rest. But tonight is Halloween and I do love Halloween the way I love Halloween.

The first thing I did when I came home was ask my daughter to come out to the pumpkin patch with me to see if there were any pumpkins. She was reluctant to do so since we were just out there a few nights ago and there were just dirt and dead vines. I did plant them late in the summer but they had gotten off to a great start. When I was on the road these past few months, Mama Bear didn't water them as much as she should have despite my phone calls, and thus my plans of having a corner of our yard full of pumpkins went astray.

I was disappointed but not nearly as much as my daughter was and that's why I snuck out into the yard the other night after she was in bed and hid a medium sized pumpkin behind the bushes and dragged the last living vine over to it. I wrapped the vine around the stem and threw some dirt on it.

When we approached the dusty corner of the yard Beans surmised there were no pumpkins and she thought it was a waste of time. I told her we tried our best and we should just look over the vines to be sure. When she saw the pumpkin behind the bushes, she was ecstatic and started yelling back to the house for Mama Bear. I quickly put my hand on the stem of the pumpkin and made a bit of a show about how hard it was to tear off of the vines. I'm not one for deception but when it comes to keeping the dream alive and making my daughter happy, well, a carefully placed pumpkin is allowable.

Maybe Mama Bear was right. She doesn't like Halloween the way I like Halloween. I was as tired as I had been in recent memory but nothing could stop me from dressing up and trick-or-treating with my daughter.

A few years back when I was on *Ghost Hunters International*, a woman sent me a photo of her young son with his hair spiked up whilst wearing an upside-down, backwards-facing visor. He was dressed up as me for Halloween. Poor bastard. He must have gone door to door all night explaining who his costume was supposed to be. Even then, the little old grannies handing out the boxes of raisins must have been confused.

I was dressed as Kristoff, the ice delivery guy in *Frozen* and my daughter was Queen Elsa. She had an elaborate costume with a flowing dress, cape, sparkling high heel shoes, and a long braided wig. I had also purchased her an Olaf head trick-or-treat bag, complete with her name stitched into it. Olaf the snowman takes his head off in the movie so it was cute, not macabre. My costume was a little simpler, consisting of an "Arendelle Ice Delivery" t-shirt, hooded sweatshirt and a knitted cap.

The little one was so excited to head out into the streets that we were actually the first ones in our area out and about. We had a wonderful night canvasing the neighborhood in search of candy, candy, and more candy.

I just love Halloween. Always have. I especially enjoy it now as a father. Just her and I out there alone, walking hand and hand in the darkness and the night breezes. We shared laughs and pieces of candy that were too good to wait to enjoy at home. We ran up front lawns and down driveways. We took an extra piece or two for Mama Bear at the houses that left the candy-filled bucket at their front door.

This year was great because it marked two years in a row that my daughter told me it was one of her favorite moments. It appears she likes Halloween the way I like Halloween, for it is a night of magic and special moments.

Saturday, November 1, 2014

We finished off last night back at home cuddled up in bed watching *Corpse Bride* together as a family. I then slept fifteen hours. That's right, fifteen hours. Guess I was more tired than I thought.

Today started with a family outing to see *The Book Of Life*. I thought it was a great film with a focus on love, sacrifice, and writing your own story, controlling your own destiny. Fantastic lessons. I'm an old romantic soul. I like holding hands. I adore snuggling. There are few things better than staring into the eyes of someone whom you truly love.

Sacrifice is something at my core. The message of selflessness has resonated with me at my deepest level as far back as I can remember and when it comes to my daughter, there isn't a thing I wouldn't do. I'm still working on writing my own story. Not just this one, but also the big story; the story of my life. As a man of faith, I don't worry about it all so much. I feel the big picture has already been written in the stars. I walk in faith, not in fear. But I still believe I have choices to make. There are things that I can do to make it a better story, or a worse one. Most importantly, I can make the story better for others so that's my focus. My happiness is not as important as the ones around me, and to be honest, I'm usually happiest when I'm helping others anyway.

After the movie, we came home and I made grilled cheese for the Beans and me. Mama Bear went out to pick up some DVDs at Redbox whilst the little one and I ate and went on to play video games for a few hours—Mario Party 9. Good times.

After all was said and done, I twisted the top off of an Angry Orchard cinnamon hard cider and went for a walk in the night air. It was cold and rainy out there tonight. You could hear the wind dancing through the treetops, ushering in the storm that will be here tomorrow.

I do love a good storm. Looks like I'll sleep well tonight also.

Sunday, November 2, 2014

There are many things to love about Sunday. My list starts with church, makes a turn at fresh hot bread from the bakery, detours to family time, and then heads straight on to NASCAR and football. This was my first Sunday home in forever and it was a magical one. Today was the first day it snowed this winter. I sat in church and watched the white stuff fall outside the window. It was so beautiful and peaceful—everything church should be.

After church, I picked up my loaf of Italian bread and ordered a pizza. My mighty Miami Dolphins were playing this afternoon against the San Diego Chargers, so I had time to play video games with Beans before that.

We decided upon Mario Party 9. She and I enjoy playing video games together. It's something we've done since she was almost three. It started with a simple *Pac-Man* and *Mappy* game, which plugged directly into the television. From there it expanded to the Mario Bros. games, and now we play together a lot. Lately it hasn't happened because she takes dance three nights a week and I've been on the road more than I've been home. But today was a day for family, and so we played for a few hours. Some of my favorite memories have been sitting on that couch playing Mario Kart with my daughter.

The Dolphins put a sound beating upon the Chargers. I was so excited to see them on television since Miami doesn't get a lot of coverage up here in the Northeast. They won 37 – 0. They were doing so well that CBS stopped covering the game in the third quarter and went to another game. That was okay, though, as it was just about time for NASCAR to start.

Before I could sit and watch the race, Mama Bear and I went to a local farm where our daughter's school puts on an annual art show. Local vendors set up tables and peddle their wares. There's food, crafts, and music. The big display is an art project put together by all the kids.

This year Beans made a cricket for the display. It was themed Starry Night, and featured an evening scene filled with creatures that come out at night. We were very proud of her, as she was of herself. I love seeing her take pride in her work. She loves art and has taken pottery classes for the last couple of summers. She's always writing stories and illustrating them. I just love to see what she creates.

This was a Sunday the way Sunday should be.

Monday, November 3, 2014

I finally was able to get back to the gym today. It was an interesting workout for sure. There was some issue with the local power so the gym only had emergency lighting and no heat. I worked out in my furry hooded sweatshirt under the low lights. Strangely, it was kind of comforting and a fine welcome back to the gym.

Tuesday, November 4, 2014

It's Election Day! Wave old glory and cast your votes, boys and girls. Elect the next criminal whom you want to take care of their friends. Oh hell, it isn't as bad as all that but isn't as good either. I look at it this way. It may not be a perfect system but it's the best one that we have and so we have to roll with it and hope to get the best people in there who can reform it. I don't get involved in heavy political talk. It's pointless to me and incites more arguments and negativity. I vote. I keep quiet. I go to work and handle the things in my life that I can handle. I help those I can help.

Work was work. It was a good day. I had the opportunity to play plumber. I like trying to do things that are outside of my realm. The hot water wasn't circulating to the back offices and the upstairs meeting area of my Rhode Island office building. Whilst the docs were doing surgery, I was in the storage room trying to figure out why the hot water wasn't getting into the pipes towards the rear of the building. It took me a little bit of time but I was able to take some things apart and pretty soon the water was flowing and the heat was rising up. I was quite proud of myself. I never bet against myself but plumbing is not an arena in which I have had many victories over the years. I guess playing all that Mario Bros. finally paid off.

After work I received a phone call from Los Angeles asking me to film another *Ghost Hunters* episode next week in Pennsylvania. I'm thankful for the opportunity but I have to think it over tonight. I need to look at my work schedule and such. In my heart, I know that if I can fit it in with my day job, I'll make it happen … just one more time.

Mama Bear was sick, so I brought home some Chinese food for her. She enjoys Chinese food when she's ill or has had a bad day. I tried to lift her spirits. I only like pork fried rice and fries. There's something about the fries from Chinese food restaurants. I don't care for fries normally—maybe a good steak fry but just once in a while. However, if I get Chinese food, I have to have some. I'll sometimes get wonton soup but I pick it apart because I only like the noodles and the broth.

Mama Bear ate and went up to bed early. Beans and I played the Rabbids Go Home video game and then did something remarkable. I'm fond of my nightly walks, and recently my daughter asked if she could join me some night. Well, tonight was that night. I left the hard cider in the fridge and instead, I took her hand in mine. Together we walked through the night air. The moon shone brightly above us as we walked and laughed and joked with each other. It was amazing. I'm so proud of her. It's crazy to think how quickly she is growing. I remember carrying her everywhere in my arms, keeping her safe and sound.

Now she's grown from a baby into a little girl and she's growing older every day. I cannot carry her everywhere to keep her safe but I have to trust that I've given her a firm foundation to go forth in this life and make good decisions for herself. Of course, I'll continue to guide her and help her grow. Daddy is never too far away … just in case.

She asks me to carry her up to bed every night after we play video games in our playroom in the basement. And even though it's up two flights of stairs and she is getting bigger, the burden is light, for I love her so much. Plus, I know these days are also fleeting.

As we were rounding the last turn to come back up our street, there, glistening in the moonlight in the middle of the road sat a random pile of poop. My daughter saw it first from afar and asked if that was poop or some leaves. I voted leaves. I was wrong. She and I had a good little laugh about the mysterious defecation as it was quite sizeable. We theorized it was perhaps from a deer that saw a car and literally had the poop scared out of him. I tried to steer the conversation away from our discovery and back onto conversation about the man in the moon but I failed. So I embraced her silliness and together we rushed home to tell Mama Bear about it.

Life Lesson: there are great moments and surprises waiting around every corner, and sometimes, there's poop. They can all be one in the same depending on your willingness to let go, smile, and laugh at life.

Well, it's time for bed. The naughty little ladies from the Lullaby League are coming down the path to the front door in my mind. The smallest one is wearing "I Voted" stickers over her nipples. What am I going to do with these ne'er do wells?

Wednesday, November 5, 2014

I had a busy day, which is pretty much the norm at this point. It started with a strong workout. I had to do a lot of marketing for the day job, which entailed putting on the dress shirt and sport coat and then going to the offices of referring dentists, handing out referral pads, and various dessert-type treats as a thank you for their continued patient referrals to our offices. Then the day finished up with taking ACLS (Advanced Cardiovascular Life Support) and PALS (Pediatric Advanced Life Support) classes in order to keep my medical certifications current.

The highlight of the day was a sugar cookie iced latte at Dunkin Donuts. Peppermint mocha is my favorite iced latte flavor, which also came out this week but this was my first affair with sugar cookie. I always order my iced lattes the same way, regardless of seasonal trends—extra flavor, extra sugar, and skim milk. I watch my girlish figure, you know. The sugar cookie flavor came with red and green sprinkles that made it simply amazing. I thoroughly enjoyed this little beverage and I look forward to many stolen moments together this holiday season.

In other news, it looks like I'm going to film for that ole ghost show. Say it with me, kids! "Just one more time." I should have my head examined at some point. I would but I know the elves wouldn't like it. There's nothing wrong with doing the show. I love investigating the spirit world, especially in such grandiose locations but I have done a lot this year and could use a bit of a respite. Oh well. I'll sleep when I'm dead. Maybe.

I have a gig to do at the Old Mill Parafest in Michigan this weekend and then I'll come home Sunday and fly out Monday night after work—this time to Pennsylvania. I haven't really reviewed the specifics. Work is work. Fly me here. Fly me there. This hotel. That hotel. Fly me home.

Working is what I do best. It's what I know how to do. It's what I have been doing since I worked at that ole Jefferson Diner in Warwick, Rhode Island, during my freshman year of high school. I've never stopped. There is nothing wrong with good and honest work. One job. Two jobs. Three jobs. Up to four jobs at a time. It's what I do. I pride myself upon being able to do what they say can't be done.

East bound and down, loaded up and truckin'
We're gonna do what they say can't be done
We've got a long way to go and a short time to get there
I'm east bound, just watch ol' Bandit run.

– "East Bound and Down" by Jerry Reed

Thursday, November 6, 2014

When asked how The Beatles enjoyed their first trip to America, John Lennon replied something akin to, "It was a plane ride, a cab ride, a hotel, and we had grilled cheese sandwiches." That was pretty much how today went. However, I reflected on two stories today. One stars my daughter and the other stars my father.

Little Beanie Boo was going to the bathroom. Like most kids her age, and her old man, Beans knows it's best experienced in the nude. "No encumbrances," as George Costanza from *Seinfeld* would say. She sat there in her birthday suit on the white porcelain throne, curly hair down over her shoulders, chatting me up about her day at school as she often does. She's still at that age of feeling completely comfortable holding a conversation whilst doing her business. I've learned to lock the door when I'm occupied but that doesn't deter her from having a conversation with me through the door.

Suddenly she leaned forward so her chest was flat against her knees. She reached back with one hand and pulled the toilet seat lid down on her back, stuck her arms out by her side and declared, "Look, Diddy! I'm a turtle!" Ha! That's my girl. And yes, she likes to call me Diddy. I'm not sure where that came from but she says it sweetly so it's all right by me.

Now … onto my father's tale.

You need to understand, my father is a big old truck-driving teamster. A former Harley man. Black hair—what's left of it—and a black beard. Throughout most of his life, he was rarely seen without a cigar clenched between his teeth. He's truly the toughest guy I know. Now he's closing in on 70 and I still wouldn't want to challenge him in a brawl. He always reminded me of Bluto from the Popeye cartoons (or Brutus depending on which Popeye cartoon you are watching).

A brief note on Popeye by the way. He came into town and took Olive Oyl away from Bluto/Brutus. They were engaged until the squinty-eyed sailor blew into town on his corncob pipe. Who's really the bad guy?

Anyhow… back to the lecture. My father recently retired, and like most people who spent most of their lives working hard to get by, he wasn't adjusting to it well. He tinkered in the barn on our old '69 Mustang. He made unnecessary modifications to his lawn tractor and snowplow. He drove my mother crazy. He painted the heads of all the nails in his barn for reasons still unbeknownst to us all.

But then one day, it finally happened … my father had a nemesis.

Many people feud with family members, neighbors, co-workers, or the guys at the bar. My father? Well, he went to war with a bird. A tiny robin, to be precise. You see, despite denying it, he's has always been a perfectionist. Perfection plagued me as a child but thankfully I've learned to let go. My father however, clings to keeping things as pristine as possible. So when he cleans the cars, he expects them to stay that way, Mother Nature and birds be damned. For several days in a row, he washed both cars in the driveway, and then returned to the house or his fortress of solitude in the barn only to emerge and find a bird had pooped upon one of the car mirrors.

He quickly became convinced it was one specific bird that returned daily to do his dirty sinful business in effort to mock my father and drive him into a maddening rage. He sat in the kitchen window and waited to see if he was correct, and sure enough, he saw this robin sit upon the car mirror, poop, and take flight.

And so, my father, age 66 at the time, devised himself a plan that would prove to be the envy of any cartoon hunter trying to capture himself a "wascally wabbit" or roadrunner. He took a handful of birdseed and placed it upon the ground betwixt the cars in the driveway. He then took a box and propped it up with a stick to which was tied a string that he then ran across the driveway, up the path, and into the kitchen window. Then, my father, Bluto/Brutus, waited for his nemesis to take the bait whilst my mother took to the phone to tell me of his exploits and how he was driving her crazy.

Sure enough, the little robin flew down onto the driveway and started to peck away at the birdseed. My father, the great hunter, was elated and pulled the string. The stick flew and the box dropped down upon the bird. However, the bird was swift and moved in such a way that the box only had him pinned down by one wing. By the time my father ankeled it out there to defeat his foe, the bird had wiggled free and flew off into the wild blue yonder, only to return again and poop on the mirrors.

This feud escalated over the next few weeks, resulting in my father borrowing a handgun from a friend of his in order to best the bird. Keep in mind; this was no BB gun but a real pistol complete with a red target laser. I was concerned, not for the bird, for my father is no Wyatt Earp but rather for the neighbors and the highway that ran across the street. And sure enough, he took to shooting, and the bird simply flew away.

The seasons changed, as we do, and the bird eventually left only to return again this year. He is convinced it's still the same bird. Classic Bluto/Brutus. That's my dad!

He also once set the eaves of the barn on fire whilst trying to get rid of a woodpecker with a ladder, a blowtorch, and a can of ether (his usual tools for the removal of bees by the way). But that, my friends, is another story.

Friday, November 7, 2014

I'm high above the clouds in aisle seat 11B aboard Delta flight DL3848 on my way to the land of golden chariots, Detroit! I have a gig to do tomorrow night in Dundee, Michigan, called The Old Mill Parafest. It will be my last paranormal event of 2015. I have two more motivational lectures on the books for the year and that should close it out.

This event should be a good time as many of my friends are going to be there. Both people from shows I have worked on and fans that have turned into friends over many miles and many smiles.

I worked this morning in surgery for a few hours before my dad picked me up at the office and dropped me off at the airport. This should be the last big week for the year as well. By that I mean I work this weekend, fly home Sunday night, work Monday, fly out Monday night to film until Thursday, and fly home to work on Friday. I don't mind the schedule much as I have had ample time to rest since last week when I did the marathon college lecture series that left me sleeping in a rental car for two hours.

I'd take a lifetime of long and dark rainy days if it meant most of my daughter's days would be sunny and filled with love, light, happiness, and health. And so, that's how I look at my schedule this week of doing this event before the quick turnaround of filming for that ole ghost show.

"Just one more time." They might as well carve that into my gravestone.

Saturday, November 8, 2014

Big event today in Dundee, Michigan, The Old Mill Parafest featuring yours truly and some of my closest friends in the paranormal community. Amongst them are Miss Kris Williams, Amy Bruni, John "The Old Man" Zaffis, Jeff Belanger, and my long-time friend and Detroit native, Mr. John E.L. Tenney.

Tenney and I have some mischief planned during our break today. We're going to film our own rendition of the infamous opening sequence for the classic television show, *Laverne and Shirley*. I have been sitting on this idea for some time and have been waiting for the right moment to do it. I have all the props secured and ready to go. This is going to be hilarious.

Speaking of hilarious, I spent a good deal of time last night taking pictures of myself in the Santa hat in various locations around the hotel. My favorite was sitting fireside whilst reading a book in the hotel lobby. Sleeping in bed with the hat on was a close second though.

Perhaps I'll bring the hat to the convention and wear it today as well. Merry mischief awaits!

Sunday, November 9, 2014

Four hours of sleep and I am back in the sky. This time it's Delta flight 790, seat 27 C on a near-empty plane. Strangely enough, there were only three seats to choose from when I checked in online yesterday. Methinks some airline hijinks are happening.

No matter. I'm on my way home sweet home. I'll have a lot to do when I get there. I have to cut the lawn, iron rake it, cast some grass seed, and fertilize it all. I also want to reorganize my shed for the winter as all the summer stuff is still in the front and Lord knows the weather is not getting any warmer for a long, long time.

I was reflecting on yesterday's event. I was quite happy with my lecture. I ended up wearing the Santa hat for most of the day, including during my one hour monologue of happy nonsense. I'm not sure why exactly, but I brought a chair up on stage with me to use as a prop. I proceeded to move it around the stage with me, sometimes standing on top of it for elongated periods of time, whilst regaling tales of randomness.

When all was said and done, I spoke a bit on the paranormal, told some personal stories from the road, touched a lot of motivation and spirituality, and tried to impress upon everyone the importance of living in the moment, every moment.

When I was walking back to my table a kind older man approached me with his hand outstretched and tears in his eyes. He wanted to thank me for encouraging others not to give up and for my work with suicide prevention and awareness. These are the people, and these are the moments, that make it all worthwhile.

Now to get home to the two little ladies I do it all for. Then I'll unpack my bags. Pack my bags. And get ready to do it all again. Just one more episode. This time, I mean it.

Never give up.

Yard work was completed, but a few outdoor tasks remain outstanding before the winter rolls in. The moon came out before I was ready, so I couldn't finish everything up.

We had an impromptu birthday party for Mama Bear. Both of my stepsons, the youngest one's sweetheart of a girlfriend, my mother-in-law, and the Beans, all sang Happy Birthday, and gave my wife her birthday presents. No one told me we were doing this today. I was lucky to have some of her presents ready and available for the occasion.

Afterwards, I took Beans up to get washed and ready for bed and let Mama Bear spend some time with her boys. They are older so they don't live with us anymore. It's nice for them to have some alone time.

What happened next I have decided to entitle: "The Vagina Dialogue".

I was getting my little one out of the tub and drying her off, and she asked me what the real name for her petunia was. "Petunia" had been the name my wife had decided to bestow upon my daughter's genitalia and I simply never questioned it, nor did my daughter, until tonight. Why she couldn't wait to ask my wife about it I'll never know, but I figured I could handle it.

Firstly, I wanted to know why she suddenly knew it was not actually called a petunia. I suspected the kids at the lunch table at school, or perhaps on the bus. As it turned out, she had lunch with my mother-in-law and started to sing a song that I sang when she was a baby crying in the crib. "You're just a little petunia in an onion patch. Boo-hoo. Boo-hoo." Why she sang this song that I had not heard in many moons is an unknown variable and will undoubtedly remain as such.

However, when she sang the song this time, she brought up to Grandma the imagery she had concocted in her mind depicting the petunia in the onion path. That's right; she imagined a solitary vagina floating above a field of onions. When Grandma laughed, Beans questioned it, and she was told her lady part was not really called a petunia, hence the question posed to me by my 7-year-old.

I explained to her that it's called a vagina. That is the correct term for it. There is nothing shameful about it but Mommy had given it a cute little name because she's a little girl and that's the way these things are. She practiced saying it a few times with a giggle and that was that. Or so I thought.

A few hours later, I was here in bed with Mama Bear watching *The Walking Dead* and I heard Beans crying in her room. I ran in there to see what the matter was and make sure she was okay. My sweet little angel looked up at me, tears in her eyes, and exclaimed, "I forgot what my petunia is called!" This occurred again about twenty minutes later and my wife had to remind her and then let her go tell Grandma that she knows it's really called a vagina.

Oh Beans… whatever will Daddy do with you?

Monday, November 10, 2014

I'm currently in Washington-Dulles airport after arriving via United flight 5745, upon which I sat in seat 6B, next to an older woman who admittedly had too much wine and proceeded to announce loudly that I was adorable. Ha! These things only happen to me. It was an interesting flight to say the least.

I have been stuck here in Washington for over two hours now. This next flight is only thirty minutes long and will take me from here to Harrisburg, Pennsylvania, but it's been delayed four times. Apparently they've been unable to get flights in here from Pennsylvania due to snow. Well, it's better that than vampires. Oh wait, that is Transylvania. I've been there, too. I get confused.

I had a tall eight dollar Blue Moon ale at one of the overpriced airport bars and went in search of food but all the food courts were already closed. I've been filling my time and starving off hunger by taking random pictures around the airport of me in my magical Santa hat. I enjoy fighting misery by making merry mischief and spreading happy nonsense. The airport is pretty empty, but still, those who remain don't even raise an eyebrow to the Santa hat. One guy gave me a thumbs up—at least I think that was his thumb. You can never tell in airports. There are some lonely and perverted people hidden in them late at night.

I should be flying out of here shortly after Cinderella's carriage turns back into a pumpkin and hopefully I'll be nestled into a hotel room in Pennsylvania by 1:30 in the morning.

Tuesday, November 11, 2014

Happy Birthday Mama Bear!

Today is my wife's birthday and sadly I'm over here in Pennsylvania getting ready to go on an investigation of some restaurant whilst my bride is back home without me. I did send her a beautiful bouquet of flowers in a fancy Vera Wang vase, and I'll be taking her to dinner at the end of this week when I get home. I do the best I can from the road.

Ah well, I can only do what I can do. Back to work.

Wednesday, November 12, 2014

Tried to sleep late, as I was a bit tired from the investigation last night. The case was a decent one. Nothing crazy but some spirit interaction.

However, sleeping late was not in the cards as my phone started ringing just before 8am. There was some question from one of our referring dentist offices and I give out my cell phone number so they can always reach me. So, here I am in Pennsylvania, half asleep and they're reaching me. When all was said and done it was almost 11am and I was able to get back to sleep until almost 2pm and now it's time to head out and film at the Old Cumberland County Prison in Carlisle, Pennsylvania.

Thursday, November 13, 2014

It's almost 2am and I have returned from tonight's *Ghost Hunters* filming, nestled snugly in my hotel bed. The Old Cumberland County Prison looked like it wasn't going to be such a great case but when I was down in the basement, which was once used as solitary confinement, things picked up. There were loud noises; items sent crashing to the ground, and the sound of footsteps coming toward me, all when no one else was there.

I'm flying home tomorrow, thankfully at 1pm, which allows me to sleep until 10:30am. Normally I try to catch one of the first flights out of here and get back home, but that leaves me running on two or three hours of sleep, and sends me home exhausted physically and mentally. This time I opted for an early afternoon flight so I could sleep a little bit more and get home feeling decent. Plus it helps that Beans has one of her dance classes after school today, which means she'll get home late and I'll get home around the same time. We can reconnect, have a family dinner with Mama Bear, and get to bed.

Speaking of which, it's time to sleep. The naughty little ladies of the Lullaby League are taking the elevator up from the mezzanine. They will be rattling my door handle soon, disregarding my Do Not Disturb sign.

Perhaps I shall write again later today whilst in flight.

United 5745 is carrying me home from Washington-Dulles airport as the sun is setting outside just beyond the wing. I'm seated in row 19-aisle seat C. Next to me in 19D is a fellow with very hairy arms. I have acquiesced usage of the dividing armrest.

I didn't write upon the first flight today from Harrisburg to DC because it's literally a thirty-minute flight. They don't even bring out the beverage cart. The flight attendant walked through with a bottle of water and a stack of cups. No time for any fanciness there.

My time in the Dulles airport was a bit briefer than it was just a few nights ago, as I only had a two-hour layover this time around, and there were no additional delays. I had time to take out my Santa hat and take some pictures—one of which was with a Christmas tree they must have just put up because it wasn't there three nights ago.

In an airport filled with stuffy old white dudes in uncomfortable looking suits and necktie nooses, I'm the guy in his late-thirties wearing a Santa hat. Very professional and mature, I know, however, I'm just not a very pretentious fellow. I'm living life a la mode, free of status symbols and elitist concepts. Sure, I can dress up in the suit and look like a handsome devil, dimple in my chin and my Windsor knot, but I would rather just be me. I'm a ripped up jeans and screen printed t-shirt kind of guy with a Santa hat for good merry measure.

When I was here on Monday night, I was intrigued by the sign that read "Service Animal Relief Area Ahead". I even took a picture with it, Santa hat and all. Now, I have traveled the world but I have never seen such a sign, and though I have seen many a service animal, I have never stopped to think about where said animals go for relief. So today, with ample down time and a cheery disposition, I went out in search of this magical relief area. And funny enough, it turned out to be one of the very few things in this life that was just how I had envisioned it; a small room with AstroTurf on the floor, covered in urine stains. Perfect.

I did find it funny that no one in the airport questioned a grown man in a Santa hat going into the Service Animal Relief Area without any visible animal, but in actuality, what would they say? I just hope no one thought I was making use of the relief area myself. Then again, why can't I mark my territory?

Mr. Willie Nelson is singing "All Of Me" into my ears, sweetly and with a knowing verbal nod. God bless you Mr. Willie Nelson, wherever you may be right now.

The flight will be making its initial descent in a few moments and I'll be turning in my little plastic cup of ice cube remnants that once chilled my in-flight tomato juice for my inner in-flight vampire. He was happy that they didn't just offer him water on this flight. A man's inner vampire cannot live on water alone, you know.

Things are going well internally. The eggnog river in my mind is high, but not alarmingly so. The live studio audience has been in great form. Jasper P. Jinglebottom is introducing new items to Jolly Good Times. I may have to look into hiring him full-time there to run things. His peppermint milkshakes are really a hit with the other elves. That reminds me, I need to order more peppermint schnapps. We don't want the natives getting restless.

Time to fold up my little plastic tray and place my seat in its upright and locked position. Let's land this big metal bird!

Friday, November 14, 2014

Back to work and back in the swing of things. Busy little day today at the office, followed by a dinner date with Mama Bear in honor of her birthday a few days ago. The Beanie Baby was sleeping over a friend's house.

It bothers me a bit when the little one stays out. I find myself walking by her room and wanting to look in on her as I usually do, only to remember she's out for the night. I know it's important for her to have time with her friends, so I try to keep that in mind.

Saturday, November 15, 2014

Tonight I went to see Mr. Bob Dylan sing his songs at the Providence Performing Arts Center downtown. Mama Bear didn't want to go but I knew several people that were going, one of which was my friend Stephanie Zabski who was driving down from New York to catch the show. Dylan fans are a good group and very dedicated to ole Mr. Zimmerman (his original surname). I've seen him around eight times or so. Stephanie has been to a Dylan show upwards of twenty times and others have seen him even more still.

We started the night at a random little bar named Aurora, which I have never been to before, but it was the only place close by that didn't have a packed house. I prefer quiet little bars to a crowded house. Aurora was showing *The X-Files* on a movie screen against the back wall, and then switched it to an ocean scene very reminiscent of an old Windows screensaver, accompanied by bizarre music. Their beers were not your run of the mill selection but rather the artsy variety. I don't fancy artsy. I settled on a white ale as my choice and it was a safe bet. I followed it up with something labeled "Teenage Dream (The Wet One)" on the chalkboard behind the bar. It wasn't everything it was made out to be but it wasn't half bad either. Just like sex, just like pizza—even if it isn't great, it's still pretty good. So, then again, maybe Teenage Dream was everything it was made out to be.

After leaving the bizarre bar, we made our way over to the show and I took my seat in the second row behind the orchestra pit. I bought a single ticket since no one wanted to go with me and that allowed me to get such a great spot. Best I had ever had for a concert.

Dylan took the stage in his usual style, quietly and with no introduction. One of the first songs he played was "Beyond Here Lies Nothing", which is actually one of my favorite of Dylan's newer songs off an album released about five or six years ago. He went on to do a few classics that he doesn't perform as often anymore—*Tangled Up In Blue* and *Simple Twist of Fate.* The tempos were different for these songs from that of their original recordings but they weren't unpleasant. He also altered a few verses, adding in some new takes on old lyrics but that's part of his enigma.

At 73, he split his time between sitting at the piano and standing behind the microphone at center stage. He was dressed a bit like an aged cowboy with his wide brimmed hat, long gray jacket with white trim, and matching trousers. The set design really complimented the man and his music. A large dark brown curtain hung in a wrinkled state around the stage in a half circle. Seven large old stage lights hung low around the edge of the curtain, whilst eight other small lights were spread throughout the stage, all of which were lit with a soft, sometimes flickering orange glow, as if Nikola Tesla was just backstage testing out his experiments with electricity for the first time.

Bob doesn't dance now but I don't think he ever did. He doesn't even walk the stage as much as he wanders it. But he does so with a quiet nobility that draws you in and holds you close. Then he stops and stares into the darkness, right hand down by his side, his left hand on his hip with his index finger extended, like an old gunslinger squinting into the setting sunlight at what may be his final showdown.

There was a brief intermission and I went to make water in the men's room. Whilst in line, I looked at my phone and I had eight text messages from my daughter. She's only seven but she sends Mama Bear and me texts on the iPod Touch when she goes to a sleepover or when I'm away. Her first five messages were about how sorry she was that she somehow got a crack in the bottom of the iPod. I wasn't mad, of course. Accidents happen and the iPod is old. I bought it for my wife back when we were dating. I wasn't concerned at all. It's just another material thing anyhow.

However, the texts she sent were so funny that I must record them here as she originally wrote them to me:

"Hay Dad I didn't know- please don't get mad but I cracked my iPod a little but it still works."

"It's near the button on the bottom."

"I'm so so sorry."

"Please don't get mad."

"P.S. I'm naked."

"Sorry about the iPod. I did not know."

"And in bed naked only in underwear."

"Good night XOXOXOXO."

Ha! I have no idea why she felt the need to include the naked and underwear talk but it was hilarious. Hilarious that is, only if she outgrows sending those sorts of messages before boys become a legit threat to

Daddy's sanity.

Anyhow, the show was a very pleasant one, and I really enjoyed the night as a whole. After the last song was played, Bob stood with his band, center stage, and stared into the darkened crowd without saying a word and then stepped back behind the curtain.

I stepped out into the night air and headed to Firehouse Hot dogs for a couple of grilled cheese sandwiches and coffee milk. Firehouse is an old train caboose that has been at the junction of Johnston, North Providence, and Smithfield for the past 25 years. It's moved back and forth across Route 44 a few times from this parking lot to that parking lot, but it has always been there for me. I remember my father first taking me there when I was a kid. During high school my friends and I went there after work at the local Stop and Shop grocery store for a bite to eat. As we got older and started going out to the nightclubs and such, we returned to Firehouse for late night fare.

Though they are known for their hot dogs, I have always ordered grilled cheese and bacon even before it was on the menu. For all I know, I may be the reason they ended up on the menu. I don't get down that way much anymore since I'm not usually out late at night. They don't open up till 6pm so when I do have late night plans, I make the effort to drive down there and keep the tradition alive.

As I sat in the cab of ole Angelina, radio turned up and the heat turned up higher, I ate three grilled cheese with bacon, and drank delicious coffee milk, whilst envisioning my previous visits and times gone by. I often reminisce upon the various stages of my life. The paths I have traveled and left untraveled. It's important to take stock of where you are, where you've been, where you are heading, and most importantly, who you are. Never look back or look ahead for too long or you'll miss the moment. I repeat this because it's so very important.

The right song can enhance the right moment. That's one of the reasons I always have music playing, even if it just in my mind. Right now the disc jockey at Jolly Good Times is playing Mr. Bob Dylan's "Shooting Star". It's one of my favorite songs Dylan does. It's also one of the few songs that always make me cry. Crying is good, for it means you still feel emotion. It refreshes and flushes out the soul, and it's a good reminder that you're alive.

Seen a shooting star tonight
And I thought of me
If I was still the same
If I ever became
What you wanted me to be
Did I miss the mark?
Overstep the line

That only you could see
Seen a shooting star tonight
And I thought of me

– "Shooting Star" by Bob Dylan

Sunday, November 16, 2014

Ah Sunday, how I do love thee. I had breakfast with my little lady whilst Mama Bear stayed in bed sawing wood. Beans wanted waffles so I made them for her. I had a bowl of Boo Berry cereal, my favorite cereal of all time. I stocked up on it after Halloween was over, as I'll have to make it last until next fall.

We played video games in the playroom together. Our games of Mario Kart have become quite spirited over the years. We are currently on the latest version of this classic game, Mario Kart 8. I couldn't help but notice today that I went from letting her win so many moons ago to trying my hardest to best her in competition, only to come in second place more times than not. I'm proud of her gaming skills and I'm also thinking I need to sneak down to the basement and practice at night while she sleeps.

Beans also came with me to church today, which I always enjoy. I love going to Sunday morning services, and it means the most to me when my little girl is there by my side. I feel like her very existence is proof of God's love here on earth.

After services ended, I was asked if I would say a few words next week as part of their stewardship drive. I don't have to make a hard play from the pulpit for money, as I would never do that anyway, nor would I attend a church that employs those practices but they simply want me to tell my story as a means of example of what the church means to me. I'm very much looking forward to it. I do love to speak to a crowd, no matter when or where but especially about the Kingdom of God, light and love.

I spent a few hours in the afternoon listening to audio recordings from my most recent investigation of that old ghost show. Then I made a little lunch for the family and set the DVR up to record NASCAR. Today is the last race of the season and the championship will be decided but I won't be able to watch it live. Several months ago, I purchased front row tickets for my family and I to attend a Disney production called *Mickey's Music Festival*, and nothing, not even NASCAR, comes before making special memories with my wife and our daughter.

The show was entertaining and the little girl enjoyed herself thoroughly. I bought her a small Princess Jasmine poseable figurine and a soft pretzel. Then I capped off the evening with a trip to the Newport Creamery for dinner and ice cream.

It was a great day for sure, but the highlight for me was just moments ago when my daughter came down the stairs into the living room and asked me to come upstairs to tuck her in and say her prayers. We prayed the Our Father together for the first time outside of church and I was quite taken with how well she had memorized it without my coaching or prodding. I try to guide and shepherd her but I don't force anything upon her, for I feel each person's path must be his or her own. So you can imagine the smile upon my face and within my soul when I heard her say the words of the prayer, knowing that she had taken it upon herself to learn them.

And now, it's time to watch *The Walking Dead*. Good night!

Monday, November 17, 2014

It was a dark and gray day filled with freezing rain and unseasonably low temperatures. This is usually what February feels like around these parts. Considering it's a week before Thanksgiving, I was surprised at how cold it was this morning.

Speaking of Thanksgiving, the turkeys at the ole Belwing Turkey Farm are in great spirits, especially since, you know … Thanksgiving. When I beeped to them this morning, several of them flapped their wings and one of them made it to the roof of their turkey hovel. Ha! I love those turkeys. I'll miss them when they all leave after Christmas. It seems like forever until they will come back again next year. (Yes. I know they won't be the same turkeys but it helps my fragile eggshell mind to think they are the same.)

I started to promote a website where you can sponsor a turkey at a farm in upstate New York. You can save their little turkey lives. Now, I'm no vegetarian. I love eating chicken and steak but I don't see why we all have to eat turkey on the same day and time each year. Who says that only the president can pardon turkeys?

Tuesday, November 18, 2014

Despite the frigid temperature I had a great morning at the gym. I really am fancying my new knitted cap. My head feels nice and toasty warm when I start my day. That's the way life should be.

The day ended the way a day should end as well. Mama Bear had a planned night out with a few of her friends, leaving me alone with Beans for a great Daddy-Daughter night. I offered to make her dinner or take her to McDonald's and after some deliberation, she elected to have McDonald's. She gets a Happy Meal with a grilled cheese, just as I did when I was a finicky kid. We don't go to McDonald's often and she's more interested in the sandwich and yogurt than fries, so I don't worry about taking her there every once in a while.

Then we came back home and played Mario Kart 8 for a long time. I helped her get bathed and ready for bed. And then, as a surprise, I had a DVD of some Coyote and Roadrunner cartoons. She loves the old cartoons just as I do. It's nice to share a bit of my childhood with her.

My lower back is killing me today as it has been on and off for a few days now. The gym made it feel better this morning but it gradually became worse as the day went on. Ah well, looks like sleep will be the medicine I need more than anything else. It's only going to be getting colder outside from this point forward, so I need to rest up, and get back to the gym in the morning to strengthen everything up. Bodies get old. Things fall apart. But if you keep yourself going in the right direction, coupled with a positive mindset, you'll do all right.

Wednesday, November 19, 2014

Today we fried a turkey at work. I never touched the thing until dinnertime. I gave it the ole Pontius Pilot and kept my hands clean. I knew I'd feel bad driving home by the turkeys if I took part in cooking one of their own. We have been holding potluck luncheons at work every couple of months, and scheduled them especially for Thanksgiving and Christmas. Lots of food, everyone together, extended lunch break. Life is good.

My favorite part of the day was lying here in bed with my little one cuddled up against my chest, just in from dance class. I went to lie in bed a bit early. My lower back was pretty tight with this early winter weather and missing the gym for most of last week due to work. I'll be back in the gym first thing in the morning. Nothing and no one keeps me down.

That is an important thing to remember too; don't let anyone steal your sunshine. Your happiness should not be tethered to anyone else. Don't let the opinions of materialistic people in a plastic world dictate who you are or who you are supposed to be.

This is your life. Live it your way.

Thursday, November 20, 2014

I reserved VIP tickets for Mama Bear and me to take the Beans ice skating at Rockefeller Center on Thanksgiving night. It should be a great end to a great day. I'm not much of an ice-skater myself but it's more about making memories even if that means bruising my firm, round apple of a hiney whilst falling repeatedly on the ice. The VIP portion of the ticketing package allows for us to enter through their VIP igloo, have a personal ice skating concierge, skate rental is included, and you get hot cocoa and freshly baked cookies. I can't wait! Attending the Macy's Thanksgiving Day Parade has been a dream of mine since I was a child, and it's coming true in just a week's time!

On the tail end of the day, I received a call from that all too familiar 818 area code. Yup … one more episode.

Friday, November 21, 2014

Merry mischief will be underway tonight! After work I'm teaming up with my cousin, Frank Smith, and together, accompanied by our Santa hats, we shall pain the town red and white like a candy cane! Let's get festive!

Saturday, November 22, 2014

I woke up early this morning with my li'l girl laying on my chest staring at me. I knew the look in her eyes. It was video game time. We had a 32-race Super Mario Kart 8 marathon. We did quite well as the Red Team, soundly beating the Blue Team. Moments like these are truly my favorites.

The good people at Church of Our Saviour had asked me to speak at the services this weekend, and so I did. It's time for the annual stewardship drive and they hoped I'd share a little bit about myself, my story, and speak as to why the church is important to me. Of course, as Sinatra would say, "I did it my way."

There were stories about my youth and the Roman Catholic Church I attended as a child, which I would refer to only as "Our Lady of the Dollar Sign". That church put the almighty dollar before the almighty Lord. The same mistake so many other churches make, hence why they're disappearing. God isn't getting small; His people just can't see Him from behind their vaults of cash. But Church of Our Saviour isn't that way and that's why I like it. They actually put money into the community and into the world and many parishioners do mission work overseas as well.

I told some jokes. I made some serious points. I left them with something to think about. And then I went home.

Mama Bear bought tickets for us to see a musical called *Ghost Brothers of Darkland County* written by Stephen King with music and lyrics by John Mellencamp. It also starred Billy Burke and Gina Gershon, who still looks fantastic and sings equally as well. It was a nice night out with my wife. We don't get much time for such things enough. The musical was great, an entertaining story with great acting. Mama Bear and I had wine in plastic cups and large soft pretzels. Classy, I know.

Greg Wise as John Willoughby.

Marianne is carried safely home by Willoughby.

Willoughby arrives at Barton Park
in his stylish carriage.

Willoughby and Marianne race past the church.

Sunday, November 23, 2014

Started the day at Church of Our Saviour delivering a lecture to the flock. This one was different than last night's, though. I don't prepare for these things. I mean, I have thoughts and ideas, but I don't write anything down. That way I can be alive, in the moment, and adapt to the crowd's reaction. I believe spirit guides me in all I do, so I don't worry about those things, or anything, really.

But what made this morning's presentation really special for me was that my daughter was there to watch. Seven-years-old, bright eyes, radiant smile, and she believes in me. "God only knows just what she sees in me...." Not now, Kenny Rogers! This is *my* moment. This was the first time my daughter saw me speak in public, and though it was just a small smattering of what I do, it was the most rewarding because she was there.

I called an audible whilst I was up behind the podium. I was going to talk about the same things that I said the night before, but then I looked down and saw my little girl sitting there—the most important person in my life, looking at me with stars in her eyes. I told the congregation about how my daughter asked me to pray with her earlier last week. How she said the Our Father from memory, of her own undertaking as I had never asked her to memorize it. That's what this church gave me—my daughter's first steps in faith, and that incredible moment, me speaking to a crowd including her, which was so very important to me. I'll be forever grateful.

Monday, November 24, 2014

I called to confirm the rental car and hotel room for the big New York City Thanksgiving extravaganza! I'm so looking forward to this. The only other Thanksgiving that stands out in my memory is the one back in 1989 when I ate mashed potatoes like a boss, and then retreated to my room to play a marathon session of Dragon Warrior for the original Nintendo. Ah, those were the days.

I have to pack up tomorrow night after work, as I didn't have time to do it today. I don't worry too much about packing; jeans, t-shirt, sweatshirt, underwear, and socks. However, I would like to bring my turkey hat, and my Santa hat but I must locate the former as it has gone wayward. The Santa hat is sitting at the end of my bed as I type these words. I keep it close so I can feel it's magic.

One more day to go and then I'll moon the turkey float!

Tuesday, November 25, 2014

Today was a blur with the sweetest ending.

I slept through my alarm this morning because my little girl snuck into our bed during the night and snuggled her way alongside me. It's hard to get up on a cold dark morning when my smiling little angel is all warm and snuggly and smells like sleep. The gym will always be there. These moments are fleeting.

After work, I took the family out to dinner and then we went home to pack for the big trip to New York tomorrow. I gave my daughter one of the smaller suitcases to pack up her stuffed animals for the trip. Amongst them was her newest acquisition, a real Beanie Baby, this one called Early Bird. It's a little red-breasted Robin she won today in a coloring contest at school. It was a cornucopia with the word "Thanksgiving" sprawled across the middle, and I must admit she really did a great job.

I was glad to see Toad made the cut for the trip to New York. He's the little fellow with the white and red mushroom cap in the Mario Bros. games. My daughter has had him in bed with her since first he appeared in her stocking on Christmas morning when she was four.

There is a great Toad story, actually. One of my favorites. My daughter was readying herself for bed a few years back and she couldn't find Toad. My wife checked the bed and her bedroom, and I checked everywhere else. Toad was nowhere to be found. My daughter was beside herself with grief. The only thing my wife could think of was she may have thrown it away in the garbage by accident when she was cleaning the house early that morning. So the simple solution was to check the garbage. Problem being I had taken the garbage to work with me that morning and threw it in the dumpster because I missed the garbage pickup that day.

And so, being a good father, I drove the 45 minutes to my office in the middle of the night and proceeded to climb into the dumpster to dig out the wayward toad. When I finally found the bag in question, there was no Toad in it. At least the lost souls who hang out by dumpsters in the back of laundromat and liquor store plazas underneath the moon and stars had a good time watching me. I returned home defeated and without Toad, without answers for my daughter. As I went to her bedside to apologize, I grabbed the covers to tuck her in tight, and what unto my wondering eyes should appear but stuffed Toad, lying right there. My daughter was elated. She grabbed him and brought him with her into our bed, where she was making a habit of sleeping.

Now she is sleeping across the hall in her own bed. Before I tucked her in tonight, I showed her a clip of me on the 200th episode of *Ghost Hunters* and another clip, of me and my oldest friend Darren in the Spartan Race we did in Amesbury, Massachusetts, this past summer. I wanted her to see the

Ghost Hunters clip because in one of the ending scenes, I kept positioning my arms in such a way that so a bracelet she made for me would always be in view, knowing when the episode aired, I could show her how I wore her bracelet on television. It was a simple black, orange and white bracelet made with these tiny rubber bands but it meant a lot to me because she made it for me. I also wore it when I filmed the Dunkin Donuts commercial last year as well.

The Spartan Race was an obstacle course event almost five miles long. It was a series of grueling physical challenges through mud and under barbed wire. Darren and I painted our faces like two of our favorite wrestlers from the 1990s. He was the Ultimate Warrior and I was Sting when he was wearing his *The Crow* movie makeup. There was only a quick frame of us in the televised event but at least we made it on television! We were also the only two people there with our faces painted like 1990s wrestlers. In all honesty, though, it was a tough challenge and one I was very thankful to surmount.

So after we said our prayers and our good nights, I told her I was proud of her for doing such a good job in school and for winning the coloring contest. I said I showed her those television clips because I want her to be proud of her daddy and to know that I love her. I closed her door and was heading off to bed when I heard he call me back. I went in and asked what she needed. She told me that she wanted to make sure I knew that she is always proud of me, no matter what I do. That puddle on the floor—that was my heart melting.

I love you little girl, and Daddy will always be proud of you, no matter what you do.

Wednesday, November 26, 2014

We made it safely to New York!

As fate would have it, I ended up getting the little red Kia Soul as my rental for this trip as well. Funny to have traveled with the family in it, as the last few times were alone, or with a pumpkin named Admiral Gourdington.

There was a horrible storm raging today that took us all the way from our house to New York. Rain, freezing rain and snow, all the way to the hotel. But, the little rental did well. I sang Christmas songs for most of the trip. Mama Bear sat silent. Beans was busy playing her video games. So, for the most part, it was much like my previous trips in the little red rental.

Considering it was the biggest travel day of the year, getting to the hotel just about thirty minutes after anticipated wasn't too bad at all. We are staying at the Marriott Courtyard on 6th Avenue, room 706. It looks like we will have an excellent view of the parade. I'm so excited!

Thursday, November 27, 2014

Happy Thanksgiving!

And a happier Thanksgiving I honestly cannot recall.

My day started at 3:30 this morning when the parade bands were warming up in the street outside. Mama Bear and Beans slept through it somehow but I crept to the window and watched them rehearse. It was amazing! The streets were empty with the exception of one or two homeless people. The bands, all dressed up, and instruments shining, played and marched in the desolate city. It had a very strange apocalyptic feel to it. I was going to go outside to witness it firsthand but it was quite cold and I didn't want to leave the hotel room in case Mama Bear or Beans woke up looking for me.

The bands quieted down by 4:30 but I couldn't sleep. I had waited years to see the Thanksgiving Day Parade and it was almost here. So I just lay in bed, waiting … dreaming. Finally, at 8am my little girl woke up and we made bagels and hot cocoa in the hotel room. I took a shower whilst Mama Bear awoke from her slumber.

The streets were lined with people waiting for the festivities to begin. The weather was cold and clear but not freezing. I was thankful for our warm hotel room and magnificent view.

When the time arrived, we were all together with my daughter sitting in the window seat and my wife and I in two chairs behind her. The Macy's inflatable star balloons kicked it off, accompanied by Thomas the Tank Engine, which our daughter made a point of telling us she was no longer into that baby stuff (as if we hadn't noticed). We cracked the window open so we could hear the bands, and I had the network coverage of the parade on the television too so we could see what celebrities and musicians were on which floats.

I was excited to see the Paddington Bear balloon. There is a new Paddington Bear movie coming out this Christmas, and I really enjoyed the books and show when I was a kid. I sported my Santa hat for some of the event, and my daughter joined in on the fun, sporting the green elf hat that Jinglebottom wears for his own social media purposes.

The parade was everything I wanted it to be, and more. There was a moment when my daughter was sitting in the window, legs crossed, just looking out onto the balloons in carefree childhood wonder. This was why I came here—in part, for me to realize one of my childhood dreams but also for my daughter to have the opportunity to do the same.

I slipped out to the McDonald's to grab us some snacks and brought them back to the room for us to enjoy before our nighttime surprises. I had purchased VIP skate packages for the three of us at Rockefeller Center. We were able to enter through their "igloo" which is where we picked up our skates and enjoyed some hot cocoa and fresh cookies. And by the way, they were delicious cookies.

I'm not known for my ice skating prowess. Truth be told, I can drive a mean racecar and I'm skilled at walking but skates and blades are not things I'm meant to use. That being said, I couldn't let it hold me back from making memories with my wife and little one. Beans had gone ice skating once or twice before and she was actually pretty good. She may be running on the ice more than skating but she gets around. Mama Bear floats around with a good deal of modest grace. We stayed out there on the ice for the better part of ninety minutes, stopping once for a cocoa and cookie break. We took some nice pictures together and saw the Christmas tree they'll light up next week.

Back at the hotel now and Beans just choreographed her own routine to "All I Want for Christmas Is You", which encompassed the entire floor space of hotel room 706, both window seats, and the countertops.

Now she's snuggled next to me in one bed and Mama Bear is in the other. It has been a great day and I have a lot to be thankful for.

Beans watching the Macy's Thanksgiving Day Parade

Friday, November 28, 2014

We all slept in a little bit today, worn out from yesterday's festivities.

There's a lot on deck today, though. I'm thinking we'll take a walk through Times Square and see what Black Friday looks like on such an engorged level as New York. Then I have tickets for us to go see the Radio City Music Hall Christmas Spectacular. I'm thinking the little one will really enjoy it since she enjoys her dancing so much. Here we go!

I have to say, New York is crowded as New York usually is, but I think Black Friday is worse back home. My personal distaste for the whole post-holiday shopping nonsense, especially nowadays when people are lined up outside of stores waiting for them to open, is strong. Family took a backseat in this society many moons ago and the allure of discount flat screen televisions only makes it worse.

We went to the multilevel Toys R Us that has a ferris wheel in it. It also has people trying to get you to try out toys and eat samples and it's all just too much. We headed over to the Disney Store where I bought a couple of stuffed animals for my daughter and thus breaking my personal tradition of not shopping on the day after Thanksgiving. I suppose this was a special occasion and I was doing it for family.

Then we headed over to Radio City Music Hall and took our seats in the fourth row of the orchestra. I keep telling my daughter we won't always have such great seats for events but for now we can and we should enjoy it. And enjoy it we did! The music was fantastic and the dancing was amazing. There were awesome special effects too, including fireworks, confetti snow, glistening streamers and a 3-D flight on Santa's sleigh.

We had a great time, and if I'm correct, which I believe I am, seeing the Rockettes inspired my daughter to put on another hotel room dance performance. As I write, I see her practicing moves and cuing up music. I better go. She likes me to play the music for her.

Headed home tomorrow!

Saturday, November 29, 2014

We drove home today after a stroll by the Empire State Building, a brief look at the Macy's storefront windows that were bursting with holiday awesomeness, and a quick stop in the subway, which is bursting with something else entirely but it helps to fulfill the New York experience.

We came home to find our Elf on the Shelf Amber had returned. It's nice to have the little plastic enforcer around but truth we don't need her to keep Beans in line. She's truly a good child and is pretty hard on herself when she knows she did something that she shouldn't, which is very rare.

Nothing against Mama Bear, but Beans takes after me for self-discipline. I was known to put myself back in the crib when I felt I had misbehaved, and I'm still rather hard on myself if I do anything I feel is out of character to this day. For instance, I responsibly enjoy a tasty hard cider once in a while. One is good, two is better, and then I'm done. I can have more and handle it without issue but I always feel bad about myself if I do. I can't explain why. It just seems like I shouldn't. Hopefully Beans and I'll outgrow this overzealous self-discipline thing at some point.

I have some holiday themed motivational lectures coming up in the next two weeks. There is a Rudolph themed one I did last year that had great reviews, but I'm not one to rest upon my laurels. So I spent some time tonight working on a new lecture based upon *How the Grinch Stole Christmas* when I came across a much lesser known holiday classic called *Halloween Is Grinch Night*, which I found online so my daughter and I could watch. It was a musical of sorts, with lots of reference to the "sweet sour winds" and putting your glasses on to face things as they are. Interesting lessons for a Halloween special but my daughter and I enjoyed it anyway.

The little lady helped me out by picking different screen captures for me to utilize in my lecture. She's so sweet and she has a good eye for visual representations that speak volumes beyond their mere animated depictions. She even suggested motivational topics I could discuss when showing the pictures. That's Daddy's girl for sure.

Tomorrow is church and working further on this Grinch lecture. Should be a good Sunday. Maybe I'll make pasta.

Sunday, November 30, 2014

Ah well, the best-laid plans and such. Never did make that pasta. But church was good.

Afterward I put the Christmas decorations out in the yard and brought the Christmas tree and its decorations up from the basement so we could all trim the tree and get festive with it. I prefer a real tree but the damn cats caused so many issues with the tree last year that Mama Bear and I decided to purchase an artificial tree at the end of the year when they were on sale. It's white and pre-lit with colored lights. I quite fancy it. Not sure I would want it up every year but I like it for now.

Darren Valedofsky, my friend since first grade and the only person who has been by my side since I was seven that's not a blood relation, came by my garage tonight and I pulled the brakes on his wife's van for him. I like tinkering on cars and such and it was nice to be able to see my oldest friend. Despite talking with him two to three times a day, I hardly ever see him. I hardly ever see anyone. I just work and spend the little bit of free time I have with my family. But that's okay. That is what this portion of my life is about—providing for family.

WINTER
DECEMBER - FEBRUARY

Monday, December 1, 2014

Ahh, December. I do love this time of year.

Finally, people don't look at me like I'm crazy for wearing my Santa hat and singing my Christmas carols. It truly is the most wonderful time of the year.

I watched the Miami Dolphins beat the Jets tonight whilst enjoying a pizza and some Sam Adams Winter Ale with my friend Jeff Belanger. It was nice to sit and talk outside of a paranormal venue.

My phone kept beeping alerting me to text messages from my daughter, telling me that she missed me and wanted to talk to me when I got home and that I had to wake her up by tickling her as soon as I came in. So when I came home, I did as she asked and was pleasantly surprised as to what she wanted to tell me. A few months back we purchased four tickets to see the Fresh Beat Band, a musical group featured on a Nickelodeon TV show, in concert at the Providence Performing Arts Center. The plan was for Mama Bear to take the Beanie Baby and two of her friends to see the show. Beans had a different plan, though. She asked me if I had anything on my calendar for Thursday night because she wanted me to go with her, Mama, and one of her friends. I asked if she was sure about that because we bought the tickets for her and her friends. She told me that she'd rather have me with her than any of her friends.

A deaf man in the retirement home on the other side of town could hear her play my heartstrings. I swear I have the most thoughtful little girl. I'm so blessed. I told her even if I had anything scheduled, I'd be glad to be there with her, Mama, and her friend. I'm sure we'll have a great night out.

I'm looking forward to Thursday night. As for tomorrow night, I have to film half of my last episode for *Ghost Hunters*. This time I mean it for real.

Tuesday, December 2, 2014

Tonight's the night! After multiple seasons of being on the air with *Ghost Hunters* I could quite possibly be filming the first half of my last episode. No matter what, it has to be my last run. A good run it has been, though.

I filmed with them starting in their second season, and then appeared on a few episodes here and there for a few years before quitting in order to get married and be home with my bride. A few years later, I was off to film with *Ghost Hunters International* for over two seasons before returning home to film a few episodes of the original *Ghost Hunters* show, and then calling it quits once again. Being away from my daughter pained me beyond words.

When I leave the office a little bit early, I'll be heading out to Boston Harbor and boarding the USS Constitution to investigate and film. It should be a grand time. I enjoy being aboard ships. I especially like the old wooden vessels. For some reason, I have always been fascinated with the back of the ship where the captain's quarters are. It just looks so awesome out there on the dark water, lights flickering on the small panes of glass across the stern. Majestic.

Unfortunately it's supposed to be a wintery mix of rain, ice and snow tonight. Good times.

Wednesday, December 3, 2014

Today is my mother's birthday. I sent her some flowers and I have gifts for her at home but unfortunately I won't have the time to stop in and see her and my dad today. Life gets in the way of the way we want things to be sometimes—most times, really. But, as the good John Lennon penned, "Life is what happens to you while you're busy making other plans." He couldn't have been more correct. God, I do love John Lennon.

I spent last night freezing my biscuits on that blasted ship for that blasted show. The case itself was pleasant but there wasn't much activity outside of some footsteps and what sounded like a girl's voice. The best part of the night for me was interacting with a family that was with us from the Make A Wish Foundation. This was the third family that I have had the opportunity to work with on the show this season.

We sit with the family, sign autographs for the kids, let them in the vehicles and check out the equipment. Then a few of us take them on a mini investigation off camera, just so they can get the feel of it.

This family was really sweet and their young child was amazing. He was a bit concerned about walking up and down the stairs throughout the ship's deck, and so I bear hugged him and told him that I would carry him up and down them wherever he wanted to go. It was great. To feel that the little guy trusted me so much was amazing. I really enjoyed spending time with them the most.

The end of last night was brutal! Trying to wind up the camera cables and put away the equipment in the ice cold rain was horrible. Especially since I had torn off a dime sized piece of skin betwixt my thumb and forefinger the night before whilst doing an oil change on ole Angelina before heading out for beer and pizza with Jeff. The cold salt air kept stiffening the wound, and every time I had to flex my hand in any way, the skin would crack and bleed. It made for a long and painful end to the night.

But the night ended as nights do, and I was able to get almost five hours of sleep in the hotel before heading back to Rhode Island for work in the morning. Not much sleep, but more than I had gotten in the past whilst filming.

This morning's commute was a fun one as I loathe Boston commuting. I was coming off of route 93 and back up onto 95 when I hit a patch of ice on the ramp and Angelina got a little sideways. I was doing the speed limit but it was just one of those winter weather type of things; early morning, cold roads, overnight icy rain, and me. It's a two-lane ramp, so it was rather dangerous as I had a white SUV on my right when I hit the ice and Angelina's back end skidded out to the right. Thankfully, I watch a lot of racing, both on asphalt and dirt track, so I know just enough about counter-steering and throttle control to have been able to brought her back pretty quickly.

God bless that ole Angelina of mine. She and I have been through it all. We once slid across a bridge right in front of the blade of a state plow truck and we spun a quick 180 to get back in the throttle before even nicking a fender.

We shall see what the rest of this winter wonderland holds!

Right now, I just want to sleep.

Thursday, December 4, 2014

Today was a crazy day. I went to pick up a friend of mine before work and I had to drive under this small stone bridge, which was a one lane, two-way road that has a light signaling right of way. Apparently the small Indian fellow coming the other way was unaware of the light and in the middle of the bridge his little Honda came nose to nose with Angelina. Good thing I keep up on my brakes!

It seemed there was darkness around every corner today. In work, out of work, everyone I came across seemed to want to steal my sunshine. These days happen. The main thing is to keep your focus and keep your spirits up, and so that is exactly what I did. I listened to my Christmas music. I had a piece of cake. I focused on my plans for the evening with my wife and daughter. And, I got through the day.

This evening we went to see the Fresh Beat Band. My daughter and her friend Morgan had a great time. We ate pretzels and I bought them plastic tambourines that lit up. They danced a lot, especially my little Beanie Baby showing off her dance moves, including her newest ones from Irish Step Dancing courses. I'm so proud of that little dancing angel.

When we were walking back across the city from the Providence Performing Arts Center to the Durango, the opening scene from the Batman backstory played through my brain as it usually does in moments like this. Thankfully, we are never approached by thugs and held up, but in moments like this I feel like the big protector. I know my wife and daughter, and her friend, feel safe because I'm there walking with them. It makes me feel very responsible and needed. And I needed that today.

Friday, December 5, 2014

Looking forward to tonight's events. My wife and I are going to dinner with a few friends of ours, and then we are heading out to see a comedian named Dimitri Martin whom I've never seen perform live, but I enjoy him on television. Should make for an enjoyable evening.

Saturday, December 6, 2014

We had a great time last night at dinner with our friends Robin and Adam. We went to the Capital Grill and then to the Veterans Auditorium for the comic show. Funny stuff. Good times all around.

Today I'm heading down to a Holiday Inn in Cherry Hill, New Jersey. My friend Rosalyn Bown is putting on an event of spiritual healing, including a mediumship course, a medium gallery reading, a presentation by my friend Clay Smith and his wife Joy, and a festive soul message brought to you by yours truly. I'm looking forward to it. Once Mama Bear and Beans drop me off at Hertz to pick up the rental car, I'll be on my way. Should be a quick five hour trip.

Well, lots of changes took place between the time I picked up the rental car and the time I arrived in New Jersey. It took me closer to eight hours than the expected five hours to arrive at the Cherry Hill Holiday Inn. I literally sat three miles from the George Washington Bridge in New York for almost two hours. They're doing construction on one of the lanes on the upper level of the bridge, which in turn caused a huge back up.

I was concerned about the dropping fuel gauge on the rental, and the increasing discomfort in my bladder. As I approached the ninety-minute mark, I couldn't take it anymore. Let's just say I was glad to have stopped at Dunkin Donuts earlier, for that large empty container was an oasis.

What? Like you haven't had to pee in a cup at least one time before.

In other news unrelated to my bladder, I decided to call an audible on the planned presentation. Though I was going to stick with the *How The Grinch Stole Christmas* theme, I decided to change the presentation style. More on that in a minute.

On a somber note, my Uncle Geno passed away this morning. My parents called me during my commute to let me know. He had been sick as of late, so it was not a surprise but still it was sad to know that this world lost such a kind soul. He looked like one of the baddest bikers on the planet, with his jean jacket, cowboy boots, Harley Davidson shirt, salt and pepper hair and beard, yet he was one of the kindest, soft-spoken guys that you could come across. The world was better for having hosted him for the last 73 years. Rest well, Uncle.

Tonight's lecture was fantastic!

I brought my laptop up to the front of the room as I was introduced and it looked as if I was going to set up a PowerPoint presentation as per usual and commence with my speech. Instead, out of my laptop bag I retrieved my Santa hat and a copy of Dr. Seuss' *How the Grinch Stole Christmas* book. I proceeded to read the book to those in attendance, pausing on various pages to discuss lessons I wanted to impress upon everyone there. It went over better than expected.

As I lay here in the hotel bed with a belly full of pizza reflecting upon the evening, I think I did well. The message resonated with a good majority of the people that came here tonight, and for that, I'm thankful.

Tomorrow morning, I'll saddle back up in the rental and head back home to Mama Bear and Beans where I belong.

And now … now we sleep.

Sunday, December 7, 2014

Well, paint me green and call me Mr. Toad because I just had a wild ride.

Hmm … will anyone get that reference? Mr. Toad is kind of an old school story at this point in time. I remember when they used to have a ride at Disney for good old Mr. Toad. Then they announced plans to close it and turn it into the Winnie The Pooh ride. I signed petitions and wrote letters. True story. I was in my early twenties writing letters to Disney to save Mr. Toad. In retrospect, I wonder why I do some of these things. A lot of these things, actually. Ah, screw it. I'm entertaining myself. Now when I go there I always feel a little guilty about enjoying the Winnie The Pooh ride. It's no Mr. Toad but I love the Heffalump and Woozles song.

Anyhow, I was just over halfway through Connecticut on my home when catastrophe happened. I was in the left lane, making up a little time, traveling behind a van that had some scriptures written upon the back of it. The van suddenly cut over to the middle lane and then pulled into the right lane and jammed on the brakes right in front of this Jeep Cherokee. The Jeep hit the brakes so hard it turned sideways and then shot across the highway right at me. The next few seconds happened in super slow motion. Thankfully the good Lord keeps a little cushion of protection around me and I have watched a lot of NASCAR so I knew exactly what to do.

I have seen a ton of races where a car goes into the wall and then shoots across the track at another driver on the bottom of the track. You aren't going to be able to brake in time in order to not get hit, and if you speed up, chances are you will still get hit so the best thing you can do is steer towards them, hoping that they will slide right past you. And so, that is exactly what I did. I jammed on the brake and cut the wheel toward the oncoming car, releasing the brake and sending the little rental flying across the highway. I don't think you could have measured twelve inches between the front bumpers of both vehicles.

The Jeep smashed hard with the passenger door against the Jersey barrier between the northbound and southbound lanes. The whole Jeep lifted up in the air and came crashing back down. The van that caused the accident started to drive away and then pulled over. I straightened out the little rental and did the same. I then called the state police and had them send a rescue and some state troopers.

Luckily no one was seriously injured despite the severity of the wreck. Due to my eyewitness account they were able to charge the driver of the van with causing the accident. And the rental and I made it home safely. No Heffalumps. No Woozles. And sadly, still no Mr. Toad.

Monday, December 8, 2014

I beeped at the good ole turkeys at the turkey farm this morning. There are much less of them these days but I try to keep their spirits up and their tiny bird brains off of their fallen comrades claimed in the Great Battle of Thanksgiving 2014. We lost a lot of good birds this year. Damn shame. Save a bird. Order a pizza.

Tuesday, December 9, 2014

Filming tonight! My last *Ghost Hunters* episode- and this time... this time I mean it. It isn't that I don't enjoy filming the show. It's just become a running joke betwixt me, my wife, my friends, Jinglebottom, and the rest of the imaginary elves in my mind that I'll never truly quit filming. I'll never quit working multiple jobs.

However, this time, I do believe we have reached the end of the road. This episode, the 13th, fulfills the season ten order the network placed. I was only supposed to do two episodes, so looking back on it now from episode thirteen is a bit surreal. I have to say, I pride myself on working hard and making every effort to do all I can for the good of my family, friends, and fans alike, but this year—well, I don't think I could have done any more. Between college lectures on the paranormal, library lectures on the same, paranormal events, show tapings, the day job, and my motivational work, I have done more than ever before and I still feel the best is yet to come.

I would say I've seen the sun but I ain't seen it shine. Play me out ole Blue Eyes will ya? Thank you, Mr. Sinatra. Thank you.

"And wait till you see that sunshine day! You ain't seen nothin' yet!" – "The Best is Yet To Come" by Mr. Frank Sinatra.

Wednesday, December 10, 2014

Last night's filming was a cold one. We were up at The Mount—the old Edith Wharton house up in Lenox, Massachusetts. Not much in the way of heat in an old mansion and a huge stable area. But it truly was my last case, so the weather didn't bother me much. I kept a couple of heat packs in my front and back pockets of my jeans. KJ the Spaceman and I saw a strange light anomaly on the second floor of the old stable area but that was about the height of the action for us. Regardless, it was a remarkable evening simply because it was the end of an era.

At least I think it is.

It has to be, for me at least.

It was also a remarkable evening for what happened after the investigation. I returned to the hotel and went up to the room. I opened the door and noticed in the shadowy distance the bed looked rather unmade. I chalked it up to shoddy maid work and stepped into the bathroom to make some water and wash my hands before unpacking.

It was then that I noticed that someone had already unpacked their stuff in my room. As I stepped back into the room I noticed that indeed, someone was sleeping in my bed. The man started snoring and I made for the door, closing it quietly behind me as not to startle him.

The front desk was rather confused by the issue, insisting that I give them the man's name. They even tried calling the room to wake him up. I just wanted to get some sleep and requested any room that was unoccupied. By the time the little lady at the front desk placed me in another room it was close to 1:30 in the morning. I was able to get two and a half hours of sleep before leaving for a long three-hour ride to work this morning.

I worked for a few hours this morning before going to the funeral for my Uncle Geno. I was a pallbearer along with a few of my cousins. It was an honor to carry such a kind man to his final resting place, knowing his soul has already gone beyond, back to where we all belong. I suspect my family members won't notice some visitations and friendly disturbances from him in the coming days. It's been my experience that many spirits check in on their loved ones for at least a couple of days after they pass on. I think they do it as a way of passage for themselves and also to try and let us know it's okay.

It rained at the cemetery. The undertaker's men stood there with the large black umbrellas over the family. We stood on plywood placed to cover the mud. I've always thought it would rain when I die. It rains a lot during big moments in my life. I find it comforting.

After the funeral I went back to my office, because until I die and it rains, I work. It's really the only thing I know how to do.

Thursday, December 11, 2014

Still wiped out from filming. I didn't sleep well last night. A lot on the ole noggin' I guess. Chest was hurting a bit, too. It does that when I haven't slept in a few days. I think I've been pushing myself a bit but alas, I'm done. This weekend will be one of rest and relaxation. Finally. And now we sleep.

Damn it, elves! Turn down the radio and put your clothes back on. I don't care what Jinglebottom said! Jolly Good Times is closing early tonight. Now turn out the neon lights and let me get some sleep.

Friday, December 12, 2014

Tonight was awesome! After work. Mama Bear and I took Beans to Trinity Rep down in Providence to see a stage production of *A Christmas Carol.* I have gone to see this play every year since I was eighteen, except one time three years ago when I accidentally bought tickets to see *It's A Wonderful Life.* It was playing in the lower theater on the same night as *A Christmas Carol* but they hadn't done that before and I guess I wasn't paying much attention when I bought the tickets online. It was fantastic in its own right. They did it as a live radio production of the story set in a late 1940's radio station. Genius.

This was Bean's second year seeing *A Christmas Carol* and she was excited. We had great seats as well—front row center—the same ones we had the year before. I personally think this year's production was one of my favorites in the last nineteen years. Well, technically eighteen. I know my daughter was hoping that Scrooge would shake hands with her when he has his rebirth and embraces Christmas, darting about the theater like an elf that has had too much eggnog. And sure enough, he did. My little girl found another way to interject herself into the show as well. When Scrooge was waiting for Bob Cratchit to come into work the day after Christmas, he made a big show about being angry that Bob was late, and then it led up to what looked like firing the young clerk—and instead Scrooge gave him a raise. It was at this point, when Bob is staring dumbfounded at Scrooge, that my daughter cutely interjected a loud. "What?!" into the script, at which both Scrooge and Cratchit laughed, as Cratchit gestured to my daughter and repeated her words to Mr. Scrooge. My little one couldn't be happier with herself, and neither could my wife and me.

After the play, some fans stopped me for some photographs, which made me feel proud in front of my family. Then I gave my daughter some money for the local food drive collection they take up at the theater door to show her the importance of generosity and thankfulness for what we have.

On the way home, I stopped and introduced Beans to Firehouse Hot dogs. She and I had grilled cheese—mine with bacon—and Mama Bear had a cheeseburger.

God bless us all … every one.

Saturday, December 13, 2014

I awoke this morning to the sound of numerous footsteps running up the stairs to my bedroom. As I rolled over and opened my eyes, I saw three small blurry figures standing in the room. As I put on my glasses, I saw it was my daughter and two of her friends from school. One of them said, "Your dad sleeps till noon?" My daughter quickly corrected her, "No, just today. It's a special day. He never gets to rest."

I appreciated her sticking up for me, but I didn't appreciate her bringing her friends into my room. Luckily I was under the covers and not laying there in my boxers for the entire world to see. That is one of the reasons I decided to do the Thanksgiving trip this year; just us three away from everything else. Doing things we want to do. They were perfect days for me and my family, the way I wanted them to be.

Mama Bear and Beans had plans with some friends that kept them out for most of the day. I did housework and an oil change on Mama Bear's new Durango. The oil change took me a little longer than it normally would have but only because I didn't have the right socket I needed to get the oil filter canister off. The Durango doesn't use an all in one filter and canister like most new cars do. Dodge went retro and you keep the canister mounted in the engine, remove the cap and replace the filter and seal ring. Some cars back in the 60s/70s had this set up. It isn't hard to utilize, as long as you have the right tools, which I didn't, but now I do.

I was able to get the oil changed and the laundry done before my family returned. I even had time to hoist up a delicious Miller High Life whilst sitting in front of the Christmas tree, Santa cap upon my head, and Pliers the cat in my lap.

I'm one happy little elf, if a bit twisted.

All right boys! Time for one more round at Jolly Good Times, on me. Then it's lights out.

Sunday, December 14, 2014

Mama Bear is snoring beside me. She and the Beanie Baby are quite sick.

This day started at 5am when Beans crawled out of her bed and into mine. Poor little thing was sniffling and coughing and hot to the touch. I gave her some medicine and some tissues and placed her back in bed with Mama Bear, who was showing symptoms of a similar illness.

I can't sleep next to one person sniffling and coughing, never mind two of them so I just went downstairs and started my broadcast day. I did dishes, fed the cats, changed litter, and took the trash outside. I watched some television and started breakfast for when the ladies finally awoke. I made red and green pancakes to promote a Christmas theme and a feeling of good will amongst everyone. We all ate in the living room whilst watching the *Frosty The Snowman* cartoon.

I had already made an appointment for Beans to see the pediatrician at their earliest slot, which wasn't until 2:45 with an on-call doctor, and I knew in my heart they both had strep throat and would need some antibiotics as soon as possible. The appointment came and went and I was right. Strep throat. The doctor didn't examine Mama Bear but birds of a feather flock together and I know my birds. I picked up the antibiotics, along with a handful of cough drops, cough medicine, and some other remedies that I'm fond of. Then I stopped at the store to pick up some pudding and snacks to help get them on the mend.

The rest of the night was spent making dinner, cleaning up the kitchen, giving the little one a warm bath, and getting them both medicated and to bed. I did squeeze in a little video game time with Beans. I recently bought a NES remix game pack that presents challenges from the old Nintendo games I grew up with presented in a new way. It's fun for me to relive parts of my youth and even more so to see my daughter enjoying herself with things from my past. It's as if the ghost of Dustin past and the ghost of Dustin present both get to hang out on the couch in the playroom and play video games with my favorite person in the world.

I'm not sure what the hell the ghost of Dustin future is doing but I pray he is doing good works and hasn't lost his mind … yet. Ah, well. Whatever it is, I'm sure he is happy. No matter what may come, I'm pretty consistent in that. You can be, too. Just appreciate the little moments and always weigh your problems versus your blessings. The perspective helps put things into proportion.

There they are, the naughty li'l ladies of the Lullaby League. They are singing a naughty rendition of "Santa Baby" and shimmying up the staircase. It looks like I best be hurrying down the chimney … to-night.

Monday, December 15, 2014

I had a day off from the office today and was planning on sleeping in but with wife and Beans sick, well, sometimes a dad's gotta do what a dad's gotta do. The one task I had to do for work was pick up our holiday ham for tomorrow's potluck luncheon. I had a merry drive in Mama Bear's Durango up to Norwood, Massachusetts, jingling all the way with the Christmas music up loud.

I was supposed to help some friends of ours move today, but they had some delays with the plan of the day, so things were a bit derailed. I was all pumped up for moving, so I went to the gym in the afternoon, not something I get to do often, and I was able to exercise my cravings for lifting things up and putting back where I found them. The only bad thing was the heat was broken in the locker room. After my workout, I stripped down to my birthday suit and almost literally froze my ass off whilst walking to the showers. Brr! Tis the season to freeze your chestnuts!

Tuesday, December 16, 2014

The Potluck Christmas luncheon was a success at work. I brought the ham along with some garlic-mashed potatoes I made at home (and by made I mean that I combined four containers of pre-prepared microwave mashed potatoes with garlic powder and butter). I can actually cook quite well, but I just didn't have the time to peel four or five pounds of spuds last evening. Ole Angelina smelled like a rolling restaurant when I came out of the gym and climbed into her cab this morning. On a side note, the heat at the gym still isn't fixed, but I have hope for tomorrow, as I always do.

Wednesday, December 17, 2014

Look Ma! No cavities!

I still call my mom after each visit to the dentist to let her know I don't have any cavities. I like to make her proud. People seem to think because I eat a lot of candy and pour sugar into everything, my teeth are riddled with cavities, but that's a falsehood. I take great pride in my smile, though I don't like to show my pearly whites in most photos. A politely cheerful grin looks best. I think I'll celebrate my dental hygiene appointment results with a multicolored, cherry flavored candy cane.

It's a sweet Christmas, indeed, my little elves!

Thursday, December 18, 2014

I'm feeling the Yuletide spirit moving and shaking these old bones! I really am enjoying this holiday season. So much Christmas! So little time!

I went through my pile of Amazon boxes that I've been hoarding in my basement. Buying gifts online is not as romantic and true to the Christmas ritual of giving as is going to the stores and experiencing the hustle and bustle of shoppers rushing home with their treasures but I haven't had much time this year, so I ordered quite a bit from the good elves at Amazon.com.

It looks like everything I need is here, with the exception of one thing I ordered for Mama Bear that came in the wrong size. I'll have to return that straight away. But everything else is in order. Of course, there's still time and I'll probably pick up another thing or two before Christmas Day. Not that I like the material end of this holiday but I do like to give gifts, as I feel it truly is better to give than to receive.

I must get to wrapping these trinkets and tokens of affection, but tonight is not the night for such things. Tomorrow won't be the day to wrap presents either, as I have to meet up with Mama Bear and Beans right after work and head to a special Christmas concert at the Dunkin Donuts Center. The Trans-Siberian Orchestra will be putting on *The Christmas Attic* promptly at 4pm, and we will be there to see it.

In other news, Mr. Jinglebottom, resident imaginary mind-elf in charge of Jolly Good Times, and my fictitious campaign to usurp Santa as King of Jingling, informed me that sadly, I'm running third to not only Santa, but also Krampus, in this year's election of King of Jingling 2014. If you are not familiar with Krampus, he is a Christmas demon of sorts, from Alpine folklore. He has a goat-like, classic Beelzebub appearance, and he carries a burlap sack along with a switch made of birch sticks to whip naughty children into shape, or carry them off with him.

Astounding really, that I would be running third to him in an election in my mind, but maybe I'm having an off year.

Merry Christmas Krampus. Ya bastard.

Friday, December 19, 2014

Today was a whirlwind for sure! Mama Bear was supposed to pick up the Beanie Baby for early dismissal from school, and then meet me at work with the tickets so that we could leave directly for the show. Just before Mama Bear wheeled the Durango down the street to my office, she realized she had forgotten the tickets. We both drove back to the house in a mad dash to grab the tickets, and then turned back to the city. We were so frazzled by the whole situation that neither of us were thinking clearly enough to realize that we simply could have reprinted the tickets at my office since they were purchased online. Thankfully we were able to pick up the tickets, grab a hot pretzel, and make it to our seats, with three minutes to spare. Life is good.

The show went a lot longer than I thought it would. The Trans-Siberian Orchestra played a three-hour set, the first half of which was the "Christmas Attic" sequence. It featured a narrator, animation on moving screens in the background, and lots of laser lights flashing sequentially throughout the musical numbers. It was well performed and presented, but I think I speak for the family when I say it moved a little bit slow. The music was great, the songs were thoughtful, but it just wasn't like their previous Christmas concert Mama Bear and I attended eight years ago when Beans was still in her belly.

The second half of their concert was exactly what I was looking for, and then some. My daughter had climbed up into my lap and was really grooving to the music. The band played not only some of their more well-known Christmas songs, but they also played some things from a Halloween album that, though I'm not too sure how it fit exactly, it did.

It was everything Christmas should be. There were flames, fireworks, moving platforms, screeching guitars, and women dancing and swinging their hair about as if they were in a gentlemen's club or as Mama Bear calls such places, the "Dirty Girl Store". Ha!

Well, maybe it isn't everything Christmas should be, but we did enjoy it, especially when they played their version of "Carol of the Bells". Totally rocking.

We wrapped up the evening with dinner and then returned home.

I had promised my daughter I'd stay with her for one night in her princess bed and it appears tonight is the night she has chosen to cash in that chip. Since the bed is about an eighth the size of the one I share with Mama Bear, and it's cluttered with stuffed animals that she insists must stay in the bed with us, I'm predicting extreme back pain in the morning.

Saturday, December 20, 2014

I'm no Suzie Psychic, but indeed there is back pain this morning and plenty of it. I barely slept, for I simply could not get comfortable, and then when I was so weary that comfort did not matter anymore, I finally passed out.

Today is a busy day for sure. I'm taking my little one to church this morning to practice for tomorrow's Christmas pageant. Despite being sick and missing the costume measurement and initial practice last weekend, the reverend said that she could still be an angel and involved in the show. The little one is quite excited about it and I am as well.

After that, I have to get my hair cut so I can keep myself looking like the prettiest girl at the dance this holiday season. Then I'm off to meet up with my cousin Franky, as we aim to keep alive a long-standing tradition, the graveside toast. Since my grandfather passed away when I was in fifth grade, the family has gathered at the cemetery on the Saturday before Christmas to say a few words and toast in his honor. We always drink Moxie as we remember him. Moxie is a very old-time soda with a unique flavor but it's not unpleasant. Over the years, the people who attend the graveside toast have dwindled, and those who we visit have multiplied. Such is life, I suppose.

I'm hoping to squeeze in a quick visit to McShawn's Tavern over in Cranston if I have some time. Saturday morning is beer and hot dog day, after all, and it has been a long time since I have had the opportunity to visit. I hope Moe is working.

And later tonight, I'm meeting up with my six closest friends since high school. This is another Christmas tradition, the guys' night out. We're in touch regularly, but with life being what it is, busy, we don't see each other very often. Some years we go to the casinos in Connecticut and take in a show. Other years we get pizza and lay low. This year it's some multifaceted type of hotel called The Dean. It has a German restaurant, a karaoke bar, and a fancy-schmancy art bar. German food is not my usual fare of choice but I'm willing to give it a try. I know I fancy their pretzels at least. Every time I visited the Frankfurt airport, a total of eight times I believe, I had a pretzel. Good times.

Sunday, December 21, 2014

Before I go on with a recount of the day, I must pause for a moment of silence for the good turkeys of the Belwing Turkey Farm over in Rehoboth,

Massachusetts.

(Silence)

Thank you.

They were some good birds. I beeped, they flapped. Lather. Rinse. Repeat. I'm going to miss those beautiful bastards, but alas, Christmas time is coming soon, and thus go the lives of the turkeys.

Today was the day of the Christmas pageant at our church; quite the big affair for the children of the parish, including my little Beanie Baby. I was excited because, not only was Beans going to be up there dressed as an angel and singing like the dickens, but Mama Bear would be in attendance as well. She doesn't usually come to services with us, so when she does, it means something to me. I don't force my faith and practices upon anyone, not even my wife. She's on the same team but she doesn't come to worship. No worries. I pray for her anyway.

Our little girl really did look angelic up there. Her curly blondish brown hair cascading down from under her golden halo, outlining her cherub face, and falling onto her white robe really added to her character. She looked so sweet up on the altar, singing the songs in her songbook, holding her flickering battery-powered candle. Mama Bear and I couldn't have been prouder.

After church we returned home to play and build a gingerbread house whilst Mama Bear wrapped presents. It was actually a pink Hello Kitty sugar cookie house but it had all the same blueprints as a gingerbread house. I made a pizza for dinner, and then we all watched *The Grinch Who Stole Christmas* movie. I do love this time of year.

You know what I don't love though? Wrapping presents.

I mean, I don't loathe it, but I don't like it very much. Thankfully there was still some magic in that ole Santa hat I found, and there was eggnog in my fridge—the two of them helped to keep me in a Yule mood. Fitting as it's the Winter Solstice tonight as well.

Looks like it's time for bed once again. Work comes early tomorrow. My gym bag is packed and I'm ready to go. But first, we sleep.

Please don't disturb, for I'm dreaming of a white Christmas.

Monday, December 22, 2014

Ahh, it's here! Christmas magic is in the air and I'm feeling groovy. I'm still very much behind in wrapping my Christmas presents. I tried my best last night but I couldn't finish them. So much to wrap, so little time.

I've alluded to this before; I don't like the commercial portion of this holiday. I'm down with Christ. I love my faith and I love the celebration of it. Yet when I look around, I see gifts and toys and trinkets, which are all fine if they're given out of love and with good nature.

As I tucked my little girl into bed tonight, after we said our prayers, I spoke with her about the holiday, Christmas, gift giving, and what really matters. I wanted her to know it's my pleasure to provide such a life where we can have gifts for Christmas for everyone in the family, but it's more important to understand that gifts aren't what matters. It's the love we have for one another that makes a difference. The kindness we show all year long. Our conversations. Holding hands. Long hugs. These things mean more to me than anything you can buy in a store and put a bow on. That's a good lesson for all of us actually, not just seven-year-old girls.

Tuesday, December 23, 2014

Do you remember the movie *Ghostbusters 2*? I'll give it to you, it wasn't as good as the original *Ghostbusters* film, but it had its own merit. Mainly, it had pink slime. The pink slime that ran underneath the city of New York fed upon emotion and then magnified it, affecting the people of the city.

Though it's the Christmas season, a time of goodwill toward men, it appears pink slime is everywhere and people are out of control. Sad really. I see it every year. Traffic adds tension to already well-worn nerves. Standing in line in stores. Squabbling over limited quantities of the hottest toy item of the season. It's all quite silly to me, but sadly I must endure it.

I just wish people would support each other, help each other, and show love to each other. We are here for a limited time. There is no reason to be so hateful, especially during Christmas. I believe that SpongeBob SquarePants said it best in his song, "Don't Be a Jerk, It's Christmas".

In other unrelated news, the polls closed tonight at 8pm and it appears I once again lost the election for King of Jingling. Jinglebottom was saddened by how much Santa crushed us, as he maintained his crown with 97% of the vote. I was just happy to get 2% and beat Krampus who had 1%.

Ah well, back to wrapping presents and drinking eggnog. Once the last bow hath been placed, I'm off to bed to dream of a white Christmas.

Wednesday, December 24, 2014

I can dream all I want about having a white Christmas, but it looks like we will be having a wet Christmas instead. It rained all day today and it's going to rain again tomorrow. I don't watch the news and I don't check the weather, but I hear it's going to be 60 degrees tomorrow. I don't think I ever recall having such a warm Christmas day. Very bizarre.

Speaking of bizarre, I missed the mailman today when he attempted to deliver a present I had purchased for Mama Bear. It was the last gift I was waiting for. You see, I had purchased a Michael Kors handbag for my wife, and then I had purchased a matching wallet/clutch to go with it. Personally, I don't care for brand names and trendy nonsense. I also believe one should not have a purse or wallet that costs more money than one can carry in it. Mama Bear thinks otherwise, and so I placed the order for these items almost two weeks ago. The handbag came in within a week's time, but the wallet was delayed until today. Of course, I was out when they came to the door to have me sign for it. Ironically, I was already at the post office mailing out something for work.

The post office closed at 1pm today, but they told me the carrier should be back by 1:30 and if I caught him in the parking lot, I could sign for my package there. Needless to say, I sat there from 1pm until 2:30 before he showed up. No worries, though. I wanted to make sure Mama Bear had a nice Christmas, and if that meant sitting in ole Angelina listening to the windshield wipers slap out the rhythm on the glass whilst Elvis sang Christmas songs to me, so be it.

After my rendezvous with the mailman, my wife and I took the Beanie Baby to go and visit my parents for Christmas Eve. Along the way we stopped and tried to have a bite to eat. We ended up going to five different places before we found a place that would serve us. All our favorite spots were either closed, take out only, or seating by reservation. I felt like Joseph taking Mary and unborn sweet baby Jesus from place to place looking for some rest. Trust me, if there was a manger I could've eaten at, I would have. Thankfully we found Chelo's in Garden City was open and happy to have us.

Our visit with my parents was quite pleasant. Funny to sit there with Nana and Papa, and remember when they were just my Mom and Dad. Sunrise. Sunset. How quickly the time does go.

I know I'm awfully busy. Work keeps me busy, keeps me on the road, and keeps a roof over my head, but it also keeps me from having the time I would like to spend with those who matter the most to me. So when I do get a chance to spend an hour with my wife, daughter and my parents, I cherish it, for it won't be like this for long. These moments are also fleeting as they were when I was a child and as they are with my child.

And now, home sweet home. Mama Bear and I have set out the presents we bought and wrapped for everyone. The cookies and milk have been left out for Santa. Beans even left carrots for the reindeer. The stage is set. Come on, sweet baby Jesus! Save this old world, which is still in chaos.

The naughty little ladies from the Lullaby League are sauntering seductively up the staircase, wearing naughty Mrs. Claus outfits, and licking candy canes in a provocative way.

I shall leave you with a slightly altered verse of a Christmas classic: "And I heard him exclaim as he rode out of site, Merry Christmas D. Pari, you are doing all right."

Thursday, December 25, 2014

God rest ye merry gentlemen, may nothing you dismay.
Remember Christ our savior was born on Christmas day.
To save us all from Satan's power when we had gone astray.
Oh tidings of comfort and joy- comfort and joy.
Oh tidings of comfort and joy.

Merry Christmas to all… and to all a good night!

Friday, December 26, 2014

The day after Christmas … always my least favorite day of the year.

There isn't really anything horrible about it but it just feels wrong.

All the excitement. All the build-up. Then, it's a quick climax and we are back to work. Back to reality. People put away Christmas cheer with their decorations. Their good will toward men gets placed up in the attic with their plastic trees and tangled strings of lights. Life goes on as usual, as it always does on the 26th of December.

This is why I don't chase material possessions in this life. There is a lot of build up for little reward. You've probably noticed these things a time or two in your life as well. You work so hard for something, you wish for it, you sweat for it, you bleed for it, and then you get it, and it leaves you feeling empty.

I took the day off of work today just to try and escape that feeling, but it found me anyway. It always does. I had emails to return from the office, texts, and voicemails a plenty. Days off aren't what they used to be. The day started the way I wanted it to though, sitting on the couch and playing video games with my daughter. She is my shining light through all of this.

I spent some time reflecting on the year past and my life as a whole. It wasn't because of the upcoming New Year, though I know a lot of people get sentimental for such things. I personally don't like the New Year. It's just a bunch of people wasting money, getting drunk, and endangering themselves and the public.

My introspection and reflection came from watching the movie *Jersey Boys*. This recounting of how Franky Valli and the Four Season came to be had a very poignant moment, for me anyway. There is a scene where Franky is traveling, counting money, sitting in empty hotel rooms, up on stage, and then doing the same over and over and over. Lather. Rinse. Repeat. This is how I feel all too often; especially this year. There's such a fine line in balancing who I am as a father and husband, and doing what I have to do to provide a nice life for them. It's complicated by my personal distaste for material things and the material world. I'm out there doing what I must do to pay the bills, all the while knowing that being a great father and husband means more than a roof over their heads, dance classes, and a new Durango. But to some extent, these things are needed as well.

I get criticized a lot by some friends and family members that I work too much; that my wife and daughter probably don't know who I am, because they never see me. If I'm being honest with you, these accusations and assumptions hurt. Truly they do. Being a good father and husband are what I pride myself on, and though I may not be perfect at either one, I'm trying my best. So when people say these things, it hurts because it's the vocalization of something that I truly fear the most. If I let the words of these people into my heart and soul, they would eat me alive. So I don't let it. I hear it, I acknowledge it, but I don't let it take root within me. Because these people, though they know me … they don't *really* know me.

I take pride in what I do, but I worry that to many, maybe even to some of those closest to me, the sacrifice of all I do is missed. It's easy to look and see the travel, the event appearances, and the television tapings as some sort of glorious lifestyle, but it's truly the most difficult thing I have ever had to do in my life. And don't get me wrong, I fully realize the scope of my "celebrity" is very small, so I can imagine what it's like for those who are in a greater demand but my life is not without its sacrifices. I know this year hath afforded me great blessings but they were not given without their price. I know the cost yet I hope next year will bring more of the same. Talk about conflicted.

I work hard, I sleep little, and I take joy in being with my family most of all. Yet, I also say I feel alive when I'm up on stage talking to a crowd. In times of confusion and conflict, even inner-conflict, I find it more important to make a list upon the sticky note in my mind about things I'm sure of.

In my mind the list goes like this:

- I'm a thankful servant of God. Where He guides me, I go willingly.
- I'm not a perfect person but I'm doing my best.
- All I do is for the good of my family.
- I have a mission in this world, to leave it much better than I found it and I'm not done yet.
- I walk in faith, not in fear.

Knowing the things on the list are all of truth, I know that I can proceed without concern. I don't need to overthink things. Do I travel a lot and work too much? Sure. But at the end of the day, when I'm home, I'm home. There's no distraction. Sure, there are the texts, emails, and calls from work but I dispatch them quickly and effectively. Nothing comes before sitting at the table and sharing waffles with my daughter or sitting on our couch playing video games. Especially not this morning as she received several new games for Christmas yesterday, so today was a lot of Disney Infinity, Captain Toad's Treasure Hunt, and Super Smash Bros. for the Wii U. And we had a grand time of it.

The last gift my daughter opened up yesterday morning was a small box containing our Disney Magic Bands, signifying that we would be going on vacation there again very soon—in just under three weeks, actually. And that box was bought and paid for by me traveling and working. That box gives the three of us a full week together in Florida, no work emails, no texts, and no distractions. It truly is a gift for all of us. And I cannot wait!

No one's life is easy. Nothing comes without a price. We all strive for different prizes. Things valuable to some may not be valuable to others. None of us are truly right and none of us are truly wrong. But we have to get along. Find what makes you happy, and pursue it. Don't let the hateful judgment cloud your vision. Don't let the labels tell you who you are. Don't let anyone steal your sunshine. You just be you. Never bet against yourself. And smile, damn it! It's only life, after all.

Saturday, December 27, 2014

Since this was the last Saturday of the year, it was only fitting that I started it off at McShawn's Pub with a Miller High Life, a couple of hot dogs, and some old friends. My friend Tom Durant was in town from California and our mutual friend John Zaffis drove up from Connecticut to meet us. It was a pleasant morning for such a gathering. We all met each other because of our mutual fascination with the paranormal, but over the years and various travels, we developed a friendship that stretches beyond the unknown.

After the meeting of the minds as McShawn's, I had to head back home to grab Mama Bear and Beans so we could head down to the Dunkin Donuts Center and see the latest Disney On Ice performance. I think this was the third of these types of shows we took in this year but they're always well done and the little one likes them so very much, so I don't mind.

After the show I came right back home and climbed up into bed, which is where I'm now. My back has been bothering me for a few days and it seems to be getting worse instead of better. I think I just pulled a muscle but I'm not really sure how. These things happen, and the best thing I can do is rest. I was told I had scoliosis as a child, so having occasional back pain isn't unheard of but I haven't had any pain in it for over a year now.

My gym routine hasn't been what it usually is, so maybe that is contributing to the issue. The cold air brought in by the winter weather doesn't help, and neither does sitting on the basement floor wrapping presents night after night.

But, these things will pass, as they always do.

Sunday, December 28, 2014

My little one had been asking to stay in the spare room of our house, and so that is what we ended up doing last night. We watched *Guardians of the Galaxy* and ate popcorn and corn chips.

Today should be a pretty simple day. Our reverend is off from church this weekend so the parish is just singing carols and reading lessons. I usually enjoy this worship session very much, but the little one and I slept in a bit too late, so we missed it. The rest of the day will be spent doing some minor chores around the house, putting away Christmas decorations, and running the lawnmowers, snow blowers and the generator, just to make sure everything is okay.

Mama Bear has some errands to run, so I'm sure the little one and I will play some of her new video games and such. Then I think we will split a pizza and finish off the leftover chocolate cake that we had on Christmas.

The last week of the year is upon us. This isn't a time to slack off. So many people become enamored with the beauty of the New Year that they write off what is left of this one. Not me. This is not garbage time. This is my life and I'm going to make the most of each day. Even though Beans is off from school this week, I have to work, so I'm going to make the most of this day that we have together.

Monday, December 29, 2014

Monday Monday.
Can't trust that day.
Monday Monday.
Sometimes it just turns out that way.

"Monday, Monday" by The Mamas & The Papas

Mama Cass was right. This day could best be described as a work-a-thon. Time to climb into bed and hit the reset button.

Tuesday, December 30, 2014

For a description of this day, see Monday December 29th, 2014 as it was much of the same.

Lather.

Rinse.

Repeat.

Wednesday, December 31, 2014

Alas, a much needed day off!

These last two days were nightmares at work. Way too many patients with way too little staff. At the end of the year, healthcare deductibles are about ready to reset, so everyone and their mother fill the doctors' offices to the hilt trying to get the most out of their coverage before the first of the New Year. Conversely, no one wants to work because of the recent holiday season, so keeping staff motivated to fight off the sniffles and come into the office is a difficult chore.

But today shall be a grand day. Mama Bear has some things to do, so it's a Daddy-Daughter day. We plan to go shopping and take in a movie. Looks like we will be seeing *Into The Woods*—a Disney movie with a twist on some classic fairy tales.

Damn it. Damn it. Son of a bitch.

The best-laid plans go awry, and so on and so forth. In the time it took me to take a shower, all hell broke loose at my office, which is technically closed. Yesterday we transferred our phone system to some new fancy operating system that utilizes ways and means other than the old school telephone lines you see connected from pole to pole. And as is the way with new technology, it still had some bugs to work out. Nine text messages and three voice messages were on my cell phone when I stepped out of the hot shower to towel off my firm apple of a hiney.

Referring dental offices couldn't get through to our office so they called the surgeons from my office personally, and then they called me. The few employees I had authorized to go into the office to do some stocking and cleaning up also contacted me. I tried to fix everything remotely by logging into the network and making a few calls. All seemed well for a little while and so I loaded up Beans and we headed to the movies. I was pulling into the theater when the phone started chirping at me through my pocket. There would be no movies for Beans and I. Whatever is in the woods would have to wait for another day.

As I was turning Angelina around to go meet Mama Bear and deliver Beans to her, something occurred to me. At this very moment, I was becoming the one thing I truly hated—every asshole father in every Christmas special that can't be bothered with his child because the office and the almighty dollar beckons. To be fair, they never point out that the father going to the office is what provides for the home, the Christmas presents, the lights and heat being on, and so forth. This is also not to say the mother isn't contributing to these things either. I'm just speaking of the old time movies and cartoons that fill my head, so don't start up with a feminist movement. I love women in the workplace. If it was up to me, women can have the workplace. I'd rather stay home.

But in the here and now, I was cancelling plans with my daughter because of an incident at work, and it was killing me. I want nothing more than to be a great father, and when I can't fulfill my commitments to my little one, well, it really hurts me. Unfortunately, this was a problem that could not be handled without my presence. I decided to try and put a smile on my daughter's face by telling her we would go to the movies tomorrow but she wasn't buying it. She wasn't crying or being unreasonable by any means, as she is an amazing girl with great sensibility, but I could tell that she was saddened by the turn of events, even if she said it was okay.

On our way to meet Mama Bear, there was a Target store, and I pulled into there to at least give my daughter some little surprise. The phones were down at work now, and they would be down when I got there. Since Beans received her first "bra" on Christmas day (it's really more of a sports bra type thing), she had been asking to get a few more, so she had one for each day of the week. Oh Daddy's little girl is growing up fast. So we went into Target and made our way to the aisle where such things were kept. Beans was picking out colors and patterns that she wanted. I didn't know what size to get her, so we had to slip them over her shirt and see what fit. The ladies in the aisle seemed to take some amusement with a clearly red-faced father trying to slip sports bras on and off his daughter as quickly as possible without making a scene.

As I drove her back to Mama Bear, my little girl looked at me and said, "Thank you for the Brazils." She meant brassieres. Ha! Oh, how I love that girl of mine. This one moment saved the day and warmed my heart for the next five hours whilst I was at work fixing the phones.

Happy New Year, ya bastards!

Should Old Acquaintance be forgot,
and never brought to mind...

Thursday, January 1, 2015

The ball dropped promptly at midnight and I was snuggled in bed with Mama Bear and Beans whilst we watched it on television.

Earlier in the evening, after I returned home from work victorious over the phones, we went to a small party with two of the little one's friends and their parents. We had steak, lobster, and lots of snacks. I ate steak, as I won't eat out of the ocean, for I have only been upon this floating rock for 37 years and I have personally urinated in the ocean enough to think of it as the world's toilet. There is dinosaur poop in there somewhere, floating by the decaying bodies of long forgotten mobsters and the city of Atlantis. Sushi, anyone? I think not.

Here we are. A new year sits in front of me with her legs spread akimbo like some wanton whore. People get giddy with excitement when they talk about their resolutions for change in the coming days. The majority of them quickly lose their luster when they realize change requires hard work. Change cannot be accomplished by sitting on the couch eating cheese balls and watching daytime television. Well, some change will happen, but it isn't the kind you want.

I don't make resolutions for the new year as a rule. I joke about some of them, like my promise to bring booty back in 2015. But for the most part, change occurs over time, and so each year that the good Lord allows me to stay here, I make continued efforts to be a better person, to be a kinder soul, to take care of those in need, to be a faithful servant to God, and to be a good husband and father.

If, whilst doing these things, I stay in shape and become a better provider for my family, so be it. But the resolutions to change, when fueled by vanity and the cravings for material possessions, often fall short quickly, for they are hollow and have little to stand upon.

That being said, I remain optimistic as always and 2015 will be a grand year for me, I'm sure. Fifteen is my lucky number, after all, and this will be the only year ending in fifteen that I'll around to witness. I plan to make the most of it.

We were supposed to go see a movie today, but Mama Bear slept in till 1pm as she wasn't feeling well, and Beans was a bit cranky after being up till midnight, so we won't be going. Me? I'm the same today as I was yesterday, and was still looking forward to going to the movies, for I'm as constant as the Northern Star. Instead, it looks like I'll work on my events calendar for the coming months. I already have eight booked from now until October and I'm certain that number will grow, for which I'm thankful. The holidays are over. My break time is done. It's back to work tomorrow and changing the world as always.

Friday, January 2, 2015

Don't stop believing it's possible for a man to change his stars. It is. This day could be the day you snatch your gleaming destiny from the rusted jaws of fate. Many will tell you destiny and fate are the same thing, but I don't see it that way. I believe fate has a negative connotation of that which is considered to be predetermined, whereas destiny is a sparkling ray of hope of what one could possibly aspire to.

Fate is death. Destiny is the life that leads to it.

Go ahead and accept your fate, whilst I achieve my destiny.

Saturday, January 3, 2015

Starting off this year right by keeping alive my Saturday tradition at McShawn's Pub. Too often through the year, I'm too busy to do the things I want to do, like meet up with my dad at McShawn's and enjoy a beer and hot dog together. So that's what I did this morning. It was brilliant.

Moe the bartender was there, and he was dancing to Salt-N-Pepa's "Let's Talk About Sex" as it was playing on the jukebox. It was a classic moment. It gave me hope for the year. I can't explain why exactly, but some things need to be felt more than they need to be understood.

Sunday, January 4, 2015

I had a blessed morning at church, even though Beans didn't come with me, and Mama Bear stayed in bed. When I'm at service alone I can focus more on the readings and on my prayers, but I like it better when my family is there with me.

I stopped at Dunkin Donuts on the way home to pick up a bagel for the little one and a coffee for my wife. I like to surprise them with little snacks and sweet treats. I also feel indebted to the good people at Dunkin since they asked me to do a commercial for them last year. A check actually showed up for it again this past week. I hadn't received one in a few months so I thought the money train had reached its last stop, but I was wrong. So happily, happily wrong.

Ain't no money like commercial money! You work one day and randomly checks keep showing up for the next eighteen months.

Monday, January 5, 2015

I didn't sleep well last night. I felt some weird spiritual stuff going on. Good stuff, but at the same time, I was trying to sleep! Ah, well. It seemed to rejuvenate me. Despite my limited amount of shuteye, I was bright-eyed and bushy tailed today. Well, I was bright eyed at least. My firm apple of a hiney is as smooth as the day I was born (I'm not hairy).

I was able to get a ton of stuff done today at the office. Check this out—Saturday, after McShawn's, I stopped into my office to tinker on the phone system to see if I could fix anything. I technically don't know anything about phone systems, but I don't back down from a challenge either. Turns out, I did pretty well! Three out of four phone lines were working this morning. Huzzah!

I also came up with some cool ideas for my various other ventures. A little bit for the paranormal and a little bit for my motivational work.

The only thing that I didn't do today was go to the gym, but I wanted to give my back a day of rest as it was sore a bit yesterday. Damn cold weather! I'll never acquiesce to aging, injury, or anything that makes me feel like less of a superhero. Tomorrow I'll be back at it. Gym, first thing in the morning, along with some new downloads of some old Elvis music. I think the King will mix in nicely with Mr. Willie Nelson, Mr. James Brown, Metallica, and Lil Wayne.

Good night, you beautiful bastards.

And thank you for your support.

Tuesday, January 6, 2015

Family game night has been sweeping the Pari household by storm. So much so that it has been every night, thus being in direct opposition to its namesake, but that's okay as we are enjoying it. Our daughter recently discovered the game of Life and that's how this whole thing started. It's progressed to encompass a cat version of Monopoly, Kids' Monopoly, and Mouse Trap. The little one is actually quite competitive and can win on her own without Mama Bear or I tanking on purpose. Sometimes I want to beat her and I can't seem to find a way to win. They grow up so fast.

Wednesday, January 7, 2015

I was pulling into Dunkin Donuts this morning to get my holiday flavored peppermint mocha iced latte with extra flavor, extra sugar, and skim milk—so I can watch my girlish figure—when I heard a crunching sound in Angelina's front end. When I pulled her into work and backed into our space, I gave it a quick look in the frigid morning air, and I noticed the lower ball joints on both side look near collapsed. It's my own fault. I changed out her upper ball joints just a few months ago and I should have done the lower ones as well.

After work, I was on my way home and had just pulled off my exit when there was a huge crunch followed by some squeaking and the brief smell of burning brakes. As soon as I pulled her into the garage at home, usually reserved for Mama Bear's Durango, I put on the space heater and jacked her up so that I could slide under her skirt and see what the matter was. Lower ball joints for sure and it looked like that old gal could use new shocks as well. I wasn't surprised. I did literally just pull off one of her rear shocks a few months back. I didn't bother putting a new one on since the mounts had rotted off. Hey, we have been together on the road for sixteen years and over 260,000 miles. These things happen.

I can wiggle the wheel back and forth due to the ball joint collapsing and when that happens, the brakes get compressed at a different angle, hence the scent of burning brake pads. I'll have to change those soon. too.

All of this is too much to do tonight and not something I want to do on the floor of my garage without a lift. Looks like I'll be taking the Durango into work tomorrow since the merry-go-round broke down.

Thursday, January 8, 2015

I'm so tired
I haven't slept a wink
I'm so tired
My mind is on the blink

– "I'm So Tired" by The Beatles

Friday, January 9, 2015

A great many moons ago when I was a young buck full of promise, raging hormones and swimming spermatozoa, I was on a date of sorts with a girl named Kelly. I was in eighth grade and she was in tenth. I've always been a sucker for the older ladies. We were at Rocky Point Park, a local place in Warwick, back when there were still local amusement parks. It was a grand spot nestled by the seaside filled with blinking lights, spinning rides, and the best damned clam cakes in the state. If you're unfamiliar with the delicacy known as the clam cake, picture a ball of dough with tiny bits of clam in it—very tiny—actually, don't think of the clams at all. Just picture a tasty ball of dough deep fried with a touch of clam juice in it, golden brown, crispy and delicious, dusted with just a bit of salt. Mmmm.

Anyhow, there I was, young, curious, and wearing a neon orange "Surf or Die" shirt with dark blue jeans that had this really awesome late 80s/early 90s strip of black corduroy up the leg. With my hair spiked up and glistening with gel, this was going to be it—the day of my first kiss. I could feel it. Just before my mom and grandmother were coming to pick us up (smooth, I know), we decided to end our time at the park by taking one more ride upon The Scrambler. Now this is a ride that goes by many names, I'm sure, but it basically moves around like you are riding in a large eggbeater being tossed this way and that way. Good times.

As we unlatched the bar on the ride and went to step back out onto the midway, I specifically remember the feel of a cool ocean breeze. I remember this so clearly because I felt it upon my firm, round apple of a hiney. Somehow, my fancy jeans must have gotten snagged on a jagged edge of the ride whilst we were being scrambled, and thus unraveled my pants. Damn it. Damn it. Son of a bitch.

Luckily my surfing shirt (by the way, did I mention at this time in my life I couldn't swim, never mind surf) was an extra-large and hung upon my small frame like a sundress, thus covering my wicked shameful nakedness.

Why am I retelling this tale now? Well, I was at work today when I received a call from my wife that young Beans had an accident at school. Thankfully she was fine but she somehow she managed to tear the seat out of her jeans. Talk about family traditions. Ha! It must be in the genes. Get it? Sorry. I couldn't help myself. Better living through puns, I always say.

Anyhow, I left work early as I had Mama Bear's Durango since Angelina has yet to be fixed, and then, with a set of new pants, we took the little one out of school as an early dismissal, went to get her haircut, and then to see the new Disney musical *Into The Woods*. My wife and daughter seemed quite pleased with the movie, but I couldn't wait to get out of the woods. I was okay with it for the first ninety minutes or so but just when I thought it was over, it started with a whole new story line and I mentally checked out.

We then went to Target to get a new desk and chair as I plan to set up an office for myself in the spare room. I need a little space where I can work on my writing and work on my projects.

Anyhow, that was the day. All's well that ends well, as they say—and speaking of which, that spikey haired kid who couldn't swim, wore surfer clothes, and was nearly bare assed at the amusement park did get his first kiss that day. It was back at the house, up against the linen cabinet, just as her dad was picking her up. She, ummm… kissed me. I was petrified. Luckily, I got over that, but I never got over older women; so much so that I married one.

Oh, what ripped Beanser's pants you ask?

The world will never know, but being that she is only in second grade, I do hope there was no kissing involved.

Saturday, January 10, 2014

I put together my desk and chair today, thus my office is complete! Now, to do office type things. Hmm let's see. I have a candle and laptop. Ah, screw it. I'm going to the gym and then play video games with Beans. See ya!

Sunday, January 11, 2015

This year isn't starting out too smoothly. All the phone and tech issues at work combined with the automotive troubles of sweet Angelina have me on the ropes. I have been beyond tired trying to fix everything and hold it all together, plus spend time with my family. So to help balance all this out, I went to church this morning with my little one and restored a great sense of inner peace.

I spent a little time looking around online today, just to see what I could see in regards to new trucks. I have had my eye on this certain blue Dodge Ram 1500 that was in the lot when I bought Mama Bear her Durango back in the fall. I could have sworn I saw her on the lot when I drove by the other day, which would mean she's a leftover and thus cheaper than a few months ago. Not that I'm going to buy anything but it's nice to dream.

Damn it. Damn it. Son of a bitch.

I went to pick up sweet Angelina at my buddy Donnie's garage, and sadly, whilst driving her home, with my daughter riding shotgun, something came loose in the front end and caused us to shoot two lanes to the left across the highway. Luckily, I felt something wasn't right and had dropped back to stay out of traffic and I was able to get her back under control before my little one even looked up from her video game. The good Lord seems to have my picture high up upon His refrigerator for some reason, because He keeps saving my unworthy behind.

I took my truck off the highway and I called Mama Bear to come pick up the Beanie Baby. No sense in putting her in harm's way. I know Angelina and I knew I could get her home. No one knows her like I do. I was able to diagnose the issue pretty quickly—the front left brake caliper randomly hung up and pulled her sharply to the side before releasing its grip on the rotor, thus sending her shooting off in that direction.

These things happen. They can be fixed. Everyone made it home safe.

That is what mattered. I'm heading to bed now, and I'll "keep on believing that tomorrow will bring a better day." There is a great song by Johnny Clegg and Savuka called "Cruel Crazy Beautiful World" that has a line similar to that in it. It's a great song to live by. I often think it's something I would like to make sure my daughter hears and keeps in mind as she lives her life; a musical star to guide her ship by.

That's another line in the song, too. Go look it up and give it a listen. I'll be here when you return.

Monday, January 12, 2015

When I went into work this morning, I was alone and I turned on the office music system. To my pleasant surprise The Beatles were playing "Here Comes the Sun". I took this as the greatest of signs, as I'm one who believes in, or rather, recognizes such things. I had played that song on repeat through a set of stereo headphones upon Mama Bear's stomach when she was pregnant to soothe baby Beans whilst she was floating in her amniotic heaven. I talked to her and told her how excited we were to be her parents and that I couldn't wait to meet her face to face.

She got the nickname Beans when she was still in utero, actually. When we went to see the sonogram, I looked at the picture and she had this perfect kidney bean shaped head. Thus, "Beans" was born, so to speak.

When she was actually born, I made sure the first song she heard here in the outside world was "Here Comes the Sun". I placed the same stereo headset in her little bassinet in our hospital room and played it for her. I hope someday to play it again when I walk her down the aisle at her wedding, should she chose to get married, assuming the world makes a man worthy of my daughter. I'm a proud father. What can I say?

The workday was only a couple of hours old when I received a call from the salesman that sold me Mama Bear's Durango. He had seen that I was trolling the Dodge websites and confirmed that the same blue Dodge RAM was still sitting in the lot and that he could get me into it for a decent price since we were almost a month into 2015 and they needed to move out the 2014 inventory.

Funny enough, last night when I had stopped at the ATM to pick up a little cash on my way to pick up Angelina, my wife actually commented on seeing the truck in the lot across the road from the ATM but since I thought all was well with sweet Angelina at the time, I didn't think it much more than a still distant dream. What a difference a day makes. After hearing "Here Comes The Sun" this morning and getting the call about the truck, I decided to go give it a look. I had a lecture to do tonight for the good people of the Tiverton, a nice little seaside town in the East Bay section of Rhode Island. But I had some time in between jobs, and so I followed my instincts and went to kick some tires.

It had been love at first sight since last September. A man and his truck, a tale as old as time, and here we go again. She has 20-inch chrome rims beneath her electric blue frame; sweet bucket seats in the cab and a 345 horsepower 5.7 V8 Hemi engine that smells like happiness and the dreams of unicorns. Yes. It's that fucking magical. (You know how much I mean this because I cursed. I don't do that often. Go back and look. Son of a bitch doesn't count. That one is my favorite.)

When we went on our test drive, it was like dancing on ice but in a manly way, if that is possible but it doesn't sound possible. Anyhow, I only had an hour to make the deal and wrap it up before I had to get to my lecture; luckily I work best under pressure and time constraints. I got a great deal on Maggie May and I'm picking her up on Wednesday. Yes, she already has a name. She has had that name since I first laid eyes upon her underneath the light of the silvery moon back in September of 2014.

I don't like to do things for myself. I honestly have a hard time with it. I can buy things for my family. I can sacrifice for others. But buying something for myself has always been a bit of a struggle for me and I didn't know how I was going to break it to Angelina.

In other news, my first paranormal lecture of 2015 went well. It was a packed house, so much so that they moved it from the library to a larger building and they still had to add seats. The crowd was great and had stayed after the lecture to ask questions until the event organizers had to usher them out. I was honored to have so many supportive and interested people there. Doing paranormal events in the last week of October is one thing, as tis the season and all of that. But to pack a lecture hall on a freezing cold night in the middle of January in a small town is something else. I never take moments like this for granted, for they won't last forever.

I finished off the night with dinner accompanied by my friend Cody DesBiens and then headed home. I pulled into the driveway to see the saddened headlights of sweet Angelina. I explained to her that I would fix her brake caliper and that she wasn't going anywhere. She was merely getting a new baby sister. Our sixteen years together has meant everything to me, and we still have a date with 300,000 miles. She seemed to understand. And I meant every word of it.

Time for sleep. The elves in my head are being a bit rambunctious. I hope they will keep it down at Jolly Good Times, the pirate-themed bar in my mind, but then again, let them celebrate, the beautiful little bastards.

Good night, my friends.

Tuesday, January 13, 2015

Tuesday the 13th could have been just as scary as Friday the 13th if it was marketed correctly. Ah, well. That ship has sailed.

Tomorrow Maggie May arrives!

By the way, she is named for the Rod Stewart song about a love with an older woman. However, she could be easily confused with Maggie Mae, which was an old Liverpool folk tune made famous by The Beatles about a prostitute who robbed a sailor. So, you know, either way it's a pretty awesome name for a truck.

Wednesday, January 14, 2015

Maggie May did not arrive today. Color me disappointed. The gentleman whom was charged with the duty of getting her registered down at the DMV failed to get a stamp that he needed, and so, Maggie May is staying on the car lot for one more lonely night. That's okay. My Big Blue Baby will be home tomorrow. Though it's a bit of a letdown, I believe things happen for a reason. If I'm meant to have her home tomorrow, I'll get her. I've waited sixteen years for a new truck; I can wait one more night.

Thursday, January 15, 2015

Woohoo! My new truck has heat you can control, not just high heat or no heat like ole Angelina. It has air conditioning—my old truck lost that function about eight years ago. I now have dashboard lights that stay on all the time, not just pop on randomly when I hit a bump and then fade back into the darkness. I have to say, Maggie May, you were long overdue. I even have satellite radio so I can listen to my "40s on 4" old jazz station.

I must admit though, I still love my dear sweet Angelina and she isn't going anywhere but I won't miss having to tuck a scarf or old sweatshirt behind my lower back to protect me from the protruding wire frame of Angelina's old bucket seat.

The guys at the dealership wanted me to record an internet video for them. They had somehow found out about my *Ghost Hunters* career in the last 24 hours and the sales team spent some time watching some of my videos online. I didn't want to record a video but I did take some pictures with them and such.

I had asked my wife to accompany me in picking up Maggie May so I could take our daughter in it as my first passenger. She is my little princess, after all, and thus she was asked to sit shotgun in Maggie May on her maiden voyage. I drove her over to her dance class and dropped her off there with Mama Bear, and I then piloted Maggie back home and we had a little conversation along the way, just getting to know each other.

Friday, January 16, 2015

This morning I boarded a flight, which is in itself, nothing unusual, however, it's only the third time I've flown out of town with Mama Bear and Beans. We're down in Disney World now and we're actually greeted as the "Royal Family of the Day" here at the Riverside Hotel on Disney property. Two ladies met us as we arrived on the Mickey's Magical Express bus and they held up a sign with our name on it. They played royal announcement music and let everyone in the lobby know of our arrival. They had balloons and a letter from a Disney Princess for young Beans. And then we took a photo and were directed to our room—no need to check in, no hassle, no nothing. It was a great way to start our vacation.

I really want this vacation to be special for my family. I'm not patting myself on the back here, but I went all out last year and worked like a dog. Sure, Mama Bear has a new Durango that we will be paying for, and I just picked up Maggie May but there's more to life than vehicles and monthly payments. I like to spend time with my family.

I have all kinds of special dinners and surprises planned for my family and me this week. But being the Royal Family was not something I could have arranged and it was a very pleasant surprise for me, too.

We spent the day at the park, hitting up our favorite rides. We started with the Haunted Mansion, and then made our way over to Space Mountain and the new Seven Dwarves Mine Ride. We met some characters and took in some fireworks, before finishing up the night with one more tour of the Haunted Mansion. I really do love that damn ride. The music, the effects—it just feels like home to me.

We were riding back on the bus tonight and my little one's head was against my side, her chin being supported by one of my hands, dreaming peacefully and I thought it's all worth it. I'm doing the best I can and it seems I'm doing all right.

That being said, I only slept for about two hours last night, as I was worried I'd oversleep and we would miss our morning Jet Blue flight to Orlando. I also spent much of this day carrying the little one around the park, so I'm off to bed.

Saturday, January 17, 2015

Wow! This day was packed with fun but a lot of hustle. I planned for us to spend a little time in two different parks: the Magic Kingdom and

Disney's Hollywood Studios. We hit some of our favorite rides over in the Kingdom, met Anna and Elsa from *Frozen*, and then had lunch at a little Italian place in Hollywood Studios so we could get VIP seats for the Fantasmic fireworks show this evening. It was a tight schedule, especially considering we had to catch busses back and forth to the various parks but, with a little bit of luck and a lot of hustle, we made it happen.

We ended the night by going on the Twilight Zone's Tower of Terror thrill ride. It was the first time for all three of us, so I wasn't sure exactly how Mama Bear and Beans would react to it but everyone seemed to enjoy it. Mostly Beans, though. That girl loves a good scare more so than her daddy, I think.

Tomorrow is scheduled to be a more relaxed day, which is good, because I could use a little down time on this vacation.

Sunday, January 18, 2015

Beans and I sneaked out to the pools this morning and let Mama Bear sleep in today. Yes, pools. Plural. There's a large adult pool next to our room that opens at 9am and there's a family pool with waterslides and waterspouts that opens at 10am. Beans and I visited both and had a splendid morning together.

We hung around the Magic Kingdom today and played this magic portal game that they have set up around the park. We also did a bit of shopping and I spent way too much on Haunted Mansion merchandise. I cannot help myself. Ah well, I have to decorate my office back home with things I like. Beans and I had some cool ghost photography done as well. They take pictures of you and overlay them with images of a skeletal-like corpses, and then the images change depending on your viewing perspective. It's really cool and something brand new to the Mansion.

Tomorrow I have a very special surprise in store for the little one. I cannot wait to see her reaction.

Have a magical night, my friends.

Monday, January 19, 2015

Bippity boppity boo!

I used a little bit of Daddy Magic and had it arranged to take the little one for a full princess makeover at the Bippity Boppity Boo Salon here at the Magic Kingdom. I've never been one to buy into that whole "princess" mentality and neither does my daughter. She corrected me when I called her princess today and asked to be called Beans. I love her. I thought it would be a nice thing to let her get her hair, makeup, and nails done by a Fairy

Godmother-in-training. Sleeping Beauty—Aurora—is her favorite of the princesses, so we had a proper pink dress for her and everything.

We then went over to Epcot Center to tour the countries and take in some sights and sounds of the world. Disney gives you these great little bracelets that make it easy to spend money. They link the wristband to your charge card and now you don't need to worry about carrying money around with you all week. Brilliant. So brilliant in fact, that I stopped bringing my wallet around with me as it was just uncomfortable.

This proved to be a problem as I attempted to buy a tasty adult beverage in Epcot's American Experience. I waited in line in the hot Florida sun and had my wife and daughter go sit in the shade to stay cool. I ordered a pretzel, a beer, and water. All seemed fine until the surly gentleman who must have left his Disney personality in his sock drawer asked me for my license. Keep in mind, he asked no one in line before me for theirs, including two gents who looked like college frat guys at best. I explained that I left it in my wallet since we were using the bands and I didn't bring it. He never made eye contact and just grumbled something to the effect of he can't believe I wouldn't carry ID with me. Next thing I knew, I walked away a tad frustrated with water and a pretzel. The American Experience, indeed.

Luckily for me, I could simply walk over to Germany, talk nicely to the beer maiden (and I brought my wife and daughter with me to show that I was in fact a responsible mature adult), and I was able to enjoy a delicious frosty beverage, responsibly.

We finished up the evening with a dinner with the princesses, also arranged with a bit of Daddy Magic about four or five months ago. The princesses all visited our table one by one, and our daughter was able to take pictures with them all.

We wrapped up the night by watching Michael Jackson in Captain EO, which I saw with my parents back when it was new in 1986. It was kind of fun to sit there with my wife and daughter recalling when I saw it the first time. Strange in some ways, as Michael passed on a few years back. I lost myself in the show for just a moment. I felt like I could have run into my childhood self somewhere in that theater.

Of course, the night would not be complete without one more run through my daughter's favorite ride, Space Mountain, and mine, the Haunted Mansion. It was the end of the night and we were able to go through the mansion a few times as the park closed. We had to tell a little fib to the ride operator because Beans is seven and children under seven are not supposed to ride through this attraction on their own, but she really wanted to. No harm was done. I was quite proud of her. Though it's my favorite ride now, I remember being terrified by it when I was a child. Oh, how times have changed.

As the bus pulled back up to the Riverside Hotel, I hoisted my sleeping daughter up against my chest, her cheek felt cool against mine in the night air, and I carried her all the way back to our room. Hey, I know I'm not perfect, and the good Lord knows I make my fair share of mistakes, but in this one moment, I felt like I was doing all right. Chalk one up for Daddy.

Tuesday, January 20, 2015

My little one and I spent some time in the pool again today. She made up a game called "Squeezy Squid" in which we take turns being Squeezy Squid, and the object is to catch the other one when they are off the ladder or steps, and squeeze them. I'm not sure where she comes up with these things but man did we have some laughs playing it.

The parks were a lot of fun, and this vacation is rolling on.

Wednesday, January 21, 2015

After our full day at Animal Kingdom and Magic Kingdom, I had one more little surprise tucked away for Mama Bear and Beans. I made reservations for the Illuminations Dessert party, which is a dessert buffet featuring sweet treats from around the world, champagne, rum punch, and an amazing fireworks display, all situated against the waterfront of the Epcot park. It really was a nice evening; and lots of fun for Beans as she was feeding the sugar free lemon cookies to the ducks and the fish by the handful. I couldn't help but laugh when Beans ordered a punch and explained that there should be no rum for her as she wasn't 21.

Thursday, January 22, 2015

Today was our last day down here in Disney World. We started it over at the Disney Hollywood Studios as Beans really wanted to ride the Tower of Terror one more time. She also wanted to do this "penny trick" where you keep a penny in the palm of your hand, and when the elevator drops you, the penny floats just above the palm of your hand. God bless her, she is so brave. I tried it, but when the elevator dropped us I was holding on to that penny for dear life. I definitely gave ole honest Abe's cheeks a good pinch.

We then went on the Aerosmith Rock n' Roller Coaster for the first time. Mama Bear sat out the Tower of Terror but she was on board for this one. I was worried that Beans wouldn't like it because of how fast it is. I should have known better. We were back in line for a second ride as soon as we disembarked from the first ride. She had me download the song, "Nine Lives" that played whilst we were on it. My little girl sure knows how to rock. She gets that from me. Mama Bear is a country girl but she likes pop country, whereas I like classic rock and true country music like Willie, Johnny, and Hank. Guys who only need first names.

We finished up the day over at the Magic Kingdom, going on Space Mountain and the Haunted Mansion just one more time. Then we browsed the Mansion gift store, which resulted in me shipping back copious amounts of Mansion merchandise to decorate my office, and I also picked up some creepy colored lipstick for Beans per her request. Between the lipstick and the Hatchet Bride doll that she picked out (her name is Constance, by the way), I'm very proud of my daughter's taste.

Tomorrow we fly home. Time for me to pack up and get us all checked in for our travel back to wintery New England. I hear we're getting snow this week and a blizzard this weekend. I wonder if any of the park personnel would notice if I just stay here and sleep in the hammock by the pool every night?

Friday, January 23, 2015

We had a very pleasant and uneventful flight home, and I'm thankful for all that we have been able to see and do this past week.

After my father picked us up at the airport and brought us back to Mama Bear's Durango, we headed for home, stopping only to pick my old pickup, sweet Angelina, from my buddy's garage. Turns out it was a little more than just the brake caliper hanging up, but she was fixed and ready to come home and meet her new sister, my Big Blue Baby, Maggie May. My daughter asked to ride with me in Angelina on the way home, so I obliged, of course. We were just about home when Darius Rucker came on the radio singing "Wagon Wheel". Now, there were many levels at work here. The song itself was originally penned by one of my favorite musicians and poets of all time, Mr. Bob Dylan. It was later recorded by Old Crow Medicine Show and it was fantastic, in my opinion.

Darius Rucker has been hot on the pop country scene these past few years and he once was part of a band called Hootie and the Blowfish. I saw them perform in an outdoor arena whilst a distant storm was moving in and lighting streaked the night sky. It was one of my favorite concerts even if I was never clear as to if Darius was Hootie or the Blowfish.

So here we were at dusk, driving ole Angelina back home after a weeklong vacation together. I was tired. Beans was full of energy, as most seven-year-olds are. And then she started singing "Wagon Wheel" perfectly. On pitch. Not fumbling a lyric. Not missing a beat. I held her hand and started to sing with her as we were pulling down our street. My voice was breaking here and there as I was choking back tears but Beans didn't seem to notice. It was just one of those moments. It was just so meaningful.

It's timeless, precious moments like these that I'll always cherish in my heart and no doubt think about whilst I take my last few breaths upon this planet someday many moons from now. Don't worry about your five-year plans; enjoy the small moments squeezed in to each and every day, for they are far more valuable.

Saturday, January 24, 2015

Whew! Once again, "I got some sleep and I needed it. Not a lot, but a little bit." It's truly amazing how vacation can wipe you out. I'm glad I'll have today and tomorrow before I need to go back to the office. Plus it's snowing outside, so it looks like I have some things to do around here. Time to suit up, fire up the snow blower, and get to business.

Snow blower worked but it was backfiring like a son of a bitch. Looks like I have more work to do, especially if that blizzard is coming on Tuesday. I should have stayed in the Haunted Mansion. It looks like they have a great groundskeeper.

Sunday, January 25, 2015

I wanted to go to church this morning but both the little one and I slept in too late. Just as well, as it appears it snowed some more overnight, which means I have some shoveling to do. Then I'll diagnose the snow blower, get the generator running, and do the mandatory fuel run to fill up all the spare tanks with gasoline in case this blizzard knocks out power for an extended period of time.

The last big storm we had here was two years ago and the neighborhood adjacent to ours was without power for almost two weeks. We were fortunate. We had a tree that fell from our property and took out a power line but that was repaired in just a few hours. I personally enjoy a good power outage. I light some candles and try to catch up on some reading. Of course, this doesn't last long as the little one likes to play board games and such, which is all right by me as well.

Anyhow, I have lots to do, so I best get to it.

The generator had a bit of an issue getting up to speed today, but I got her straightened out. It looks like the only real issue with the snow blower is the spark plug needs to be replaced. I'll pick one up tomorrow during my lunch break.

I have 27.5 gallons of fuel reserves stored out in the shed. And I also stopped to pick up the obligatory milk and bread. I never understood why these were the items that you stock up on in case of an emergency. Personally I prefer pizza and pumpkin pie. But it just so happens that we were low on food since we were on vacation for a week, and we needed milk and bread. I guess we could make French toast.

Ah well, I think I'll watch the Elvis 1968 Comeback Special and then get some sleep. I want to hit the gym before work in the morning.

Rest well, you beautiful bastards.

Monday, January 26, 2015

Well kids, here we go. It's snowing outside as I write this. It's just about 7pm, and it has been snowing for most of the day but the accumulation has been nothing to talk about, until now.

I got in and out of work without too much hang up. I was even able to stop and pick up a few extra bags of rock salt at the hardware store that I'll use as ice melt in the days to come.

I have my snow gear laid out and ready to go. Two pairs of socks, work boots, pajama pants that I wear under my jeans, a t-shirt, a thermal shirt, and a thick hooded sweatshirt, all beneath my puffy jacket. And of course, I have a pair of gloves, and the pièce de résistance—my skull faced ski mask. Why? Because you need to have a bit of fun and happy nonsense despite the severity of any situation you could be facing.

Looks like I better fire up the old snow blower and get this party started.

Round one is done. It's just a few minutes before Cinderella hour and I did one pass over the driveway with the snow blower, followed by three passes with the shovel. After the first few inches were removed, it just kept coming down but not enough to warrant utilizing the noisy snow blower at such a late hour.

There will be more coming overnight and throughout the entire day tomorrow. My plan is to get up at 4am and hit it again. If I do a pass with the snow blower every four hours, I should be able to stay ahead of it.

Time to shower and grab about three hours of shuteye. I won't let this storm get the best of me.

Tuesday, January 27, 2015

Damn it! Damn it! Son of a bitch!

The snow blower done up and died the moment snow touched it just around 4:30 this morning. This resulted in a small cloud of profanity occupying the area just outside of my garage for about ten minutes, before I gave up on trying to fix it and just set forth with my shovel in hand and my headphones on. Flames—literal flames—shot from the exhaust. It sounded like a fuel problem the way it was breaking up. Either that or an electrical short of some kind. It worked last night. This morning? Nothing. I decided not to let it cloud my mental clarity for now. Without the assistance of the snow blower, I was in for one hell of a day. Man versus nature, without the aid of a machine; perhaps that is how it should be.

The day started off well enough. The waning darkness gave way to the gentle light of dawn as my plastic shovel first scraped the black asphalt beneath the nineteen plus inches of snowy white carpet. The lamppost shone a wonderfully soft golden glow across the frozen crystals that stretched the length of my driveway and beyond. My task was there before me and neither of us had much else to do. I reached down in my jacket and turned up the music on my iPhone. I started with a little Frankie Valli and the Four Seasons, mixed in a little bit of Mr. Elvis Presley, my favorite Jewish folk singer Mr. Bob Dylan, and a dash of Metallica.

Three and a half hours later I was about halfway done with my driveway and I was seriously contemplating why the hell I have such a long and wide driveway. Strategically parked, I honestly believe you could fit close to twenty cars in it.

What was worse than only being halfway done after three-and-a-half hours, was turning around and seeing that the area you just cleared was already sticky with about an inch more of freshly fallen snow. The ice froze to my eyelashes, and as you know, that's God's way of telling you, "Don't worry that it's only 8am. You're in a blizzard. Go in the garage and have a beer." And so, being a good little Christian soldier although not perfect, I did as I thought I should. Thanks for having my back, God. I appreciate it.

Two-and-a-half-hours and two cold Coors Banquet beers later, I was listening to Lil Wayne and Leon Redbone sing duets in my muddled mind. I finished the driveway, only to see it now had about two to three inches of freshly fallen snow back where I first started around 4:30 this morning. And so, our little hero cued up The Beatles, slung the shovel over his weary shoulders, and snow-shoed it back to his point of origin.

Since the snow was only about a fourth of what had fallen the first time I had to clear the driveway, I was able to clear the whole thing in an hour, which was just in time to do the two back stairwells and their landings. When you are in the backyard clearing landings and stairwells, it dawns on you that you need to shovel a path to the fixture where the oil man pumps oil into your tanks, so you're shoveling snow more than two feet deep across the length of your yard.

At this point I thought I was triumphant, but then I remembered the front path had not been cleared, and if we were to get visitors, packages, or Jehovah's Witnesses, they would not be able to get to our front door. And so, a shoveling I did go. By the way, I don't mind visits from Jehovah's Witnesses. I find them to be quiet kind. They can witness what they want, and I can witness what I want, and together we can share a nice spot of tea.

After shoveling the front path, it was time to go across the street and clear the mailbox. This is the worst of all the tasks, for you see, when you live in a rural neighborhood, the mail carrier is not required to get out of their vehicle to deliver your mail, so if you want your bills, your candle catalogs, and mail order pornography, you need to shovel a spot in the snow big enough for an entire car to fit. What makes this a particularly daunting chore is by this time the town plows have cleared the streets, so the snow is now packed tightly and waist-high, creating a frozen wall of misery between you and the mailbox. Good times. By the way, I don't get mail order porn. It's just funnier to write such things. I have the internet like everybody else.

By the time I was done, it was time to do the driveway once again. Old Man Winter was in good form today—I have to hand it to the cantankerous bastard. He had me on the ropes.

I honestly don't know how I did it, but in total I spent four hours outside in the snow last night, and then eleven straight hours outside in the blizzard today, which boasted wind gusts of up to 50mph. I ducked in the garage only two or three times, when my eyelashes were freezing, when Beans brought me down a bagel, and when Mama Bear brought me SpaghettiOs. Other than that, I never stepped foot in the house and I honestly never felt cold or tired. And for those of you with a morbid curiosity whom are wondering what I did about the call of nature and the recycling of those beers, well, I can tell you this: like most men, I enjoy writing my name in the snow. And being the fancy boy that I am, I write in cursive.

Now I'm back safe and warm in the house with proper facilities that don't allow one the creative space to write his name, nor anything else, in cursive or print. However I did get to take a lovely hot shower that made me realize just how cold I must have been outside. My hands themselves hurt to open and close, there is a pain in my chest reminiscent of when I spend all night filming only to sleep two hours and go back to work, and my firm round apple of a hiney was so cold to its core that I felt as if I was defrosting two frozen hams.

Time for rest! The good Lord knows I need it as it's still snowing and I have to get to work tomorrow. I'm turning my brain over to the elves at Jolly Good Times, the pirate-themed bar in my head, assuming that they aren't frozen solid in the egg nog river.

And to all a good night!

Wednesday, January 28, 2015

Now that I've had twelve hours of sleep and time to think about it, I've never seen Jehovah Witnesses out during the wintertime. Is it a seasonal thing like Girl Scout cookies? I'll have to make a mental note upon the yellow sticky pad in my mind to ask my Jehovah friends. Hmm… it appears Jinglebottom, the elf in charge of Jolly Good Times, has been tinkering with the yellow sticky pad. There's something scribbled here about a blowup doll and … oh, that's just disgusting. I can't even relay that message. Damn elf.

Now here's the problem I have with living in New England. Thankfully this winter has not been a bad one until now, and even with one big snowfall, it isn't that bad compared to some I have been through. It took me three hours to shovel the driveway and clear the paths and clean off sweet ole Angelina and Maggie May. So before I even get in the truck to go to work, I feel like I've already worked. New England is great because you have all four seasons, but with each season comes an ass-ache of its own.

Ready, kids?

Spring

Task: Planting the grass.

Problem: It rains like a son of a bitch in the beginning of spring so if you plant too early, all your seed gets washed away. Then suddenly it gets hot as hell and you have to constantly set timers for sprinklers to ensure that your little grass plants are getting enough water.

Summer

Task: Cutting the grass.

Problem: If you were lucky enough to grow grass in the spring, you now have to maintain it. Cut it too short and it'll burn in the unrelenting scorching summer sun. Let it grow too long and your wife will yell at you, your neighbors will mock your poor landscaping skills, and your manhood will shrink down three sizes too small like the heart of the Grinch.

Fall

Task: Raking the leaves.

Problem: How many damn leaves are there?! Raking the leaves is not a horrible chore. It's fun, actually. They're light, crisp and smell nice. It gets to be a bit of a pain when they get speared on the rake like some sort of sacrifice and you then have to stop raking and bend down awkwardly to remove said sacrificial leaf, but when you are done, both you and the leaf are heroes.

Now it's time to bag the leaves. You have nice little neat piles of leaves, right? Sure, you do. But now you have to get them into bags. You can try to put the bag in a barrel, but after you put in a few armfuls of leaves, the bag starts to billow up from some strange air pressure and then the bag slips off the side of the barrel and leaves are in the bag, and out of the bag, and on the ground. It's a nightmare.

So screw the barrel, you can just use the bag—except the bag won't stay open. Once you get the plastic bag positioned just so, you bend over awkwardly yet again to pick up a huge armful of crisp leaves, and along comes a wind gust that either closes your bag or blows the damn thing down the street, as your wife yells at you, your neighbors mock your poor landscaping skills, and your manhood shrinks down three sizes too small like the heart of the Grinch.

Winter

Task: Snow shoveling and simply surviving.

Problem: It's cold, it's wet, and neither of those things are any good. You shovel only to get snowed upon again and again and again. Then after you shovel you get to drive to work. If you can avoid people sliding and smashing into you during your morning commute, your reward is eight hours of work before you can drive back home in the same hazardous traffic conditions. Congratulations.

People think Hell is hot. Satan sits there laughing at you whilst demons prod you with iron pokers and all you can do is gnash your teeth in anguish. Let me tell you something, people are wrong. Hell is cold. It's a freezing cold icy driveway with 50mph gusts of wind, and you must shovel snow for all eternity whilst demons prod you with icicles and all you can do is gnash your teeth in anguish; but don't worry. Satan isn't there because it's fricking freezing and he is too smart to hang around that place.

There you have it, kids. Life in New England.

Thursday, January 29, 2015

My Big Blue Baby is back home! Okay, with all the blizzard and snow nonsense I failed to mention some things.

I refused to drive my new truck, Maggie May, in the snow. I know it sounds ridiculous as she is four-wheel drive and Angelina is not, but Angelina and I have been through sixteen winters together. She's a ballerina. I know how to dance with her across the icy roads of misery and misfortune that are the winters of New England. That gal looks out for me and I look out for her and God handles everything else. We have history. And I don't want to get salt and sand all over the Big Blue Baby. She's still shiny and new, and although Angelina doesn't look her age, she's a hardened bird that can handle the harsh substances of the winter roads. Maggie May isn't ready yet.

Since Maggie May wasn't going to be out and about on the roads, I brought her down the way and into the dealership last night because she had a faulty speaker in the passenger door that had to be replaced. After work today I picked her up and she sounds as pretty as she looks. She's tucked safely in the back corner of the driveway away from the trees and the salt and the snow.

In other news, my father and his friend came over the house today to fix the old snow blower. I had no idea they were going to do it and I'm quite thankful they did so, as we are getting more snow tomorrow and then again on Monday.

Didn't I tell you New England winters were a bitch? Ah, well. To everything, turn, turn, turn … right?

Now, depending on your age, your disposition, and the style of your underwear, those words there could be in reference to a 1950s song by folk singer Pete Seeger, a song made famous by The Byrds in 1965, or Chapter 3 of the Book of Ecclesiastes. Regardless of your particular favorite, or even mine for that matter, I do believe the words to hold a great truth in the seasons of New England, and the seasons of our lives, "To everything there is a season, and a time to every purpose under the heaven."

I bid you a good night, my friends. I'll write more tomorrow, unless Jesus bugles me back home. But I hope not, for I like to think I'm still in the summer of my life.

Friday, January 30, 2015

I was able to meet up with my friend, fellow writer, and paranormal enthusiast, Jeff Belanger this evening. I do enjoy spending some time unwinding and exchanging ideas over pizza and beer. As a matter of fact, anything done in the company of pizza and beer is rather enjoyable.

I'm looking forward to this weekend. I have quite a bit to do for the around the house and I have to put the final touches on my book *What's Next* that Jessica sent back to me in its final edited state.

It's also Super Bowl weekend, pinning the New England Patriots against the Seattle Seahawks. Being a diehard Miami Dolphins fan means I have to support the Seahawks over our division rivals the Patriots. Unfortunately I live in a house with two women whom I love despite their poor taste in football teams, as they are both Patriots fans. Needless to say, I'll have to keep my Seahawks allegiance quiet. I know the Patriots will win. The bastards.

Saturday, January 31, 2015

It was a classic Saturday morning. I started it with a bowl of Boo Berry cereal before I headed out to get my haircut. The same woman has been cutting my hair for the past twenty years now. I'm not sure what I'd do if she retired. She knows exactly where my cowlicks are and how to handle them. When she goes away on vacation, I just let it grow until she returns. There's nothing like going in the salon and resting your head back in the sink whilst you get your hair lathered and rinsed—your worries and troubles swirling down the drain behind you.

I brought my new truck Maggie May out today. The Big Blue Baby and I picked up my dad after my haircut and we went to McShawn's Pub over in Cranston for a few hot dogs and beers. I introduced my father to Fireball Whiskey. Normally he will not drink whiskey but he enjoyed the cinnamon flavor and ordered a second round. We took a picture together at the pub and then went on a few errands before I returned him home.

I went in the house to say goodbye to my mother and then it happened. My father came down the stairs holding his Elvis painting. This was a huge deal. This painting was a point of contention between my parents for over thirty years. It's a beautiful oil painting of Elvis in his white jumpsuit against a black background and his ring actually sparkles thanks to some inlaid crystals and just a bit of glitter, and a frame dusted with 18-karat gold surrounds all of this majestic beauty. It's as beautiful or horrible as it sounds, depending on your vantage point. My mother has always hated it and had fought to get it removed from the home. I was honored to take the King home with me. Sadly, my wife and daughter seem to hate it as my mother did. My wife told me not to bring it in the house and my daughter told me I could hang it up in the shed. I snuck Mr. Presley up the staircase to my office where he can hang peacefully and without worry of criticism.

It's done! I just finished reviewing the final edit of *What's Next.* This book of mine was sitting in my nightstand drawer for around two years. I scribbled it all into a composition notebook that had Captain America on the cover. It was all written whilst in flight going from event to event and trying to make a living. It chronicles my time after leaving the *Ghost Hunters International* show, coming home, trying to pay bills and working on getting a new show of my own on the air. It's partly autobiographical and partly motivational. I'm very pleased with the way it came together, especially the closing chapter and epilogue. I do hope that people will find this book enjoyable and that the message will resonate with my readers.

Sunday, February 1, 2015

Super Bowl Sunday is here! Truthfully I'm more excited for the food I'll prepare than I'm for the game. My Miami Dolphins haven't been to a Super Bowl since I was born so there isn't that much to get excited about. I'll spend most of the game rooting against the Patriots, which is also enjoyable, but not as much as supporting your own team in the championship game. My Dolphins will rise again in time.

Speaking of time, the big game is starting soon and I have some cooking to do! Let's see, there is pizza, doughboys, tortilla chips and cheese dip, those little hot dogs wrapped in the puff pastry….

The Patriots won. My wife and daughter are happy. I pretended to be for the little one's sake, but Lord knows I loathe the Patriots. We Miami Dolphins fans have a saying, "There's always next year." I know it well, as I've been saying it since I started watching the NFL back in 1984.

Monday, February 2, 2015

It's Groundhog Day!

Groundhog Day delights me in many ways, none of which I can explain. I just find the whole nonsense of it delightful. This past Thanksgiving, I went to New York City and see the Macy's Thanksgiving Day Parade, which was something I always wanted to do. The next thing on that list of necessities is to travel down to Punxsutawney, Pennsylvania, and witness Punxsutawney Phil, the prognosticator of prognosticators, get pulled from his comfortable home like a baby out of a uterus, and falsely predict the weather. What a tradition!

Fun Facts: A groundhog is also known as a woodchuck, which is also the name of my favorite hard cider. They are sometimes called whistle pigs, which is just a fun thing to say and a silly little notion in itself.

Everything about this "holiday" appeals to the kid in me. Chock full of nonsense and happiness. Long live the furry little weatherman, the groundhog! The little fellow saw his shadow this morning, which sadly means it looks like I have six more weeks of shoveling snow ahead of me. Oh well, you can't blame the messenger. It actually snowed another seven inches here today, so it looks like the furry rodent was right. Oh well, at least I closed the office so everyone could stay home safely.

I just got myself all excited just thinking about Groundhog's Day. That settles it. I have to start planning that trip!

Tuesday, February 3, 2015

I had a meeting after work with the two doctors that run the practice to discuss some ideas and such. Things look bright for me on the home front as their COO. I have to work on some ways to develop and grow the practice further, and I'm sure I'll figure it out.

In other news, I just hung up with a production company who wants to cast me for a new paranormal show. They have some interesting ideas to make it different from what is already out there, which is good. With my contract I can appear on anything I wish, should I choose to do so, but I'm rather picky so we shall see what comes of this. It's nice to still be not only a viable option but also a sought after option for new television projects. However, between my day job, my lecture series, my private events, my convention appearances, and trying to be respectfully selective regarding whom I work with and what I do, it isn't easy for me to do much more than I already am.

Speaking of which, Marc had my website updated for me yesterday. It looks like I already have ten appearances listed on paranormalrockstar.com with a few more pending. I'll be returning to some old venues that asked me back time and time again, which is truly an honor, and I like to think it says something about me as an entertainer and host. There are some new places on this list too, which is also good. I'm still trying to get some motivational bookings inked for 2015, but that will come in time. I just have to stay with it. There isn't any harm in trying to help people, whether you help ten thousand or just ten. It's still a worthy goal.

This year is starting to unfold herself before me like the gentle petals of a flower, or that of a young bride in her bedchambers, both of which are very nice blessings and should be treated as such.

Wednesday, February 4, 2015

Some days go by like inchworms, methodically and mostly unnoticed.

I appreciate inchworms. One blew into the window of my office on a leaf in late spring last year. I'll never forget it. The little green fellow landed right in front of my keyboard as if he floated in on a dream. I took the time to watch him and his little inchworm ways. I appreciated the moment for it gave me great perspective. Here I was typing away and trying to get my daily grind done so that I could go home and see my family, only to get up again in the morning to hit the gym and do it all again. Lather. Rinse. Repeat. And then here was this little green inchworm, going about what little green inchworms must go about. His struggles in comparison to mine may seem miniscule to me, but to him I'm sure they are equally important. As a child weeps for the loss of a stuffed animal, a rich man weeps for the crash of the stock market. Importance is a matter of perspective.

I watched the little green fellow for some time before I placed him back on his leaf, brought him outside and placed him at the base of the tree, and wished him well. When days go on that seem unimportant and methodical, I think of that little inchworm and know that we all serve some greater purpose for things that are unseen from our tiny and focused perspective. No day is wasted. No moment unimportant.

I just hope that if my leaf lands on the keyboard of some unperceivable giant whilst he is busy doing some unperceivable giant things, he doesn't squish me or put me in the trash receptacle.

Thursday, February 5, 2015

I spoke with Marc this morning about the contract option for the new show I was asked to be a part of. He and I agreed it wasn't in my best interest for several reasons and so we let that ship sail. It's important to know what ships to board and which ones to let sail quietly into the sunset or sink to the dark depths below.

I was quite contemplative today. I still am. It was a pleasant enough day with light snowfall that didn't accumulate too much, but I took ole Angelina into work anyway as I didn't want to risk the Big Blue Baby in the snow. The good folks of Rhode Island and Southern Massachusetts seem to forget how to drive in such conditions. Suzie Snowflake was dancing with Jack Frost just outside the thin pane of glass in my office window. I watched and pondered. I pondered and watched.

I have spent so much time shoveling, snow blowing, and cursing the snow these past few weeks that I haven't had much time to enjoy the beauty of the season, for each season that comes and goes does have its share of pain and sorrows but they all have their own beauty and whimsy as well. I must make note not to overlook such things. No man knows how many seasons he has left.

There is something melancholy about the snowfall in the nighttime. It's peaceful, sure, but there is a quiet sadness beneath its blue hue as it slowly falls upon the white hillside under the moonlight and lantern-shine. Sadness itself has a bit of beauty to it. Sadness is a real emotion. It's tangible. None of us live a life free of it. It's a great commonality. There are things in this life that we all must go through. No one is exempt. Fear. Struggle. Doubt. Loss. Pain. These things happen. They are inescapable and that is okay.

One of the things I often mention in my motivational lectures is when you're in a trying time, it may help to stop thinking, "Why me?" and replace it with "Why not me?" We are all broken together and that's all right. That's beautiful. We all get our moment in the sun; some of us just have to wait longer for the clouds to clear, and in truth, there is nothing wrong with cloudy days anyways.

Smile, damn it! It's only life, after all.

Friday, February 6, 2015

I know we all think our children are the best, but here are some great quotes from my daughter to make her case:

"Daddy did you see the new commercial for Chuck E. Cheese? First off, they redesigned Chucky so he looks like more of a rat than a mouse. Then they redid the song he dances to and it's just horrible. That place is really going downhill."

"I started a new club at school today. It's called The Tooth Wigglers Club. I'm the president and I made my friend Grace the vice president. We have eleven members so far. I teach them about teeth and show them the best techniques to wiggle out their teeth."

This next one needs a bit of a precursor. You see, my wife and I like to joke around with Beans and today we thought it was funny to tell her that she'll be getting a new little brother or sister. When I told her that Mama Bear was pregnant she quickly replied, "If you are pregnant Mama, you better sell it." Ha! All of these quotes came within two hours of me being home after work. For a seven-year-old girl, she's truly funny. She must get it from me unless you ask my wife of course, who still protests that I'm not funny.

Saturday, February 7, 2015

Today was Snugglefest Saturday! Beans decided last night that today we should just snuggle all day while we play video games, watch movies, and TV shows.

The day was off to a horrible start as I had a text from work asking me to pick something up from the Massachusetts office that we needed in the Rhode Island office on Monday morning. I decided I'd better do it today since there's another snowstorm coming through in the next few days. Of course my unscripted and unexpected sojourn to the office was an interruption to Snugglefest Saturday.

We started the day with video games on the couch in the playroom; mostly Mario Kart 8 and Rabbids Land for the Wii U. Mama Bear brought us down some breakfast. We had cinnamon rolls, pancakes, bacon, tater tots, and toast. Only I ate the bacon because Beans still is keeping up the idea that she's a vegetarian. She doesn't like the taste of meat. She also doesn't like the taste of vegetables. Then we watched some television for an hour or two before I made a dash to the office and returned home. The rest of the day was spent playing video games and watching some old *Muppet Show* DVDs of the original television series. Mama Bear made soup and worked on a photo-book of our recent trip to Disney World. I made doughboys and pizza. It's hard to beat a day like this.

Long live Snugglefest Saturdays!

Sunday, February 8, 2015

It looks like we are going to get hit with another snowstorm today that will carry on until Tuesday. I feel like this winter will never end. There are piles of snow along the roadsides and in parking lots that are easily ten feet high. Oh well, I think I'll take ole Angelina into work tomorrow as the Big Blue Baby shouldn't be out in such weather yet. People think me crazy for not driving the four-wheel drive vehicle in the snow, but Angelina is a sure-footed Sherpa in such weather.

Monday, February 9th 2015

Brrrrrr! Enough already with this damn snow!

Tuesday, February 10, 2015

Now, you have to understand, my father is from a different time. He was born in the 40s, raised in the 50s, blossomed in the 60s, and pretty much has never aged since. I'm pretty sure he still thinks he's 21 and there isn't anything wrong with that. He dances to his own beat, and he is one hell of a dancer. He's a hard worker, a great tinker, and one badass ole goat. What he isn't, is a doctor, or even someone trained in first aid.

Growing up, my mother and I joked that when there was an issue of any kind, he would turn to his own Holy Trinity—Vicks VapoRub , Vaseline, and duct tape. If your nose was running, if you had a cough, if your chest was congested, or if you had a fever, all you needed was Vicks placed generously upon your chest or under your nose. Dry skin? Chapped lips? Cut yourself and bleeding profusely? Put some Vaseline on it. And any household or automotive issue could be solved with a few strips of shiny silver duct tape. His tape wasn't the name brand though. It looked similar and behaved about the same but it was a heavily discounted product he bartered for at the flea market on Sunday morning. It was like his church. He strolled the halls and visited with the vendors each week. He haggled and traded time and time again. He was a master at his craft. The old man's barn is still heavily stocked with bungee cords, tape, and random knickknacks from the flea market.

This weekend he was working on his old snow plowing tractor and he cut his finger open on a piece of steel and it started to bleed profusely. So what did he do? He smeared a layer of bearing grease onto it and kept working. So today, three days later, he finally went to the walk-in clinic to have it looked at, mostly due to the constant prodding of my mother. They wanted to give him stitches but of course he wouldn't let them. Instead he just flirted and joked with the nurses and was given a tetanus shot before being released back into the wild.

Wednesday, February 11, 2015

My daughter, the President of the Tooth Wigglers Club, had a victory over her canine tooth last night! She has been waging a wiggle war with it for a few weeks now, sometimes twisting it to the point of bloodshed. Finally, she got the dang thing out. I heard the Tooth Fairy gave her five American dollars for it. Talk about cost of living increases. I got a dollar as a child and I was happy, damn it. But, as Mr. Bob Dylan sang, "The times, they are a changing."

Thursday, February 12, 2015

Two words: roof rakes. For you see, it's still snowing. It snowed today and it's going to snow all weekend—another possible blizzard with at least another foot of snow. The fluffy white stuff is piling up everywhere. My driveway looks like the Olympics luge.

Sadly, not everything is as much fun as shooting down the driveway in the morning. The snow is also piling up on top of the rooftop. Snowcapped roofs are fine and actually look quite beautiful but the weight of the snow over time can prove to be problematic. Now, I'm not one to take part in the sensationalistic nonsense that the media puts out there about house roofs collapsing all over the place. My house is solid and the roof is only about two years old, so there's little to worry about but it's still a good idea to take some of the weight burden off of the house. This idea is not particularly appealing to me but it is to my wife, or more accurately, to my mother-in-law who lives in the attached dwelling.

There are three ways to do this: hire a crew to go up there and clean it off to the tune of $1,800, go up on the icy roof myself and shovel it off, or get a roof rake. The roof rake is a shovel on a bent pole. It's nothing fancy. But purchasing one in New England after the blizzard we just had, and the one that may be coming, is like trying to find a unicorn and taking it for a proper saddle fitting down at the leprechaun stable.

I called several stores but they have been without them for weeks. I tried ordering them online but they are sold out. Again, it's a small shovel on a curved pole that you stretch up above your head, place onto the roof, and pull the cold snow down on top of you like a frozen white blanket of death. And somehow these things are out of stock everywhere.

However, the good Lord, despite my mistakes and wayward ways, He keeps my picture up on His fridge anyway. I was making my calls and found a place that was getting a shipment of five roof rakes in today. They agreed to hold one for me.

Guess who has a unicorn with a tiny custom-made saddle, baby?!

Friday, February 13, 2015

Bring on the black cats, broken mirrors, spilled salt, and all of that happy horseshit because it's Friday the 13th. I take no precautions on this day. Superstition is superstition and that's all there is to it.

Tonight I'm taking Mama Bear down to the Foxwoods Casino in Connecticut for dinner and a show. We have reservations at a fancy prime steakhouse, and then we're going to see Craig Ferguson, a comedian I enjoy quite a bit. He had a late night talk show for ten years that just wrapped up in the end of 2014. I truly enjoyed the show but Mama Bear didn't, so hopefully she'll enjoy his live show more.

But first, I must rake the roof!

Damn it! Damn it! Son of a bitch!

It was only three degrees out there this morning. Three degrees! And there I was like some sort of idiot standing near testicle-deep in the snowdrifts whilst pulling cold piles of frozen white misery down upon my head. Damn roof rake. Ah well, at least my mother-in-law will stop driving my wife crazy about the snow on the roof, and thus I won't be driven crazy.

Am I freezing? Sure, but it's a small price to pay for mental clarity and a bit of rest. And now, to work I go!

Saturday, February 14, 2015

Happy Valentine's Day!

Mama Bear and I had a great time last night. Our dinner was delicious. We had candied bacon, followed by steaks, and "Drunken Donuts". They literally make you fresh donuts and then provide you with liqueur infused icings in which you can dip your donuts. What a wonderful, wonderful, wonderful idea.

Craig Ferguson was hilarious! He even had characters from his old show involved. And yes, Mama Bear seemed to enjoy herself as well.

Our little one was sleeping under the watch of my mother-in-law when we came home. My wife decided she wanted to pick her up and carry her to bed. I don't think I realized how big our little Beans had grown until I saw her in my wife's arms with her feet almost dragging on the ground. Of course, Mama Bear is a petite lady at 4'10", but still, our little seven-year-old is gaining ground fast.

In other news, I submitted my first motivational book *What's Next* to the publisher today. I uploaded the text and the cover and now I await the draft copy that needs my approval before final publishing. I'm terribly excited.

It has been snowing all day. I've done the obligatory cleaning of the driveway, paths, and stairwells. It's going to snow right through tomorrow too. High winds and about a foot of snow, but it still can't get me down because tonight is the NASCAR All-Star Race! NASCAR is back baby. Thank God. Vroom! Vroom!

Sunday, February 15, 2015

Today I:

- Used the snow blower
- Shoveled
- Raked the roof

- Shoveled again
- Cried a little bit
- Shoveled some more

Dear God, please let it stop snowing. Thank you. – D. Pari

Monday, February 16, 2015

I was hoping to start back at the gym this morning and really focus on my new and improved routine for this year. What I was hoping to do and what I actually did were two different things. When the temperature is in the low single digits and the wind is howling outside your bedroom window like a freight train, it's a bit difficult to get motivated enough to come out from under the covers. I suppose it's just as well since I'm still sore from the four hours of snow removal yesterday. But tomorrow is another day and I have already set up my protein shakes and a new playlist.

Staying fit is important. I don't need to walk a runway or do a photoshoot but I do need to stay healthy so that my wife and little girl can rely upon me for years to come.

Part of a healthy lifestyle is sleep, which it's time for now.

Tuesday, February 17, 2015

Winner! Winner! Chicken dinner!

Today was pretty awesome for sure. I had a stellar workout this morning. There is just something magical about exercise. I felt strong physically, charged up emotionally, and just well overall.

I came home from work today to see that my wife and my daughter shoveled the driveway whilst I was at work. What a great surprise! It was very nice of them and I really appreciated it. I don't like to bother them with that sort of thing normally, silly male pride and all, but it was a very strange snowfall today so I suppose it was a time for strange things. It was light and fluffy and looked like the cottony fibers of spring dandelions; it was very peculiar indeed.

And Mama Bear made chicken wrapped in bacon for dinner, so yes, there actually was a chicken dinner. Anytime you have one meat wrapped inside of another meat, you are winning in a big way. This was one hell of an awesome day.

Wednesday, February 18, 2015

It's looking like I'm going to be having a very, very, very busy year. I already have nine or more events scheduled for the paranormal side of things and today I received two inquiries for the motivational side of things. And as if that was not enough, I opened up my email to find a new contract for the 11th season of Ghost Hunters that is set to start filming soon. Hmm … just one more episode? Sound familiar?

I'm already filled with conflict once again and we aren't even fifty days into the new year. I'm not sure what is expected of me in terms of obligation to the show. Last year I just agreed to do episodes as they became available. This contract reads as if they want to lock me in for every episode. Though it's very flattering to be wanted, I'm not sure I'm ready for that level of commitment. My day job is what has made everything possible for my family on a consistent level. The show is what has made it possible for me to do home improvements, take my family to New York City for Thanksgiving and to Disney World just a few weeks ago.

If I have to choose between one or the other, I have to stay with the day job as I'm a gentleman and I believe in dancing with the girl that brought me to the ball. I have always despised the old adage of not being able to have your cake and eat it too. What the hell are you supposed to do with cake if you can't eat it? That's just absurd.

Then there's the heartstrings issue, of course. Even reading the contract makes me miss my daughter and she is just across the hall in her bedroom. I asked my wife what to do but Mama Bear said just to ask for more money. Keep in mind I didn't even tell her the financial details of the contract. I should have made her my agent.

Ahh, well, this is too much to decide in one night's time. I'll sleep on it. Pray about it. And in the end probably end up flipping a coin. No matter what, I'm thankful for the opportunities.

Thursday, February 19, 2015

Damn it! Damn it! Son of a bitch!

I was bamboozled! I set my alarm for 5:13 this morning, as I'm not one to wake up at customary times like 5:00 or 5:15. I feel the little oddity of getting up at off times gives me an intangible edge on the rest of the normal world. Anyhow, I got up at 5:13, I ankled it on over to the bathroom and slipped and slid into my gym clothes, headed down to the kitchen to grab my protein shake, and I was off to the gym. Right? Wrong!

I opened the garage door to four more inches of snow. Grr! I attacked it with furious shoveling, followed by mean-spirited snow blowing, and then I finally acquiesced to the notion that I would not have time enough to go to the gym before work today because we were starting early at the office.

On my way back into my garage with my shovel slumped over my shoulder, I noticed my neighbor across the street was shoveling her equally large driveway alone. I said to myself, "You know what you've gotta do, cowboy." I sometimes refer to myself as cowboy when I'm trapped in my inner monologue. And so, I went across the street to see if I could be of assistance. Her husband was out of town on business and she was just trying to get at least half of the driveway cleared so she could get her own vehicle out. I told her I would handle it and I went back to my garage and fired up my snow blower again. I tell you this not to be boastful, but merely as a story of what we should do as humans. We should help each other. We should care for one another. We should always walk forth with a kind smile and a helpful heart.

The workday is done and now I'm here at the dance studio waiting for my daughter to finish her class. She is only seven years of age (seven-and-a-half if you ask her) but she's dancing in the production group with the fifteen-year-olds. I'm quite proud of my little Bean-head. Mama Bear had something to do with her mother tonight, and so here I sit with the other dance moms. Of course, I'm sitting here with my leather motorcycle jacket and a NASCAR shirt featuring a pin-up model, so I don't quite fit in. Luckily I'm notable for being on a silly little reality show, and so all is forgiven and people love me! Ha!

They are all very nice actually but I can't talk about sequined costumes and other dance companies. I'm in to this for my daughter. I watch her practice at home. I help her stretch. I practice moves with her while my overprotective inner-dad screams, "No! It's way too dangerous!" but I do it just the same. I go to as many of the competitions as I can, and I always make the big recital even if it means I have to drive all night to get there.

I'm quite proud of her. She's in school all week and is a great student. She's well beyond her grade in reading and even fancies writing and illustrating her own books. And then she's here at the dance studio three nights a week for an hour or two at a time with my wife. She really does love performing on stage. Her first recital was when she was just turning four. She made a big show of bowing to the crowd, and when the rest of the girls were exiting stage left, she stepped forward to the edge of the stage and blew kisses to the crowd. I wonder from whom she gets all that charisma?

I just love spending time with my daughter. Almost any man can be a father, physically speaking. But it takes love, time and much more to be a dad. Of all the accomplishments in my life, if there is more than one to begin with, the one I'm most proud of is being a dad. The precious moments I get to spend on this great big spinning rock with my daughter are amongst the most pure, the most joyous, and the most love filled than any others in my life. I would walk through the fires of hell and back for that girl, and I wouldn't utter one single word of complaint.

Here is a little aside about life. This is it. You, right now, are living your life. And some day, you will be dead. A 5-foot corpse, give or take a foot. What will you be remembered for? Who will remember you? Does any of it really matter?

You're damn right it does. It matters greatly. Each step you take each day makes smoother or rougher the path for those whom come after you. You can leave a legacy for your family. You can be remembered fondly, or you can be remembered as a curmudgeon. No one lives forever, though the pharmaceutical companies are making a pretty penny off of prolonging our lives, though the quality of it often swirls around the drain before we do.

Here's my point, if I have one at all, and I think I do. Do something with each day of your life. Don't wait forever to make your impact. The little things do matter. They may in fact matter more than the big things, because like tiny snowflakes, they pile up over time, and make quite an impact. Trust me.

Christian author Max Lucado is currently running a little social experiment called "100 Happy People". The concept is simple, for a forty-day period, you try to make others smile by acts of kindness. You can record these acts in a journal for review. You can share these acts on social media to inspire others. It's pure and beautiful. I have been enjoying it quite a bit. But I'm going beyond the forty days. I'm going the distance. I started a long time ago and I'm going to keep it up until I'm in the grave. I compliment strangers. I sincerely ask people how their days are, and I listen intently. I smile at children (not in a creepy way). I'm known to give hugs, not always to great results, but I hug anyway. I shovel driveways for neighbors. Each day of my life is spent, and will continue to be spent, trying to help others. For what greater purpose is there than to be of service to all. Being of service without a catch. Without need for thanks. Without need for repayment. Just being helpful. I love it and I live for it.

Friday, February 20, 2015

We had an employee appreciation dinner after work today. It's always nice to feel appreciated and to show others appreciation.

Take nothing for granted.

Saturday, February 21, 2015

My father has almost every tool known to man in his big red barn. One thing he doesn't have, however, is a roof rake. We are expecting a heavy and wet snow tomorrow—surprise, surprise—so I went down to their house this morning with my roof rake in order to clear the piled up snow from some of the house and the lean-to adjacent to the barn.

Ten minutes into my snow removal efforts it became apparent that we would need some of those other tools in his arsenal because the roof rake broke. One of the stabilization arms tore clean off. Thankfully we were able to modify the brackets and repair it with some nuts and bolts frankensteined from projects in the past. Ten minutes later the other stabilization arm broke off, and we had to repeat the lifesaving procedure. Two hours and two repairs later my work was done and the roofs were raked clean of their great white oppressor.

My dad and I celebrated at McShawn's Pub with hot dogs and beer. Life is good.

I was so excited to surprise my daughter with tickets to see Monster Jam tonight. There is something special about sitting in a loud arena as oversized trucks drive over smaller vehicles and fling dirt everywhere. Beans and I have been going to see the monster trucks since she was about three. Mama Bear came with us once down in Stafford Springs, Connecticut, a few years back but mostly it's just Beans and me. We have seen them several times at the Dunkin Donuts Center in Providence, and once last year at Foxboro Stadium in Massachusetts.

Tonight's show was a local one in Providence but it almost didn't happen. I met my wife and the little one at a roller skating rink where they were attending a birthday party whilst I was helping my parents with their snow problem. Beans and I hopped in ole Angelina and made our way to the city for the show. It was a sloppy snowy night with snow mixed with freezing rain, creating a wonderfully wintery mess on the roads. My wife told me to take the new truck since it has four wheel drive, but I went with my old truck as I was worried about some sliding into Maggie May out in the snow. Plus the Big Blue Baby doesn't like this kind of weather yet. She still has that new truck smell.

I cut across Federal Hill, a well-known area of Providence, and shot down Bond Street, a tiny side street that I normally utilize on my way to the Dunkin Donuts Center. Unbeknownst to me, they closed this street as they utilized it to pile up a mountain of snow from neighboring parking lots. I didn't find this out until I was halfway down the hill and saw the mountain of transplanted snow for myself. I spun my truck around and tried to make it back up the hill. No dice. Angelina's motor hummed and her tires spun but we only slid backwards into the snow mountain. I quickly dismounted my sure-footed steed and placed my rubber floor mats beneath her back tires in attempt to give her some traction. I dug out the snow with my bare hands. I turned the tires. I kept it in low and said my prayers.

God must have been busy or was keeping me safe from some other catastrophe because Angelina wasn't going anywhere. My little girl was looking on the verge of tears as Monster Jam was starting in thirty minutes and there we were stuck in a snow bank, just a five-minute walk from the show. I tried calling AAA for towing assistance but there was an extended wait time on hold due to the storm, and after fifteen minutes ticked by, I hung up. I went on-line and submitted a tow-assistance request for AAA, only to find they couldn't be there for three hours. My heart sunk. The show would be done by then.

I wrote a note saying we were stuck in the snow bank and would be back in three hours to meet AAA. I placed it on an old Frisbee I had in the back of the truck cab and placed it in the window. My plan was to just leave her there, go see Monster Jam and then walk back afterwards to meet the tow truck driver.

I was just about to step out of the truck and lock her up when I thought better of it. It's still an active street up to that point, and it would break my heart to leave Angelina cold and alone in the storm. I called Mama Bear to come pick up Beans and take her to the show. I figured I could sit in the cab of the truck in the darkened roadway and listen to the winter wind whip across the windshield backed by the golden tones of Mr. Willie Nelson singing sweetly through the speakers.

Fifteen minutes later, Mama Bear arrived at the same time Beans told me she didn't want to go without me. I walked up to my wife's Durango to see what she thought we should do, when Jose, my AAA angel, showed up from behind a blinding mix of headlights and wind-driven snow. Five minutes later, Beans and I were back in the cab of Angelina, having had her towed up to the top of the hill. I gave Jose ten bucks, though he didn't want to take it. I insisted because I wanted to show my sincere appreciation for his assistance.

We made it to Monster Jam having only missed a few minutes after opening introductions. Beans and I had a great night together, and we had a fun little story to tell.

Life is what you make it. Even a simple snowy night can lead to adventure and new memories.

Sunday, February 22, 2015

There's something magical about standing in front of the oven whilst a cake cools in front of you. It brings me right back to my childhood. It's a cold one out there today. I started the day by making blueberry pancakes for Mama Bear and Beans, followed it up by shoveling over an inch of wintery slush from the driveway, and just finished making what I'm sure will be a wonderfully delicious funfetti cake with hot pink frosting. Mama Bear and Beans are out right now, so I figured the little one would be pleasantly surprised to return to a freshly baked cake in one of her favorite colors. Not to leave Mama Bear out, I did the laundry and the dishes too.

Standing next to the oven, the heat coming out of it as it cools down, I'm reminded of my Nana's house as a child. My mother's parents had a fantastic floor vent in the living room where the heat would come up from the furnace. It was a fancy looking metal grate that had to measure somewhere around two feet by two feet, if not three by three. I remember being a kid and hearing that furnace kick on. I would scramble to sit on the grate and feel the forced hot air come streaming up all around me.

Life moves pretty fast, enjoy your memories, but don't forget to make new ones too.

As for me, I'm going to wait for my girls to get home so we can enjoy some cake.

Monday, February 23, 2015

It has been very cold this winter. A cold winter means turning up the heat and paying high heating bills. At least, now it does. I keep the heat up to make sure Mama Bear and Beans stay warm and well. However, many moons ago, single D. Pari would keep the heat very low. I recall being in my old house with my clothes on, and a robe on top of that. I would walk from room to room with a jar candle instead of leaving lights on. Candles provide heat and warmth, and all for a lot less than oil heat and electricity. There were days when it looked like a monastery in my old house. Assuming that monasteries look like they do in my mind with pillar candles everywhere.

I still like candles and if it was up to me, I'd be all about keeping the heat low and the lights off but I can't do that to my ladies here. Luckily for me they both like it cold at night as they get very hot under the moonlight, I suppose, or they both like to go to bed fully clothed. Beans sometimes wears her pajamas with the feet on them. We call it her sleep sack.

So in the morning when I got up, it was chilly. I put on my robe and went around the house opening the window blinds and putting the heat up. I even have an app on my phone that looks like a candle, so when I wander the morning stairwell in my robe and slippers, holding up my candle app, I look like a modern day Ebenezer Scrooge. I think I shall bring back that classic Dickens look when I get a bit older. I'll get one of those long nightshirts with matching stocking cap. I'll wear some fluffy slippers and patrol the halls via candlelight.

I've great plans for my twilight years. I'm going to get really weird. I'll be getting a Bull Terrier named Seamus and he and I'll go for walks on Sundays after church. We will get meatball sandwiches at the local shop and sit under a tree whilst we ponder the bigger questions in life.

Hang in there, Seamus dog of the future! Daddy's coming!

Tuesday, February 24, 2015

I finally talked with the guys at ye old ghost show corporate about the new season. I was honest in telling them that I appreciated the offer and that I'd indeed like to be a part of the new season, but I was concerned about signing a contract that locks me in for thirteen more episodes. I like to think they were honest in saying I was always really good on the shows, both *Ghost Hunters* and *Ghost Hunters International*, but I had really dialed it in during season ten and they'd really like to have me back. There's a contract to negotiate and such, so of course they could just be pouring a little buttery praise upon me, but hell, praise is praise. I'm like a dog hanging his head out of the car window, easy to please, and looking for a leg to hump. Scratch that last part. Scratch my belly. God, I'm a mess.

The production company is sending me the shooting schedule so I can give it a look over and see what investigations I'll be able to join them on this season. I feel pretty good about my decision. We shall see how it plays out. 2015 is well upon me. One more episode. Buckle up, kids. Here we go again.

Wednesday, February 25, 2015

I woke up to about four inches of fluffy white misery this morning. I was all revved up and ready to go to the gym. Then I saw the driveway and my trucks asleep beneath a blanket of snow. It took me the better part of an hour-and-a-half to clean everything off and get to the gym but I made it in time to have a decent workout before work. I have to admit, I couldn't help but think how nice it would be to live on a tropical island and sell hot dogs on the beach for a living. This winter has been the worst one in my lifetime for sure.

My daughter's dance schedule has resulted in a little dinner routine that Mama Bear and I have worked out without any discussion. On dance nights, Mama Bear leaves something in the crockpot and I come home from work and make the side dishes and Beanser's dinner. She still has my diet at her age, which consists of pasta and pizza, pizza and pasta.

Tonight I put dinner together whilst dancing around the kitchen to a little Mr. James Brown. It was magical. We then had a nice dinner together followed by some cake. Afterwards I did dishes to the melodic sounds of that beautiful redheaded gypsy bastard, my friend and yours, Mr. Willie Nelson. Somehow the musical dichotomy of Brown and Nelson seemed a perfect pair for this evening. Mama Bear and Beans don't seem to care for my music, or my dancing, but I honestly think underneath their irritated façade they love it and someday when I'm gone, they will remember it fondly.

Thursday, February 26, 2015

Take a break from reading this and go listen to Elvis sing "King Creole". You're welcome.

Friday, February 27, 2015

My daughter came home with this song that she wrote at school.

I'm on my way
And I'm here today
Standing tall
Trying not to fall
But it's tough to be a girl
And for the whole world I'm feeling so sad
I'm in the dark saying Help! Help! Help!
I'm in a trance
Help! Help! Help!
It's tough to be a girl
I don't know about you
Is it tough to be a boy too?

She is seven-years-old and writing her own songs already. The lyrics have some depth as well. She is a thoughtful little Beanser.

Saturday, February 28, 2015

I've got some thinking to do about this new *Ghost Hunters* contract….

SPRING
MARCH - MAY

Sunday, March 1, 2015

I finished reviewing the final proof for my new book, *What's Next.* I'm so very excited to make it available for everyone to read. As I've said, I know it won't be a *New York Times* Bestseller, but I believe it will indeed help at least a few people. And whilst one walks through this life, it is charged unto him to do just that. I toiled long and hard on my book, as did my friend and editor, Miss Jessica Jewett, the Duchess of Atlanta (unofficially, but officially so).

I'll be releasing this to the public as soon as Create Space uploads my final proof. I believe in the power of this little book. I think it can do great things. If nothing else, I have high hopes. I have high hopes. I have high apple pie in the sky hopes! Great. Now I'm hungry.

Monday, March 2, 2015

I enjoy listening to Christmas music when I drive alone at night. There is something magical about it. It transports me outside of myself. It is almost like watching a movie of my life.

Tuesday, March 3, 2015

Still weighing out my options regarding the show…

Wednesday, March 4, 2015

Still snowing. I signed the contract for Ghost Hunters season 11.

Thursday, March 5, 2015

Still snowing.

Friday, March 6, 2015

The final proof of *What's Next* was approved and uploaded today. Hopefully good things will come of this for many others.

Sunday, March 8, 2015

It's the calm before the storm. It's out there. It's brewing. It's coming. Circling me like a giant shark playing with its prey. *Jaws* was on tonight. It's such a classic movie. A truly timeless masterpiece littered with incredibly written dialogue and stellar acting. Plus there's a giant shark!

Sharks make me uneasy; not that I come across them often, thankfully. It may sound silly but even pictures of sharks in the ocean with their mouths open wide make me a little weak in the knees. I think it's more the feeling of being powerless to defend myself more so than the shark itself, for I think they are magnificent creatures. I love watching *Shark Week* every year on television. I'm fascinated with their anatomy and their abilities, but I still don't want to go swimming with them.

My favorite scene in *Jaws* is when Quinn and the guys are sitting in the Orca singing, "Show me the way to go home…" and then you hear the thump of the shark ramming the boat. That's how I feel now. I'm sitting there in the hull of the ship of my life, knowing that shark is out there swimming, slowly, methodically, and it will soon come crashing into the hull of my boat and attempt to destroy me.

January through March is my quiet time. I work my day job. I work on my books. I work on my lecture materials. I spend time with my family. I absorb the moments spent with my wife and daughter like a sponge soaking up water with a seemingly unquenchable thirst because I know these times are fleeting. Life itself is fleeting. Moments slip by each and every day. So I try to make the most of this time that I have here whilst I have it.

In the first week of April, I'll be back on the road filming again, and balancing it with my day job. Then the weekend events will start up. And April showers will turn into May flowers, which will in turn yield to the dog days of summer. Summer leads to October and I'll be busier than ever.

There will be long drives to give lectures, flights to events, and probably a cold night or two in a rental car. But for now, I won't think about the shark. I'll ignore its sharp white teeth waiting to tear me away from my family and separate us like flesh from a bone. I won't look into its black, lifeless, doll-eyes that will mirror my vacant eyes upon the sleepless nights that will surely come. No, I won't think about the shark any more. I'll simply sit here in the hull of this ship, have a drink, and sing a song, for this is the calm before the storm.

"Show me the way to go home..."

Monday, March 9, 2015

I was reminded this weekend of the time my mother kissed that beautiful redheaded gypsy bastard, Mr. Willie Nelson. Now, I'm sure in his time, and probably still today, ole Willie has pressed his lips against many a lady but my mother is the only one I know of personally. This was some time ago when I was back in grade school; I want to say fifth grade feels about right. My mother won a radio contest to meet Willie Nelson; she added the kissing part herself.

My mother isn't much of a drinker, you see, and she and my dad had stopped off for a beverage or two before going to the meet and greet prior to the concert. My father recalls my mother running her fingers through his hair. Willie's hair, not my dad's. My father lost the majority of his hair many moons before. My mother apparently commented on how clean it was before asking Willie for a kiss. He supposedly checked with my dad prior to the deed, which would make sense as my father has always been a strapping man who could handle a group of rowdy drunken bikers by himself, never mind one straggly country singer with a heart of gold.

And as Forrest Gump would say, "That's all I have to say about that."

Tuesday, March 10, 2015

Neil Diamond tonight!

Wednesday, March 11, 2015

Wow! Neil Diamond was amazing last night. The guy is 74-years-old and he took the stage a singing and a dancing! Through some magic of the universe and the love of God, I ended up with a floor seat eight rows from the stage instead of four rows from the back. Life is good.

Thursday, March 12, 2015

I spent an hour last night doing an internet radio interview to help promote my first event of the year coming up next month in Salem, Massachusetts. I spent some time talking about my new book as well. I did another interview tonight for a friend of mine who was doing his show for the first time. We talked about my beginnings in the paranormal, my path to spirituality, and the motivation behind my *What's Next* book. When it was all said and done, I made my way upstairs and stepped into my daughter's bedroom to kiss her good night. She was drifting off to sleep already, but opened her little eyes when I went to kiss her on her head.

Usually she listens to Christmas music on her iPod speaker system all night, but lately she has been mixing it up with a little bit of Disney music as well. When I came into the room "Do You Want To Build A Snowman" from the movie *Frozen* had just come on. I love that song. It makes me cry sometimes. I admit it. I can't deny it.

Music is so near and dear to my soul. It speaks my emotions when words fail me. This particular song makes me think of how quickly my little one is growing up. I remember sitting in the movie theater with her when *Frozen* first came out and getting out of work early one day so I could meet her and Mama Bear at the *Frozen: Sing-A-Long* at the theater as well.

I realize now, despite all the snow this year, we never built a snowman. That saddens me. Most of the snow was icy, or it was too fluffy, or it was just too dang cold out. Beans isn't a big fan of getting cold. Neither am I but I must make a point of building a snowman with her at the next opportunity, which hopefully won't be until the end of this year.

I kissed her gently and let her know I love her and I'm proud of her. When I was closing her door I told her that she makes me happy. I think it's important for her to know that. Even if we didn't build a snowman this winter, we had a lot of fun.

Friday, March 13, 2015

Happy Friday the 13th everyone!

Spill some salt. Walk under ladders. Walk only behind black cats. Break some mirrors. Celebrate in style.

I took Mama Bear and the Beanie baby to dinner at The Old Grist Mill Tavern in Seekonk, Massachusetts, tonight. It was first established in 1745. It was then destroyed in an accident in 2012 when a tractor-trailer over turned and ruptured a gas main that connected to the restaurant. They rebuilt it and opened it again, much to the joy of my daughter who has always wanted to go there for dinner. I guess she needs to try the grilled cheese and pasta with butter everywhere.

I reserved a nice table near the window so we could watch the little waterfall that runs alongside the restaurant. I enjoyed a large ribeye steak and a huge slice of warm blueberry pie. Wife and Beans enjoyed themselves, which made me happy. That is what it's all about.

Saturday, March 14, 2015

Little Beans and I went to the Father and Daughter dance tonight. Technically they now call these things a Sweetheart Dance but I'm from a different time and so I call it what I remember it to be.

My little one was all dolled up in a black and red dress with a furry black shawl over her shoulders. I wore my black pinstripe suit with a red dress shirt and black tie. We looked killer. I'm always so proud of my little girl. I really enjoy accompanying her to things like this. It isn't often we get nights out together. We danced, we played, we lost the 50/50 raffle, and then we went out for pizza. The first time we went to this dance, she was in kindergarten and we won the 50/50 raffle. Since then I think the little one has it in her head that we should always win it. But win or lose the raffle, I always win because I get to spend the night hanging out with my daughter and having the best time. Even if it means for most of the dance I stand by on the sidelines of the gymnasium floor holding a warm Capri-sun, half a cup of goldfish crackers, and tiny heeled shoes that were "not good for dancing, running, or playing" with her friends.

It's no bother. I would hold the world upon my shoulders for her.

Sunday, March 15, 2015

Beware the Ides of March! Ahh, the oracle, the seer, Vestricius Spurinna; if only Emperor Julius Caesar had listened. D. Pari fun fact #712: Caesar and I share a birthday and Italian heritage.

Boy, do I love Sundays. Unfortunately I slept through church today. I actually slept for over twelve hours, but I guess I needed my rest. I was such a ziggy piggy! I made mini raviolis and garlic bread for my NASCAR feast today. It was delicious.

Monday, March 16, 2015

The headlines in the news lately have all been hate driven. It's racist issues, a sexist issue, or a gay/lesbian/transgender/bisexual issue. It all seems so foreign to me. I don't know how long it will take for everyone to just get along in peace. How much longer must we walk this world fighting each other over little differences instead of celebrating our humanity and reveling in what makes us a bit unique?

Everybody's talking about
Bagism, Shagism, Dragism, Madism,
Ragism, Tagism, this-ism, that-ism
Ism ism ism

"Give Peace a Chance" - John Lennon

I'm with you, John. Give peace a chance.

Tuesday, March 17, 2015

Happy Saint Patrick's Day!

Now don't get me wrong, I enjoy a tasty adult beverage in a responsible manner, but I don't like celebrating with over indulgence. I prefer to reflect upon the saint behind the holiday. It's in that manner that I refer you to one of my favorite prayers, Saint Patrick's Breastplate.

I arise today
Through a mighty strength, the invocation of the Trinity,
Through belief in the Threeness,
Through confession of the Oneness
of the Creator of creation.

I arise today
Through the strength of Christ's birth with His baptism,
Through the strength of His crucifixion with His burial,
Through the strength of His resurrection with His ascension,
Through the strength of His descent for the judgment of doom.

I arise today
Through the strength of the love of cherubim,
In the obedience of angels,
In the service of archangels,
In the hope of resurrection to meet with reward,
In the prayers of patriarchs,
In the predictions of prophets,
In the preaching of apostles,

In the faith of confessors,
In the innocence of holy virgins,
In the deeds of righteous men.

I arise today, through
The strength of heaven,
The light of the sun,
The radiance of the moon,
The splendor of fire,
The speed of lightning,
The swiftness of wind,
The depth of the sea,
The stability of the earth,
The firmness of rock.

I arise today, through
God's strength to pilot me,
God's might to uphold me,
God's wisdom to guide me,
God's eye to look before me,
God's ear to hear me,
God's word to speak for me,
God's hand to guard me,
God's shield to protect me,
God's host to save me
From snares of devils,
From temptation of vices,
From everyone who shall wish me ill,
afar and near.

I summon today
All these powers between me and those evils,
Against every cruel and merciless power
Against every knowledge that corrupts man's body and soul;
Christ to shield me today
Against poison, against burning,
Against drowning, against wounding,
So that there may come to me an abundance of reward.

Christ with me,
Christ before me,
Christ behind me,
Christ in me,

Christ beneath me,
Christ above me,
Christ on my right,
Christ on my left,
Christ when I lie down,
Christ when I sit down,
Christ when I arise,
Christ in the heart of every man who thinks of me,
Christ in the mouth of everyone who speaks of me,
Christ in every eye that sees me,
Christ in every ear that hears me.

I arise today
Through a mighty strength, the invocation of the Trinity,
Through belief in the Threeness,
Through confession of the Oneness
of the Creator of creation.

After all, three is a magic number.

Wednesday March 18th, 2015

Faith is a powerful thing. It is a personal journey. Yet it is not something that anyone should be ashamed of or afraid to talk about.

Thursday, March 19, 2015

I woke up last night in a terrible state. I was covered head to toe in hives, only my face and my man parts were spared, for which I'm very thankful. I took copious amounts of Benadryl and rubbed Benadryl lotion all over me. I then passed out and suffered the dreaded Benadryl hangover when I awoke for work this morning. The hives had gone away, but sadly returned again in the late afternoon but they were different this time, blotchy and sporadic. At least I'm no longer a glorious shade of hot pink.

Friday March 20, 2015

The damn hives came back. Sum 'bitch…. Or in this case sum 'itch! I am not sure what the cause of this is but I best be getting to the bottom of it for even my bottom is itchy.

Saturday March 21, 2015

Saturdays were made for cartoons and big bowls of cereal. It just feels right.

Sunday March 22, 2015

I was offered the opportunity to travel down to Martinsville, Virginia, next weekend to catch the NASCAR race with my buddy John Helfman. He's the one that does all the marketing for my favorite driver Kurt Busch and he has his hands in a few other teams as well. I wasn't going to go because I have a Disney Institute management course this week that will take me out of town for two days already, and then I'll be filming with that old ghost show next week. After some internal debate and the weighing of cons versus pros, I decided to take Helfman up on his generous offer and booked the flight. I'm going to be working like crazy from next week until November anyway; I might as well throw myself a sendoff party in true style.

In other medical news, I went to a dermatologist about my recurring hives and he placed me upon a 24-hour allergy medication and a steroid to keep things under control. So far so good, except I'm a bit on the grumpy side and very hungry. Grumpy is very out of character for me so I apologized in advance to Beans and Wife. Hungry is not out of character for me but not resisting the urge to eat is. I can't wait to be off this medication. Unfortunately it's going to take two weeks. Ugh! Oh well, I can add and drop weight like no one's business. Once this runs its course, I'll run to the gym.

Monday March 23, 2015

Not going to write much today. Side effects from the medication are making me crazy! My heart is racing. My hands are shaking. And no matter how much I want to, I cannot sleep at night. I made it through the whole day on less than two hours sleep. My mind is tired and my vision is blurry, now if only my body would acquiesce to sweet slumber.

Tuesday March 24th, 2015

I don't get sick often. Sniffles and coughs happen but I don't pay them any mind as they are so few and far between. I can work all day on cough medicine better than some people could work on their best day. I haven't received a flu shot since I was sixteen and I haven't caught the flu since then either. Coincidence? I think not.

When I do take ill, it's usually kidney stones. Family trait, I'm afraid. I've done all the tests and cut out all the triggers, yet they still come around every few years. They come around every year if I drink a lot of iced tea, so that delicious vixen and I have had to part ways.

So here I am with this mystery allergic reaction still looming beneath the surface. The meds are keeping it at bay but they are really playing with my head. I have been able to control the irritability but I've been eating a few more donuts than usual.

Wednesday, March 25, 2015

I'm aboard U.S. Airways flight 4467 aisle seat 10C. This little baby is taking me to Philadelphia where I'll spend the rest of the day lounging about my hotel room until the Disney Institute management course tomorrow. I didn't stay at the hotel holding the seminar, as it was a bit cheaper for me to stay just a bit down the turnpike and save the company some money. The company probably wouldn't care but I'm a frugal little fellow. Plus, I do like to drive. Driving always gives me time to clear my head. A soul alone is often a good thing. One needs introspection.

Here at the hotel and the damn hives came back! Luckily they are only on my calves but they have me worried. I have NASCAR this weekend and I have to film next week in addition to my day job. That is a lot of hustling for one man. I can handle it for sure. Lord knows I have done that and then some just last fall. However, an itchy, hungry D. Pari is not one that has been tested quite so thoroughly … yet. Going to try and go to bed early tonight. Like before 8pm early. Maybe I just need rest.

Thursday, March 26, 2015

Well, the damn hives went down over night. Huzzah! I didn't sleep so well due to feverish night sweats and acid reflux. More side effects, I suppose. Ah, well. Each day is open unto enough misery as it's. I shall speak no more of it. Today is my management seminar with the good people of the Disney Institute. Time to get my learn on.

I'm aboard U.S. Airways flight 4537 aisle seat 11D. The gent in 11F is sleeping—mouth agape, head pressed against the plastic window. Ah, life. I'm on my way home from my Disney Institute course after a few flight delays. No worries though. These big old mechanical birds fly and die when the good Lord says they should. As a rule I do my best not to fret much about delays, except for that one time I ran full speed all the way to the gate and they had given my seat away because they didn't think I'd make it. That bothered me. I had my throttle pushed all the way to rabbit for that one.

But this flight delay was no big deal. Everyone will be asleep when I get home and there was a certain piece of pizza making eyes at me from the food court anyhow. Plus, I was at the Philadelphia airport. An airport I know oh so very, very well. I did all the necessary things. I went to Chick-fil-A. I had a mojito at the Asian bistro. I visited the men's room, which still possesses, in my own humble opinion, the best use of natural lighting in such an airport facility. A magical moment occurred when I was washing my paws and preparing to leave the restroom. The custodian came sauntering in, in true sauntering custodial fashion. A short, stout little man with black skin and white whiskers. He was singing "Love Me" as sung by Mr. Elvis Presley. Well, not being one to miss an opportunity such as this, I picked up on the next verse and together we serenaded two or three very lucky patrons who were sitting on their own porcelain thrones whilst we imitated the King. It was a remarkable moment in my life. I may never know the custodian man's name but we bonded in the night under the natural bathroom light.

In regards to today's course, I must say the Disney Institute seminar was fantastic! I highly recommend them. I was never a big Disney kid. I went to the park once when I was just about seven or eight-years-old and it was a grand time. I enjoyed Winnie the Pooh cartoons and Mr. Toad's Wild Ride, but that was the extent of it. I cried when my father made me go in the Haunted Mansion. Now you can't get me to leave the damn place. Oh how times change. And as I mentioned, they also replaced the old Mr. Toad Ride many moons ago. Godspeed, Mr. Toad. Buckle up.

The course was really well run and I have a ton of great ideas to bring back to my office. I want to rewrite our books, focus on values, communicate a clear vision and leave a legacy. Truth be told, I've always wanted to leave a legacy. Out of all the characteristics people say I have, "kind" is the one that gets mentioned the most and it's probably the one I'm most fond of as well. There's no reason to wander through this world without a smile for all you meet and a hug for all you greet. My catch phrase as of late has been "Smile, damn it! It's only life, after all." I stand by it.

I sat front and center today, much unlike me of the past that would pick the seat in the back closest to the door for easy access escapes. Whilst in discussion with a lady at my table, I pitched myself as a motivational speaker and exchanged contact information. Talk about you do, and do what you talk about. And above all else, always be hustling.

For my participation in the class I even earned a li'l Mickey Mouse figure that is currently nestled in my laptop bag at my feet beneath aisle seat 10D. It was a great day. Truly.

The only reason I wish my flight didn't get delayed multiple times would have to be my inability to stop eating on this dang medication. I had donuts because, well, I love donuts. I ate a king sized bag of Reese's Pieces for really no good reason. I'd be willing to wager I haven't eaten Reese's Pieces since I was a kid watching the movie *E.T.* with my dad in the theater. And now here I sit bending my in-flight Gummy Bears into multiple naughty positions in some attempt to set a record for the Gummy Bear Mile High Club. What is wrong with me?

Oh well, at least there isn't any sort of monster out upon the wing like the one that plagued my friend Mr. William Shatner in that old episode of *The Twilight Zone*. What? I can't say Mr. William Shatner and I are friends? Well, I'll have you know that we tweet back and forth quite frequently. I'm sure I'm glorifying our acquaintance relationship but he did ask me for autographed items for his celebrity charity auction and he sent me these tweets whilst I was waiting for tonight's flight:

❖❖❖

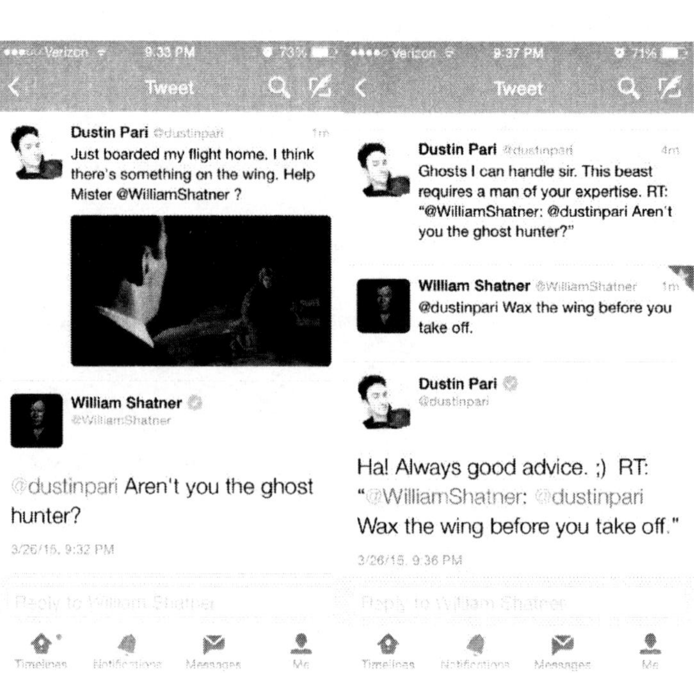

That's right, boys and girls. Captain James Tiberius Kirk and yours truly! (Seriously, he's, like, the nicest guy.)

Southwest Flight 1456 is taking me from Rhode Island to Baltimore, Maryland, where I'll meet up with my friend John Helfman and his wife who I have yet to meet. Seat 16E is where I'm planted. It's a middle seat. Yes, I know. On Southwest you don't get to pick your seat beforehand. Instead you get to pick your seat when you get on the plane based upon your ticket number. Your ticket number is dependent upon when you checked in online, or if you paid the extra money to board in the first few numbers. It's all a scam, kids. Don't believe the hype.

It's all fun and games aboard Southwest until someone claims the last non-middle seat. I created a little stir by executing a brilliant breech of etiquette whilst boarding. I was in the mid numbers of the B group. This is the group that always has to make the tough decisions. Do you take the front row that has been left vacant because there is no storage space? Do you hop in the first middle seat you see that is wedged betwixt tow people that look fairly normal? Or do you risk it all and head to the back, hoping your quick guesstimate of how many people are in line in front of you versus the amount of aisle or window seats left vacant in the back? Tough questions, my friend.

I tried a little something new. I gambled on the long haul, which isn't new for me. But when I did get to the back and there were still frantic mid-late B group people looking for those cherished seats of aisles or windows, I took the last open row and chose…. the middle!? Now, I can never be sure, but methinks I heard the nice flight attendant gasp. That's right! I took the middle! The middle seat in an empty row. What the hell, you say? Row 16 was mid-plane but was occupied by two flight attendants in discussion whilst the B group shuffled by. When I approached, they moved along, leaving row 16 vacant. By thinking quickly and taking the middle seat, I made everyone following me come to the harsh reality that the choice isn't aisle or window. The choice is, do I want to sit next to someone whom my arm has to brush against for the duration of the flight? That, my friend—that is the decision! And when given the decision, people will shuffle by and hope on sitting without having to touch anyone. And now I can sit here with this whole row to myself. Don't hate the player. Hate the game.

I think that's what the kids say. If it isn't, don't tell me. I don't want to know.

Saturday, March 28, 2015

I spent last night at the Helfman's home. They were very kind to host me there for the night. They have a great basement room that is completely dark and silent. It was as if I slept in a sensory deprivation chamber. I slept like a rock, and the good Lord knows I needed it.

Today was a pleasant road trip from Baltimore, Maryland to Martinsville, Virginia. It was about a 5-hour ride but Jon, Ange, and I had pleasant conversation about everything from living positively, NASCAR, and thoughts on the afterlife, and so the trip went by quickly.

We settled in at the hotel and I watched some television shows about UFOs. I enjoy that type of stuff quite a bit. I have a tattoo of the typical "gray" alien on my left calf. It was my first tattoo I ever got. He has great big eyes, sneakers, and some tattoos of his own. Originally he had a question mark on his belly, but over time it became a weird squiggle, so I had tattoos put on him which gave him a cool punk rock sort of look.

I remember spending countless hours in high school reading books about Project Blue Book and various report files. For hours on end I would lay out by the ocean at night and listen to the waves lap up against the shore in Jamestown whilst watching the skies in hopes of seeing an unidentified flying object. I watched the movies like *Fire in the Sky* and *Communion.* I later spent the better part of a weekend in conversation with Travis Walton whilst at a convention in Michigan. He was the gentleman abducted in the real *Fire in the Sky* story. He autographed a copy of the book for me.

My own UFO encounter came a few years back. I was driving through Indiana in late October of 2010. I was doing the college lecture tour circuit, as is still customary for me in the fall. I remember clearly that I was listening to a radio broadcast discussing the rescue of the Chilean miners trapped underground and rescued just a day or so before. It was around one or two in the morning and I put the hammer down to make up some time along the interstate as I raced on towards the next night's lecture spot. The road was desolate and dark. The stars were shining brightly ahead of me, and then it happened! What I laid on my back and prayed to see for years in my youth was there in front of me. Straight ahead of me in the night sky, a light appeared. It was shaped in an arch, like an eyebrow in the sky. Bright red on one side and brilliantly white on the other. There seemed to be a sliding brightness denoting motion from one end of the arch to the other, and then a solitary object that lit up in front of me like a flashlight and hung there for just a few seconds. It shot dramatically to the left and streaked across the night sky and out of my vision faster than anything I had ever seen before. I shut off the radio and just drove in silence for some time, feeling small, and thankful.

This just in! Due to an error in email communication it turns out I don't have to film this coming Monday night as I thought. Instead I have one more entire week at home before having to go back on the road for *Ghost Hunters*! Woo hoo! One more week! One more week!

Tonight was awesome in a way that only nights like this can be. The Helfmans and I went over to the bowling lanes near our hotel. The NASCAR officials put together a bowling tournament with some of the racecar teams. I spent the night eating greasy bar food and drinking cider with Jon and Ange, a local driver Josh Reeves who is a friend of mine, and members of the #78 Furniture Row racing team. One of the guys was a *Ghost Hunters* fan and had lots of questions. The team spotter (the person who communicates with the driver throughout the race about his position on the track amongst the other cars and what's going on around him) seemed to take a liking to me and invited me up to watch some of the race from his position at the top of the track. Tomorrow is going to be an excellent day for sure!

Now I shall unwind with some Oreos and milk... and more shows about aliens. Don't judge me. I cut back on the damn prednisone today, so I ate a lot less. I feel good about that. I shall celebrate with cookies.

Sunday March 29th, 2015

Woohoo! What a day! What a day! What a day! I picked up my NASCAR credentials this morning at 7am and the day just took off from there.

It was a very cold morning at the Martinsville track but the sun was shining and that gave me hope. Thanks to Jon and some connections that were made at the bowling lanes last night I had breakfast in one of the infield kitchen tents. The tent was run by a woman named Kat who cooks up breakfast and lunch for several of the top NASCAR teams. I had a bowl of scrambled eggs and hash browns as I walked through the garage area with Jonathon and his wife Ange.

I then met up with my buddy Josh Reeves and we walked on the rack together through turn two and down the backstretch. I took a pretty sweet low angle shot of the backstretch in the morning sun. I was really alive and happy in the moment, sure to be aware of every sense like how the cold air felt against my skin, the brightness of the sun as it shined down on the silver aluminum seats in the stands. The smell of fuel and the oil seemed to dance upon the air in the garage area and the sounds of the engines roaring to life, disrupting the silence. And taste? Well, Martinsville is known for its hot dogs, and they did not disappoint. I had two.

My NASCAR hero Kurt Busch showed up and went over into his hauler. He called for Jon to go in and speak with him, and within a minute's time Jon motioned out the back of the trailer door for Ange, Josh, and me to come inside. It took all I could not to run. Such a fan I am! I felt as giddy as a schoolgirl. I was fortunate enough to have met Kurt before but it still thrilled me to do so again. I was really over the moon that he remembered who I was as well. "That guy from *Ghost Hunters*," might as well as be my middle name at this point in my life. Hey, you dance with who brought you. No shame in that.

Kurt was recently reinstated to NASCAR and rightfully so. I won't go into the specifics of the nonsense that kept him out of the driver's seat of the #41 car for a few weeks this year but let's just say that justice prevailed. Hanging out in the back of the trailer Kurt was funny. We talked about the outcome of the race the week before where he was leading with mere laps to go when a phantom caution was called which ended up costing him the win. He joked about it with good nature. He offered us hot cocoa and tea. As we said our goodbyes I wished him luck, and then sheepishly asked for another picture together, to which he kindly obliged.

I attended the drivers' meeting that takes place before each race. Jon and Josh joked that it was the one thing you would be excited to do only once in your life. Jon escorted me over to the meeting tent and brought me inside. He took his leave and left me standing there at the edge of a row of seats where Jeff Gordon, Dale Earnhardt Jr., and Kasey Kahne sat. Literally, Jeff Gordon was one chair away from where I stood. Jimmie Johnson sat one row up. One row back was Clint Bowyer. A few rows behind him sat Carl Edwards. The list goes on and on and on. It was amazing! All these incredible drivers, guys who I have watched race each Sunday from my couch, now sat all within my view, and many within arm's reach. It was like a dream.

What happened next had to be one of the funniest things I think I have ever witnessed. It was just as Jon and Josh had said it would be. There were the most talented drivers in the world and they watched what's equivalent to a driver's education video. A narration instructed the drivers about rules and regulations of the track. They were told where to turn into pit road and how fast they could go. They were told how to signal to other drivers when they needed to change lanes and drop to the bottom of the track. It goes on and on, and the funniest part was they watched it quietly and some with intense focus. It just seemed a very strange juxtaposition. Then everyone stood and they closed with a prayer. I liked that. I took a lot of pictures during the meeting and I wished Clint Bowyer good luck on my way out of the tent as he and I were walking together. Crazy. Simply crazy. How the hell do I get myself in these situations?!

I walked back out onto the track and took some pictures with Kurt's #41 machine before he slipped into the driver's window and started the engine. Jon had given me a radio and headset to use so I could listen to Kurt's verbal exchanges with his crew chief during the race. I watched the race from the infield at turn two. I could see the cars when they came out of the turn or pulled off of pit road and raced onto the backstretch. It was amazing. I stood there for the better part of 300 miles before Kurt slid a lap down due to a set of ill-timed scuffed tires his team had placed on after he lead for a good part of the race.

Shortly after that we took our leave from the track since we had to drive back to Maryland that night. Jon, Ange, and I listened to the rest of the race on the radio. Denny Hamlin won, Kurt finished on the lead lap in 14th. I'm now nestled in at the Helfman's home and I have a flight coming up at 6am, which will have me up at 4am. As I drift off to sleep tonight I'll count my blessings for they are so numerous. Today was a great day.

Monday, March 30, 2015

I didn't write on the plane this morning because I was content blissfully sitting against the window in the exit row and listening to Kermit Ruffins play sweet New Orleans jazz music. I didn't get a lot of sleep last night but I did get a belly full of McDonald's pancakes at the airport this morning so that makes up for it. I don't eat a lot of fast food but I do love McDonald's pancakes. They remind me of the days when I was a child and my dad sometimes brought me to McDonald's on weekend mornings when he was home and Mom was sleeping in. They weren't many times but I remember them fondly. I asked for extra butter then and I still have to ask now. I'm not sure why they are so incredibly stingy. One pat of butter per pancake is simply not enough.

Anyhow, I landed in Rhode Island this morning just around 7:30am and went right into work. I'm exhausted. And I'm sunburned. It was only around 45-50 degrees at the track at its peak yesterday and so I didn't feel the heat of the sun but it found me standing there in turn two and placed a bright red memento upon my forehead and neck. Maybe this is where the term "redneck" initiated.

Tuesday, March 31, 2015

I'm so very blessed. Things are not always easy for me but things aren't meant to be easy. Through struggle, we become strong. Through that strength, we grow. It's because we grow that we are able to rise to new heights and achieve our dreams.

And so, as I reflect upon this past weekend and all the fun I had, I know the shark is out there. I'll be heading off to film next Monday night right after work. I'll film for two days and then get an early morning flight back to the office on very little sleep. I'll do this for the better part of the year. It won't be easy. I'll struggle. I'll grow stronger. I'll rise to the occasion and do what is necessary to provide a better tomorrow for my family because that is what I do. It's all I know how to do.

I still have the rest of this week to enjoy time with my family and this weekend we go to Hershey Park for Easter. The shark will have to wait until the bunny leaves before he can attack me in the Orca.

Tonight was a great night. Mama Bear was sick unfortunately, but Beans and I had an incredible time watching *Mary Poppins*. Beans has been asking for me to sit and watch this with her since I had to go away to the Disney Institute course last week. Time with her is the only thing that can beat a NASCAR weekend. I also am quite fond of Miss Mary Poppins as well. It's a great movie with an even better soundtrack. I still sing that, "Chim-chiminey, chim-chiminey, chim-chim-charoo," song on a regular basis. There's something whimsical and mysterious about it that resonates with me. I remember my dad taking me to see *Mary Poppins* when I was a kid. He was on the road a lot when I was small, as I have had to be as well; family tradition, I suppose. Chim-chim-charoo.

Wednesday, April 1, 2015

I've never liked April Fool's Day. I still don't. I don't like playing pranks and the like. I don't like foolishness. I'm a happy nonsense kind of guy.

Thursday, April 2, 2015

I'm all packed and ready for what is to come. The family and I are leaving for Easter weekend tomorrow afternoon, so that was suitcase number one. When we return Sunday night, I'll have to prepare to leave to film for *Ghost Hunters* on Monday. I don't think it's a great idea to drive home five-and-a-half hours from Pennsylvania and then pack for a flight the next day, so I did it all today, hence suitcase number two.

As the wise magician Professor Hinkle said in *Frosty*, "Busy! Busy! Busy!"

Friday, April 3, 2015

I have to work this morning and then pick up the rental car so I can drive Mama Bear and Beans down to Hershey Park for our annual Easter weekend trip. We have been doing this for the past five years now. It's a tradition that I look forward to each spring. What's not to love? Family time, rollercoasters, and chocolate. Life is good!

Saturday, April 4, 2015

What a day! The family and I spent a good six hours at Hershey Park. This was the first year Beans was categorized as a "Hershey Bar", which was the height requirement necessary to be able to ride the majority of the rollercoasters at the park. She's quite the daredevil and rides things that would have petrified me as a kid and still give me pause today. Of course, I ride everything she wants to go on, as I want to be there to experience things with her. Mama Bear does very well with this as well. There are a few select rides that she won't attempt but most she will go on at least once.

The big ride this year was a rollercoaster called Sidewinder which starts by pulling you backward and straight up in the air so you're looking down at the ground. It launches you forward through numerous loops and twists and turns before pulling you up another vertical ramp where you stare at the clouds waiting for the sudden drop that sends you flying backwards over the same track you just traveled. Needless to say the little one loved it.

It was a wonderful time for me. I truly enjoy these moments the most. No work, just family time and fun. This is what it's all about. That shark is still out there circling, trying to remind me of what is to come next week, but I'm not paying it any mind. Now is my time. I'm not going to be a tree in the stage show of my life. I'm living in the limelight baby.

Interesting night at the hotel. Beans and I played in the pool as we usually do, and then we grabbed fresh cookies from the lobby and brought them back to the room to share with Mama Bear. But tonight we also sat as a family and watched the History Channel, which was showing a series on the Bible and Christ. I was glad to see not only Beans show interest, but my wife as well. I don't force the faith on either of them, so it means a lot to me when they come to me with questions and such. I do my best to answer them honestly and encourage them to learn more. I like to think I'm doing a good job. I believe that you teach the lessons of Christ by example and not by force. I wish more thought that way. If so we might be living in a much better world. I'll continue to do my part and pray for the rest.

Sunday, April 5, 2015

A blessed Easter Sunday! He is risen. I do love Easter. It brings hope, and I'm a big fan of hope. Hope is that little warm ray of golden sunshine that brightens our coldest day at our darkest hour. Without hope we should surely perish.

The Easter bunny found his way to our hotel room once again. He left two dozen plastic eggs willed with small toys called Shopkins for young Beans. She also received a large basket filled with books, stuffed animals, and chocolates, which she kindly shared with Mama Bear and me. She's very good-natured and shares by her very nature. It makes me proud to see her behave as such.

The family and I will enjoy one more day at Hershey Park and head back home in the afternoon.

Time to go hit some rollercoasters!

Monday, April 6, 2015

United Airlines flight 4375 is taking me from Rhode Island to Illinois in seat 23C—the aisle seat on a tiny plane, my favorite type. I'm off to film the first episode of *Ghost Hunters* season eleven. Here I go again. Speaking of which, Whitesnake is on my iTunes singing just the song for the occasion:

Though I keep searching for an answer
I never seem to find what I'm looking for
Oh Lord I pray you give me strength to carry on
Cuz' I know what it means
To walk along the lonely street of dreams
Here I go again on my own
Going down the only road I've ever known
Like a drifter I was born to walk alone….

Indeed "one more episode" has extended itself throughout all of season ten's thirteen episodes, and now into season eleven. I literally came home last night from Hershey Park, changed suitcases, and went to my day job this morning knowing that it was going to be off to the airport afterwards and on the road until Thursday. This truly is the only road I've ever known.

It has never been just one job for me for the majority of my time in the workforce. It's a family tradition. One that I hope will end with me, that's for sure. I hope to get little Beans a good college fund and hopefully she will be able to pursue whatever career path she so chooses. I'll always be proud of her, no matter what she chooses, but I hope her life will be a bit easier than mine has been thus far. Not that I'm complaining mind you. I'm quite grateful for all the opportunities that the good Lord has provided me with. I don't mind hustling and making things happen, but a little sleep once in a while would be pleasant as well. Oh bother, I'll sleep when I'm dead. Let's make things happen now!

I'm excited to get filming actually. I haven't been on an investigation in a while now. I was supposed to help out with one locally a few nights ago but life got in the way and so I couldn't make it. I do enjoy my time interacting with the spirit world but my interaction is not limited to time doing investigations for television or not. My spiritual life is interwoven betwixt prayer, investigation, and happenstance. I won't trouble you with the story here, for it is quite detailed and a tad bizarre. Lord knows I wouldn't want anyone to think me more off than they already do. Let's just say I have friends on the other side and I appreciate their interaction. There are signs that come my way. There are messages. Sometimes there are even voices in my head, besides those of imaginary elves at Jolly Good Times and the live studio audience in my mind. I'm thankful for the guidance I'm given no matter how it comes. If there's one thing I've learned, it's that you cannot trust the majority of your fellow man but you can trust your gut. I truly believe our instincts know the right and wrong thing to do most of the time. Why we choose to go against our internal guidance and ourselves is beyond me. Let God be your steering wheel, not your spare tire.

I'm also excited for my in-flight Caprese sandwich nestled in my carry-on bag. This little treat is becoming a regular thing for me. I had one a few weeks ago when I was flying to Pennsylvania for my Disney Institute course. I was glad to have it, too. My flight was delayed and I ended up sitting around in an airport that was basically closed up shop for the night leaving me without anything to eat outside of vending machine fare.

I've said before that I often feel like a real life Paddington Bear. He travels around with a smile, a kind heart, and an innocent approach to life and its experiences. He also travels with a marmalade sandwich under his hat. Smart bear. I trust you see the similarities. I quiet fancied the adventures of Paddington as a child. I read the books and I watched the animated show. If you recall I was quite excited to see the Paddington balloon in the Macy's Thanksgiving Day Parade last year and recently the family and I went to see the new Paddington movie as well. It was a jolly good show. Beans and Mama Bear seemed to enjoy it too. I can't seem to get the taste for marmalade but other than that, we're practically identical.

I can't help but sit here and think what these next few months will hold for me. I'm not normally the type of person that likes to think too far ahead. I'm a day-to-day guy. As they say, "Each day has enough troubles of its own." I prefer to say that each day has enough wonderful moments of its own but I was outvoted when they were putting together popular sayings. Tis true though. Each day is filled with opportunity. Opportunity that may never come to you in quite the same way again, so you might as well get off the couch and take a chance on it.

Always bet heavy on yourself. Life is a game of inches my friends. I'll say it time and time again because it's so very important. Don't get psyched out by that "big picture" and "five-year plan" nonsense. No one is promising you five more minutes, never mind five more years. Play the cards you have been dealt to the best of your ability now. Enjoy each moment. Savor the sunshine, dance in the rain, and give the bastards hell! Never acquiesce to misery and those who revel in it like swine in slop.

You want to be happy? Be happy. You want to be sad? Be sad. "It's not that easy," they will say. Yes, it is. You're not a slave to your yesterday. Your circumstances can only influence you as much as you allow them to. Sometimes you have to lift your head up, keep your eyes on that horizon, and smile in pure defiance of the darkness that surrounds you. No one can steal your sunshine unless you let them.

Ah well… there I go again. Simmer down, soapbox boy! I can't help myself. These are things I believe in.

But, as I was saying before I was derailed onto track #9 where John Lennon was singing and Bob Dylan was playing his harmonica for a boxcar full of hopeful hobos and dreamers, I'm not one to look too far down the tracks. I don't even check weather reports unless I'm going to a NASCAR race and even then I give the meteorologist little credence unless the meteorologist is Punxsutawney Phil, of course. That little fellow is based in pure science.

And so, I won't look ahead but simply embrace the day and each moment that makes it up. I shall close this writing for now. I'll listen to the sounds of Mr. Willie Nelson as he sings "A Little Old Fashioned Karma" sweetly through my earbuds. I'll sip my Dunkin Donuts iced latte made with extra mocha flavor, extra sugar, a shot of coconut and skim milk—I watch my girlish figure, of course. This winter cannot last forever and bikini season is coming up you know. (Side note: my dear little wife refuses to order this sweet coffee concoction for me. I can't help that I'm a fancy boy with good taste.)

And now, to stare out the window and make pictures out of the clouds, for who knows if I'll be able to do so again. Till next time my friends—be kind to all you meet and have a smile for all you greet.

Tuesday, April 7, 2015

Tonight is investigation night. I tried to sleep as late as I could in the hotel but I ended up getting up at 7:30am anyway. That's when my daughter usually gets up and the absolute latest I get up for work if I'm not going to the gym first. I took the opportunity to call and chat with Mama Bear and Beans before they started their day, and then I tried to get back to sleep but was unable to due to a faulty air conditioning unit in my hotel room. Even though the temperature wasn't very warm outside in Indiana, my room was too warm for me to sleep. I like cold rooms and warm blankets. I rang down to the front desk and asked for the maintenance man to come fix it … twice.

A fire alarm went off when I was in my room. Now kids, don't do this at home, or anywhere else, but when I'm in a hotel and the fire alarm goes off, I usually don't bother getting out of bed. It's not a very unique occasion. At least two or three times a year there is a fire alarm in the hotel. And if you go downstairs to ask if the hotel is indeed on fire, the hotel staff will make you go outside and wait for the fire truck just in case. You end up standing there like a child participating in a school fire drill, freezing your naughty bits off and praying for the infernal ringing and buzzing sounds to cease. And so, I just stayed in my room, looked out the window and stayed on the alert for the scent of smoke. After ten minutes, I got bored and wandered out into the hallway and met up with some members of the production crew for *Ghost Hunters* who were also buying time. No one went downstairs to the desk. We all know better.

There was, however, one time and only one time, in all my years of traveling and listening to hotel fire alarms scream through the night like the banshees of Ireland, the hotel was indeed on fire. The incident occurred a great many moons ago, so many now that it seems like another lifetime. It had to be season two or three of the show, which places it back about eight years, and we were filming at the Crescent Park Hotel in Arkansas. It was a great hotel and a wonderful investigation. Afterward, I was in my room enjoying cartoons and cereal, which makes me think it was a Saturday morning, and I heard the sound of my buddy Sully who did audio for the show yelling my name. I went to the door and there he was, beer in hand, telling me the building was on fire. I thanked him kindly and was about to write it off as him just having a laugh at my expense when I saw the lights of the fire trucks pulling up through the great windows of my room. It truly was a grand room; I recall it had a big four-post bed that rose high up in the air like the firm hindquarters of a well-proportioned lady.

It just so happened that the lovely Crescent Park Hotel and its big bottomed beds were hit by lighting that night, or more accurately, the rear portion of the roof was hit. I'm not sure if I was thinking clearly at the time due to a cereal sugar high or because I was exhausted but I left my room and made my way to the parking lot where a local newspaper was taking photos, and there I was wearing my shorts but no shirt and holding my trademark upside-down visor in my hand. And that was the only time any hotel I have stayed in was actually on fire.

Time to head to tonight's investigation. Tonight it's the Old Lake County Jail, which housed such notorious bad guys like John Dillinger. I think it'll be a good. Most old prisons and such are good for paranormal activity. I don't think Johnny D is there, though. I'm not sure where he's haunting these days but I'm starting to wonder if he is hanging out with the hotel maintenance man that never showed. Come to think of it, maybe it was he that pulled the fire alarm earlier today. That scoundrel.

Wednesday, April 8, 2015

Yesterday's investigation was a lot of fun. It was nice to get back in the saddle again and do some paranormal research. I'm short on time today, as I have to pack up my hotel room so that I can leave right from tonight's investigation and get to the airport in Chicago for 4am and catch my flight at 6am. Then I'll change planes in Philadelphia and get back to Rhode Island in time to go to work for the day. So, unless I can get a little sleep on the plane, it looks like I'm staring down a thirty-plus hour day. Dear Lord, give me strength.

Thursday, April 9, 2015

I'm sitting blurry-eyed in aisle seat C27 aboard U.S. Airways Flight 4617 taking me from Philly to Rhode Island. I didn't write aboard my flight from Chicago because … well, I barely remember that flight. I think I nodded off once or twice for twenty minutes or so. Once this flight lands, I'll go directly to work. I won't pass go. I won't collect $200.00, though I do hope this insanity pays off at some point. Oh well, at least the first episode of the season is in the can. Now I just have to do this a dozen more times. I can almost see my own words scrolling up through my eyes like the credits of some old movie from the 1940s.

"Stay focused."

"Life is a game of inches."

"Eyes on the horizon."

Friday, April 10, 2015

Well, I got nine hours of sleep last night after being up for 35 hours. I could have used a few more hours to be honest but I can make this work. Normally I only get six hours of rest anyway.

After work yesterday, I basically dumped out my suitcase into the laundry basket and loaded it up again as I have to go directly from work today up to Salem, Massachusetts, to do SalemCon. It's a first time convention that involves me being at a VIP party tonight, on the floor tomorrow morning meeting fans and friends, and then I'll do my lecture and finish it all up with an investigation which runs until midnight.

I'm looking forward to going up to Salem as it's one of my favorite places to visit. It isn't so much the history of witch persecution as I personally find the whole matter to be a bit sad knowing that these people were tortured and killed for nothing. Giles Corey, a man who was pressed to death during the famed witch trials, is a bit of a hero to me. I know I have mentioned before how his words "more weight" are somewhere etched on the backside of my heart. I truly feel I can carry the weight of the world and then some. There may be some signs of wear and tear starting to creep in along my edges but I'm not paying them any mind.

Anyhow, I must get going. I may have slept through the gym but I have to get to work!

Saturday, April 11, 2015

Just back from my dinner break up here in Salem. Many of my friends are up here, including Jeff Belanger and Cody DesBiens, and so we went to Salem Beer Works for dinner. (I also went there last night after sneaking out of the VIP party for a little bit.) I love Salem Beer Works! Not only do they have incredible blueberry ale that they serve with fresh blueberries in it but they also have delicious steak tips.

This morning went very well. I met a lot of people that had some really kind things to say about my motivational work. My new book *What's Next* outsold my paranormal books 2:1. I also debuted my new shirt that reads "Smile Damn It… It's Only Life After All" designed by my good friend Jeff Ouimette. The shirt has a skeleton key on it that works within the design of the word "smile". Shirt sales were good with the white version of the shirt outselling the black one, which is a big deal in the paranormal world as black shirts may be the glue that binds everyone together. You think I'm kidding but I'm not.

My whole mission is to change the world, and injecting a bit of happiness, light, sunshine, and white t-shirts into the paranormal community is a step in the right direction.

Well, my belly is full and I'm a happy boy. It's time to head over to my station for tonight's investigation. I'm going to a place called "Whynotts" that sells wands for witches and wizards. It's a cleverly designed Harry Potter themed place.

Wands at the ready!

Sunday, April 12, 2015

I was supposed to stay at the Hawthorne Hotel last night after finishing the investigation but after getting back from the investigation I realized I could pack up and get home just before 3am. I wasn't looking forward to the late night drive as I was still a bit tired after filming this week but I wanted to be home when my daughter woke up this morning. She had a dance competition yesterday, which I still feel bad that I was unable to attend. Mama Bear spent the better part of the day with her assisting with costume changes and makeup. (I still don't like that they wear makeup because I'm trying to keep my little girl little.)

Her dance troop did very well, winning two Gold level ribbons and one High Gold. She and her group were also invited to perform locally at the theater in Twin River Casino. She was very excited to show me her ribbons and tell me about it this morning and I was excited to hear it even though it was at 7am. Luckily she allowed for me to go back to sleep afterward. I crashed until high noon and then made pancakes for the little one and me. We then spent the next three hours playing video games in the basement playroom. Mama Bear was a bit sick and slept on the couch. I made her some soup and more pancakes for Beans before retreating upstairs to watch the NASCAR race from last night, and catch up on some things for work.

I'm still a bit worn out from the week, but I'm hopeful that hitting the gym in the morning will get me back on the right track.

I apologize that these last few days have been mere recaps without much further insight, but I have been exhausted. Maybe that is the insight: exhaustion will clog up your brain and choke your creativity, eventually leaving you wearing tissue boxes upon your feet and an open bathrobe whilst you stand there gazing in the mirror choking your chicken.

Monday, April 13, 2015

Deep thoughts today; too deep to handle now. I think I'll simply wade in the shallow end with the other kids and attempt to put it into words tomorrow.

Tuesday, April 14, 2015

All right, it's time to take the water wings off and just dive right in. By no means is this a pity party, as I don't allow for pity, and I'm not one for your typical party. But here you are, here I am, and someone told me that I should allow for others to see the man behind the curtain once in a while so they know he's real, that he breathes, that he bleeds.

Well, I need to be Superman for my daughter … or Batman—I'd rather be Batman. I favor Bruce Wayne over Clark Kent because I fancy a good vengeance story, plus he has such wonderful toys. Anyhow, I like to be Batman for my daughter as I want to always be her infallible and invincible superhero but in the end I'm just a man. And that is actually what is troubling me. I've been working like a dog lately and a quick glance at my calendar and my contract shows it's just the beginning. I'm not complaining. I'm thankful. I'm blessed. But man, I feel awful. Not just tired, though I am tired, too. It's more of a scheduling issue between things I want to do and things I have to do. Life is like that, though, for all of us.

There's a great prophet that I have had the pleasure to know in this life, my dear Uncle Bub. I lived with him for the summer of my senior year of high school whilst my parents were rebuilding the second floor of our home. He and I had great conversations late at night as we listened to The Beatles, Bob Dylan and Willie Nelson. We often discussed living life in shades of gray. Not quite conforming to what is necessary, not quite doing whatever you want to do either but existing somewhere in between. That's the dream.

Right now, I'm once again back to doing what I know how to do best—work my sweet, firm, round apple of a hiney off because that's what I have to do. What I want to do is hang out with my daughter every day and go on family vacations to tropical beaches and amusement park resorts all across America. What I need to do is find that gray area.

Sadly, right now all I can do is what I have to do. There is no shame in hard honest work, and I'm proud to do so. But I'm also very troubled as I'm missing things my wife and daughter are doing together that I simply cannot be a part of due to my work schedule.

Little Beans is quite the talented and dedicated dancer. I'm thankful she's healthy, strong, smart, kind, and beautiful. (I'm proud. I know.) I'm glad that Mama Bear takes the time to bring her to all of her practice sessions, her competitions, and her recitals. I do my best to get to as many of these things as I can, yet with my day job, filming, and my weekend events, I barely have time to attend any of her competitions which I know mean a lot to her and it would be nice to be there to see them and spend time with her and my wife.

I make it a point to not take any bookings on the day of her dance company recital as it's a great moment for her and I love to be there to share in it with her. I usually sit there with tears in my eyes and I don't care who knows it. Yet even missing the regular competitions is difficult for me. Not being home for dinner together at night wears on me. The loneliness of the hotels and life on the road, though familiar to me, and at times very strangely comforting, is tiring.

Despite all that, I do I feel it is never enough. I feel like I'm never a good enough son to my aging parents as I'm not able to visit them often. I feel as if I'm not a good enough husband as I'm not home with my wife often. I feel like I'm never a good enough father because I miss dance competitions and various activities. That last one really cuts me to the bone. I often feel like I have the weight of the world on my shoulders and the only thing I can do is soldier on as I always have. Work all day. Work all night. Send the paycheck home to pay for the house. Pay for the trucks. Pay for the dance lessons. Pay with my lifeblood.

Trust me, I know there are worst ways to make a living and that there are people with things far worse than I have them, but we all have our struggles. The loss of a toy to a small child is no less important than the loss of a crown to a king. In this life, I'll forever be the small child. I don't even want to be a king. For kings are snooty, old and tired of spirit, and that's something I can never be.

I must be careful to guard my thoughts. That's why I don't let others see behind the curtain very often. It isn't due to some plastic bravado and macho nonsense; it's for my own survival. For you see my friends, it's true the tongue is the rudder for the soul. How you talk about your life, how you see yourself in it comes to shape you and your future. Can a man change his stars? Yes; quite easily, all too easily actually. Most often people change their lives for the worse as they wallow in darkness and misery like a pig delights in rolling in its own filth.

Though it's important to be aware of one's own shortcomings and serious issues so that you can take ownership of them and thus defeat your inner demons, it's quite another thing to constantly bellow your misery and sadness out to those around you like a the town crier of colonial times.

Talking about winning the lottery isn't going to ensure you'll win but talking about how sad and miserable you are will in fact make you sad and miserable. You can bet on that. So when things are tough, and they often are, I take it in stride. I put a smile on my face in pure defiance of the darkness. It's not a fake smile, for I truly have a lot to smile about. We all do. Make an honest and serious list of your haves and your have-nots. You'll soon see that you have more than you thought. God provides for even the birds and the insects, so of course He provides for us.

I know there are going to be missed dance recitals. There are lonely hotel rooms waiting for me to unpack and pack and unpack once again.

The long black road is out there, my familiar mistress, waiting to take me far and away from my family time and time again. I'll travel it. I'll dance with her. I'll do what needs to be done; for I know that when I'm finished there will times of great merriment with my family.

I'm sorry, dear uncle Bub. It appears I'm failing in living in shades of gray. It seems that I spend weeks upon weeks in the black. Then I get to spend some cherished time in the white. I suppose if you mix it all together, maybe I'm doing all right after all. Still, the struggle is real but through struggle comes strength and growth. When all is done, I'm going to be one big and strong bastard with shades of gray in my hair.

Wednesday, April 15, 2015

Happy tax day, America! I celebrated the only way I know how. I listened to The Beatles sing "Tax Man" and I went to the post office to send out my tax payment at the last minute possible. To quote a true lyrical master, Lyrics Born, "This is fiscal harassment! They keep touching my assets!" A pun well done.

I don't know what's going on but I'm beyond tired. Thinking of turning in early. Rest well my friends, and if you die, do as The Beatles suggest and "declare the pennies on your eyes."

Thursday, April 16, 2015

Wow! I was more tired than I thought. I slept over eleven hours. Sadly this means I missed out on the gym this morning but I feel great. It looks like I have a busy day on tap. Time to get to it! "What do you think I do, write letters all day?" – Steve Martin in *The Jerk*.

I left work early today so I could watch Beans perform in reading theater at school. Reading theater is a small group of children who perform a dramatic rendition of short plays while on stage. It's designed for children to work on voice projection and conveying emotion through inflection and gestures. I was so proud of our little Beans today. I met Mama Bear there and together we sat in the front row and watched as Beans read her parts with pride, and in true Beans fashion, gave a wonderfully dramatic bow when she was done.

Just a few days ago, I was writing about how difficult it is for me when I have to miss these types of things, so I was very happy to be able to share this moment today. After the production was over, I spoke with the two teachers who oversee the activity and they both said acting comes naturally for Beans, she's a good reader, and a talented girl. Mama Bear and I are so very proud of her. I joke that she takes after my wife, as Mama Bear is very quiet and barely talks, while yours truly … well, you know.

Random middle of the night thought: what if crop circles were just graffiti being done by teenage alien pranksters treating mother earth like the walls beneath a highway overpass?

Friday, April 17, 2015

There are few things more relaxing than getting home early from work on a Friday, popping the top off of a cold Miller High Life, and watching NASCAR qualifying. Well deserved, I think. This weekend should be a good one. I have to get a lot done, as I won't have many weekends home in the near future. I have to do oil changes, get vehicles inspected, and rake the dead grass out of the lawn, plant grass seed, and fertilize said grass seed. I purchased all of the seed and such today on my way home from work. I'll go tomorrow to get oil and filters and the like. I don't mind doing that type of work; I actually find it rather peaceful.

Mama Bear and Beans are out on a play date so I'm home alone with the cats. My daughter's four stinky, smelly cats. Luckily I love her, and so I tolerate these furry little monsters. I'm rather fond of them, actually. Each one has its own personality, its likes and dislikes. They're okay, but I like to play like I don't like the smelly little furry bastards.

Hey look, my beer is empty. We can't have that. Waitress! A refill please. Oh, that's right, I'm the waitress. I hope I'm also a good tipper.

Saturday, April 18, 2015

I underestimated the leaves. Serves me right. I once wrote a poem called "My Father Versus The Leaves" back when I was in high school and fancied myself a poet. It basically speaks to him raking and cursing and dying, whilst the leaves pile up upon his grave.

And so, as I struck out to seed and fertilize the lawn today I was met with piles of leaves that were hidden by the winter snow. I raked up four large lawn bags full of the crispy little bastards but many more remain. This was my first day of spring; a day when the weather was nice and I was home with time enough to enjoy it and get some things done. Not all can be done in a day anyhow. I was able to get Maggie May my Big Blue Baby inspected.

I also took my 1990 Daytona, Angel, in to get her inspection sticker. I'm still going to sell that car but man it is fun to drive. I tried to sell it before the winter came in last year but it rolled in fast, the snow was relentless, and so my little Angel sat in the driveway and waited for everything to melt and for the birds to sing.

I also did oil changes for Mama Bear's Durango and my old pickup truck Angelina. I enjoy doing oil changes. I find the whole task soothing. It's a simple thing to do and is quite practical. There is a reason that Angelina has over 270,000 miles on her- I take care of her.

Of course, you can't spend all day doing chores, tasks, yard work, and vehicle maintenance. One must have a little bit of fun. I took Mama Bear and Beans to the movies to see the Disney nature film, *Monkey Kingdom.* It was very enjoyable. Disney has a knack for storytelling and we all learned a lot about the hierarchy of the groups in which monkeys live. It was very interesting to see how they treat each other and mistreat each other. Perhaps we aren't that evolved after all?

Back home Mama Bear and I spent some time outside and I daresay it appears Beans nailed riding her bicycle without training wheels! We're all proud. She already started asking me what time we can get up and go out bike riding tomorrow morning. Something tells me I better get my rest.

Sunday, April 19, 2015

As expected, Beans woke me at 7:30 this morning and asked to go bike riding. She ended up falling asleep in bed with Mama Bear and me last night when we were watching the third *Night At The Museum* movie. We have enjoyed that series quite a bit but I think my little daredevil wore herself out yesterday racing her bike down the street and down our driveway hill.

I was able to calm her down long enough to have breakfast and get off to church. She stayed home with Mama Bear this week. I never force either of them to go to church. When they want to come along, I'm happy to have them there with me. I believe you're to show the Gospel to people, not shove it down their throats.

Right after church, I found myself running up and down the street trying to keep up with my daughter and her bicycle as she was racing back and forth, back and forth. I do go to the gym every day but I'm not a runner by any stretch of the imagination. However, I'd run to hell and back if that's what my daughter needed me to do. Luckily for me today's task wasn't to hell and back. I may want to rethink my cardio routine though for it seems that this will be a new thing I am required to do. Being her Dad is fun as it is constantly challenging me to adapt to new things.

Monday, April 20, 2015

It's important that we forgive people in this life. I know a lot of people have a tough time with it and that's why I bring it up here. There's no one in my life that needs forgiving, at least not that I know of. If they do, then they are forgiven. Yes, it's that simple.

"Now listen here chipmunks to this advice...", said David Seville to Alvin and the Chipmunks.

If you want to go through this life with a smile on your face and a happy heart, you must forgive others. You have to do this for yourself more than you do for them. Hell, half the people that have wronged you probably don't remember doing it anyway, if they ever did at all.

There's an old Buddhist proverb. At least I think it's Buddhist. If not, now it is. Anyhow, there's a little story about two monks, one old and one young. The old monk and the young monk wander as monks do between the time they take to meditate in the garden and make pretzels. (Side note: I wanted to be a monk at one point in my life in order to do those things, but then I learned they don't exactly make pretzels and there would be no intimate encounters with the ladies—not even holidays. The deal was off.)

So the monks came across a woman at a river who asked them to carry her across. The old monk obliged and the lady took her leave. Hours later, the monks settled down for meditation, or pretzel making, depending on your version of the story and your understanding of monks. One thing was for certain, they were definitely not making sweet love to the ladies. The young monk then told the old monk that he couldn't believe how rude the lady was, for she did not thank him for carrying her across the river. The old monk informed the young monk that he carried her across the river and was done with her, whereas the young monk had been carrying her ever since they departed.

It's not a mind-blowing concept, but its simplicity is where its beauty dwells. Those who don't do right by us must be let go so that we can move on with our lives. It's easier to move forward when you are not looking backward.

I know that there are those in each of our lives that do some truly horrible and despicable acts. Very few of us, if any, get through this life unscathed. I get it. It sucks. Some people are not deserving of forgiveness. But the forgiveness isn't for them. You don't even need to call them up and tell them that all is forgiven. As I said, many who have wronged us aren't even aware of their misdeeds. You just need to look inside yourself and pour out that bottle of poison you have carried for so long within yourself. Life is too short to spend it carrying the burden of hatred, anger and resentment. Don't allow those who have hurt you to do it again. That is just foolish. Forgive, yes. Forget? Only as it pertains to allowing yourself to move forward. Don't permit it to be a recurring act.

Remember my friends; you are not a slave to your yesterday. A victim once does not mean a victim for life. Your scars are just proof that you are one tough sum'bitch and that you are a survivor. So be a survivor. Stand up. Dust yourself off. Rip off that label placed upon you and crush it beneath your feet as you walk bravely forward with your eyes on the horizon.

Tuesday, April 21, 2015

My new shirts came in! Huzzah!

I closed my last literary misadventure *What's Next* with the phrase "Smile, damn it. It's only life, after all." It's a phrase I've used for quite some time and one that I truly believe. It seems my little turn of phrase has resonated with the masses, and by "the masses" I mean the good people who have read my last book. As the new season of doing events and such has started to take shape I decided to change up my merchandise offerings and thus I had a few boxes of these shirts printed up in various colors.

I had some of these shirts at my last event up in Salem a few weekends ago but I only offered them in black and white at the time. I wanted to amp it up a bit and flood the world with happy nonsense, hence my new shirts in a rainbow of colors from hot pink to neon orange. If you are going to smile big and bright, your shirt should echo that sentiment.

Wednesday, April 22, 2015

Stay the course. Stay the course. Stay the course.

I keep telling myself to stay the course, as I fear my mind is letting big picture fears seep into my mental landscape. Things have not been easy financially as of late. Coming out of my slow season (December through March) is always a bit difficult. Events and things start to pick up for me in April and then by October all is well again.

Getting by is an issue for me as well my friends. Just because some of you may have seen me on television doing paranormal investigations with *Ghost Hunters* or sipping lattes for Dunkin Donuts does not mean I swim through my bank vault like Scrooge McDuck, but Lord knows I wouldn't mind the opportunity. I don't need to be rich per say, but knowing that the monthly overhead is always taken care of and I can get a pizza whenever I want a pizza, which is often because I really like pizza, would be nice.

Alas, I'm thankful for all the opportunities that I have been given and so I don't mind doing it all, but damn, it would be nice if it were just a tad bit easier. Bah! Humbug! Things aren't meant to be easy. Easy does not inspire growth. Growth only comes through pain and struggle. I must be due for a growth spurt.

I'll be driving down to do an event in Pennsylvania for my buddy Marc Tetlow on Friday. The event is at Pennhurst, a group of old buildings that once served as an asylum and such. I get foggy on what is what as for the better part of ten years now I have been walking around old castles, jails, school houses, mansions, hospitals, and asylums in over twenty-some-odd countries. At some point, it all blends together like the mocha and coconut flavor syrup in my delicious Dunkin Donuts iced latte.

Anyhow, I'll drive down in a rental car right after work on Friday and return home in the same rental car on Sunday. I'll try and soak up some family time on Sunday evening before unpacking my bags and re-packing my bags, as I'll then go to work on Monday morning and fly out to film for the television show after work.

My sleepy brain started to worry about what money is coming in, what money is going out, when I'm coming in, when I'm going out, and when I'll have time to be with my family and perhaps enjoy a short walk in the warm spring air with a cold hard cider.

Silly brain. Focus upon loftier things not of this world. Family is fine. The rest is just material world necessities that mean very little. As for the work schedule, I'm a juggernaut. Eyes on the horizon, shoulders squared, and ready to carry whatever burden necessary for those I love; feet firmly planted on the ground, head softly dreaming in the clouds. There is simply no stopping me because I'll never give up.

Thursday, April 23, 2015

It was a very busy day today. Work was chaotic but I handled it well as I keep my ducks in a row. That's a lie. I don't have any ducks. I did a have a turtle once, but he didn't wander around very quickly, or much at all.

Friday, April 24, 2015

No time to chat, for like the White Rabbit in *Alice In Wonderland*, I'm late. I'm just getting out of work and I must get to pick up the rental car and Miss Kris Williams, a fellow *Ghost Hunters* and *Ghost Hunters International* alumni. She's driving down from New Hampshire to meet me. I'll safely shepherd us down to Pennsylvania for tomorrow's event at Pennhurst.

I hope she likes my eclectic mix of music, as I abide by the old *Supernatural* road trip adage of, "Driver picks the music, shotgun shuts his cakehole." Personally I like to say pie-hole.

Dang it! Now I want pie.

You'll be glad to know our last stop before the hotel was a gas station that had mini pies on sale. Two for three dollars! I bought two coconut cream pies, which I'm now enjoying from the comfort of my hotel room. Sweet dreams!

Saturday, April 25, 2015

Over two hundred people came to the event tonight. I met many new friends and spent some time with some old ones as well. We just finished up the meet and greet and the question and answer panel. My new t-shirts sold like hotcakes, which coincidentally is what I had for breakfast. (McDonald's. of course.)

It appears *What's Next* is really coming into its own as well. A lot of people picked up their own autographed copy tonight and even more came through with kind words about it after already reading it. I do hope this literary misadventure does as well and helps a lot of people.

Time to head off to the investigation after a quick stop at the Wawa gas station to fuel up my belly with a BLT and crispy chicken sandwich.

I'm Ziggy Piggy!

Sunday, April 26, 2105

It was a pleasant ride back home from Pennsylvania today. Miss Kris Williams seemed to enjoy my music and apparently my driving doesn't scare her like it does my little wife. I knew I wasn't a bad driver. I may drive a little on the quick side and I handle the car like I'm finishing the Daytona 500 but I'm a very responsible wheelman.

Speaking of NASCAR, I watched the race my wife recorded for me after I took Mama Bear and Beans to dinner. My favorite driver Kurt Busch won the race in Richmond, Virginia! Huzzah!

Monday, April 27, 2015

Worried man
Papa is a worried man
There is no way that I can see
That I can feed my family
I don't own a money tree
I don't own no land
– "I'm a Worried Man" written by Johnny Cash

Mr. Willie Nelson is playing that song as he occupies the elite suite betwixt my ears on this flight. I'm in seat 21E aboard Delta flight 1409, which is carrying me from Rhode Island to Detroit, Michigan. This is an exit row seat with plenty of leg room. I'm changing planes in Detroit on my way to Cleveland, Ohio. I don't recall ever being to Cleveland before but that doesn't mean I haven't yet. I sometimes recall being places I've never visited except for perhaps on a dreamer's holiday. I'm lucky I even know where I'm half the time, for I'm well known to take mental leaves and flights of fancy.

This flight isn't fancy but the Asian businessman next to me is dressed quite fancily in his pinstriped suit and shiny shoes. He's visiting the Land of Nod and perhaps chasing unicorns or sailing the seas of root beer in his own dreams. I'm wearing an Iron Man t-shirt, ripped up blue jeans, and I'm wide awake, sitting here in the exit row, occasionally looking at the clouds on the wing and occasionally typing this here literary misadventure.

The flight attendant looks like a corporate version of my good friend and Detroit native, Mr. John E.L. Tenney. John and I have some events coming up this year. I look forward to reuniting with him. He's one of the few people who seem to think like I do. Or perhaps I think like he does. No. No, that's impossible. John is crazy whereas I'm just another guy on the lost highway.

This little trip should start out promising, turn interesting, and leave me exhausted. This will be the second episode that we have filmed for the eleventh season of *Ghost Hunters*. I don't know what episode it'll be when they air it, as they do things in any order they decide. They haven't decided to even air the ones I filmed last year but I'm sure they'll come soon.

I just finished up my hot dogs from the Coney Island Express in the Detroit airport and now I'm aboard Delta flight 5181, which will bring me to Cleveland. I'm squeezed into window seat 6A and typing on my Mac like a Tyrannosaurus Rex if a Tyrannosaurus Rex decided to type. I wonder what story matter a Tyrannosaurus Rex would write about? Probably not a book about building killer biceps.

Most times I enjoy being just over 6'1" but not when I'm on a little plane with hardly any room. The guy near me is also very well dressed, just like the gentleman from the orient on my previous flight. This guy is your generic old white guy, except he's wearing opal cuff links. I complimented him on them. He dismissed me with a terse thank you. I suppose well-dressed guys don't care what guys in jeans and an Iron Man t-shirt think about their cuff links.

Oh well, I shall land soon enough as this is a short flight of just about thirty minutes. Good thing, too, as I have also finished eating my in-flight gummy bears and my Oreos.

I do like to eat.

Tuesday, April 28, 2015

Tonight I'll investigate the old Midwestern Railway Preservation Society B & O roundhouse and a few passenger cars that they have restored there. Should be a good time. I love trains. There is a certain nostalgic romance to them. I often feel that I long for the 1940s, which is interesting as I was not alive until 1977, at least in this form. But I love music from that era, railway travel, and war stories.

I've traveled on trains a few times here in the United States but never a great distance—mostly from Rhode Island to New York and back for filming and events. I did travel in Europe on them quite often. I recall a very early morning train ride to Venice that took three hours or more but I figured I would never be a mere three hour train ride from Venice so I might as well make the most of it.

When it comes to trains, some men like the engines, other the passenger cars, but me? I'm a caboose man. I like my trains like I like my women, with a strong caboose.

Wednesday, April 29, 2015

I didn't get back to the hotel until 4am this morning. It was a long evening but a lot of fun. Walking around the old train yard with the moonlight reflecting off of the old engines and passenger cars was really a pleasant experience. I felt a bit closer to all those old hobos and Mr. Bob Dylan who once sang about all those old hobos. I think I could have spent some time riding the rails back in the day.

Ah well, 'twas is another lifetime or a dream I once had I suppose; for now I must focus upon this lifetime and what is here and now.

Good morning, America. How are you?
Don't you know me? I'm your native son.

—"City of New Orleans" by Arlo Guthrie

Time to go to work as tonight I'll be investigating the old Gray's Armory just around the corner from the Cleveland Indians baseball stadium.

Thursday, April 30, 2015

High above the clouds on U.S. Airways flight 824 in aisle seat 19C as it brings me from Cleveland to Philadelphia. Once again, it appears my knowledge of the Philly airport will be quite handy as the turnaround time betwixt flights is tighter than a hot dog in a bun.

There's a lot going on in my sleepy head today. The old elite suite between my ears is a mess. It appears that Jinglebottom and the elves in there had a grand party last night at Jolly Good Times. The floors are sticky and I can't be sure, but I think they somehow got a cat. It's just too much to make heads or tails of at this moment.

I made it back to the hotel for 2am last night which allowed for three hours of sleep before heading to the airport to start this two flight trip back to my day job and then home to Mama Bear and Beans.

I'll try and write more on the next flight. I need to get at least thirty minutes more of sleep. Hopefully Jinglebottom can rouse the rest of the elven brood and clean up my mind before it's go time.

I felt like I just closed my eyelids when the tires of that last flight screeched down on the ground in Philly. A quick ten-minute walk to familiar gate C22 brought me to U.S. Airways flight 4617. Sadly there was no time to stop at the good ole Chick-fil-A or the little Asian sushi bar that makes those great mojitos but there will be other times for that I'm sure, as long as the good Lord permits and I keep getting booked on flights through Philadelphia.

I'm perched up in aisle seat 4D and wide-awake. It appears that my elf-in-charge, Mr. Jasper P. Jinglebottom, has managed to get the pirate-themed bar in my mind cleaned up. He even did some work down along the banks of the egg nog river. The place looks nice; almost respectable. A little warm tomato juice has satiated my in-flight vampire and I'm good to go for the day, which is a good thing as it's straight to work when this bird touches down in Warwick, Rhode Island.

Friday, May 1, 2015

I slept about eleven hours last night. Talk about awaking feeling refreshed. I don't think I realize the wear and tear I'm putting on this body of mine. I feel good for the most part. I get a little pain on the left side of my chest from time to time, but I think it's more muscular; perhaps an intercostal muscle—between the ribs—than its cardiac muscle. Either way,

I'm not going to worry about it. I don't worry about things.

I think I look healthy. There was a photo taken of me at the last investigation and I have to say, I was rather proud of the way I looked. My body looks strong and my face looks peaceful. I think that sums me up.

Saturday, May 2, 2015

With limited weekends available to me this year, I have to make the most of them in terms of vehicle, home and yard maintenance, as well as family time. Today was going to be a busy day; I knew it from the start. The highlight of which was going to be seeing Beans perform with her dance troupe at the East Providence High school. I normally don't get to see her dance competitions and so I had asked my manager to cancel my appearance at tonight's Houghton Mansion event in Adams, Massachusetts, so that I could see my little one perform. I have only cancelled an appearance once before and it was for the same reason. I try not to take a booking on a day I plan to see my little girl perform, but sometimes dates change on her end or on my end, and these things happen. Marc and I extended free tickets to those who were planning on coming out tonight to another event we are doing later in the year.

Anyhow, back to my day. I wanted to take my '99 Mazda pickup, ole Angelina, up to get her inspection sticker done this morning but I ate cereal and sat on the couch with my daughter instead. Then she and Mama Bear went to her musical theater rehearsal and so I hit the gym and then came back and took care of the yard. I experience moments of Zen when I simply wander around my property picking up sticks and branches and move them into the woods. I saddled up my ride-on lawn mower for the first time this season. Thankfully she started right up. I listened to Elvis and enjoyed a nice cold beer whilst giving the grass its first trim of the year.

I raked everything up and was preparing to drop some grass seed and fertilizer when I received a text from Mama Bear saying that today's dance competition was moving along quicker than usual and so I better get down to the location if I wanted to see our little girl on stage. I drove Maggie May, my Big Blue Baby, and due to a slip in time, I had to push my new girl to speeds with which I have not yet tested her. Thankfully that new Hemi engine did not disappoint.

I watched Beans up there on stage as I sat in the audience trying not to cry. Neither of her performances was sad by nature, but I just get all proud and choked up seeing her up there. She's only seven-years-old still, yet she does her performance in front of everyone, fearlessly jumping and flipping through the air. She's simply an inspiration to watch. I also enjoyed watching Mama Bear watch her. It was nice to see her excited as well since she puts so much time in with her at practices and such.

Beanser's troupe won three trophies and a special judge's ribbon. She went to the front of the stage to get one of the awards and once again I felt that familiar lump in my throat as I tried to hold back tears. I'm a pretty tough guy. I have never been one for all that alpha male, dominant monkey nonsense. I don't think that sort of false bravado proves anything. But I'm physically "strong like bull" and I can take a ton of pain, of the mental, emotional and physical variety without even a groan. Yet my heart melts with everything that little girl of mine does. I just can't help it.

She has another dance competition tomorrow as well. Between my work schedule and her dance schedule it's looking like a rough couple of weeks for us both.

I think I'm going to keep my writing and all other extraneous things to a minimum this week and spend as much time with her as I can. If the following week's entries are curt, you will know why.

Sunday, May 3, 2015

I look around and I see little monkey men in their little monkey suits trying to drive a flashier car, have a fancier watch, and build a bigger sandcastle than all the other monkey men in the sandbox. Many of them climb over one another, step upon one another, and even kill one another merely to advance their perceived position and have the shiniest rocks or the biggest banana.

At what point will we all realize that the things we are told are of value in this material world, with its plastic people and their plastic opinions, mean very little?

I know do what we must do to get by in this world. We have to play the game. We have to go around the board again and again, pass go and collect our $200, which doesn't go as far as it once did, but this human experience is about so much more than that. The things you own end up owning you, my friends. You are meant to use the machines, not the other way around. What is truly important never comes with a price tag. Things are only as valuable as you perceive them to be. Sundials tell time, as do high priced wristwatches. Economical cars get you from point A to point B, as does an exotic sports car. You can work your whole life trying to buy enjoyment, or you can simply enjoy life.

Me? I enjoy walks with the ones I love in fields of bright yellow flowers. I long to someday be sitting by a lazy river in the South, sipping a mojito and listening to a band play New Orleans jazz just off in the distance beneath an ivy covered gazebo.

You can keep you Lamborghinis. I'll keep my dreams.

Monday, May 4, 2015

If I hear one more person say, "May the fourth be with you," today…

Tuesday, May 5, 2015

Pretty sure I was the only guy working out with Christmas carols playing through his earbuds this morning. I can't help it. I'm festive. Even if it's Cinco de Mayo, I'm celebrating with Christmas music. My only wish is that I had a mug of eggnog to hoist up in a festive toast.

Wednesday, May 6, 2015

Having a tough time not thinking about the workweeks that lay ahead. Yes, weeks—plural—as there's no break in them until the end of the month. Stay in school, kids. Oh wait, I stayed in school and I still have to do all this stuff. Hmm… be an astronaut, kids. Come to think of it, I wonder how astronauts get paid? Do they receive a stipend whilst in training? Do spacewalks pay more than mere moon missions? Are their bonus incentives? Alien hush money? Astronaut ice cream sponsorships? If I ever meet an astronaut I hope he or she is ready for some questions. In the meantime I'm having Jinglebottom place "Astronaut Ice Cream" on the yellow sticky note shopping list in my mind. This must be purchased soon.

Thursday, May 7, 2015

Nothing but commercial jingles from my youth have been in my head today. I will do you the favor of not putting them in yours.

Friday, May 8, 2015

Beans had a pajama party at her dance studio tonight and so Mama Bear and I went out to dinner whilst waiting for her. Beans had a great time and came home with a tie-dyed shirt she made. Mama Bear and I came home with our bellies full of steak.

Saturday, May 9, 2015

Hallelujah! I took ole Angelina to get her inspection sticker this morning and the ole gal passed the test! I was quite proud of her. There aren't many sixteen-year-old pickup trucks that can still coast through inspection without backing out of the garage in shame; the "failed" sticker on their windshield like a scarlet letter.

Together the ole gal and I bounced around the back roads near my home as we ran errands. We stopped at the graveyard so I could take a little stroll and she could idle her engine for a bit. I do enjoy my walks through the cemetery so very much.

I had a lot of things to do this day since I'll be gone pretty much from Monday the 11th until Saturday the 30th of this month. Luckily Beans had dance practice and musical theater, so that meant her and Mama Bear were out of the house for most of the day, which allowed me to do all I needed to without feeling guilty for not spending time with them.

I handled all of the yard work; cutting the grass, planting more seed, covering it, fertilizing it, and watering it. Then I took to getting the laundry started and washing down Maggie May in the driveway. Both trucks were a bit dirty and needed a good bath. Beans came home in time to help me wash Angelina and my 90 Daytona ES called Angel. She's on her way to my parents' home tomorrow so my father can see to selling her. As much as I love Angel, I simply have no time to drive her. I tried to sell her in the short few weeks before the winter hit but I simply ran out of time. I hate to see her go, but I don't want her to rot away in my driveway either. Looks like we will have one last ride together.

I finished the day by playing video games with Beans on the couch in the playroom. Mario's Super Sluggers was the game of choice. We had some epic baseball battles tonight. She's quite the challenger. I don't have to let her win, rather I have to play my best to try and mount a victory for myself and Waluigi. Mama Bear hates that we play video games but I think she misses the amount of bonding that we do. It isn't about the games themselves; it's about the time we spend together—the laughs, the jokes, and the teamwork when we play a cooperative game. We have a great time. I started her on video games just before she turned three. She played Mappy and Pac-Man on a simple plug-and-play system. These are some of my favorite memories.

Sunday, May 10, 2015

Happy Mother's Day! Beans made breakfast in bed for Mama Bear today. She wouldn't even let me come downstairs to help. She made a toasted bagel with butter, a bowl of cereal and iced coffee. She didn't notice that the coffee pot wasn't plugged in, so she thought it was broken. She improvised though and made it by simply pouring the coffee grounds into a plastic tumbler and mixing it back and forth with milk, water and sugar. It's the thought that counts. Mama Bear didn't try it. I took a sip out of sheer curiosity. It had a watery granola texture to it. God bless our little girl. We went as a family to visit my parents and then off to have some pizza before returning home to clean up the flowerbed, as this is what Mama Bear wanted for Mother's Day. Twelve large bags of yard waste and numerous bug bites later, I quickly informed Mama Bear and Beans that for Father's Day, I'd just like to sleep … and maybe some of Beanser's homemade iced coffee.

Monday, May 11, 2015

US Airways flight 5174 is presently carrying me from Providence to Charlotte, North Carolina. I'm in aisle seat 20D as Mr. Elvis Presley is singing "Promised Land" in the elite suite betwixt my ears. The King is in good form today. He sounds strong and full of moxie.

I too feel strong and full of moxie, which is a very good thing as today starts my nineteen-day work marathon! Yesterday was my last day off until May 30th. As Yosemite Sam, the world's roughest toughest bad man who ever crossed the Rio Grande, once said, "Yah, mule! Yah! Yah!". Of course, he was riding a camel at the time, but still, the sentiment rings true.

This little flight is just the first of the day, as I'll be changing planes in Charlotte and then heading to Detroit. We are filming there and nearby Ohio for the *Ghost Hunters* show. I'll film tonight and tomorrow in Detroit and then Wednesday night at the other location. I'll film all night on Wednesday, well into Thursday morning, before returning to the airport in Cleveland and flying back to work for 9am. I'll work at the clinic all day on little to no sleep, go home, pass out, get up early on Friday, and drive back to the airport to catch a plane headed to Ohio once again—this time for an Ideal Event for Marc Tetlow.

Why not just stay in Ohio? Why fly in and out of the same airport in less than 24 hours? Good questions.

I have to put in time at the day job, as I cannot simply abandon my office. Working for MSL Facial & Oral Surgery has been very good to me for the past fifteen years and I can't simply check out now. Living the dream, but dreaming very little.

May all your dreams be wet ones, my friends (I'm sorry for that line but it had to be said as I actually say it quite a bit). Speaking of sleep, I barely slept last night. I was so itchy from the bug bites I received as my reward for cleaning the flowerbed that I simply could not rest without scratching. I usually don't sleep well on any night before I have to fly out but that wasn't much of a bother to me this time, as I knew I was going to the gym and to work before my flights today. It's only those early morning flights that interrupt my peaceful slumber.

Ahh, the King has gone on to sing his version of Mr. Bob Dylan's "Don't Think Twice, It's All Right". He is doing the extended version, too.

Over twelve minutes of Elvis singing Zimmerman's lyrics in escalating and descending tones of pure vocal honey. It doesn't get much better than that.

The lyrics seem vaguely fitting as well:

I'm heading down that long lonesome road, girl,
Where I'm bound, I can't tell.
Goodbye is too good a word, girl,
I'll just say fare thee well.

When the rooster crows at the break of dawn,
Look out your window, baby,
I'll be gone.

The captain turned on the seatbelt sign and the flight attendant is preparing the cabin for landing. I suppose I should prepare myself as well.

Till the next flight my friends, don't think twice, it's all right.

On board US Airways flight 2067 headed to Detroit two hours late. I boarded the plane on time and slipped my little caboose into window seat 10F that happens to be the exit row with the extended leg room as there is no seat in front of it. None of this was by accident, my friends. I urge you all to check in 24 hours before and select the best seat available.

I was a little concerned at first when the gentleman sat down next to me in10E as he smelled quite reminiscent of my cats' litter box. I mean, I miss the furry little bastards when I'm away, but not that much. I was relieved to find out he was in the wrong row and thus had to move. Whew. A literal breath of fresh air.

My sweet victory was short lived, however, when who should occupy 10D and E but a very young couple who was hopelessly in love and showed it by making out for the majority of the two hour delay I just spent seated on the Tarmac. Now don't get me wrong, boys and girls. I'm all for love. I don't even mind a well-done public display of affection. A grand sweeping gesture of passion and romance is the stuff that makes the world go 'round. Incessant pecking and suckling, however, grows to be quite annoying after the first few minutes. I comforted myself by thinking in the unlikely event of an emergency in the aircraft, I'd probably have not one, but two oxygen masks at my disposal as I envisioned the young lovers pulling off some Romeo and Juliet style crash position sharing one mask, leaving me with two oxygen masks whose bags may not appear to be fully inflated, but oxygen is flowing.

Whilst we are on the subject of unlikely events, if I was in such a situation where I was about to make a fiery exit from the heavens, I think I would prefer to have nitrous oxide flowing through the masks instead of oxygen. If not nitrous, could the oxygen at least be scented like coconut so I could possibly imagine I was nestled betwixt the tanned and firm bosom of an island girl who just finished making me coconut pies? It's not that much to ask for, is it?

Anyhow, here we are, up in the clouds once again and now I really want pie. I had to let the production company know that my flight was running behind. I was mostly concerned about dinner, truth be told. There are few things that cause me discomfort in this life, and not eating is one of the ones that top the list. I don't overindulge most of the time, especially on travel days, so every meal is important as I work long and hard. I've already been up since 6am, hit the gym, and went to work all on a protein bar and a beautifully crafted maple frosted donut. Since they are expecting me to go right from the airport to film the investigation that will run into the wee small hours of the morning, dinner cannot be overlooked. I kindly requested that a small cheese pizza be available for me when I get in so I won't be hungry all night. I do love a good pizza, just nothing too fancy. Cheese or pepperoni do me just fine, especially if it's made with the little pepperoni that curl up and trap their own oils in themselves. That's the good stuff right there.

I delivered pizza for a few years back when I was working my way through college. It was one of four or five jobs I had—yes, all at the same time. I loved the job itself. It was for a little place named Nino's in Cranston, Rhode Island. I drove my little 90' Mitsubishi Eclipse around listening to my music and eating all the mistakes that the kitchen made. The money was decent and it was actually rather fun. You never knew who was going to answer the door, or what they would or wouldn't be wearing. All the drivers talked and had their favorites. My pizza muse was a well put together brunette mom in an affluent neighborhood that despite knowing she ordered a pizza, was always unaware of it being delivered and would answer the door in a towel, her bare shoulders still glistening with drops of shower water. All this and she tipped well too. Good times for a young fellow like me back then.

This flight has gotten very turbulent and has distracted me from my memories of yesteryear. I enjoy turbulence quite a bit. These are the flights that make you really feel like you're flying. Being buffeted by the strong winds this way and that way; it really tests your gumption.

I don't like those oversized planes where I feel like I have been sitting on a sofa with a bunch of strangers for the past hour and suddenly I'm walking out of the living room with wings into a new and foreign land.

Give me stormy weather! Give me thunder, some gray rain clouds, and then throw in some lightning for good measure. Let me know I'm alive and soaring high above the trees and that everything I experience every day could be taken away in a blink of an eye and the drop of a half inflated oxygen mask that really should be pumping out nitrous, or at least smell like tanned coconut boobies.

Tuesday, May 12, 2015

I know what I've been told
You gotta work to feed the soul
But I can't do this all on my own
No, I know I'm no Superman
I'm no Superman

—"I'm No Superman" - Lazlo Bane

Indeed, I'm no Superman, but I try like hell to not show any weakness. I'm no spring chicken either. On a long enough timeline my kryptonite will surface and bring me to my knees, but I haven't seen any sign of it yet, so I'll just pick up my cape when it's ready at the cleaners and continue on.

Night one of investigation for the show is done. It ended up being a later night than I thought. I'm not sure I did anything of value last night as I investigated the Toledo Yacht Club in Ohio. I was terribly overtired just from life itself, not to mention the extensive travel it took to get out here after a long day at work. This exhaustion resulted in me being terribly distracted by my own humor; what can I say, I amuse myself.

Wednesday, May 13, 2015

I finished up filming at the Toledo Yacht Club around 3am or so, and was snuggled in the hotel bed by four this morning. My hotel room is interesting. They are remodeling the Holiday Inn Express and my accommodations are fresh and clean, yet they remind me of a beach bungalow if it was designed by the IKEA store. Regardless of the room's alien appearance, I must have slept quite well as I awoke with creases in my face and torso—signs that I never moved all night long. Good signs, as even Superman must sleep… I think.

I ate breakfast at the truck stop restaurant when I woke up at high noon today. I do love truck stop food. Always reminds me of my dad and my first travels on the road with him in one of the big 18-wheelers. The scents of asphalt and diesel fuel also remind me of my father as that's what he smelled like every day when he came home from his job at Cardi Corporation where he worked as a dump truck driver for most of his life.

Now my dad is retired, and I have taken up the torch as the father who is often on the road traveling for work. Based on my family history, I'm a third generation father who makes a good majority of his living, providing for his family, by having to be away from them on the road.

When I was home earlier this week, I found a scrap of paper upon which my now seven-year-old daughter had written a song called "Magazine Cover". The lyrics of which are as follows:

This girl's got some sass
And a little, little class
But you'd never see me on a magazine cover
You might see me on the road
But never ever on a magazine cover

She has been leaving little notes and song lyrics here and there around this house, but this one really resonated with me as more than likely you might see me on the road but never ever on a magazine cover.

Thursday, May 14, 2015

I'm exhausted and squeezed into seat 7C aboard Delta flight 5051 that will take me from Detroit back to Rhode Island, at which point I'll go right back to my office and back to work. I was only able to get 87 minutes of sleep last night, or this morning if you want to be exact, so today should prove interesting. Jinglebottom and the elves in my mind were up all night partying.

Back here in the land of reality we filmed long into the wee small hours of the morning at a place called The Whitney, a stately old home in downtown Detroit. The building itself was really something to behold. Such beautiful architecture and old stained glass windows, one of which was an original Tiffany, all in stark contrast with the current condition of its surroundings. I still believe in the Motor City. Detroit may not be as glorious as it once was, but it will come back, it just needs a little time and tenderness. Stay strong, Detroit!

Up here in the air I'm just glad not to be near anyone that smells like kitty litter. I'm also glad not to be near anyone who is connected at the lips of another person. Those flights out here were something else but it's usually not that bad. However, I do dream about perhaps being able to travel just once more up in the first class cabin. It's been years since I've been up there. When I was on *Ghost Hunters International*, I had so many frequent flyer miles that I was bumped up quite often, which came in quite handy on those long overseas flights.

It wasn't quite like I imagined, though. I always thought it'd be a bunch of stuffy old guys in suits sipping the finest champagne whilst wearing their top hats and monocles, twisting their mustaches and watching the stock ticker. Apparently I imagine anything associated with the affluent members of society to be easily representable by the old guy on the Monopoly board game box. Of course, what I imagine and what is reality hardly ever coincide. Such disappointment. Oh well, this may not be Boardwalk but back here in coach it isn't so bad. I'm not in jail; I'm just visiting.

Friday, May 15, 2015

Aisle seat 18C is where I'm at as U.S. Airways flight 4482 tears a hole in the sky bringing me from TF Green airport in Rhode Island to Philadelphia International airport in Pennsylvania, my home away from home.

I don't think I'll stop neither for a mojito nor for a chicken sandwich, as is usually my custom, but only because it's currently 7am and a bit too early for such things. If I change planes in Philly on my way back home Sunday, I'll indeed have both of those things as long as time allows, for such things are delicious and should be enjoyed whenever possible.

Got kind of tired
Of packing and unpacking
Town to town
Up and down the dial

Maybe you and me
Were never meant to be
Just maybe think of me
Once in awhile

I'm at WKRP in Cincinnati

—Theme from *WKRP in Cincinnati*

Well I may not be on WKRP in Cincinnati, Ohio, but I'm aboard U.S. Airways flight 4611 in aisle seat 18C headed to Cleveland and I'm quite tired of packing and unpacking. I had to do that exercise in futility last night after getting home from my day job. I unpacked from filming and then packed the same empty suitcase with fresh clothes and some merchandise I'll need for the event at the old reformatory prison in Mansfield, Ohio, this weekend.

Tonight and tomorrow night I'm doing an event for Marc Tetlow and Ideal Event Management. I do enjoy these events quite a bit. I'm looking forward to meeting many new people and seeing some old friends. The only unfortunate thing is that these events mirror the television investigations in that they go to the wee hours of the morning as well, and I'm still tired from filming this week.

I didn't sleep as well as I wanted to last night. I was very tired, but I stayed up to spend time with Wife and Beans after I finished preparing for today's trip. Time at home was really limited this week, so I wanted to make the most of it. Of course I also woke up every hour on the hour as well, fearing that I would oversleep and thus miss my flights and the event. I can't seem to squelch that internal alarm of mine. It goes off like that every time I have a flight coming up, and lately I've had a lot of flights coming up.

Maybe my life would have been different if I was a radio DJ like those on the old WKRP television show that I enjoyed watching as a child. Funny enough, it was that show that is responsible for me pursuing a degree in television and radio production, thus working as an intern at WPRO-AM radio where I was an overnight board operator for the syndicated *Coast to Coast* radio show with Art Bell. I sat there and listened to stories about the paranormal, building my knowledge, whilst waiting to play the local commercial breaks. Obtaining my video and radio production degree also allowed me to work at WPRI/WNAC CBS and FOX news in Rhode Island. It was my video equipment skills coupled with my paranormal knowledge that would eventually lead me to a position on *Ghost Hunters*, *Ghost Hunters International*, and all the lectures and event appearances that came along.

So, I suppose a big thank you is in order to the good staff members of the fictitious WKRP radio station. Without Doctor Johnny Fever and Loni Anderson's amazing breasts, I may never have watched the show and thus never pursued a degree that would define a large part of one of my careers, and my life.

Saturday, May 16, 2015

Just up the road from my hotel here in Bellville is a little old train with a little old dining car and a little old man who runs it as a diner. It's called the Buckeye Diner and let me tell you, boys and girls, it's well worth your time. Tell them Dustin sent you and they will say, "Who?"

Friday night's event at the Mansfield Reformatory went very well. It's been a long time since I've visited. The last time was when we first filmed here for *Ghost Hunters* and I had marked a black X over one of the cells in which I'd heard quite a bit of commotion. I was glad to see the X was still there and it had become a part of the tour as well. No one can say I haven't left my mark in this world.

In all honesty, I truly cannot remember doing an event style investigation where there was so much paranormal activity and so many people having strange experiences. From people seeing shadows to guests getting scratched, it was quite the night to remember. Lucky for me, as my memory is not the greatest when it comes to things other than restaurant locations and song lyrics, I get to take people around the old prison again for night two of the event. There were over two hundred attendees last night and another two hundred set to come through the doors this evening.

I'm looking forward to doing the event again tonight. I enjoy these things quite a bit, even if they do leave me tired, especially after the week I had. Last night a gentleman came up to me after the Q&A session and told me that I should be a stand-up comedian as he found me naturally funny. I almost asked him to call my wife and tell her those comments as little Mama Bear stands by her opinion that I'm definitely not funny. I don't think I would ever be a comedian but this is by far not the first time I have been given this compliment, so I think my wife's point isn't valid since her evidence to back it up is greatly outweighed by logic, reason and popular opinion.

Sunday, May 17, 2015

Welcome to the jungle
We've got fun and games

– "Welcome to the Jungle" by Guns N' Roses

It's only fitting as one is blazing a path through the home of the Rock n' Roll Hall of Fame in the early morning to hear the unmistakable tones of Axl Rose pumping through the speakers of the rental car. It was a dark morning complete with bouts of torrential rain and thick patches of fog. Perfect for me to drive to the airport after having about eighty minutes of solid shuteye in the bank thanks to last night's investigation event.

I booked these early morning flights because I have to get home to see Beans in her first ever musical stage performance. She's playing two roles in *Suessical the Musical* and I really don't want to miss it. And so once again, we find our hero flying high above the clouds, this time upon U.S. Airways flight 4587 in aisle seat 15D. I'm sleepy but doing okay. I have been a little bothered by a bit of chest pain that comes and goes as of late. I attribute it to sheer exhaustion, as it only seems to bother me after midnight once I've been up doing an overnight or two for the show or for an event. I'm sure everything is okay and so I'll skip the trip to the doctor and save myself the co-pay.

I just need sleep.

Last night was particularly taxing on me. I filmed three nights this week and finished the second night of a two night event. I started feeling fatigued a bit early on but did my best not to let anyone else know about it. The show must go on, after all. I realize I'm not an actor or any great showman but I'm proud of what I do and the interaction I have with the people that come to these events, so I couldn't just sit back and mail it in. Light the lights and prop me up on stage if you have to—the show must go on.

As I was approaching the Cleveland International Airport this morning Pink Floyd came on the radio with their song "Time". It's a classic tune and one of my all-time favorites. The *Darkside of the Moon* album plays with the smoothness of a baby's bottom; if the baby was also crawling out of a Salvador Dali painting and drinking a bottle of Captain Morgan. I recall sitting in my bedroom on many nights during high school just listening to that cassette tape play over and over and over again as the red and blue lava lamps I had on each side of the stereo moved along with the beat.

The lyrics for "Time" seem incredibly appropriate for this moment, including the beating heart in the background.

And you run and you run to catch up with the sun but it's sinking
Racing around to come up behind you again
The sun is the same in a relative way, but you're older
Shorter of breath and one day closer to death

That last line is true, but hopefully it's still far off. Remember, kids, nothing is promised to you, no matter how young you are. It could be later than you think.

Monday, May 18, 2015

Mama Bear and Beans, though loving, did nothing to help me rest last night. Since Mama Bear had a migraine, she went to bed when I did at 5:30 last night. Beans came in our room as well, so she and Mama could watch TV. I tried to sleep for a few hours but eventually acquiesced to the reality that no one was being thoughtful of how tired I was, and so I dragged my pillow into the spare room and had a not-so-restful night there. (We have a ghost. He likes to shake the bed. Bastard.)

Tuesday, May 19, 2015

Unbeknownst to me, I recorded my favorite EVP to date on this last case. (That's Electronic Voice Phenomenon for those of you not in the know. Spirit communication recorded but unheard at the time.)

I was investigating with my buddy KJ McCormick in the carriage house of the Whitney home in Detroit last week and after a series of odd noises and what sounded like a footstep, I asked if the young lady could come closer to us so that we might be able to hear her voice. The response I recorded said, "I can't walk anywhere."

I have been thinking about it since I heard it whilst reviewing the audio recorder. Her voice had a very hollow, yet very human tone to it. She sounded sincere, but what does she mean? In the afterlife we physically don't have to walk anywhere? She personally can't walk anywhere? I have no idea. I don't think we are meant to know all the answers, but I was glad to know that somehow I communicated across the void betwixt this life and the next.

Wednesday, May 20, 2015

There was an episode of the show *South Park* I saw many moons ago that stays with me and surfaces at random times. It was about "underpants gnomes" that steal your underpants. What else would they do?

The characters of South Park finally follow the underpants gnomes and get them to divulge their plan.

Step One. Steal Underpants
Step Two. ???
Step Three. Profit

With all the work I've been doing of late, I feel I'm mired in step one, stealing underpants—metaphorically of course—knowing somehow this will all work out and result in profit. I'm not sure how it will work but I trust in the underpants gnomes. Perhaps I should not trust in false animated prophets in matters of profit. I've put trust in lesser things, and it always turns out okay as long as I keep my faith in God.

Thursday, May 21, 2015

I was having a conversation with a friend of mine about growing up. When I was a kid, I really thought that if someone was an adult that meant they had it together. It wasn't until I made it to adulthood that I realized that screwed up children often grow up to be screwed up adults and raise more screwed up kids. Ah, the circle of life. Someone get Mufasa and the rest of the Lion King cast over here to sing with me.

Dear God, why is it that I can best relate to life by referencing movies, music or commercials, and furthermore, why are they mostly cartoons?

Anyhow, I don't view myself as screwed up. On the contrary, I think I'm rather well adjusted. I'm good in any situation I have come across. I have never felt powerless or utterly defeated in a situation. Does that mean I win all the time? Hell no. But I never feel fear in any situation.

I was once in a plane somewhere in South America that lost an engine and altitude quite rapidly. People were screaming. I sipped my wine. It's not like I want to make a fiery exit from this world but I'll be damned if I go out screaming. I know Jesus and John Lennon are waiting to greet me on the other side, and I hope one of them has the forethought to bring a pumpkin pie.

Anyhow, back to the lecture at hand. I was shocked to find out in my young adulthood that many adults were just faking it. They didn't have themselves together more than anyone else I knew. This was comforting and also unnerving at the same time. For example, when I go to the bank, I don't want the teller that keeps making mistakes and has to cross things out on the paper statements she slides me over the cold marble countertop. I want someone that knows how to cash my checks and manage my accounts. I'll let someone step in front of me in line at the bank just to avoid a teller who gives me the vibe of confused and easily defeated by the challenges of life. I'm no Suzie Psychic when it comes to picking up on these vibes; I just go by simple visual cues. If their hair is disheveled and their outfit is a mess, they're a good candidate to avoid. If their head is slightly tilted back, their eyes focused intently on the task at hand, and their mouth slack jawed, I'll be sure not to deal with them in any matter of important business, be it finance or ordering an iced latte. I don't want my money screwed with and I don't want to pay a few bucks for a lousy coffee that is light on the sugar and syrup. These things are important.

This method of discernment proves to be a little trickier when I have to call a company on the phone, but if the representative that picks up sounds like a cantankerous individual or perhaps as if they are a few fries short of a Happy Meal, click and I dial again. I call it phone roulette. I keep dialing until someone picks up with a cheerful voice and pleasant disposition.

Those who dwell in darkness and linger in hate won't participate in the stage show of my life as long as my firm, round apple of a hiney is sitting in the director's chair. Life is too short to deal with those who are only going to cause you aggravation or make you a lousy coffee. Be selective in whom you deal with.

Friday, May 22, 2015

My exit row seat is 10F aboard U.S. airways flight 1777 heading from Rhode Island to Washington D.C.—my least favorite of all airports. It's just a quick changeover to my second flight that will take me to Louisville, Kentucky, for tomorrow night's Ideal Event Management event for old man Tetlow. (He isn't really that old. Just a few months older than me actually, but I like to give him hell because I love him like a brother.)

I've been enjoying the extra legroom and my view out of the window whilst trying to distract myself from the pain I feel in my heart. Thankfully the pain is not physical as it was at the beginning of the week. Though I never achieved the marathon of sleep my body so craved, I slept enough and hit the gym every morning, so I feel pretty good. No my friends, this time it's an emotional pain as the heartstrings are being plucked to a sour melody for tomorrow is little Beanser's eighth birthday and I'll be without her, stuck in an old tuberculosis hospital known as Waverly.

My little girl is even walking and dancing in a parade through Seekonk tomorrow with Mama Bear as a part of her dance studio. I wish I could be there to see it and be a part of it, but I have to do the gig. Life on the road and all that happy horseshit. Beans and her song on the little scrap of paper were right. "You might see me on the road but you'll never see me on a magazine cover."

I think I'll have been on something like fifteen flights in the last two weeks after this weekend is over. That is a lot of sitting next to strangers, half awake, and half alive. I feel like I'm living my life in airplane mode lately. Someday I may in fact walk past my own ghost in one of these empty airport terminals.

Little Beans was crying last night after we said our prayers and I said good night. I felt horrible. She told me I have been going away too much lately. I can't disagree with her. All I want to do is be home with her playing video games on the couch and snuggling up to watch movies together. But, being a provider is my role. I do a fair job of it. And so I put on my brave face and told her that this is what Daddy has to do to keep our home, to pay our bills, and fund our family vacations. I told her not to worry and that Daddy would be back very soon. My heart breaks every time she cries, but I can't let her know that. I do let her know that I would rather be with her, but me getting emotional would only make it worse, and so I soldier on behind a confident mask of bravery in the name of sacrifice.

I have to be honest here, though. This sucks. I don't mind not sleeping. I don't mind waking up in a hotel room and not knowing where I am. But not being there for my little girl's birthday breaks my damn heart.

I remind myself how lucky I'm to have the opportunities I have to provide for my family. We aren't rich by any means, but through scraping, struggling and hustling, the bills get paid every month. I'm healthy enough to do all that needs to be done. My efforts allow for Mama Bear to be home with Beans. Nice home. Food in the fridge. Lights and water are on. Everyone is healthy. Can't ask for more than that. There will be other birthdays, and we can always celebrate when I get home.

Well, writing this has been very therapeutic. How about that?

Saturday, May 23, 2015

Happy birthday, Beans! Daddy loves you even when he's so far away.

I'm feeling rather refreshed this morning as I have finally caught up on my sleep. I think I may have slept for just over nine hours last night. Good times.

So tonight is the event at Waverly and that will be all fun and games, but first thing's first. I must find a good pizza place. Work will always be there, but pizza, like the love of a good woman in her youth, is fleeting.

Sunday, May 24, 2015

All these damn flights over the years, you would think I'd have glimpsed a UFO at least once, damn it. Elusive little buggers. Yes, I do believe aliens exist. To think we're the only intelligent life forms out here spinning through the universe is arrogant. To think us "intelligent" may also be a stretch. It all depends on perspective. I'm sure a dog thinks itself brilliant in comparison to the cat and vice versa. Then again, I only slept two hours last night, so take my ramblings at your own risk.

I'm high in the sky with the apple pie hopes of some small ant trying to move a rubber tree plant. And now I want pie. Pie for breakfast? Damn straight. Pie anytime. Of course I don't think this airline serves pie. I don't think any airlines serve pie. Damn shame. Mile high pie. That's what I'm talking about, boys and girls. Get yourself a slice.

U.S. Airways flight 5628 was delayed in getting off the ground due to a broken toilet. Yes. Toilet. These things happen. There are two poopers and two wings on this here plane. We can fly with one toilet. I wonder if the aliens ever have to ground the mother ship due to a busted crapper? The world may never know.

It was a bit of a sprint down to gate E8 to catch my connecting flight, U.S. Airways 5251 to Providence but I'm happy to say I made it. In my years of running across airport terminals from gate to gate as Jasper P. Jinglebottom and the other elves in my head mock the White Rabbit from *Alice in Wonderland* and sing merrily, "I'm late! I'm late! For a very important date!" I have experimented with many songs of my own to fuel my heroic sprints. As of late, I've found "MmmBop" by Hanson to be a sure thing. I have yet to miss a flight whilst listening to that song, plus it keeps me in a cheery mood as I run down the people movers and hurdle wayward traveling toddlers toddling about as wayward traveling toddlers do.

I'm writing to you nestled comfortably in exit row seat 15D flying through a cloudy sky as Mr. Willie Nelson sings "Uncloudy Day" in the elite suite betwixt my ears. God bless that beautiful gypsy bastard. His lyrical genius has brought so much comfort to my old soul over the years.

I'm happy to be headed home to Mama Bear and Beans. They will be at a cookout when I land. I'm not sure if I'm going to go meet them there or just head home and rest up for our reunion. I still have some birthday gifts to give our little one. Mama Bear gave her some of the gifts yesterday, and I also sent her some sunflowers so she knew Daddy was thinking about her from far away on her special day. However, there are some gifts that I tucked away for when I get home. Video games are one of our things, so I picked up the new Kirby game to give her upon my arrival.

Hmm… go to the cookout or go home? Beer and hot dogs versus a hot shower and bed? I kind of want to go to the cookout as I never attend social functions anymore and I don't want people to think I've completely lost my marbles. I don't want them to imagine that I'm walking around my bedroom wearing a silken jade kimono and empty tissue boxes upon my feet. Why is it that I imagine myself wearing a silken jade kimono and empty tissue boxes upon my feet?

I'm rather tired and I don't know how much of a polite party guest I would be if I attended the cookout. I know I would be the talk of the party if I showed up in that silken jade kimono that I have in my mind. But without said kimono, and without sleep, I may not be much of a polite party guest.

Here's another issue, and perhaps the real issue, the only issue. This whole being on television thing is not really me. I'll spare you the usual disclaimer: thankful. Respectful of the spiritual world. Great opportunity. Most of my friends have known my very well and for many years, whereas my wife's friends have only known me since our marriage and thus conversation topics are limited, and since not everyone knows someone on a television show, it usually falls to that. And in itself that is all well and good, but it's still not me.

David Allan Coe, one of my favorite country artists, was known for his own special brand of showmanship, or lack thereof, depending upon whom you ask. His Rhinestone Cowboy persona is legendary. He would sometimes ride a motorcycle out on stage dressed up in a flashy outfit and start his performance as this almost alter-ego. Kind of like me and the Paranormal Rockstar, me and Jinglebottom, me and other various personalities who won't allow themselves to be listed without proper compensation or litigation will ensue, and sue they will.

In his song "Long Haired Redneck" Mr. David Allan Coe drops the line "I've been the rhinestone cowboy for so long I can't remember…." and that line hits home as often times I feel as if there are truly two people here, if not more. And no, it isn't a multiple personality disorder; it's a damn survival technique. I do my events to the best of my ability no matter what is going on behind the scenes of my green eyes. Yesterday was a great example. I was hurting for missing my daughter's birthday. I touched upon that a few days ago. What I didn't even write about yesterday was being concerned for my mother who was home and very sick. She's been battling with CHF and COPD for many moons now and there are good days and bad days. Yesterday was a bad day. But, outside of my buddy Tetlow and one or two good friends, no one at that two hundred person event ever knew a damn thing about it. I smiled. I sang. I danced. I told some jokes. I posed for pictures. None of this was disingenuine, for when I no longer want to do these things, if the day comes that I no longer care, I simply won't do these things regardless of the payday. But last night, I wanted to be there, and so I did the gig even though there was pain in my chest, both physically and metaphorically, and no one knew it. The show must go on. I have a few people out there that depend on me and this poor boy isn't going to let them down—ever.

But if you ever want to know what it's really like behind the eyes of the "Paranormal Rockstar" and my imported leather bracelets from Bangkok, beyond Jinglebottom and the elves at the Jolly Good Times pirate-themed bar in my mind, take a listen to Mr. David Allan Coe's "Another Pretty Country Song." It's about as close to my soul as it gets.

I bought this rhinestone suit in California
These boots came all the way from Mexico
This Cadillac ain't nothin' son, you ought to see the Greyhound
I bought to take my band from show to show

Seen my face a thousand times on TV
And heard me on your local radio
And in your eyes I see the admiration there for me
But son there's something that you ought to know

Well, I've got to take a drink to keep from shakin'
Motel rooms ain't nothin' like a home
Money can't make love grow any stronger
When you leave your woman home alone

She can't raise the children with no daddy
She can't love a man that's always gone

It takes a whole lot more than pride
To keep your feelings locked inside
While you sing another pretty country song

(I've seen your face a thousand times on TV
I've heard you on my local radio)

It's true I took some pills to stay awake, son
And this diamond ring I wear is just for show
I've got a little cabin in the country
When I'm not on the road that's where I go

Try and put my feelings down on paper
Right or wrong the show has to go on
I can cry deep down inside and keep on smilin'
While I sing another pretty country song

But I've got to take a drink to keep from shakin'

Note: I've never taken any pills to stay awake. I use sugar for that.

On second thought, maybe I'll go to the cookout and say hello and sing "Another Pretty Country Song", as I know the show has to go on. Though I must admit, the idea of being at home in a silken jade kimono sounds pleasant. I imagine it would feel heavenly as it tickles across my man parts, if I don't wear my unmentionables of course, but there I had to go and mention them.

Monday, May 25, 2015

Memorial Day! I totally forgot I had this day off. I just assume I work through all holidays as I did back in my days working for CBS and FOX news. I remember eating hot dogs at a gas station in Pawtucket on Christmas one year. It wasn't quite feasting on the prize-winning turkey that Mr. Scrooge sent to the house but it wasn't all that bad either. I like hot dogs.

Speaking of which, I plan to cook some hot dogs on the grill today. I also would like to visit the cemetery for a relaxing walk, perhaps straighten up some gravestones and American flags.

Time to shower up and get ready for the day! I think I shall listen to Mr. Kermit Ruffins whilst I lather, rinse and repeat today. I do love my New Orleans jazz.

Well, Mama Bear's list of things for me to do today wasn't in sync with my list of things to do today. I ended up uncovering the pool, cutting the lawn, and trimming the hedges. I don't need a list. Were these things what I wanted to do today? No. But I would have done them anyway as I know what needs to be done and I'm a responsible person. I had to have a talk with Mama Bear about the lists as I find them to be emasculating. You want me to do something, just ask. I was probably going to do it anyway.

The highlight of the day was having a little Hello Kitty ice cream cake and singing Happy Birthday to Beans. This is her second birthday celebration this week, but the first I have been able to be a part of. She has her big party with her friends this coming weekend. Must be nice to be eight. Life is a party.

Tuesday, May 26, 2015

I'm wiped out. The captain in my mind has turned on the "fasten your seatbelt" sign, as he is exhausted and switching to autopilot. Assume crash positions. Take care, and tempt not the fates.

Wednesday, May 27, 2015

Yee-ha! I'm fully recharged and ready to go. I had a great workout today and the first half of my day has been going quite well. After work today I have to get home and start studying my firm round apple of a hiney off as I have an anesthesia assistant certification examination to take tomorrow. I have had the book to study for six months now, but if you've been paying attention, I haven't quite had a lot of down time these past six months. So, can I learn everything I need to learn in one night? I never bet against myself.

Tonight will be one of those forgotten nights of my life. But right now it's very real.

It's almost midnight and instead of studying at home, I'm still at work. I have my New Orleans jazz music blaring throughout the office sound system. Kermit Ruffins is singing "Drop Me Off in New Orleans" and playing beautifully on his horn. I'm drinking an Oreo flavored iced latte from Dunkin Donuts. It's delicious. It's beyond delicious. It isn't a good night, but I'm trying to make the best of it.

Turns out that my plans were not in sync with those of the universe tonight. Just before the workday was over one of the x-ray imaging servers crashed in my Massachusetts office, thus I'm still working. We can't start surgery in the morning without x-rays that's for sure. I have been working on seven different workstations and the main tower with one of our IT guys. I try to study in-between installing, uninstalling, and reinstalling software. I'm taking a little break now so I don't go crazy … or you know, more crazy than usual. I'm counting on my ability to learn things by osmosis to get me through the test tomorrow at this point. I did this same certification ten years ago, and I have been working as an anesthesia assistant for over thirteen or so years now. I must know something.

Thursday, May 28, 2015

Woohoo! I do know something after all. I passed my test and as Mr. James Brown would say, "I feel good!" I celebrated by leaving the testing center and going to the gym on my way home. As I hit shuffle on my music to get my routine started "All Right Now" by Free played in the elite suite betwixt my ears. Indeed it was. Everything was all right now.

At Jolly Good Times, the imaginary pirate-themed bar in my head, Jinglebottom (Head Elf in charge) popped the cork on a fresh bottle of rum and toasted me, before mooning me; the classless little bastard. Ah well, at least he recognized my achievement.

Friday, May 29, 2015

So the filming schedule for next week changed and no one told me until just now when the production company called me to confirm flights. I was supposed to fly out Monday night or Tuesday morning to film Tuesday night. Now they want me to fly out Sunday to film Monday night. I have a ministry lecture at the church I attend on Sunday, and Mama Bear has plans of her own, so I can't make the Sunday flight. They agreed to fly me out Monday morning. I'm having a hard enough time keeping track of things on a day-to-day basis as is, I really can't accommodate for last minute changes on a mental level.

Many moons ago actor Jim Carrey starred in a movie called *The Truman Show*. It was really a fantastic film in my humble opinion. It was about a guy whose whole life had been a reality show unbeknownst to him. The cameras were hidden. His friends were all actors. The viewers of the show had t-shirts and buttons that read, "How will it end?" and I'm starting to wonder the same thing.

Saturday, May 30, 2015

What a day! What a simply fantastic day. We held Beanser's eighth birthday party today at a place called Mockingbird Music Studio up in Mansfield, Massachusetts. It was a great time. Beans was able to record a CD of her own, along with twelve friends. She sang her favorite country song "Riverbank" by Brad Paisley , along with current pop hits like Taylor Swift's "Shake It Off".

Mama Bear stresses herself out leading up to these parties every year, but she always does a great job. She makes the chocolate pops, the cupcakes, and the snacks. She plans the activities (because recording a CD isn't activity enough). I was there to set up, break down and facilitate everything in between. Beans had a great time as did her friends.

After the party was over I had one more surprise in store for my little girl. Despite her vocalizing her dislike for NASCAR every Sunday when I watch it, she has shown interest in actually going to a race. Of course she is still too young to go sit at a full NASCAR race at the top level, but I figured it was time I brought her to the local short track for her first race. So after the party was over and everything was cleaned and packed up, I took her with me to Seekonk Speedway to experience her first race the same way I did when I was a kid. We had pizza, hot pretzels and frozen lemonade. The racing was good and the car she picked to win the feature event crossed the finish line first. It was great just to sit there on the backstretch as I have done so many times before, most times with my dad, sometimes with both my parents and often times alone as I had gotten older, but this time I was sitting there as a dad with my eight-year-old little girl, and it was amazing.

We stopped at McDonald's for a grilled cheese as she still doesn't like hamburgers just as I still don't like hamburgers. We talked about the races. I told her about how I drove one of the top level NASCAR racecars at the track in Pocono, Pennsylvania. I told her about the time I drove in the demolition derby at Seekonk Speedway and finished somewhere around 15th in a field of at least fifty cars. When I was done I had four flat tires and a fire under the hood. She asked questions and I told her stories. Life is good. I do love time with my little one, and it was nice to carry on the family tradition at Seekonk Speedway.

Sunday, May 31, 2015

Today was a whirlwind of nonsense. It started with a strongly worded email from the production company about travel accommodations and scheduling. I thought it was directed at me due to my travel schedule having to work around my day job but apparently there were issues with other cast members as well. It was the kind of email that, if I were a weaker person, would have ruined my whole day. But, me being me, as whom else can I be, I was quick to shake it off.

I'm always ready to fight for what is right in regards to things that truly matter. If it was addressed to me specifically and composed in a proper manner that dignified a response, then of course I would respond. But as it sits, it's something that does not truly matter, and thus I simply let it slide.

As a rule, I don't respond to the loud bark of smaller dogs running back and forth on their chain guarding their 4x6 yard. If the email becomes a bigger issue and is brought to my attention I can still quickly dismiss the entire matter, as I have done nothing wrong. The bottom line is this my friends, if you are honestly doing your best, then what can they fault you for? Being too awesome? Guilty as charged! Slap the cuffs on me bailiff and I'll go willingly.

On to brighter matters for we all know the tongue is the rudder for the soul and as captain of this beautiful sum' bitch I'm steering her into clearer waters.

I gave a lecture after church services today. It's often serendipitous how these things work out, for you see, I'm not the type of fellow that prepares too far ahead. That being said, in church today I knew I was going to speak about the importance of prayer, how we look for spiritual guidance, our need as Christians for relationship with God through Christ, and how the Holy Spirit is there to offer us support—all we need do is ask. As it turns out, the readings and the sermon today were about the Holy Trinity and signs that God is interacting with us. Everything was on point with what I had thought I would talk about. Sweet Christmas! I do love when God sets me up like that. I kept it short as it was a hot day and church basements aren't known for being cool and comfortable for long periods of time. But I dare say twenty minutes' time, I got all the messages conveyed that were placed upon my heart to those who gathered to listen, and I even threw in a few personal stories and anecdotes as well.

I always feel great after giving one of my lectures, be they paranormal, motivational, or inspirational. Most times I don't even recall what is was I spoke about. It's as if I'm often not present in my head when I do most of these things. Come to think of it, it's as if I'm not present in my head most of the time, but somehow it all works out okay. I believe in numerous mental picnics, and though the floors in the elite sweet betwixt my ears are often sticky like the those of a second run movie theater, there are no ants at these mental picnics and flights of fancy of mine.

After church, Beans and I played video games on the couch and had snacks. I did a little yard work and Beans counted caterpillars whilst we waited for Mama Bear to return home. As it turned out, Mama Bear's outing with her friends went long so Beans and I called an audible of our own and headed out to the movies. We went to see Disney's *Tomorrowland* and followed it up by grabbing a pizza on the way home as Mama Bear called to say the power had went out due to some intense storms that crept in whilst we were in the movies.

We were driving in Maggie May, the Big Blue Baby, in the pouring rain as lightning streaked across the sky. Beans was so excited. She told me that she only had seen lightning once before. I can't explain it, but I was in awe for a moment when she said that. Here she is, my big girl at eight years of age. My best friend in the world that is growing up too fast for all intents and purposes, yet I forget there are still many simple things she does not have much experience with. Here she was alongside me, my talented dancer, my excellent student, my brave girl, simply staring at lightning with wonder, as it's still a relatively new experience for her. I was comforted to realize there are still many opportunities for me to teach her new things, and to be there with her as she experiences all that this life has to offer.

I have always fancied lightning myself; fascinated with it since I was a child about her age. It reminds me that no matter how dark things may seem at times, there is often a spark of light that shows us a brighter tomorrow, and all we have to do is believe.

SUMMER
JUNE - SEPTEMBER

Monday, June 1, 2015

Damn, it's already June? I remember going to Disney back in January of this year. That was pretty fun. Since then? Shoveling, work, lawn care, a NASCAR race, and more work. I'll add to the yellow sticky note in my mind, "Have some fun." I'll ask Jinglebottom to pencil it in right under task number three "Donuts". Donuts are always on my to-do list.

It's 8am and I should be squeezed into middle seat B back in row 23 on my way to Kentucky by way of Charlotte but the flight is delayed an hour due to storms and the crew not getting their required time off. This little twist of fate will make for a very interesting morning as I had an hour and fifteen minutes between flights in Charlotte, and they close the boarding door ten minutes prior to take off. So let's see here, if I do the math … carry the one … yup, five minutes. I have five whole minutes to sprint two terminals and 27 gates to my connecting flight to Kentucky, assuming all the people in the 22 rows before me can get off the plane in a timely fashion.

Like Presidents George Washington who came before me (as I'm Mayor of Popsicle Town and president of my own mind, for the time being at least) I shall not tell a lie. The little hiccup of travel this morning is a tad bit concerning only because of the email that was sent yesterday. It appeared to be a harbinger of misery, and it looks like its prophecy needed only 24 hours to come to fruition as it pertained to same-day flights on investigation nights.

But, I'm also a man of my word, and thus it shall not ruffle my beautiful feathers. As my Nana Annette Smith often said, "Oh dear, bread and beer. If I was dead, I wouldn't be here." Granted, I'm not sure that applies terribly well, but it mentions two of my favorite things: bread and beer. And so I'll simply allow for the thought of those things, and my sweet old Nana to bring me comfort.

I still dial my Nana's phone number from time to time only to hang up, as she has long since been deceased and her number now someone else's, but it still brings me a bit of comfort to think I can call her like that. I remember being a little tyke of five or six calling her at six or seven in the morning when *Pooh's Corner* came on television. It was an early Disney show about Winnie the Pooh that I got up to watch whilst my parents slept in on weekends. I called my Nana and held the receiver up to the speaker so she could hear the opening theme song and then I would relay to her what was going on in that episode. I thought she and I were the only two people up in the whole entire world. Ahh, youth, such wonderful thoughts are born there. I choose to stay in that youthful mind.

I do miss my Nana. She may no longer be with me physically, but spiritually I sense her around from time to time and occasionally will catch the scent of her perfume on a wayward autumn breeze.

Good ole U.S. Airways flight 885 finally tucked its wheels into its underbelly and here I'm in the sky once again. I'm not fancying this plane that much. It's one of those super-duper jumbo bastards that gives the effect of sitting in someone's living room that you don't particularly care for, but they have poured you some cheap scotch, and now you are stuck watching slides of their family vacation with no polite way out. Not that I have ever actually experienced it. I believe that memory is twenty or so years before my time.

Looks like I'm going to have a total of fifteen minutes to get to my next flight as they said we will be getting in ten minutes early. Of course, there is always a yin to a yang, and this time Mr. Yang has moved my flight down an additional six gates. Time to cue up Hanson's "MmmBop" and make sure the lug nuts are tight on the rickshaw, as our hero is going to have to be at maximum speed if he is going to make it to his connecting flight this time.

Huzzah! I made it! There was an extended delay getting off of the plane, which left me with closer to ten minutes to make the marathon run, but I made it anyhow, with laptop bag and carry-on in my hands. Flight 5605 is on its way to Louisville, Kentucky, and I'm sitting in seat 4D. Glistening with a bit of sweat, but sitting here despite the odds.

"That's how you're going to beat 'em, Butch. They keep underestimating you." – Butch the Boxer in *Pulp Fiction.*

I found myself trying to help a woman via Twitter with an issue this morning that seems to come up quite a bit lately. Regardless of her circumstance, as this truth is applicable in all of our lives, the lesson is this: people will continue to treat you as you allow them to. This lesson is a tough one for me as well since I often overlook the slights of others and write them off as the interactions of young souls who simply are drowning in a material world and don't know better.

But, there is a time when all of us must stand up to someone, be they friend or foe, and show them the line in the sand. We all should be treated with respect, as we should in turn treat others. The old biblical teaching of, "Love your neighbor as you love yourself," will always ring true regardless of what religion you may or may not subscribe to.

At times it may even seem easier to confront those whom we don't see eye to eye with than those whom we consider friends, family and miscellaneous loved ones. But no matter where they are in your social circle, inside or out, you may have to not only tell them what is acceptable in how they treat you, but you may have to show them as well. To not do so and simply sit idle and complain about it, makes you at fault for allowing it to persist. This is your life. Take responsibility and let them know whom they are dealing with and how you would appreciate they do so.

A king may be treated like a king merely due to his crown, but he is respected based upon his actions and how he treats others.

Tuesday, June 2, 2015

I'm up! It's 4 o'clock in the afternoon. I feel like hell, but I'm up. I'm not one to normally sleep late into the afternoon but as I did not get to sleep until almost six o'clock this morning, and I've been working like a regular dog, I'll allow it. Sadly my hibernation has cost me physically as I'm dehydrated, fevered, and a bit light headed. Nothing a quick skip out for breakfast cannot remedy.

Wednesday, June 3, 2015

"Yesterday has ran into tomorrow, wrecking every dream we've ever known." – "Lately I've Been Thinking Too Much Lately" by David Allan Coe. Indeed yesterday has run into tomorrow, Mr. Coe. That sort of thing happens when one does not have ample time to rest. However, watching the sunrise from above the clouds is always awe-inspiring. Whereas conversely, not sleeping a wink last night is always maddening. There seems to be a struggle betwixt my sleepy mind and my awake self on this fine day. Internally I'm quiet, but externally I'm animated and a bit manic.

I'm onboard U.S. Airways flight 4681 in route to my least favorite airport, Washington-Dulles in D.C. on my way home, or make that to work, back in Rhode Island. My aisle seat is 7D next to Captain Starbucks in 7F. He's the typical Starbucks customer in my mind. Tight sweater. Pompous goatee. Air of arrogance. Now, now—I do know a few good people who drink that bitter mermaid swill, so I won't hold it against you dear reader if you are on team burnt coffee as well. Me? I'm a Dunkin Donuts guy. Speaking of which, I cannot wait to get a nice iced latte when I get back home. Dulles airport does have a Dunkin Donuts; it's one saving grace.

This should be among the last marathon shifts I have to do without any sleep. I believe we have two more cases on the road that will require me to do this turnaround one more time. Then again, that "one more time" thing is what started this whole mess almost a year ago.

I wonder if that lady who had the Lambchop sock puppet show is still alive? Perhaps that song that never ended finally ended after all. Man, I should really get some sleep sometime soon. My brain barely functions right when I'm rested; it's a damn mess when I haven't.

I hope work isn't too crazy today so I can go home at a decent hour and sleep. Mama Bear will be at dance with Beans when I finally arrive. I wish they would just be home as I'm looking forward to seeing them and I don't know how long I can stay awake.

"Picture pages, picture pages. Lots of fun with picture pages. Lots of fun with crayons and your pencils." That was from the *Picture Pages* activity show that was slammed between the cartoons I watched as a kid. They were hosted by comedian Bill Cosby, who, incidentally, was in trouble recently for having "fun" with his pencil.

We all have some skeletons in our closets, I suppose. Some much more serious than others. That's what closets are for. Unless you ask my wife of course, as our closet has been relegated to holding her shoes—mountains and mountains of shoes. There are even shoes in some shoetree-like device under our bed. For a petite woman with two even more petite feet, she sure has a lot of things to put them in. Sometimes if I stop and think, I wonder if I wouldn't have to work so much if she didn't have so many shoes. But as Mr. David Allan Coe sang oh so sweetly, "Lately, I've been thinking too much lately...." Is it possible a country singer who once spent time living in an old hearse outside of the Grand Ole Opry wrote the soundtrack for my life thirty years prior? Not sure but all the lyrics seem to fit as of late.

Anyhow, as it pertains to the wife, if shoes are what she wants, then shoes are what she gets. Everyone deserves to be happy. I don't care much for shoes myself. I have what I need and that is enough. I'm not into pursuing multiple material things of moderate variation. I prefer to spend my money on… hmm… good question. It once would have been answered with parts for old muscle cars, cases of beer and them there dancing girls, but all that was before I was married. Now, I just enjoy vacations with my family and the occasional NASCAR race. I have a race coming up next month actually. I look forward to it.

I wish I could sleep on these flights but it just never ends well for me. I can sleep pretty much anywhere but planes are difficult. My neck always ends up sore and my sinuses congested. I wake up with my contacts dried out and then I can't stop blinking, which not only makes me look absurd, but it makes it very difficult to get off of the plane and find my next flight. I've tried that silly, horseshoe collar looking pillow that I see many others utilize, but it doesn't work for me.

Oh bother, it I'm being instructed to lock my tray table and return my seat to its upright position as it's time to land in the worst airport ever.

U.S. Airways flight 4478 is cutting through the clouds on its way to Rhode Island. Aisle seat 6C is treating me well. My mind is off somewhere in a field of dandelions and minstrels. My body is lost somewhere between there and the clouds.

I was thinking about the investigations from these past few weeks and months before. So many black shadows and white ladies, ebony and ivory, over and over again. Why are these the more common claims that society has reported time and time again? Also, why are all these spirits, if they are such, alone? Very rarely do I ever hear claims of people witnessing two children, two ladies, two black shadows. There is never a Noah's ark of spirits. Everything is always alone, except for the rare battlefield time slip, so on and so forth.

I think I shall place it upon my list of questions to ask God when Jesus plays the triangle and calls me to supper, supposing I get invited to dinner and that I'm given the opportunity to ask questions. There's an equally fair chance that I won't be able to ask questions and God just tells a series of knock-knock jokes. That would be okay with me as well. Come to think of it, it might be preferable.

Ah there it's. The captain of the plane has buzzed in with his local weather report for Rhode Island. Talented fellow the captain is; pilot and meteorologist. I'm not sure the point of it all. I appreciate the information, but it's a little late for me to dress accordingly now, as all my clothes are in a bag under the plane.

Thursday, June 4, 2015

Landed yesterday.
Worked all day.
Worked late.
Had to get up early for work today.
And now.... now I sleep.
Lather. Rinse. Repeat.

Friday, June 5, 2015

Strange happenings outside the ole homestead last night. I was all snuggled in bed, dappled and drowsy and ready for sleep. I just started to say my prayers and there were sounds coming from the woods outside that sounded like a swirling symphony of dogs growling and snarling. I looked out the window but saw nothing as the sound grew louder and louder. I made my way downstairs and there was the sound of a knock on the front porch. I opened the door, but still there was nothing there. I made my way outside looking for signs of animals or anything, but all was well. I went back up into bed and there was a beeping and buzzing sound coming from the woods once again. As I stood up there was a piercing light, and then nothing. Strange. Yet, somehow strange has become a constant in my life.

Saturday, June 6, 2015

If you no longer have the passion to do what you're doing, stop and look elsewhere. Time is short. This is your life. And it's later than you think.

I went to the racetrack tonight to watch some cars go in a circle while I ate pizza and drank an ice cold beer. There is something about screeching tires, burning rubber and the smell of racing fuel that soothes my soul and just feels like home; another short track Saturday night. I should have been a racecar driver. Everything about it appeals to me. The speed. The roar of the crowd. The traveling across the country from racetrack to racetrack. Vroom!

Sunday, June 7, 2015

Today was a bike ride with my daughter followed by watching NASCAR on television. I'm a simple man, but I'm happy. I prefer to live life uncluttered.

Monday, June 8, 2015

There are some days where I just like to observe the world and not take part in it. Today is one of those days. On such days I find myself thinking of odd things, like nipples. They are on your body, but try as you might, you cannot control them- yet let a cold breeze blow through and boom! Nipples!

Tuesday, June 9, 2015

People keep saying I'm a bit quiet these past few days and it's because the planet Mercury is in retrograde. I sometimes think there could be some truth to planetary pull and their effects on us furless little monkeys. No matter what, I suppose Mercury in retrograde isn't as bad as any issues that might creep up Uranus.

Wednesday, June 10, 2015

When dealing with negativity I think it's important to remember in this life, as in the spirit world, there is dark and there is light. I simply use the darkness to shine brighter rather than allowing it to dim my bulb. No one dims my bulb!

Thursday, June 11, 2015

You cannot live this life for anyone else. You can care for others. You should care for others. But you cannot live your life according to anyone else's playbook. This is your time. Don't worry about those who doubt you, just continue to believe in yourself and stay on your path. Don't ever aim to harden your heart because something or someone in this world has cruelly broken it. It's the world that needs fixing.

I was putting my daughter to bed tonight and she started telling me about this boy in her class that plays the imaginary banjo. I cannot express how intrigued I am by the mere idea that there exists a child who plays an imaginary banjo. The world needs more people like that.

Friday, June 12, 2015

I'm finally starting to feel like my old self. I'm not sure what was going on but it was strange. I think I just needed a spiritual oil change. I feel rested and recharged. Good timing, too, as tomorrow is my daughter's dance recital. I'm very excited for her and so incredibly proud. I taught her how to power slide across the kitchen floor like a rock star on stage when she was only two, so I like to take credit for her dancing.

Speaking of taking credit, I hope the last few entries with their little nuggets of joy were enough to get you through. There are some deep truths in there, and hopefully some words to help when I'm no longer here. Let me toss one more out there for you before we return to our regularly scheduled programming: don't allow for negative people to spread miserable nonsense into your life. Take control. Take responsibility. Dismiss those who are bringing you down. Cut your anchors and sail away.

Saturday, June 13, 2015

Today was my daughter's big dance recital. The recital is broken up into three separate shows as there are so many kids, dance numbers, and family members coming to see them. Beans was doing some of her dance troupe numbers in the second show, and then again in the third show along with additional dances she is a part of, so I elected to go to the third show. She and Mama Bear were there all day as they assisted the other kids in the first show as well. I have to hand it to my wife, she has been doing a ton of work in getting everything ready for not only my daughter, but for the fundraising activities of the dance school as well. I'm sure she is glad it's all over now, as am I since I have to deal with her being stressed all week.

One great thing that came out of my wife's volunteer efforts was not having to stand in the dreaded line an hour before hand in order to get a decent seat. Since she was there, we had front row seats waiting. As far as the dances went, I couldn't have been more impressed with our little girl. There she was on stage, a little eight-year-old ball of energy with bright shining eyes and a big smile, dancing with girls almost twice her age in many numbers. Not only does she get the dance moves right, and in rhythm, but she manages to flip through the air and still express emotions on her face that reflects the theme of the song. I almost made it through this year without crying. I was super discreet about it, so much so that I dare say my wife didn't notice. I can't help myself. Five years of dancing, five years of crying.

At the end of the night she was presented with a special achievement award from Miss Ashley who runs the dance studio. She gave a nice little speech about how Beans is a dedicated dancer, a hard worker, always present at practice, forever with a smile on her face, and that she encourages others. Yup, that's my girl all right. Then the lucky little bugger also won the 50/50 raffle, which she has done at other events before, too. She was beaming with joy, as was I.

Sunday, June 14, 2015

The big shark is circling the Orca boat of my life again. Tomorrow starts day one of a 17-day work and travel marathon that will see me filming in Pennsylvania, flying back home to work a shift in Rhode Island, only to then hop in a rental car and return to the Keystone State so that I can do an event there Friday and Saturday. I know what is coming. I'm just going to take it moment by moment and make the most of the day.

Monday, June 15, 2015

Strong winds are buffeting U.S. Airways flight 4563 as it carries me in aisle seat 16C to the city of brotherly love, Philadelphia. It smells like SpaghettiOs on this flight, which is not necessarily a bad thing, just not what I expected.

Whilst flying home from Italy one time, I was seated in the last row of the plane next to a small villager that had the distinct aroma of warm ketchup emanating from beneath his arms. You haven't flown until you've flown next to the man who sweats ketchup. He reminded me of my days working as a dishwasher at the tiny Jefferson Diner in Warwick, Rhode Island. I always was slightly disgusted by the scent of the dishwasher steam when a plate was placed in it that had a lot of ketchup on it. Pre-rinse, my friends. Pre-rinse.

And so, as promised, day one of the 17-day marathon hath begun. I worked in my Massachusetts office this morning and then drove ole' Angelina down to the airport in Rhode Island just before the sun went down. I had no time to enjoy the sunset today, but yesterday's was fantastic. I had spent the day with my daughter as Mama Bear was celebrating the success of the recital with a few of the other dance moms.

Beans and I started the day with waffles, and we then filled our time with video games and playing in the pool together. At the end of the day I made us dinner and we headed out for an ice cream come together at a little place named Sundaes on route 44 in the East Providence/Seekonk area. She had a cone of soft serve strawberry and I had a cup of amaretto ice cream with chocolate jimmies. (You may know them as sprinkles but if you're from Rhode Island, they're jimmies—why, I don't know.)

We sat on the open tailgate of ole Angelina, eating our ice cream treats and talking with each other as the sun sank down behind the horizon. It was a simple thing, but it was easily one of the top five moments in my life, and I hope God made note so that he can have the angel editors include it in the highlight reel they play for you on the bus ride to heaven. Lord knows I need some highlights; it can't just be a montage of me working various jobs and not sleeping. They can play that one if I don't garner an invite to the after party upstairs. I can hear the voiceover of the hell montage now, "Congratulations, mortal! You've worked your ass off but did nothing good of note, thus, you're going to hell! Dress for warm weather. And oh yes, it smells like warm ketchup down here."

And we have begun our descent. Into Philly, not hell unless the pilot really screws something up.

Tuesday, June 16, 2015

I spent a good part of the day in the hotel pool this morning after working out. It was really refreshing and relaxing as I was there all alone, the natural light pouring in and reflecting off of the serene water. I had brought my laptop which I set up over in the corner of the makeshift natatorium. I floated around and listened to Mr. Willie Nelson charm my soul as his honey soaked tones bounced and echoed off the tall white walls of the vacant space. As Willie put it best, "Classify these as good times. Good times."

Wednesday, June 17, 2015

Investigated an old quarantine station just outside of Philadelphia, Pennsylvania, last night. It has long since been vacated by humans and now inhabited by numerous raccoons. Speaking of raccoons, I best put some fancy product underneath my eyes or I'm going to start to look like one. All work and no sleep are starting to show.

Thursday, June 18, 2015

Worked all night investigating some place. So tired I'm not even sure. Oh, it was the old homestead of the good Doctor Physick. It was a cool case with a lot of interesting history for me especially as I have worked in surgery for so many years with some of the things he invented.

I haven't slept at all. I went right from the investigation at 3am to the airport so that I could catch my 7am flight back home. I wouldn't go to the airport so early normally, but the hotel was over an hour in the other direction, so by the time I would have arrived back there, it would have been time to turn around and come back here.

I had a plan to get in the airport early and sleep at the gate until it was time to board, but the airport had other plans. Security was closed until 4am, so I had to stand off to the side and wait. Then I could not board the shuttle to the terminal I needed to be at, so I stood there until 5am. I finally was able to get to my gate just shy of 5:30 but without time to get any real sleep and so I just sat there and watched the sky start to brighten like a vampire waiting for death.

The worst part of this whole ordeal is not only will I have to work when I land back in Rhode Island this morning, but I'll then have to get into a rental car after work and drive back to Pennsylvania (where I am right now) and do an event tomorrow morning. Phenomenology 107 is in York. It's one of those moments that cause me to question what the hell I'm doing with my life. One thing is for sure, I'm not sleeping it away!

Friday, June 19, 2015

I ended up going home last night after I picked up the rental to have dinner with my wife and daughter. I have missed them so very much this week. I figured even a few hours at home was better than nothing. I ended up sleeping for three hours before getting back up and saddling up the rental and heading Southbound.

I drove down well into Connecticut when the Sandman started pounding on the side door of my mind. I decided to play it safe and I pulled off into one of the roadside food and fuel stops and slept in the driver's seat of the rental for two hours. I woke up to my phone alarm and headed here to York. Upon arrival I was told by the young lady at the hotel front desk that I couldn't check in until 4 in the afternoon. It was 8am and I had to be fresh, clean, and smiling in front of those who came to see me at 10am. Luckily there was at least one more rabbit in this old silk I found, and I was able to sweet talk my way into a clean room in less than sixty seconds flat. Ahh, that ole Pari charm!

The day went well, considering I only had five hours of interrupted sleep over a three-day period. My friend Jeanette Aulet, whom I'm sure is going to be a famous special effects makeup artist someday, came down to the event and did my makeup for me. Did I say makeup? I mean face paint. Yes. Face paint is much manlier.

As I may have or may have not mentioned before, this is my third go around with reality television. People are more and more interested in what I have to say as of late and the new episodes of the show haven't even aired yet. This time around I'm having more fun, taking myself a lot less seriously, and thus getting a little weird with it.

Jeanette made me up to look like one of my favorite movie characters, Jack Skellington from Tim Burton's The Nightmare Before Christmas. When it was time to do my part and appear on the panel of guests to speak about this or that, I showed up in full-face paint to the complete surprise of everyone else.

I was very tired and I'm not sure I answered any of the questions correctly, but I know I spoke honestly and from the heart. I recall saying something about how, "Dustin Pari doesn't need reality television and reality television doesn't need Dustin Pari." I went on to say how you need to know whom you are and what you stand for. Don't allow yourself to be taken advantage of or manipulated. I closed with a profound statement about how we are given this incredible human experience with which we can do truly amazing and awe inspiring things, but most of us simply nine to five it, and ride the couch watching television and numbing our minds.

I may be taking myself less seriously. I may be in face paint. I may be sleep deprived. But I do take who I am and what I stand for very seriously. I'm here to inspire others, to provide hope, to shine light in the darkness, and above all, to ensure others never give up.

Saturday, June 20, 2015

I may be on the verge of extinction. On the bright side, I'll make for one hell of a fossil.

Sunday, June 21, 2015

A crazy storm was moving in yesterday so I hopped in the rental and started back late last night in hopes of staying ahead of the storm and make it home for Father's Day. The first hour of my journey home was lit up brilliantly by lightning streaking across the darkened night sky. It was truly beautiful. My favorite weather is a good thunderstorm with lots of lightning and pouring rain, the kind of rain that almost hurts when it hits your skin.

I made it from Pennsylvania, through New Jersey and through New York, and halfway through Connecticut before I had to get some sleep. That damn Connecticut has gotten me twice on this trip. I'm sure it's a grand state and all, but out of all the roads I have driven over the years, driving highway 95 through the constitution state tests my constitution every time.

I grabbed a two or three hour nap and was awoken by pouring rain. I pulled the driver's seat back up and headed out again. I avoided two cars that spun out of control due to pooling water on the roadway, and made it back in time to have breakfast with my dad on Father's Day. We went to the International House of Pancakes together. Some of my best memories with my father have been made over breakfast. I finished up, said goodbye, and then I went home and tackled my little girl with kisses. Out of all the things I have done in this life, being a father to that little Bean-head of mine is the one I am most proud of.

Monday, June 22, 2015

Recovering from sleep deprivation. We will resume with our regularly scheduled programming tomorrow … maybe.

Tuesday, June 23, 2015

A tornado warning is in effect for Rhode Island and southeastern Massachusetts right now. I have only seen tornados whilst driving through Indiana before, never back here at home. However, much like everything else, I'm not worrying about it much. Worst case scenario, I end up in Oz singing duets with the Scarecrow. I do fancy that "If I Only Had a Brain" song. Fun fact: I once played the Cowardly Lion in my fifth grade production of *The Wizard of Oz* back at good ole Monsignor Bove Elementary School on Branch Avenue in Providence. I daresay I was the hit of the show. My artistic delivery of the line, "Courage!" was well received.

Alas, we aren't in Kansas anymore, Toto.

Wednesday, June 24, 2015

The house is still on the foundation and there's no dead witch under it, so I guess my dreams of winged monkeys were just fancy filled dreams after all. Too bad. Miss Garland and I were getting along quite well. I suppose I'll just have to meet her at the fair in St. Louis.

Thursday, June 25, 2015

Six months until Christmas Eve! I love Christmas Eve. There is hope. There is peace. It's quite magical. I recall one grand December 24th evening when I was a child where it snowed. There are few moments more perfect than snow on such a special night.

Friday, June 26, 2015

Leaving work early and heading down to Fishkill, New York for Hudson Valley ParaCon. I have to be at the VIP party tonight. At some point I need to put sleep on my calendar. I keep hearing grand things about sleep and I would seriously like to find some time to try it out for myself on a regular basis.

Saturday, June 27, 2015

I was feeling pretty good this morning as I had only one adult beverage at the VIP party last night, as is customary at such things. Then I drank a few glasses of water and some chocolate milk. I'm not one to overindulge, especially not when I'm on the clock in front of fans, friends, and guests. I hold nothing against those who party it up, as all are welcome to do as they please, but I do like to look around and see who is lying face down on their table or hiding behind dark sunglasses in the morning.

I met many kind people today. I moved some copies of my last two books, autographed pictures and a few t-shirts. I also went over to the Red Line Diner and ate a delicious grilled cheese and bacon, followed up with some pie, which is also customary for me. I have to do the ghost hunt thing tonight. In all honesty, I'm not really looking forward to it, only because it runs until 2am, and when you have been standing on your feet for twelve hours entertaining anyone who comes your way, it makes for a long day.

Sunday, June 28, 2015

Wow! I was not expecting last night's ghost hunt event to go the way it did. I was over in Museum Village. It was an artsy area with little one-room recreations of old time life. I was in the livery building with my trusty Radio Shack AM/FM radio scanner set up for others to listen. It didn't take long before I established communication.

The spirit present did something I have never had done before. It rattled off the names, sometimes first, sometimes last, and sometimes both, of many researchers and investigators I have worked with both on and off of television. It even identified John Zaffis as "Ziggity", a nickname that many of us call him. It then repeated a name over and over that I did not recognize. It was the name of one of the gentlemen in the room with me. When he identified himself I asked if the spirit knew the man. It said it did not, but gave a woman's name instead, and repeated it again and again. Turns out the woman's name was that of a young lady who passed away earlier this week, and she was a friend of the gentlemen whom was with me. He was quite taken aback. I asked who it was speaking, figuring it was someone who had passed previously that was helping her as she was new on that side. Instead of a familiar name, I was told "Angel".

Not knowing what to think, and quite startled by how strong and clear the connection was tonight, I asked if it was a person named Angel or if it was an angel. At this point the radio, which is programmed to stay on a permanent scan, locked onto a channel that sounded like static mixed with classical music of some sort. The external speaker I use grew louder and its green indicator light became very bright, and then nothing. It all shut off completely. Very odd, indeed.

I left the investigation and went to the diner to gather my thoughts and get some blueberry pancakes, and some blueberry pie. Blueberries are my favorite berry and I needed some comfort to process all that had happened.

Monday, June 29, 2015

I'm going out with some friends tonight for pizza and beer. I'm still rather exhausted from this past weekend, and the weekend before that, and the weekend before that. But I'm alone so much; it will be good for me to get out with my crew. I've known all these guys since high school and one of them since first grade.

I work a lot. That may be an understatement. I assist in surgery a few times a week, but I also spend a fair amount of time in my office, alone. I usually start my day at the gym, alone. I drive from state to state, event to event, empty hotel room to empty hotel room, alone. I eat alone at all night diners. And by the time I get home, everyone is asleep, so even though I'm not alone, I often feel it.

So, tonight will be good for me, as although I'm strong as a bull and hard as a rock, I rather not be an island.

Tuesday, June 30, 2015

I worked all day and then drove down to Connecticut to film *Ghost Hunters*. It was our first case here in New England, which is supposed to be making things easier for me with travel. The case itself was not the most memorable, but we did film a new opening sequence for the show tonight. The production crew filled the basement with smoke and dry ice, creating a very spooky effect. They then lit up some bright lights, which took a few tries as circuits kept blowing but was eventually straightened out. The end result was our figures walking through lighted fog, our shadowy silhouettes stretching through the distance. Very cool, indeed.

Wednesday, July 1, 2015

I only slept about three hours last night as filming went long and then the lady at the front desk of the hotel seemingly needed to turn two keys simultaneously and obtain secure launch codes before she would issue me my room key. I drove back up to Rhode Island and worked all day. I'm now heading back to Connecticut to film another case tonight. I forgot how difficult this turnaround is. At least when I'm far away on the road, I can sleep in as late as I want to on this day. Sadly, that was not the case this morning, and thus I'm heading into another investigation after working a full day on two-and-a-half hours of sleep.

Thursday, July 2, 2015

I think I'm back on the brink of extinction. That being said, if I can find an appropriate bed of sediment to utilize for my final resting place, I may yet make for one hell of a fossil.

Friday, July 3, 2015

A day off! Sweet Christmas! I thought it would never come. I think the last day off I had was the first weekend of June. I spent over seven hours of this day working in the yard, cutting the lawn, trimming the edges, pruning the hedges, and fertilizing the whole lot. But all of that matters little for there was a moment today that shined so brightly it was beyond anything else I could've imagined.

My little Beans has been in theater camp this week at the local YMCA. Mama Bear and I went this morning to see her performance put on for the other children at camp, staff, and parents. The production was a few selected scenes from *Grease*, in which our daughter played Rizzo, the smart-mouthed tough girl, leader of the Pink Ladies.

Kids are the best litmus test for a theatrical performance as they are as honest as it gets. I have seen my daughter perform her dance routines at various stages and theaters across New England, but I have never seen her act outside of the walls of her elementary school. I was amazed! She was perfect and then some. Not only did she nail all of her lines, but she also delivered them with emotion, clarity and a whole lot of sass. And not only did Mama Bear and I think she did well, but the crowd did too. The kids were hanging on her every word, and they applauded her loudly at the end of each scene.

Afterwards we met the theater director who said Beans was very blessed and definitely had a gift for performing. Several parents stopped us to say that our daughter had something special. I was so proud of her. I don't know why I was given such an incredible little girl to look after, but I'm so very thankful for it.

Saturday, July 4, 2015

"Oh say can you see…."

I spent a little time today at the cemetery, as I believe that July 4th should be spent, at least partly, in reflection for those who came before us. Those who served in our military. Those who died in service. Those who shed tears for loved ones who were far away from home, and perhaps never returned. The freedoms that we are blessed to have in this country, in these United States of America, have been paid for with the blood of many. It may not be a perfect land to live in. It has its faults. But of all the lands I have visited over the years, this is my home, and I love it.

I bought some sparklers and little pop-its for my daughter. Mama Bear and I sat on the front steps and participated in our own little celebration of our country. It wasn't quite as elaborate of some of the firework extravaganzas you see at your local ball field or on television, but it was just right for us.

Sunday, July 5, 2015

Today was simple.

- Church
- Oil changes
- Wash trucks
- Play in pool with Beans
- Evidence review for *Ghost Hunters*
- Watch NASCAR

Church was great. I had not been able to go in about a month due to my schedule, and I know I won't be able to go for another month, so it was important for me to attend. I also received a special birthday blessing, which is coming up next weekend.

Oil changes are where my day became derailed. Two out of three oil filters crumpled and broke when I was trying to get them off. The sun was beating down, I was sweating, covered in grease, squeezed underneath these trucks, and nothing was going right. I'll tell you this, from now on, no matter what special is being offered at my local auto parts store, I'll always buy Fram oil filters. This was the first time I had other filters on my vehicles, and what usually takes me an hour to complete (all three vehicles), took the better part of three hours. There was a small cloud of profanity that may still be lingering in the driveway. I'm just glad Mama Bear and Beans were in the pool far from my little tantrum.

I cooled down by washing all the trucks and then following up with a shower before joining Beans in the pool. The rest of the day went along without any issues, with the exception of an exceptionally long NASCAR rain delay.

Back to work in the morning. No day off in sight for two weeks.

Monday, July 6, 2015

No one gives Eskimo kisses anymore. You know, "Eskimo kisses" where you rub noses playfully with the other person. I'm bringing it back. Eskimo kisses all around!

Tuesday, July 7, 2015

Some days I feel a little too pressured to sit down here and write something profound, and so, here it is: Something Profound.

Wednesday, July 8, 2015

I slept ten hours last night. TEN HOURS! That is almost unheard of.

Thursday, July 9, 2015

Lots going on and even more coming up! I have an event this weekend in Tennessee, followed by an event next weekend in Rhode Island, NASCAR in New Hampshire, and then an event in Pennsylvania. But, as the little mice in the animated holiday special *'Twas the Night Before Christmas* sang, "You hope, and I'll hurry. You pray, and I'll plan. We'll do what's necessary, cuz' even a miracle needs a hand." Speaking of which, I better pray for a good long while tonight. With my upcoming schedule, it looks like I could use a miracle, or at least a hand.

Friday, July 10, 2015

Beans just fell asleep. We watched the second of the Harry Potter movies, *The Chamber of Secrets*, tonight. I just started getting her into the franchise. I read all the books back when they came out many moons ago. And now, at eight years of age, my little one is enjoying these same tales with me. I enjoy them even more so now as she lays snuggled between my chest and left arm to watch them.

Now I have to pack for tomorrow morning's trip to Chattanooga. I should be able to get about four hours of sleep in if I time everything just right. These early morning flights are not my favorite but they do allow for me to spend a night home like I had tonight, so I'm not complaining.

Good night, my friends. Mischief managed.

Saturday, July 11, 2015

I'm aboard U.S. Airways flight 1831 on my way to Charlotte, and then to Chattanooga. I'm comfortably stretched out in exit row seat 10F by the window. This is my favorite seat as there is no seat in front of me, which in turn allows a tall glass of water such as me to stretch out his 6'1" frame.

I'm doing a gig tonight for Tetlow at the old South Pittsburgh Hospital in Tennessee. I've never been there before, nor has old man John Zaffis whom I'm working with tonight, so it should prove interesting if for nothing more than change of venue.

Also, since I have not been here before, there should be lots of new friends and fans in attendance. Speaking of new friends and fans, I'm quickly becoming a fan of the young lady seated at my ten o'clock position. She's wearing a little light colored sundress and dark colored underpants. She keeps getting up and bending over in dramatic fashion in front of me for some reason. It's like she is advertising those underpants. Hey, I may be married, and I try to always wear the white hat like a good little cowboy or the pope, but I'm not made of iron and I do have eyes you know. I fancy sundresses. Yoga pants are all the rage these days. They're very tight-fitting pants, but apparently the lady folk find them very comfortable, as there is an army of them strolling about in the same black yoga pants as the next gal. Me? I'm a sundress man. Very fashionable, very stylish. I love when Mama Bear sports a sundress.

Ahh, well, back to writing D. Pari—stay focused.

It's actually quite the distracting flight. It's chock full without an empty seat to be found, except for the one next to me. "This must be the day that all my dreams come true," as Bob Dylan penned in one of my favorite Dylan songs "New Morning".

Though there are not any other empty seats on this plane, judging by the malodor that is plaguing U.S. Airways flight 1831, there must have been a lot of empty shower stalls this morning. As for me, I'm a gentleman whom enjoys a good thorough wash in the morning, and often at the end of the day as well. Lather. Rinse. Repeat.

Well, it appears the captain is preparing to put down the landing gear and thus I shall continue this literary misadventure on the next flight.

Here I am on U.S. Airways flight 5179 exit row aisle seat 8D. This has been a pleasant day for travel, if you aren't counting the stench on the first flight. For I shall tell you this, there is light and there is darkness for you cannot have the sweet without the sour. You can however choose which one you look upon more frequently. I could remember the foul malodor that seemed to fester in the very seat cushions of that last flight, or I can remember the young lady who really needs to rethink her choice in color of undergarments. I shall remember the latter, with a smile.

This giant metal bird will take me into Chattanooga, Tennessee. I don't know much about Chattanooga, but I do enjoy singing: "Pardon me, boys. Is that the Chattanooga Choo-Choo?"

Speaking of singing, the talented Mr. Kermit Ruffins is currently recording in the elite suite betwixt my ears. He is a grand jazz musician from New Orleans, a place I often escape to out of the back door of my cerebellum. I enjoy taking a mental picnic there. I wear a white linen suit and sip mojitos that are brought to me via animated alligators. Mr. Kermit Ruffins plays "When I Die You Better Second Line" with his band, just off to the right there in the ivy-covered gazebo across the river. It's one of my favorite places to take imaginary vacations.

I once took a real vacation to New Orleans during Mardi Gras when I was in my early twenties. I went with my longtime friend and co-conspirator Mr. Richard P. Fredette, AKA "Mr. French".

We had a grand time for sure. Each morning Mr. French and I awoke in our hotel, readied ourselves, and we would strut on down to Bourbon Street to buy a fishbowl, a hurricane, or a three for one priced coconut rum and cola. We wore our beads. We exchanged them with young ladies. Then we sauntered back through the dirty streets to our hotel room and take a nap, only to awaken and arise again like Nosferatu when the sun went down and party time had begun once again.

One night there was a great moment of raw passion between one young lady any myself. We had seen each other here and there throughout Mardi Gras and exchanged pleasantries, and then, one magical night, we bumped into each other and kissed passionately. That's all there was to it. Just one stolen moment in time. One freeze frame from my youth that I hope ends up in the slide show of my life when I get to watch the highlight reel at the pearly gates with Saint Peter and friends. I never even knew her name, but I never will forget that one simple kiss.

"Give me a kiss to build a dream on, and my imagination, will thrive upon that kiss. Sweetheart, I ask no more than this, a kiss to build a dream on." It was sung best by another famed New Orleans musician, another personal favorite, Mr. Louis Armstrong.

There is even a better memory, or at least a more laughable one that stemmed from that trip. The French and I were going about our morning routine. We had just left some bar that was playing Kid Rock's hit at the time, "Cowboy", whilst some young lady in a wet t-shirt was dancing on stage. The show was enjoyable, but a man must have his nap, and so we took our leave and rambled back to the hotel.

I wasn't even wearing a shirt on this day, just shorts, beads, sunglasses and a smile. With fishbowl of coconut rum and cola in hand, and Mr. French in tow, I ankled it into the lobby of the building and headed towards the elevator as to access my room. Mr. French somehow got detained by the security guard at the door and was yelling something to me as the doors closed and the little "bing" had sounded. Up, up, up went the elevator. I was still singing the lyrics to "Cowboy" quite loudly. When the doors opened up on floor 24, I was greeted by a fetching young lady sitting at a desk wearing formal business attire. When I inquired as to the whereabouts of my room, she laughed and asked where I was staying. I gave her the name of the hotel and my room number, at which time she informed me the hotel was the next building over. Good times. Good, good times.

Listen up, chipmunks, to my advice. I don't condone a lifestyle of drunkenness and debauchery. I believe in enjoying myself within reason and being responsible at all times especially now that I have been married for many moons to Mama Bear, and I want to be a good father and role model for Beans. If I go out now a day, it's a one or two drink maximum, and I don't enjoy adult beverages around my daughter regularly. However, this is your life. You have to enjoy yourself and create stories at some time or another. Have a day of slightly joyous over-celebration responsibly. Wander into the wrong hotel. Kiss with passion, even if you don't know her name. Best do it when you're young if you can. And absolutely do it before they lower you into that hole in the ground at your local cemetery or they sprinkle your ashes in the Haunted Mansion ride at Disney World.

Sunday, July 12, 2015

HAPPY BIRTHDAYYYYYYYY TOOOOOO MEEEEEEE!

That's right boys and girls, in the immortal words of Mr. F.T. Snowman, "Happy Birthday!"

Today I'm 38-years-old, or at least that is what they tell me. I think I look younger, feel older, and embrace the mind of a very distractible nine-year-old child. Perhaps it averages out to 38 in the grand scheme of things.

I'm sitting in the Chattanooga airport, the same one I left less than twenty hours ago. I did the investigation gig last night, slept just about two hours, and now I find myself here at gate one, awaiting permission to climb aboard U.S. Airways flight 5165 to Charlotte, on my way back to the airport in Rhode Island.

My two hours of beauty sleep was actually interrupted halfway through when I could have sworn my alarm went off and it was time to go, and so I did. I got up, showered, shaved, and put my contacts in, only to realize it was all in my head and I still had the better part of an hour left to sleep. So I took the contacts out and climbed back in bed until the alarm went off for real. That's one way to start your birthday… in a land of confusion.

Oh! I almost forgot. Funny thing happened on the way to the airport this morning. I saw the Chattanooga Choo-Choo! Well, that is to say, as I was pulling into the airport there was a train rolling along the tracks adjacent to the airport, and so technically I just saw a train whilst in Chattanooga, but it's my birthday damn it, and that train will be what I want it to be. It was filled with happy hobos playing the mouth harp, drinking whiskey, and singing songs of old man Zimmerman. The boxcars were filled with unicorns and wet dreams. A fine morning it was. One hell of a way for a man to start his 38th year.

And now, for my next trick, I shall make my way onto the plane and tuck myself into seat 6A.

That last flight was too tight to type. The gentleman that was squeezed in next to me had the distinct aroma of cheap aftershave, expensive scotch, and lies. Let us just say I'm glad it was a quick flight.

I'm now happily planted in aisle seat 19D aboard U.S. Airways flight 5133 on my way back to Rhode Island. I'm not too sure what is going on upstairs in my mind. I think Jinglebottom, Head Imaginary Elf in charge, has neglected some duties up there at Jolly Good Times, as it appears the peppermint dam has sprung a leak, the eggnog river has once again overflowed, and the elves are all bare-assed and skinny dipping. This is going to take me some time to clean up. Maybe I can get some shuteye later today. In the meantime, here are some random magical musings:

- When I fly, I often look out the windows hoping to see aliens on their way back from the grocery store.
- I hope I don't get that scared old person look on my face when I become a ripened tomato. I'd imagine they were just frightened young people, too.
- Tomorrow is not promised to you, so you might as well get weird with today.
- The Snoopy Sno-Cone Machine is pure magic wrapped in plastic and filled with ice.
- I have always been a fan of those movies where the main characters do something to make them switch bodies. If that happened to me, I'm pretty sure one of the first things I would do is get a really embarrassing tattoo on my new body, so when we switch back, the person knew I was there.

I've never been one to make a big deal out of my birthday. I always felt like it was a personal New Year's Eve, and I'm not a fan of New Year's Eve. This year seems different, though. Normally I do this strange internal retrospective thing where I look at where I'm at financially, where I'm at with my spiritual life, my relationships—both professional and personal, and I compare and contrast where I am with where others are, and where I think I should be.

Now it could be sleep deprivation, it could be the alignment of some distant heavenly bodies, or it could be my own personal growth and awakening, but this year, well, as Clark Gable most famously said in *Gone With the Wind*, "Frankly my dear, I don't give a damn." I'm where I am. I'm here because this is where I have to be right now. There's no sense in comparing where I was last year, last month, last week or even yesterday with where I am today, because I am not even the same person today. This is now. This is my life. This is the only moment that truly matters. This moment cannot change the past, but it can sway the future, so I need to pay attention to now, not yesterday.

I cannot compare my life, my finances, my brick-a-brack collection with that of anyone else, for even if we are of the same age, we are not at the same point in our journey. Just as we all read at different speeds, we all live at different speeds. There is no sense in comparing my Chapter 15 with someone's Chapter 27. I'll get to that point in the story when I get to it. Right now I have to live this part out. And live it, I will. Live it, I am. We're often holding up our full-length lives where we know every inner thought, every behind the scene secret, and then compare our lives with the highlight reel of others that they carefully edit, enhance, and present to us.

Don't buy that bullshit. Just be your own bull. Live your own life. Destroy a china shop or two if you have to, but live your life your way, as only you can.

And so, as the pilot switches off autopilot in the front of the plane, as the flight attendant prepares the cabin for landing, I'm preparing myself for this, my 38th year on earth, the island home of my spirit. The journey thus far has been quite remarkable. I am thankful for it.

I don't know what tomorrow holds. I don't care to know. I'm not comparing any aspect of my life with anyone else's, nor am I comparing it with the ghosts of my own Christmas pasts. This is my day. This is my now. This is my life. I'm just going to have some fun and get a little weirder with it as time goes on, simply because it amuses me.

Someday, if I make it to be a wrinkly old man, whose face reflects one of a joyous life well lived, and not one masked in fear, maybe then I'll look back a little more introspectively, but not now. This is my time.

Happy birthday to me, for I am one beautiful bastard.

Monday, July 13, 2015

I slept twelve hours last night! It was an excellent gift given to me by my wife and daughter. Peace, quiet, and sweet slumber. Yesterday was excellent, actually. When I finally came home from the airport I found Mama Bear and Beans were out in the pool. I went in to drop off my luggage when what to my sleepy eyes should appear? Homemade birthday decorations from my wife and daughter that decorated the walls of our kitchen. There was even a banner. One sign my daughter made listed words that described me. "Fun, love, hardworking money maker" were some of the words that she wrote. That's my girl, appreciating her daddy. We all played in the pool for some time and then Mama Bear cooked on the grill. Beans had selected a nice red velvet cake for me. The girl has good taste.

At work today, they had a chocolate cake for me along with a card with some very kind sentiments about appreciating all I do for my work family. It made me feel good to be regarded so kindly by those whom I manage and look after on a day-to-day basis.

Ah well, another year in the books. Time to get working on this one. Thirty-eight and feeling great!

Tuesday, July 14, 2015

And today I was in my other office, the one in Rhode Island, and they had a white cake for me there. Three days. Three cakes. This year is starting off pretty damn sweet!

Wednesday, July 15, 2015

BRILLIANT!

I was sitting in my office today listening to a little Christmas music and taking care of business when I had a wonderfully brilliant idea. This winter, Dustin Pari will host the first ever "Winter Wassailing" event! The plan is to invite people to a limited ticket event where they will come with me to go door-to-door Christmas caroling on some snowy winter's evening. Of course, I hope there will be snow, but I cannot guarantee snow—only Santa can do that. The fee will be small, to cover the simple printing of the song booklets and some candles. And afterward we will all gather together for hot cocoa and Christmas cookies. Whatever money is raised will then be donated to the American Foundation for Suicide Prevention and for the church that I attend. I already have my man Marc Tetlow working on the details. This will be amazing!

Sweet Christmas!

Thursday, July 16, 2015

Sometimes I sit and ponder deep things. Things that most people probably glaze over whilst traveling through this human experience. Things like do young hippopotamus girls ever look longingly at young rhinoceros boys and vice versa? Do the father hippos disapprove of such things? Alas, the world may never know.

Friday, July 17, 2015

Busy day for ole D. Pari today. I had an inspired workout thanks to the musical sytlings of Mr. Eazy E and Mr. Leon Redbone. I'm pretty sure I'm the only fellow who has a gym playlist that consists of those two exclusively.

Now to pack up for tomorrow's Ocean State ParaCon event. The hustle continues. I'll sleep when I'm dead, maybe. I think that God gives us jobs in heaven. I'm kind of hoping He will let me have my one day of landscaping the sky, and then transition me to the bakery department.

Saturday, July 18, 2015

The ParaCon was a great time today. It was a rare treat to do an event here in the state of my origin. Plus, the little tent they had me set up under was right on a little pond of sorts in Harrisville, so the view was quite pleasant.

As promised, here on my third run in paranormal television and my tenth year of doing events and such, I'm getting weird with it. Today's lecture, *Magical Musings of a Madman*, was a hodgepodge of paranormal ideas, motivational moments, and absolute happy nonsense. All of this presented by yours truly, who started off the lecture wearing a glimmering, shimmering, dazzling cape akin to that of Mr. Elvis Presley.

My buddy Cody DesBiens, who once did a stint as an Elvis impersonator, had the cape as part of a full outfit and was kind enough to lend it to me for my weirdness du jour. Cody even cued up the Elvis entrance music at the last minute so that I could make a grand entrance. I waited through the three musical cues in the wings of the theater, and then went out, back to the crowd, cape up, then turned and took a knee at each corner of the stage before starting my shenanigans.

The stage had a great little rim of lights that were mounted on a thin rail of a wall that separated the stage from the crowd. Being part mountain goat I decided to pace along this little area during my lecture to lend to a heightened sense of danger and misadventure, or just because it seemed like something to do to entertain myself whilst entertaining others.

The microphone they handed me was muted at the time I came out, but since I project my voice quiet loudly, I decided not to use it but to keep it with me as a prop; a prop that I kept with me the entire time because if you are going with a gimmick, you have to stick with it.

Now I have to think about what to do at the next event.

Sunday, July 19, 2015

It's race day! I'm heading up to Loudon, New Hampshire, with my cousin Franky and my buddy Joey D'Antonio. Joey and I worked together back when I was a Cardiac Level Emergency Medical Technician for MedCare Ambulance. We have stayed friends over the years. He even did a stint working with me at the oral surgeon's office, where I'm still employed. Joey has gone on to be a fire fighter for the city of Warwick. We both are married with children, so we never see each other. But we text and we get together once a year for this race. It's always a grand time. Merry mischief awaits! I may even allow for Jasper P. Jinglebottom, head elf at Jolly Good Times to come on out of my head and have some fun. He deserves a break, as do I. Vroom! Vroom!

Monday, July 20, 2015

Yesterday was awesome! Thanks to Jonathan Helfman down in Baltimore, my buddies and I had Hot Passes for the race yesterday and thus hung out in the garages before the race. A kind woman called Kat whom I met at the race earlier this season in Martinsville, Virginia, runs a traveling kitchen for the Hendrick Motorsports and RCR teams. Since she's a sweetheart and a *Ghost Hunters* fan, she feeds me breakfast. Well, not literally. I feed myself, but she allows me to eat there. Cousin Franky, Joey D, and I had a hearty breakfast and then went back to checking out the cars in the garages that were getting ready for pre-race inspection with the NASCAR officials.

My favorite driver Mr. Kurt Busch was standing by to do a live interview by his hauler when we walked by. I had caught his eye and he gave me a wave and said hello just before the interview started. We hung around until he was finished and I introduced him to my cousin. Joey D was lurking around the back as he doesn't like to bother people of notoriety. I assured him that Kurt was a great guy and it wasn't an issue. I wished Kurt luck and the boys and I wandered back out to the truck in the parking lot for a little pre-race celebration.

There was some celebrating with choice adult beverages in a responsible manner, or at least as responsible a manner as can be expected considering the location and circumstances. It became apparent that we needed to eat and so, being a grill master himself, Joey D, wearing the sparkly green hat associated with Jinglebottom, thus completing the illusion of my mental fantasy, manned the grill as cousin Franky looked on in admiration of the little elf's skills.

A nice cold bottle of Dr. McGillicuddy's Mentholmint was passed around as Mr. Jerry Reed sang "East Bound and Down" through the speakers of the truck.

We packed up the coolers and set the grill to the side to cool before making our way back to the track to watch the race in the sweltering sun. Kurt's brother Kyle ended up winning, with Kurt finishing up in tenth position.

I didn't have another adult beverage once the race had started, so I drove Joey's truck Stella back home as he lay sleeping in the backseat wearing the Jinglebottom hat. Remind me to tell you the origin story of the hat at some point as it also has a bit of magic and whimsy to it. About an hour into our return trip Joey woke back up and joined cousin Franky (who now has also come to be known as Day Drinking Franky) in a series of sing-along road trip songs. We belted out the classic rock tune "Joy To the World" by Three Dog Night along with Mr. Willie Nelson's country classic "Whiskey River" as Stella tore up the asphalt, white lines flickering by, all the way home.

It was a good break for me. A rare day off, as you have probably come to see. Funny enough, we are now approaching my busy season. Reach up and pull them straps down tight kids, they are about to drop the green flag.

Tuesday, July 21, 2015

Change is in the air today… and it smells like Turtle Wax.

Wednesday, July 22, 2015

I went to the movies last night with Mama Bear and Beans to see *Minions*. It was a very enjoyable evening. The movie was funny and had an excellent soundtrack. I am so glad that I have my daughter for so many reasons, one of which is that I can go see all these animated movies without anyone thinking I'm a bit strange. Let them think I'm strange for other reasons. Lord knows there is a variety to choose from.

Thursday, July 23, 2015

There are days it seems I've fallen out of the S.S. Happy Nonsense and been cast adrift in the darkened seas of swirling salty misery. This was one of those days. But I do what I do. I flip the Etch A Sketch over and start again. I smile in defiance. I don't allow the gray clouds of dark minded people to stay in the blue skies of my mind. This is my life. I decide if I'm happy or not. And I choose happy. And now I choose to go into my basement and pack for tomorrow's trip to Pennsylvania for this weekend's event in Erie.

Friday, July 24, 2015

U.S. Airways flight 4018 held a little surprise for me this morning as I was unaware that I'd be traveling with Miss Amy Bruni whom I have known for many moons and done many an event and television program with. She is doing an event in Pittsburgh and so we are on the same flights today. I'm nestled back in the exit row, seat 8F. She is not seated next to me as I'm next to a gentleman with very hairy arms, which is making sharing the armrest uncomfortable.

I'm trying to distract myself with thoughts about what little bit of strangeness I'm going to bring to my lecture tomorrow. I have recently purchased a pair of dark jeans that are all torn up and bleached, creating a very nice mid 1980s look. Mama Bear disapproves. I bought a teal shirt that looks to have been kissed by a giant pair of hot pink lips, which also creates for a very nice mid 1980s look. Mama Bear disapproves. I'm toying with wearing a touch of eyeliner to assist in creating a very nice mid 1980s look. Mama Bear really disapproves.

I tried to explain to my wife that the whole idea is to break this mold of guys on paranormal television currently. We don't all have to wear black shirts, stand with our arms folded, look angry, and puff ourselves up with false pretense and bravado.

I'm a happy soul bouncing through life and getting a little weird with it, if only for my own entertainment and self-celebration. Hence the title of my lecture tomorrow night, "Dustin Pari presents: Getting Weird With It". I want everything that I do to reflect my inner light and unique brand of strangeness.

Now that I have my outfit all planned out, what the hell should I talk about?

U.S. Airways flight 4533 is bouncing from cloud top to cloud top from Philadelphia to Pittsburgh. I'm relaxed, sipping my in-flight tomato juice to satiate my in-flight vampire, and I'm listening to Christmas music. This is the life. It may not be the one that I dreamed about as a young boy, but then again, seldom do our dreams and realities ever match up. I like to think I've done well, though. The important things are in place. I may not be the starting quarterback for the Miami Dolphins. I may not be a NASCAR driver. But, I have been a part of television, both in front of and behind the camera for most of my life. I work in health care and help a lot of people. My motivational and my Christian work seem to hit home with some wayward souls. My wife and daughter are healthy and have a warm home with electricity and clean water. All good things.

Comparatively, speaking as it relates to dreams and reality, it may not be a wet one, but my life is closer to that than it is to a nightmare.

All right, captain, let's bring this bird in for a landing!

Saturday, July 25, 2015

I went down to the lakeside last night for dinner and watched the sun melt away. It was a most beautiful moment; one that I'll cherish. I don't get out to Lake Erie often, and the locals tell me that they are famous for their sunsets, and with good reason.

Today was convention day for the LiveParanormal SuperCon. I met a lot of nice people. Many of my friends were there. The weird genius of Detroit, Mr. John Tenney was in attendance. Ms. Rosalyn Bown, the sweetest girl in New Jersey, was there. My good friend Mr. Clay Smith and his wife Joy were also present, and we actually shared a few glasses of Captain Morgan rum together last night. Well, Clay and I did at least, because we are pirates. Joy drank wine because she is a proper lady.

Lecture time was a lot of fun for me. I stopped peddling my wares and returned to my room to shower up and perform a costume change before delivering my lecture, *Getting Weird with It.* I wore everything as I said I would yesterday. My outfit did make for a very nice mid-1980s look. I sent a picture of it to Mama Bear but she didn't reply. I suppose she didn't approve. Oh well, I'm entertaining myself anyhow.

Time to get ready for tonight's investigation event, which will land me back here in the hotel for about 2am. I originally was taking the first flight out of Pittsburgh tomorrow but I'm opting to sleep in and take the later flight back. I have to film this week and I'll need all the sleep I can get. I know it is out of character for me to rest and catch a later flight but I am exhausted.

Sunday, July 26, 2015

I'm flying high in the sky but sadly without apple pie. United Airlines flight 3790 is taking me from Steel City to my least favorite airport, Washington-Dulles. I can't complain, though. Remember that early flight I changed my mind on? Well, it ended up having some issues and had to make an emergency landing in Philadelphia this morning. Miss Amy Bruni was aboard and said the passengers had to assume crash positions and everything. I'm glad to report that everyone was fine and the plane landed safely, all be it in the wrong airport and earlier than expected.

This plane is a newer one. The seats are thinner and more plastic than cushion. It's like flying in a modern office building. Yeah, exciting, right? What happened to big seats and those sexy birds of yesteryear?

I think I shall just crank up my Christmas music and let Alvin and The Chipmunks play a few songs in the elite suite betwixt my ears for the duration of this flight. The rest of you chipmunks should heed Dave Seville's advice: you better be good and you better be nice.

United Airlines 3761 is making its way across a cloudy night sky illuminated with lightning bolts and magic. This is my favorite flying scenario. Small plane. Stormy weather. Mr. Elvis Presley taking care of business in a flash and serenading me from the elite suite betwixt my ears. He is currently singing "I Want You, I Need You, I Love You", a song that he recorded in the studio after getting off of a flight that almost crashed not once, but twice; Just another reason why you have to love the King.

I'm in seats 12C and 12D as I just so happen to have chosen wisely and selected an empty row for myself. This little flight will drop me off back in Rhode Island where I'll slide behind the wheel of ole Angelina and drive home for a few hours' sleep before hitting the gym and going to work. This week I go back to filming for that ole ghost show again as we start to shoot the remainder of the season eleven episodes. I don't have any events this coming weekend but the week after will be a huge undertaking as I travel to the northern part of Michigan for an event at Kewadin Casino. It's always a stellar event, but a bit of a pain in the hindquarters to get to.

But, as the Master Of The House from *Les Miserables* sings merrily, "Travel's a curse." Truth be told, I have yet to see the show, but I'm rather fond of the song itself. I listen to it at the gym a lot.

Hey! Donovan has slid into the studio and is playing "Season of the Witch" for the live studio audience in my mind. They seem to be enjoying it. The song lends to a certain sense of whimsy that is beneficial for most everyone to experience. Funny enough this was the song the DJ at Jolly Good Times was playing in my mind when I awoke this morning. It can only mean one thing … fall is coming. One more month until crunchy leaves and pumpkin flavored everything.

The ass end of the year is my favorite part, as the ass end of a woman is also my favorite part. I cannot tell a lie. Strange to think this year is approaching its last quarter pretty soon. We will also be ending our literary journey about the same time. I hope you have enjoyed it thus far.

Stay tuned, my friends. More madness is to come.

Rest well and tempt not the fates.

Monday, July 27, 2015

It looks like I have a long couple of weeks on deck, which is nothing new. I do have this upcoming weekend to myself, so that will be nice.

I may have to use one of those days to scout a new place to work out. When I went into the gym this morning there was a sign on the door stating that they would be closing at the end of August. The building will be repurposed and all memberships cancelled. I'm going to miss the old place. I have been going there for the better part of five years now. I kind of like how empty it is, but apparently that has led to its end.

The best part of the day was taking a nice leisurely walk around the neighborhood with Mama Bear and Beans. We were apart all weekend; me with my event and Mama Bear and Beans with the National Dance Competition. I find walks very pleasant and they are a nice opportunity to reconnect in natural conversation without electronic distraction.

Tuesday, July 28, 2015

Investigating an old library down in Westerly, Rhode Island, this evening. Should make for a good time. My buddy Cody DesBiens investigated the place recently and he told me a bit about it. I'm just happy it's so close to home. I'll be able to hit the hotel right afterwards and get some rest before driving up highway 95 and back to work in the morning.

Wednesday, July 29, 2015

Did I say I was going to get some rest? I should have been more specific. I slept for about three hours and headed back to my office. Unfortunately there was quite the accident on the highway this morning and so what should have been a quick 45 minute ride ended up being a scenic two hour tour of the back roads of southern Rhode Island since the highway was complete gridlock. I spent most of my time in thought about loftier things as I have found focusing upon traffic is never a good way to spend one's time.

Tonight I'll drive down to Connecticut after work and investigate an old theater. Should be a decent evening. At least it's a clean and safe building to be in, but to be honest, I never have much luck in theaters.

Thursday, July 30, 2015

Last night I had the most fun I have ever had on an investigation. My buddy KJ McCormick and I were not able to investigate until well after midnight due to the filming schedule and team rotation, so by the time we actually started we were very wound up and terribly silly. At first there was the matter of some sensor lights that we just couldn't seem to get to stay off. Then we became lost and turned around in the dark once we managed to get the lights off. The area we were to focus on was a hallway about fifteen feet in length, not a very expansive location to do research of any kind in, yet KJ said he wanted to try an experiment.

He walked down to the end of the hallway aglow in city lights coming through the window. He then crouches down, and very seriously asks if I could see him. I laughed and assured him that yes, indeed, I did see him. He then followed up by asking if I could see him if he was clear or transparent. I completely lost it in a fit of uncontrollable laughter. Clear or transparent? Of course I couldn't see him no matter where he was if that was the case. That was it. That was his whole experiment. I couldn't stop laughing and he was on the floor doubled over in hysterics. It became catchy as our audio and camera operators were also laughing along with us.

We finished up the night with a fun run wearing our "Buddy Bands" which are white headbands that I wrote our names on in black permanent marker. It's goofy and silly, but it brings us joy and I'm seriously hoping that they will use this footage when they edit the shows. I think it'll bring a great bit of joy to everyone who sees it.

I'm quite exhausted from filming these last two evenings but I have to drive up to Canton, Massachusetts, this evening to film additional segments for the new open of the show. Afterward I'm meeting up with some friends of mine for some pizza and beer. I don't think it will be a terribly late night, as I have had minimal sleep since Monday. There may still be some magic in this old hat I found but I'm not sure how many more rabbits I can pull out of it. Goodnight sweetheart… it's time to go.

Friday, July 31, 2015

Busy weekend in the works! Beans has a birthday party to attend and then we're hosting some of her friends at the house for a play date on Sunday. I want to be selfish and have nothing but family time this weekend, but I have to let the little one grow socially and have time with her friends too. She's quite the social butterfly and plays well with everyone, especially kids older than her.

I have to catch up on yard work and some personal landscaping. I have a hair appointment for tomorrow morning. I may pencil in a brief stop at McShawn's Pub for a tasty adult beverage as well. This life I'm living sure has been a lot of hustling and struggling. Taking time to celebrate responsibly is important.

Above all, I'm looking forward to sleep. Glorious sleep.

Saturday, August 1, 2015

Little Beans and I watched the new movie *Home* on DVD last night. Mama Bear didn't make it through it before nodding off herself. It was a great movie. Beans really liked it. I fell asleep with her tiny head on my chest and her little hand in mine. It made me feel good as I have been struggling with being away so much. It's nice to spend time with her.

Life on the road is the life I know. Working two or three jobs is what I do well. It takes me away from those I love the most, sure. But it does allow for my family to live in a nice home, in a good neighborhood, and for my daughter to attend a well-regarded school. My sacrifice makes it possible for the little one to take her dance lessons that she likes so much. Working day and night allows for us to have such nice vacations each year. And so, I work. It's what I do.

Well, I'm off to get my haircut and get all fancy and man pretty. I'll stop and get a Miller High Life at McShawn's and then head home to cut the lawn and such. When all is said and done I'm planning on taking Mama Bear and Beans to get some ice cream.

Sunday, August 2, 2015

I was able to return to church today. I haven't had the opportunity to go in several weeks due to my schedule. My reverend is on sabbatical for the summer, but the fellow who was substituting for her this weekend was quite enjoyable to listen to. He was an older gentleman, and his entire homily centered upon sharing pie with others, so he is all right by me!

I ended up making a pumpkin pie last night before bed and it cooled overnight. I had some for breakfast. I'm sure I'll eat more as the day goes on. I know it's still summer, and pumpkin pie is a fall food, but I'm ready for it, so I'm starting my fall season early.

My daughter's play date went well today. She had two of her friends over from dance. Mama Bear had the house spotless and she made snacks for the kids. I ordered pizzas and filled up buckets of water balloons for them. I was even able to get in on the fun for a little while, too. Then they went in the pool whilst I settled in front of the TV to watch NASCAR in Pocono.

I listened to some audio from this week's investigation for that ole ghost show. The new episodes will start airing on the 26th of this month. It's interesting to me, being someone who has worked on the production side of things for so many years previously, to sit and see how they put together the show after being a part of it in front of the camera.

Another big week is on deck. Work followed by flights out to Michigan for the big MI-Paracon in Kewadin Casino at the end of the week. It's a huge convention with lots of good people. The only thing I don't like about it is how smoky the casino is. I find myself holding my breath when going from the vendor room to my hotel room. There are few things I like more than fresh air.

Oh! I almost forgot. I always sing karaoke at this event. I should pick out what song I shall sing this year. I have done The Beatles "Twist and Shout", "Jailhouse Rock" by Elvis, and the last time I was there I sang a duet with John Tenney. We sang "I Got You Babe" by Sonny and Cher. I think I was Cher. Or maybe we both were.

Monday, August 3, 2015

In just a month's time, I'll be done with this literary misadventure. I do hope you have found parts of it enjoyable, others laughable, and somewhere in betwixt those moments, perhaps you found a little bit of inspiration.

To be quite honest, I'm feeling a bit exhausted today. I have touched on this before, I think. I try to be everything to everyone, and still have some time left for me to be me. Sadly, the latter part of that previous statement has been proving more and more difficult to do. It's not just the endless onslaught of work that is wearing me down either. It's more the maintenance of connections, relationships both professional and personal, wearing me down of late. I hate that I don't have enough time for all the wonderful people in my life, especially those whom I sacrifice my life to support and care for.

I wish I could just take a day and take my daughter to the aquarium but she's busy with various dance, theater, and craft camps. And me, well, when the hell aren't I busy? Perhaps I'm just too hard on myself. I do a lot with her and Mama Bear. In this past year alone there have been great little moments. There have been Daddy and Daughter nights. We spent Thanksgiving in New York. We had a great Christmas at home. We went to Disney in January. We went to Hershey Park for Easter. We spent countless nights playing video games on the couch. We went to the movies a lot. Not bad considering I travel almost every weekend and work two jobs most weeks. But nonetheless, I want to do more. I want to be everything for her and for everyone.

I feel bad that my grandmother, now in her 90s, is alone at most times. I call her once a week, but I can never seem to find the time to go see her. My parents, whom I talk to daily, will go weeks without seeing me as well. Little Mama Bear is often asleep by the time I get home, if I get home at all. My friends are a series of text messages and quick phone calls squeezed in between. As for me? I'm still half expecting to pass my own ghost in a lonely airport terminal on my way home from somewhere I can barely remember. Another lonely hotel room. Another cab ride. Another flight. Another night. Another life.

I worked at Nino's Pizza on Atwood Avenue in Cranston, Rhode Island for a few years in the late 90s. I am sure I've mentioned it before. If you are ever in the neighborhood be sure to get yourself a pepperoni pizza there. I delivered pizza mostly, but I also helped to prep things from time to time. When it comes to raw dough, which I love to eat, there is one thing that you have to remember, if you stretch it too thin it rips, it tears, and falls apart. I'm feeling like thinly stretched dough lately. Delicious, but almost see through due to over stretching.

I think I'll take it easy tonight. I'll grab a cold Angry Orchard Cinnful Cider from the fridge in the garage, and take a walk as the sun sets behind the tree-lined horizon. I'll say my prayers in thanks before I go to bed. I'll wait for those magical knitting angels of the Lord to fly in through my bedroom window, stitch up my heart, and get me ready for another day. For there is no sense in thinking much further than that. Each day is good. A blessing. I just need a little more time.

Tuesday, August 4, 2015

I awoke to a yellow sky around 5am. If you've ever seen the movie *Something Wicked This Way Comes*, it kind of felt like that. Something strange was blowing into town; I could just feel it in the air.

By the time I grabbed my gym bag, fed the cats, and made my way out of the garage door and to Maggie May my Big Blue Baby, it was as dark as night and pouring rain. Even with my headlights on and windshield wipers on high, I could barely see. Lighting flashed across the blackened sky and people of ancient times were saying prayers and sacrificing small barnyard animals to make up for whatever it was that they had done to anger the gods.

I was low on fuel and pulled up to the gas station as there was another flash of lightning which caused the power to go out, thus rendering the gas pump flaccid with a weak stream like that from an old man's penis. Luckily I had enough fuel to get to the gym and go to work. Not many people were there, which was not surprising considering the storm of the century was brewing and the gym was closing at the end of the month. Regardless, Mr. James Brown played me through an inspired workout and left me saying, "I feel good." I lathered up and showered down in the empty locker room.

As I opened the door of the gymnasium to step out into the parking lot golden rays of sunshine, blue skies, and chirping birds greeted me. This must be what it's like to be a Disney princess, I thought to myself, because who the hell else could I think things to anyways. Maybe Jasper P. Jinglebottom, Head Elf in charge of Jolly Good Times, the imaginary pirate-themed bar in my mind, now complete with swinging pirate ship gondola ride. I guess I could think things to him.

It seriously was like I left a darkened tumultuous world behind and stepped out into the world specifically reserved for filming advertisements for feminine hygiene products. Do I ever get that not so fresh feeling? Sure. From time to time. Perhaps I'll walk through a charming field of sunflowers and think about my vagina maintenance. So serene. So perfect. This could be heaven. I hopped into Maggie May and together we charted our course through this magical wet dream reality to the office, for even in my dreams it turns out that I must work.

The dream quickly became a nightmare, as dreams often do. The highway was a parking lot. A short section of the road which usually takes me about seven minutes to traverse had taken an hour. I made a bee line for the nearest feasible exit to navigate some back roads to my place of employment. I quickly became aware of the reason for all the hub-bub. It appeared that, whilst I was at the gym working on my vanity muscles, the storm raged on and caused large amounts of destruction throughout areas of Providence, Warwick, and Coventry, just to name a few places.

Keep in mind that I worked for many years as a field cameraman for CBS and FOX News locally in Rhode Island and southeastern Massachusetts. I covered many a hurricane and snowstorm. Never in all my years had I seen a storm cause so much damage and without warning. Trees were snapped in half or simply uprooted. Power lines were down everywhere I looked, some still dancing on the ground alive with electricity. There were no functioning traffic lights that I saw on my journey. I witnessed several trees on top of houses. I saw a man standing in disbelief at the edge of his driveway, his neighbor's tree fallen through the fence and on top of the roof of his fancy red sports car. Many streets were flooded.

Luckily Maggie May stands very high and thus I was able to get through some areas that others simply could not.

Through it all, I was encouraged to see people working together, directing traffic around fallen trees and letting each other know which roads were impassible. It's nice to see people coming together to triumph over adversity rather than tear one another apart.

The side roads took me another hour to circumnavigate before arriving at work, only to find the power out there. We were able to get the generator up and running and thus able to continue our business day, with limited lighting and less than adequate amounts of air conditioning.

At the end of the workday we were still without power, as was most of the initially effected area. I still needed to get fuel for my mule as there was no way Maggie May could make it home without some gasoline. The dashboard display was telling me that I had seven miles worth of fuel left in her belly. The search was on!

The gas stations closest to my office were all closed. One after another I drove up to them hopeful and coasted away wondering how this was going to turn out. I was reminded of a poem I wrote many moons ago when I was around 22 or 23, I think. It spoke about living on dreams, faith, and vapors, relating both to my trusty steed and me. I remember the closing line being something akin to, "will I make it home, or just stall out around the bend," which remains a good question, still today.

I finally found one gas station that was open. The line was longer than that to see Santa Claus on Christmas Eve when all those last minute believers who don't want to take the chance on waking up to an empty stocking line-up and swallow their pride and disbelief. I sat there and idled a good fifteen minutes saying my prayers and inching forward to the next open pump, all the while watching the station attendants come out and put red bags on pump handle after pump handle, denoting which pumps had run dry.

I had chosen well and was next in line when the gentlemen in front of me opened his trunk and unloaded several red plastic containers to fill up with dead dinosaur juice. The absurdity of the whole thing occurred to me at that point. There are other gas stations open just two towns over, a whole fifteen minute ride in Rhode Island yet these people are so small minded that they need to get all the home generator fuel here. I had no choice. Maggie's big Hemi engine couldn't make it that far. That was my oasis—my liquid ticket home.

With all his plastic tanks filled up and securely placed in his trunk, the man ahead of me attempted to leave as a car pulled in from the front and tried to take his place. I let the size of the Big Blue Baby speak for me and simply rolled forward into my spot at the pumps. It was my turn to see Santa, damn it, and he was going to hear my case for being a good little boy this year. As I put a cool twenty American dollars of the finest Middle Eastern oil into my tank, an elderly woman screaming took me by surprise. I glanced over to pump number seven and witnessed a tiny woman, stooped posture, wrinkled skin, pale white skeleton hand, attempting to wrestle the gas pump nozzle away from a forty-something year-old gentleman who was actively pumping fuel into his car. They began to shout and swear at each other as a station attendant ran out to separate the two of them. A cloud of profanity hung in the air. I replaced my nozzle quietly and climbed up into Maggie May's cab and thought about the strange changes I had witnessed in mere hours. On my way in to work, people were working together in the power outage. Now they had turned into jackals, attacking each other for the last bit of food on the prairie. The power will be back soon, I'm sure. At least I hope so, for at the rate that these people are de-evolving, there isn't much time left before we slide back into that germ infested tide pool of genetic nectar that spit us out.

Wednesday, August 5, 2015

The power was on at my house by the time I got home late yesterday afternoon. A few birch trees fell down on the back of the property but they were already weakened by the endless onslaught of snow last winter anyhow. Amazingly, the rickety fence that runs along the back of my property withstood the high winds and magically dodged all the falling limbs. The damn fence is falling apart, rotting in some areas, but it's stubborn as the day is long. It stands there in defiance of nature and my wishes that it simply lay down so I can file an insurance claim. I know how this will end, this dance between the old fence and I. There will come a day when I tire of getting the little gray box of tack nails out of the basement and going around to my neighbor's side of the property with my hammer and carefully mending the old fence. I'll get estimates. I'll review quotes. I'll pay too much anyway and a new fence will get erected. The old fence will move on to its final resting place at the dump. And within a few days of its mighty erection, the new fence will fall over under the crushing blow of a fallen tree limb. The old fence, in its grave at the garbage pile will then laugh and cackle and mock me from somewhere beyond.

Best night ever! That was what my daughter said anyway. I needed a win so I wasn't going to argue with her. Mama Bear had a meeting for Beanser's dance troupe and the upcoming National Dance Competition in Disney next year. This left Beans and I with a Daddy and Daughter night.

I made my famous pasta medley that she adores. It's nothing more than the bottom third of whatever boxes of pasta have been sitting open in the pantry cabinet mixed together with a lot of butter and a sprinkling of salt, but it's delicious.

For dessert I served raw cookie dough; chocolate chip. Beans had prepared homemade popsicles, so we ate those as well. Then we went subterranean and played some video games whilst riding the basement couch. Afterwards we retreated to the bedroom for two huge bowls of buttered popcorn and some cartoons. After she brushed her teeth and snuggled up between my left arm and my body, her head on my chest, she told me this was the best night ever. I think she was right.

There are nights when God talks to me through my prayers. Sometimes He sends signs. Other times He just lets my daughter say what I need to hear so that I know I'm doing okay.

Thursday, August 6, 2015

I'm crammed in middle seat 10E on my flight from Providence to Detroit aboard another Delta flight.

It was kind of sad at the old gym this morning. There were only two other guys there with me and the young kid that works the front desk. The building is being repurposed at the end of the month and most of the members have moved on to other places already. I'm sticking it out until the end. I'll miss the place. I feel as if I'm in the best physical condition that I have ever been in. My posture looks good. My back is feeling great. The heart gets a little wonky when I don't sleep much due to filming, but there's not much I can do for that right about now. My daughter says I look "beefy" and that I have bigger muscles than the other daddies, so I must be doing something right. It was the best compliment I have ever received.

I went to work with all of my traveling bags as I have to fly out to Sault Sainte Marie after work tonight. The Michigan Paracon at the Kewadin Casino is always a great time. This will be my fifth appearance there in six years. I'm slated to do a lecture there with my brother from another mother, Mr. John Tenney. I have some strange stuff planned for our audience. I have my makeup bag and my Santa hat with me, just in case these things are needed. Either should make for a happy nonsense experience. This is my third time around with this television notoriety and I'm getting weird with it- as advertised.

This middle seat is too much. I'll write more on the next flight.

I hope we have a grand turnout for the lecture. The casino's theater is a beautiful one and I'm thankful to present there, usually to a packed house. As I was saying, I have some things planned. I have some good friends and longtime supporters that come to this event faithfully, so I want to ensure they are entertained and have fun. Hopefully everyone will have a great time. But if they don't, I'll comfort myself in the words Hank Williams III sang, "Not everybody likes us, but we drive some folks wild."

Oh! And the buffet! I almost forgot the buffet. The good people at the casino usually give me food vouchers to use at the restaurants there. They have a buffet that is decent, but their dessert bar is spectacular. Pies of all kinds, shapes and sizes! (It may be the real reason I do this convention every year.)

El Capi'tan—land this bird and get me to the buffet pronto! Daddy needs some pie.

Friday, August 7, 2015

Wow! Day one of this convention played out better than I thought. The place was packed. I sold out of *What's Next* and had to start taking orders to send out when I get home. Half of my "Smile Damn It… It's only life after all" shirts have been sold as well. The people up here in Sault Sainte Marie are always so kind and supportive.

I have just returned to room number 535, my room for the event. I think I'll take a nap and then wake up and shower before going back down to the casino floor to do some karaoke.

Yawn! It's just before 2am. I was supposed to nap for two hours. Oh well, I guess I needed the rest. It's just as well since I have my lecture tomorrow and I'll give away every ounce of energy I have then.

Saturday, August 8, 2015

John Tenney and I rocked the lecture today! Although we have known each other for about six years or so, and appeared at countless events together whilst traveling the circuit, we never did a lecture together before.

I ended up painting my face like Paul Stanley from the legendary rock band KISS. This was a last minute decision. I was in the shower this morning and Doctor Love came on my iTunes, and suddenly it just made sense. As a coincidental aside, back when I was single D. Pari I often changed my outgoing voicemail and included a musical interlude. For quite some time it was the opening riff and lyrics to Doctor Love. "You need my love, baby, oh so bad. You aren't the only one I've ever had."

John didn't object to my face paint, as I did check with him first since it was a joint presentation. He sat with me in the green room backstage and discussed topics we could talk about whilst I applied my makeup following a step by step on-line tutorial on the subject of Paul Stanley's face paint.

We hit the stage and talked about how it's okay to be weird in life. We discussed what we do as paranormal researchers and how it should be about celebrating the persistence of life rather than the notion of death. I touched a little bit on some of my motivational lecture topics. John told some personal stories that related perfectly. We had a lot of laughs and even a few manly hugs at center stage to show people that it's perfectly acceptable for two heterosexual men to express care for each other.

After the lecture our tables were visited by many lecture attendees who wanted to tell us how much they enjoyed our presentation, a few even a bit teary eyed as the subject matter resonated with them so deeply. I wish I could tell you exactly what was said, but since it was an unplanned and unrehearsed lecture, I honestly have no idea.

The day wrapped up with a VIP dinner where I was able to sit with some fans and chat for some time. I made an effort to visit each table to try and talk with as many people as possible and wish them a proper farewell.

I stopped by the karaoke bar and belted out Mr. Elvis Presley's "Suspicious Minds" in duet form with a fan that stepped up to help out in the sudden absence of my buddy Jeff Belanger who was supposed to sing with me. It wasn't my best performance, but people seemed to like it anyway. Those people were drinking, thankfully.

Alas it's 11pm and time for bed. I have to be up at 4am to catch the bus to the airport and start my trek back home. I have to work all week, and I'm filming Tuesday and Wednesday night.

Sunday, August 9, 2015

Delta flight 4637 is carrying me from Sault Sainte Marie to Detroit this morning. I was to sit in seat 12A but was asked to switch to accommodate other passengers who wanted to sit together, so I was moved to seat 1D. Not only is 1D a pleasant little seat by the window, it's also next to 1C which is currently occupied by Mr. Ernie Hudson, an actor most notable for his portrayal of the character Winston Zeddemore in the hit film *Ghostbusters*. Ernie and I have met before at these conventions but have never had opportunity to talk at length. This is that opportunity, so I'll write more later on my second flight.

I'm tucked away in 7F against the window of Delta Flight 816 on my way back home via the airport in Rhode Island. That last flight was a nice surprise. I spoke with Ernie about what I do and he had a lot of questions about the places that I go and such. I told him about the various countries and castles I filmed in over the years. Jeff Belanger prompted me to tell him about the Winston Zeddemore statue idea that my best friend since first grade, Darren Valedofsky, had proposed to be erected in Rhode Island, complete with a plaque reading, "If there's a steady paycheck in it, I'll believe anything you say," as was a notable quote in *Ghostbusters*. I don't think Darren will ever get the statue erected, but Ernie wasn't against it and Jeff offered to pitch in $25 for the project.

I'm looking forward to getting home today. I should have time to play with Beans, hang out with wife, and watch NASCAR. They are racing at Watkins Glen in New York today. I don't think I would ever want to go to that track to watch the race as its road course layout makes it hard to watch from one place, but it's one of my favorite races to watch on television.

Busy week ahead… stay tuned!

Monday, August 10, 2015

I try to never let anyone know the hurt I suffer and the emotional pain I rise above. But underneath this superhero cape with extra starch there are many bruises and scars.

Maybe it's just because it has been a long year. Maybe it's because I'm sleep deprived. Maybe it's just because today was a tough day. Whatever the reason, I'm glad I'm home and have the opportunity to rest. Tomorrow I have to film again, and I must start the day with a new perspective.

Tuesday, August 11, 2015

Weeds are flowers. Nightmares are dreams. It's all perspective, and it's not what it seems.

Wednesday, August 12, 2015

Last night we filmed in New Bedford, Massachusetts, at the old Fort Tabor down on the waterfront. I was working with my buddy KJ and we found heroin addicts in a hole underground during our investigation. At least I think they were heroin addicts. They were definitely on some sort of drugs. I didn't want to ask a lot of questions and get into specifics. I have found that when one encounters drug addicts, especially those who have chosen to live the subterranean lifestyle, it's best to keep some distance. The police came and arrested them. That was a first.

I went home and slept two-and-a-half hours before getting up and going back to work this morning. I'm filming again after I get out of work. I may not sleep much, but at least I don't sleep in a hole.

Thursday, August 13, 2015

I ended up sleeping at the office last night. We filmed at an armory in East Greenwich, Rhode Island, until somewhere around 3am this morning and it didn't make sense for me to drive by my office in order to head home and lose 45 minutes each way that could be spent sleeping. Luckily we have a nice meeting area with a couch long enough for me to stretch out on. I had my gym bag with me too, so I was able to shower this morning and simply walk downstairs to the surgical floor and be on time for work. It wasn't the best night's sleep I've ever had but it was five hours of sleep and more than I have had in a few days so I'm not complaining.

Friday, August 14, 2015

What a day, thus far! I was able to leave work a bit early as my little one was part of a musical today and I really wanted to surprise her there. She was in camp the last few weeks as part of the Little Folks Theater. They did a modern twist on the *Three Little Pigs* story where they take on human traits. My daughter was little pig number one, who went to market … the stock market. That was one of her lines. She really projects so well when she's performing. Her pig character struggled with being greedy. She was hilarious. She sang her songs and nailed all her lines. She really shined in the dance portions of it as well thanks to all of her training. I couldn't be any prouder.

Now we're packing up and heading up to New Hampshire for the weekend. Here we go on the holiday road!

Well "Holiday Road" was right as that was the theme song to the old *National Lampoon's Vacation* movie, and this trip is starting to look like one of Clark W. Griswold's misadventures. Traffic was a nightmare. It's never smooth sailing going through Boston but today was ridiculous. We were on the road early enough since I was out of work at noon, but apparently everyone in Boston left work early as well, which resulted in a six-and-a-half hour trip for what should have taken three hours at best. But I made the best of it. I cranked up my music and sang my songs. Beans took turns playing her iPad and playing her Nintendo 3DS. Mama Bear looked at me sideways when I was singing both the male and female parts of "Summer Nights" from Grease; good thing she doesn't travel with me often or she would really start to think I was a weirdo.

The little rental car started showing some issues that I'm hoping won't become a problem. I'm not a fan of all these new fancy car keys and electronic nonsense. The car is not recognizing the electronic key when I try to start it. So every time we stop, I have to say a little prayer that the damn thing will fire up again. So far so good, but it takes a bit of coaxing and many presses of the button.

We arrived here at the hotel around 9:30pm only to find the hotel sold out because they gave my room away by accident. The woman at the front desk was a nervous wreck, and I have my suspicions that she may have been drinking. They checked someone else into my room, which means their room was still vacant somewhere in the hotel. The solution seemed simple enough, but she couldn't figure it out on her own. I suggested I just take the vacant room that was meant for the family in my room, but this was somehow not making sense to her. After two other people came over to help her, they decided to just put my family in the room the other family was supposed to use. Brilliant. Bloody brilliant. Why didn't I think of that thirty minutes ago? Oh wait ... I did.

So now I'm here in our room, getting ready to review the remaining evidence for that ole ghost show. I wanted to get it all done last night but I just couldn't keep my eyes open long enough. Mama Bear and Beans are curled up in one bed and I'm curled up here in the other bed with my laptop. Oh well. These things must be done, and then I'll be able to rest.

I best get going for tomorrow is Santa's Village! I cannot wait. I love it there! We get to feed the reindeer, ride the Yule log flume ride, shoot the humbugs, eat lots of cookies, listen to Christmas music, visit with Santa....

Saturday, August 15, 2015

I'm plumb tuckered out! The little one just relinquished her grip on me for the night after keeping me in the hotel pool for over an hour. That's no small feat after walking around Santa's Village all day. We rode all of our favorite rides, we met Santa, fed apples and crackers to the reindeer, and I think I'm still buzzing from all the gingerbread cookies, fudge, and other snacks we ate.

Beans made me laugh today in a way only she can. When it was our turn to meet Santa she told him that she'd like a pink iPod for Christmas "with lots of megabytes". Santa let out a hearty chuckle and said she was the first child he had met that had ever asked for something so specific, and that she knew more about computers than he did. That's my girl.

We finished up the night by getting some popcorn, snuggling in the hotel bed and watching *Teen Beach Movie 2* on the Disney Channel.

More fun is on tap for tomorrow. Time to go dream of sugar plum fairies.

Sunday, August 16, 2015

Home sweet home! What a day. We went to Story Land today. A lot of the rides are too little for Beans but she likes the Roar-O-Saurus, the Polar Coaster and a handful of other rides too, so that makes it worth it. They have a flume ride called Bamboo Chutes that we go on over and over again. My favorite attraction is Dr. Geyser's Remarkable Raft Ride. It is a large round raft that rotates and bounces along a water filled track and through a misty cavern. Statues shoot water and random geysers pop up along the course, all which eventually leave you soaking wet. It's frigging fantastic. We went on it a couple of times as it is so much fun, even if you end up with a soggy bottom.

This was the weekend I needed. I was really struggling there for a bit. Being away from my family always wears me down. I'm all for sacrificing to ensure they have a better life but I want to be a part of it, too.

Monday, August 17, 2015

It was a rough day today, and not because it was a Monday as I don't subscribe to that nonsense. I just always have a difficult time the first day away from my little girl after spending time with her. Ah well, the day is over and she is snuggled up on my left arm. I have a busy little week ahead of me even though there isn't any filming or any conventions on deck right now. Off to bed. Off to dream. Off to places where things aren't what they seem. Then again, things very really are anyway. None of this is real.

Tuesday, August 18, 2015

I just got in from dinner and drinks with my buddy Cody DesBiens and our friend Miss Tiffany Rice. I had a prime rib pot roast that was amazing. And pumpkin beer! Finally! The season is here and pumpkin beer is everywhere. My favorite is Southern Tier Pumking Ale with a little cinnamon and brown sugar around the rim of the glass. I'm a fancy boy.

We sat outside as the sun set whilst a young gentleman played some great classic rock selections upon his acoustic guitar. It was one of those magical evenings betwixt friends. It felt timeless, like the world outside of us was frozen. We laughed a lot. We shared stories. It was great. Even the waitress enjoyed herself. Once she found out that Cody is an announcer for the Boston Red Sox, Tiffany is a spirit medium, and I … I'm whatever the hell I am. I suppose we are quite the eclectic group. Plus, you know, there was pumpkin beer.

Wednesday, August 19, 2015

I came home and tamed the lawn today. I had forgotten I hadn't cleaned it up since the crazy freak storm of a few weeks ago. There were a lot of branches and even some full sized tree limbs that had to be broken up, cut up, and moved.

Next week at this time I'll have made my return to television, as the new episodes of *Ghost Hunters* will finally air. I have to do some publicity interviews for them over the next few days. I have been promoting the upcoming episodes right along via social media with some little pictures I made up.

I'm thankful for all these opportunities that continually come my way. I work very hard to make the most of them. And I'm constantly thinking of what's next. I'm not sure when I'll rest and just let things be but I don't see it coming anytime in my near future. I like to stay busy. I've got big plans. The best is still yet to come.

Thursday, August 20, 2015

"Straight outta Compton…" I'd write more lyrics but they are quite vulgar; artistically vulgar, but vulgar nonetheless. They were written by a rap group called N.W.A., one of my favorite groups to listen to when I was a kid. Recently a movie about them came out. I went to see at the theater tonight. I was really surprised at how well the film was put together. The way the music was interlaced with their story was very well done. It may seem funny to others that I would draw inspiration from such a movie, but it's riddled with it. The story of struggle, pain, and growth is one that resonates with me at my very core.

Amongst the musical artists that made up N.W.A. were Eazy-E and Ice Cube. Both were very talented in their own right. Eazy was the showman where Ice Cube was the lyrical genius. Both of which had their strengths on and off the microphone depending on your personal preference. When I was younger, I cared more for Eazy. He had a great look. Dark sunglasses, the hat down low, black gloves—he just looked cool. As I grew older and learned more of the story of the group, how Ice Cube did most of the writing and was screwed out of most of his money by Eazy and their manager, my respect for Ice Cube grew.

Throughout my life, I've always identified with secondary characters. I support Donald Duck over Mickey Mouse. I like Daffy Duck more than Bugs Bunny. Starscream should have laid waste to Megatron and been the leader of the Decepticons. And so, as I sat and watched Ice Cube up there on the big screen, I couldn't help but feel that he was the one I could most identify with.

In my life, I am the show. When I take the stage at my events, I'm Eazy. But in my jobs, in filming, in many positions I have held over the years, I'm always placed as the guy behind the guy. I struggle with that a lot because I know I can handle my own. And watching the movie inspired me to move along and step out further in my life and take control of some situations where I still have opportunity to do so.

I want to do more with my motivational lectures next year. Once I get through my busy season and into November, I'm going devote more time to getting things lined up for 2016. This year I have not done as many purely motivational lectures as I have in the past two years. Filming and additional paranormal lectures have limited my ability to do all the things I want to do to help others. I have been able to drop a lot of my motivational tidbits into all of my appearances, and my platform is growing, so I can't really complain about that. Once *Ghost Hunters* airs again next week my social media numbers will start to rise, and from that I can reach even more people with my message and help to change the world. I just have to be patient, and have a plan. So once November comes, I'm going to get moving on the blueprints of my future.

I may be just a white boy from Rhode Island and not a rapper from California but I'm going to do great things. My best is still yet to come. I honestly believe that and I won't stop until I make it a reality.

Friday, August 21, 2015

"Auntie Em, where's Toto? It's a twister! It's a twister!" – Johnny in *The Wizard of Oz.*

Well, I didn't drop a house on a witch but today was a whirlwind that's for sure. It was a crazy busy day at the office. I was on the clinical floor and in surgery all day as we were shorthanded and so I didn't get a chance to do a lot of the things that I needed to do. Oh well. "There's always tomorrow for dreams to come true. Believe in yourself, come what may." Clarice the doe in the *Rudolph the Red-Nosed Reindeer* claymation special. But that's another show entirely.

I picked up some Chinese food for Mama Bear on the way home. I spent time with Beans playing video games. I did another promotional interview for the upcoming season of that ole ghost show next Wednesday. I also did one yesterday and I have a couple more coming up over the next few days. I don't mind doing them. I actually enjoy being interviewed quite a bit. I like to answer the run of the mill questions with off the wall replies. It keeps people thinking and it lets them know that I'm not their average monkey. I'm a space monkey. Well, I like astronaut ice cream at least.

Saturday, August 22, 2015

My cousin Kayla is getting married today. I haven't been to a wedding in some time. You may have noticed that I travel a lot, so there isn't a lot of time back home and very little time to attend weddings. However, I have spent too much time at funerals and too little time at weddings. I'm excited to go to celebrate love tonight.

Sunday, August 23, 2015

I've been giving a lot of thought to my future. Of course, not so much so that I'm missing the present but in those empty moments after prayer before I go to sleep, that is when I'm planning.

The show's premiere is this coming Wednesday night. I'll be in every episode for season ten and I'm finishing up filming for season eleven in the next month or so. Then what? Well, that is what I'm working on.

I really want to work on my motivational speaking first and foremost. And then, there is the unknown. I have some ideas I'd like to see take shape and I'll continue to work on them. The only thing I know for certain is I don't know. And in a strange way, that is comforting, because it also means that anything is possible. Anything is possible. Amazing.

Monday, August 24, 2015

Beans in sleeping on my left arm. Her head is resting on my shoulder. I've been holding her like this for most nights since she was born. I know it can't last forever, but I do enjoy it so.

I'm traveling out again next week to do some filming for the show. I wish I could just stay here and hold her, though. Such is life, I suppose. I can't think about it too much or the pain becomes unbearable.

As the Allman Brothers so famously sang, "Lord I was born a ramblin' man. Trying to make a livin' and doin' the best I can. When it's time for leavin' I hope you'll understand. I was born a rambling man."

Tuesday, August 25, 2015

Double Stuf Oreos may lack an "f" in their name but they are simply delicious. Especially with milk. Mmm…

Wednesday, August 26, 2015

Tonight is the night! *Ghost Hunters* season ten premieres this evening at 9pm here on the Eastern seaboard. I have mixed emotions about it today. I kind of have that day after Christmas feeling when I've been looking forward to something and it just slipped by. I know it's just a television show, and whatever people like about it or don't like about it, none of that matters. I worked hard. Making the show itself is not difficult for me. The investigation part comes natural. Each episode is just a small snapshot of so much more that people don't see. Each show. Each flight. A delayed plane. A cab ride. Another hotel room. Another packed and unpacked bag. Another sleepless night. Back to work. Lather. Rinse. Repeat.

Recognize the afterlife or not, believe in spirits or don't, it matters little. The work put into making the show is hard. And so, with the show airing in just a few hours, I can only think about all that went into it. All of my efforts that have gone into breathing life into it, for nothing comes to be on its own.

I was asked to live tweet the episode tonight and interact with our fans on Twitter. I'm looking forward to that. I joked around that I wasn't sure what they wanted me to do and I'd only comment on the commercials I liked. I do like to bust the cojones of the network brass.

WOW! The editors did a great job on the show. The premiere was the investigation we filmed at the Wild Turkey Distillery in Kentucky. I was surprised at how many people were online tweeting during the show. The outpouring of support for the program and my return to the show was simply amazing. I'm so thankful for all the kind words that were shared with me this evening. There was this one scene that I was surprised they put into the show. KJ and I were discussing one of the claims of a woman getting her bottom pinched, and the conversation had turned to the style of undergarments the young lady may have been wearing. It seems to have to been quite the hit with the fans. What can I say? Everyone simply seems to be nuts about butts.

Thursday, August 27, 2015

The gym was desolate today. I was literally the only vehicle in the parking lot. I still parked about halfway to the door as is customary. I often like to think I'm a survivor at world's end. I'm the type to still stop at stop signs and do things as society had them set up to be. I like order, to a point. I had a spirited workout and feel really good. I think I shall do something out of the ordinary today.

I decided to leave work early and meet Mama Bear and Beans at the Roger Williams Zoo today. I haven't had enough time to do the things I want to do this summer, or, well, pretty much at all, and so a change in the routine was necessary. We had a great time seeing the animals and walking the park together. It's one of my favorite things to do. It may be simple, but why can't simple things big and important things? Change your perspective my friends.

Tonight I'm doing my first ever Periscope session. I'm really looking forward to it. These new social media apps allow for pictures, live video, and a lot of interaction. I'm hoping to do a little something to help others. I think a twenty minute motivational session via this new periscope app could be just the thing some people need to put a little smile on their faces. I have another interview to do after that as well. But first, yard work must be done! Beans has a play date on Saturday and so things need to look all ship shape or Mama Bear loses her mind.

Friday, August 28, 2015

I do think last night's Periscope session went very well. There was a wonderfully overwhelming response to it. I wasn't really sure what to expect but overall I have to say that I am rather pleased with it. I must plan to do more of these things.

I tore the skin off of the inside of my thumb whilst doing yard work yesterday. Not only was it painful and difficult to shower last night, but it made going to the gym this morning impossible as I can't really lift anything with my hand this way. Thus, my last day at my old gym was apparently yesterday. But, perhaps that was the way it was to go. Quite fitting actually. It was nice having the place to myself yesterday. It's how I shall always remember it. Hopefully I can heal up quickly and be ready to go to my new gym on Monday morning. I'm usually quite the quick healer so it is possible that Monday will be a reality.

We are nearing the end of this old book, just a few days left now.

"Ain't it funny how time slips away." – Willie Nelson

Saturday, August 29, 2015

I started this day with a trip to McShawn's Pub to see Dad and share some time together over a few cold Miller High Lifes and some hot dogs. They changed the brand, though, and once again downgraded the quality of the buns. I hate to complain as they are complimentary but it was nicer when they had the natural casing hot dogs and the fresh hard Italian rolls. But still, it was great to sit and talk with my dad. There was even a very rare surprise appearance from my Uncle Bub. My Mom's brother, whom I'm sure I mentioned a time or two in this literary misadventure so far. He has always been an inspiration to me. He's been sick over the last year or so and it was even more special that he made it out with us this morning.

I played some David Allan Coe and some Willie Nelson on the jukebox and talked with my uncle about how love is often wrapped in delicate pain. My dad swapped car-racing stories with some of the regulars there. It must be just about 20 years now that I have been visiting McShawn's Pub, and it holds a special place in my heart, even if the hot dogs aren't what they once were. Hell, none of us are quite what we once were.

My uncle was looking at his arms and pointing out how he now has those random black and blue marks, and some age spots that older people get from time to time. He referred to himself as having polka dots. I told him it was limited edition skin packaging, to which he repeated "limited edition" and we had a good laugh.

I parted ways with my uncle and McShawn's. My dad brought me to see a tree in Goddard Park, down in East Greenwich, where he met my mother back in 1968. There was a certain tree that she and her friends were hanging out beneath when he first rode through on his motorcycle. They dated for seven years and were married for two when I came along in '77.

Tomorrow I have it set up for my parents to renew their wedding vows beneath that same tree. My family and I are meeting with the priest and then bringing him over to the park as a surprise to my mom. My dad will bring her over to meet us there. And beneath the branches of a personal romantic landmark, my parents will renew their wedding vows in front of Mama Bear, Beans, and me. It should make for a nice afternoon.

Beans was having her play date when I came home. She and her friends were in the pool. Mama Bear was on the deck supervising. I went out back and made buckets filled with water balloons for the girls to throw at each other. I heard one of the young girls say that she wished her dad was like me. That made me feel good. I must be doing something right after all.

Hot damn! William Shatner sent a tweet to me today saying he watched the season ten premiere of *Ghost Hunters* this past week and he welcomed me back to the show. That made me feel pretty damn special, I have to admit.

Sir Elton John is seated at the white piano off in the corner of Jolly Good Times, the imaginary pirate-themed bar in my mind, and he is singing "Can you feel, the love, tonight?" into an old microphone that smells a bit like beer and a lot like eggnog. I must talk with Jasper P. Jinglebottom (Head Elf in charge of my mind) to go ahead and order a new microphone. If we are going to have such talent like Sir Elton John dropping in from time to time, we should clean the place up just a bit.

When good things happen, I believe you should pass it along and not hold on to it for yourself. And so, tonight I went down to an event the local members of the TAPS home team (the paranormal group originally associated with the show) had in Mystic, Connecticut. I wasn't slated to be there. No one currently on the show or any other show was to appear but I thought it would be nice to surprise the old team and any of the guests who were in attendance. It's always good to brighten the day of others, to do something without expecting anyone do something back for you, and to never forget where you came from. Stay humble. Hustle hard. Dream big. Never give up.

Sunday, August 30, 2015

Today I took Mama Bear and Beans to meet up with Farther Roger, who also was the priest who officiated my marriage. Is that the right term? Officiated. Sounds like a sporting event. Ah well, "all the world's a stage" and so on and so forth...

Father Roger followed us up to Goddard Park and we waited for my parents there. Beans brought Nana some flowers when she arrived. I helped my mother out of the car and my dad brought her over beneath the branches of the very same tree where they first met back in 1968. The ceremony began and my wife took photographs for us. I saw my dad start to get tears in his eyes, which is something I think I have only seen two or three times before. It was really something special to be there and see them hold hands and repeat their wedding vows from over forty years ago.

As they were finishing and my father was about to kiss his bride, a small parade of classic cars from the early 1960s were driving through the parkway behind them. It couldn't have been more fitting. It was truly a beautiful day and a perfect moment. One I'll always cherish.

Time to pack my gym bag, as I'll be going to my new fitness center for the first time tomorrow. I'm rather excited about it—all new equipment, all new routines, and a whole new me. I had spent over five years at the old World's Gym on the East Providence and Seekonk line. I have good memories there. I prepared myself for a Spartan Race within the walls of that gym and I finished the race in good form. I worked through a dislocated rib there. I'm still not sure how I dislocated it. Come to think of it, I may have dislocated the rib there as well. There were days there with no hot water, and some days with no water at all. I should probably work on my definition of good memories.

I also need to pack my suitcase, as it's time to film for that ole ghost show once again. Those two episodes I originally signed up for will go for the full duration of two seasons—26 episodes. I have to head down to Delaware tomorrow after work for—all together now! "One more episode." Dear Lord, what am I doing with my life?

Mammas don't let your babies grow up to be cowboys
Don't let 'em pick guitars and drive them old trucks
Make them be doctors and lawyers and such. – Willie Nelson

Not too long ago my father reminded me that as a child he told me to go to college and not grow up to be a truck driver like he did. Don't drive all over the country hustling a buck here and there.

Well Dad, I followed your advice, but it appears that the song remains the same. It must be in our blood. There are worst things we could be.

Monday, August 31, 2015

Here we are once again flying high in the sky with the apple pie hopes of that little ant who knew he could move that rubber tree plant. I always liked that song as a kid, and now that I have lived a good chunk of my life, I know why.

U.S. Airways flight 4521 is bouncing through the late afternoon sky much to the disdain of the nervous lady precariously perched in aisle seat 14C just diagonal from me as I'm relaxed in aisle seat 15D. Every time we hit a bump, her right hand reaches down nervously from her iPad solitaire game to grab the armrest in a fevered panic. Personally I enjoy bumpy flights as they remind me that we are flying, I'm alive, and nothing is promised.

Here's a little perspective for you, and I understand some people simply cannot get outside their own heads as of yet, and thus are nervous and scared of, well, pretty much everything. I've been around enough to know your energy is best spent controlling what you can control and just roll with the tide on the rest of the shit. Struggling in situations that truly cannot be changed, big picture act of God stuff, there's no sense in getting tense about them and worrying your pretty little head.

As far as bumpy flights go, I roll with it. Mr. Willie Nelson just checked out of the soundstage in front of the live studio audience in my mind after playing a mind blowing set. Mr. David Allan Coe is on his way out of the green room. The concert plays on and I sit here in this faux leather chair with my head back against the headrest, just letting it play from side to side as we bounce atop the clouds.

Did you ever stop and wonder why drunk drivers often survive accidents and injure or kill the others involved in accidents? They're so out of it that they don't know what's going on and never tense up or stiffen against the impact. Unbeknownst to them in their illegally incapacitated state of inebriation, their limp bodies actually protect them. As a disclaimer, I obviously don't condone drunken driving. I don't condone drunkenness at all. I actually loathe being around those who have stayed too long at the fair. I'm just giving you a real life example of how it's better to sometimes acquiesce to the strong tides and wait until you have a fair chance of swimming back to the coast before you waste all of your energy treading water in a winless situation.

Shifting gears, let me tell you a bit about how things have progressed today. It was a rough start to the morning after a restless five hours sleep. Beans kept me awake looking for wayward stuffed animals. Mama Bear had me patrolling the house for imaginary intruders in the home. Even when there's rest, there's no rest. Oh well, I like being the protector of the family and finder of lost items anyhow.

The new gym looks to be a grand place. I hope it'll prove to be a good fit for me for years to come. A few of the morning regulars from the old gym work out there as well, so it was nice to see some familiar faces. The guy I talk fantasy football with is there. The guy who likes to tell me old war stories is there. One of the guys who watch me a little too closely in the showers is also there. He must just be admiring how much I care about hygiene. Cleanliness is next to godliness, they say!

Work was work as work often is. There were staff shortages and office issues, but nothing I couldn't handle in short time. I was in surgery all morning assisting with anesthesia. I did seven cases before the morning was done. I then ducked into my office for an hour and hammered out things that needed hammering. After that it was off to the airport and Delaware bound. I'll film tonight. I'll film tomorrow. I'll get two or three hours' sleep tomorrow night when we wrap investigation, and then I'll be back on a flight home this Wednesday morning for our last flight together. It hasn't been easy but I hope you've been enjoying it.

So that's it. You are up to date. U.S. Airways flight 4521 is still bumpy. The lady in 14C is losing at solitaire and grabbing the armrest as if she can save us all, and I'm here bouncing along and listening to old country music that soothes my soul.

So as Mr. David Allan Coe wants you to know, "If you're big star bound, let me warn ya' it's a long hard ride."

Back at the hotel here, a Sheraton, nice place. It would be nicer if I wasn't locked out of my bedroom, pantless.

My fancy room is divided into two sections. There's a bedroom with a killer air conditioner and a front room with two sitting chairs, a television, and the bath. I was in bed working on some of the emails that I send to libraries in effort to scare up some local paranormal lectures for the fall, when I remembered I hadn't brushed my teeth after eating that last little mini pocket-sized pie I bought at the grocery store. Now, since I was in bed, I wore no pants or undergarments as I like to be free. I did, however, have a shirt on that read "Mr. Incredible". The air conditioner was up high to freeze my bedchamber so I sleep better, but since I was sitting up in bed and on the laptop computer, I had said shirt on to keep my nipples relaxed. I find it very hard to write or do pretty much anything with aroused nipples.

As I went to brush my teeth I pulled the dividing room door closed as to maintain the integrity of the air conditioner's hard work in chilling the bedchamber and I went about brushing my teeth. After a few minutes I emerged from the bathroom with fresh minty breath, a "Mr. Incredible" shirt, and no pants, only to find the dividing door had somehow locked behind be, leaving me in a bit of a conundrum.

I tried my best to jiggle the door open. I took a pen from the hotel room desk and jammed it in the little pinhole hoping to unlock it and return to my bed, but as fate would have it, nothing would do. So, standing there bare-assed in the front room, I picked up the phone handset and dialed zero for the front desk. I explained my unfortunate situation and they sent someone right up. I dashed into the bath and grabbed a towel to wrap around my nether regions as to not startle the hotel help, lest they think this was some ill-fated attempt at a sexual romp.

The gentleman came in with a pair of scissors, which also made me glad I had thought to put the towel around my waist as no man is comfortable with his twig and berries out when scissors are around. The gent jammed the point of the scissors into the door and viola, my bed was once again accessible. I thanked the man kindly. He in turn said nothing about my attire and went back to his lonely post at the front desk.

Life is an adventure, and sometimes, just sometimes, strange things happen when you are separated from your pants.

Good night!

Tuesday, September 1, 2015

I awoke to twelve text messages on my phone from my office. Even my days off aren't really days off. Not only am I working here in Delaware, I'm still working back at my office in Rhode Island. No worries, though. It comes with the territory. As James Brown once sang, "I paid the cost to be the boss," or in my case, I'm still paying it.

Tonight is investigation night. I'm just going to hit the gym and go grab a late lunch before the festivities begin. When we start filming, there isn't a dinner break until around 10pm, and I'm admittedly not very pleasant when I'm hungry. If I'm really hungry, or really hot, it's best to just give me a little room. Right now I'm a bit of both as it's 90 degrees and very humid here right now, so it's best we resume this writing a bit later.

Ahh … a small steak followed by a cold pumpkin iced latte from Dunkin Donuts and all is right with the world once again. I'm a very easy man to please. Someone once said that all I ever needed was to be fucked, fed, and put to bed. Truer words about me might never have been spoken. Yes, I cursed. I do that from time to time. And in actuality, that was a quote so I didn't say it at all.

At the sound of the tone it will be three o'clock and the time that I must leave to go and film this investigation. *Beeeeeeep.*

Wednesday, September 2, 2015

Most of our lives we've been outlaws
Slept with our backs to the wall
I'm a rambler, I'm a seeker, and we're gettin' weaker
A whole lot more likely to fall
We're tired of the rocks and the brambles
Those barbed wire fences and all
And we're lookin' for a home life and clean smellin' sheets
And all the soft places to fall

– "All the Soft Places" by Willie Nelson

Mr. Willie Nelson and Mr. Merle Haggard are singing this song sweetly in the elite suite betwixt my years whilst I'm seated in aisle seat 26C aboard U.S. Airways flight 1844. I was supposed to be in 25C but the gentleman in 24C was reclined fully whilst we were sitting on the tarmac and that's never a good sign for a smooth flight. I slipped back into an empty row in an effort to have a more enjoyable inflight experience, for this will be our last flight together, my friends.

Today marks the last day in a year of writing. I hope you have enjoyed the journeys, the ramblings, and my own special brand of happy nonsense. Perhaps somewhere in my musings you have found inspiration, or at least some consolation.

I filmed all last night at an awesome case, an old Victorian mansion turned museum in Delaware. It was one of my favorite investigations that I have ever been a part of but it also left me completely drained. The almost three hours of sleep I had before leaving for the airport this morning probably didn't help much either. So I am indeed, "…lookin' for a home life and clean smellin' sheets, and all the soft places to fall."

I'm literally hurting this morning. Physically, I'm exhausted. Mentally, I'm muddled. Emotionally, I'm spent. I'm barely keeping it together. Hardly holding back the tears. You want to see the wizard behind the curtain? You want to see the knife wounds in the back of the superhero that he hides behind his cape? Now is your chance. Personally, I wouldn't look. I like an air of mystery. I need to believe in magic. I maintain my childlike innocence and defend it fiercely.

Remember kids, the death of Santa Claus is your own.

I'm really feeling the pains of life on the road today. Not even my red Betty Flintstone vitamin is helping. Usually that Stone Age hottie can make everything all right. I remind myself it's okay to be hurt from time to time, as long as you don't let it define you. This is as real as it gets, my friends. I've been running on faith and vapors for some time now. There may have been some magic in that old silk hat I found but I'm not sure how many more rabbits I can pull from it. But, I won't stop trying until my dying day. When my last breath escapes my body, that will be when I rest. So yeah, I'm tired. I may be down, but I'm not out. This rodeo is far from over. Send in the clowns. They're already here.

Dang it. The brain seems to be slipping. I think Jinglebottom is running old cartoon clips in the movie theater of my mind. The floor is sticky with spilled soft drinks, but at least the popcorn is fresh. I have to try harder to focus. It may be difficult to do on such little sleep, but I have done it before and I'll do it again because it is all I know how to do.

I keep saying the best is yet to come, and trust me it is. And so I'll flip over the old Etch A Sketch in my mind and start fresh again. Lather. Rinse. Repeat. Here we go.

I believe the future is bright as it pertains to my motivational work. I may not be the best self-help guru out there, but in the circles I run, I'm the only one we've got. Until the good Lord anoints someone else to step up and take the reins, I'm happy to do it. If I have made a difference for just one person, one life, one soul, then I have done well.

Regarding my faith, I remain a sleepy little angel with a busted wing. My halo is a bit bent and rests on my head tilted to one side. But I love God. My prayer life is strong. Day to day, I do all that I can to help those around me. I try to live a life according to the teachings of the Bible and the examples set forth by Christ. I'm not perfect, and that is okay.

One thing I've learned in this human experience is you should never begrudge someone the little comforts they may need to get through this life, for you don't know their whole story. It's for God to judge, not us. We are to walk through this life, helping those we can, and trying our best. And so, that's what I'm doing. I like to think I make God smile from time to time and I piss off the devil as well.

As far as the show goes, will there be a season twelve? Will I be a part of it? Is this my last go round in paranormal reality television? I don't know. And I don't need to know. No sense in worrying about what tomorrow may bring, each day has enough troubles of its own.

This life of mine isn't all sunshine and rainbows, but it's the one I've got and it's a pretty darned good one. I smile in defiance on difficult days. I take the burden and ask for more weight. I'm proud of my endurance and eternal optimism. I urge all of you to be aware that there always is a sunny side of the street; you just have to look for it and be willing to make the journey to get there. Don't be afraid. Walk in faith, not in fear.

Beans started the third grade today. Mama Bear sent me pictures of her all dressed up and ready to get back to school. I remain forever thankful for my family, and extremely proud of my little girl. I hope that in all that I do I make her proud. She's the reason I do anyway.

This literary misadventure has now chronicled one trip around the sun for me. God willing, there will be many more to come but only He and John Lennon know for sure. I've been living on the road for the better part of ten years now, and I feel like Mr. Willie Nelson is the only one who understands me. Hopefully, after reading this, perhaps you do, too.

Speaking of Willie, I think he will entertain us with just one more song before we say our farewells. He is just getting settled here in the elite suite betwixt my ears. Tune up that guitar and play us out, you beautiful redheaded gypsy bastard!

And the devil shivered in his sleeping bag
He said traveling on the road is such a drag
If we can make it home by Friday, we can brag
And the devil shivered in his sleeping bag

- "Devil In A Sleeping Bag" by Willie Nelson

And to all of you, thanks for reading. Thanks for believing. Never give up… for there is always hope.

If you need me, I'll be out here on the road.

Audio Appendix

- " Shotgun Wille" – Willie Nelson
- "Alive and Well" – Willie Nelson
- "Copa Cobana" – Barry Manilow
- "Nobody Told Me" – John Lennon
- "Theme from Mr. Belvedere" – Leon Redbone
- "Banana Boat Song" – Harry Belafonte
- "Bloody Mary Morning" – Willie Nelson
- "Another Pretty Country Song" – David Allan Coe
- "Need A Little Time Off For Bad Behavior" – David Allan Coe
- "Much Too Young" – Garth Brooks
- "Rubberneckin"– Elvis Presley
- "I've Got The World On a String" – Frank Sinatra
- "Pancho and Lefty" - Willie Nelson
- "Alive and Well" - Kenny Chesney
- "Dust In The Wind" – Kansas
- "Carry On Wayward Son" – Kansas
- "Hallelujah" – John Cale
- "Simple Man" – Lynyrd Skynyrd
- "I've Got a Lovely Bunch of Coconuts" – Merv Griffin
- "Funny How Time Slips Away" – Willie Nelson
- "Turn The Page" – Bob Seger
- "Royal Pain" – The Eels
- "Shooting Star" – Bob Dylan
- "Simple Twist of Fate" – Bob Dylan
- "Tin Man" – America
- "What Should I Be" – Garfield Halloween Special
- "It's My Lazy Day" – Willie Nelson
- "Good Times" – Willie Nelson
- "Three Is a Magic Number" – Blind Melon
- "Mouthful of Cavities" – Blind Melon
- "Bring The Noise" – Public Enemy & Anthrax
- "MMM Bop" – Hanson
- "Trip Along" – Tripping Daisy
- "I Won't Last a Day Without You" – The Carpenters
- "I Can't Smile Without You" – Barry Manilow
- "Run, Run Rudolph" – Chuck Berry

- "Daydream" – Lovin' Spoonful
- "Driving My Life Away" – Eddie Rabbit
- "I Love a Rainy Night" – Eddie Rabbit
- "You're My Best Friend" – Queen
- "Here Comes The Sun" – The Beatles
- "Taxi" – Harry Chapin
- "Fool On The Hill" – The Beatles
- "East Bound and Down" – Jerry Reed
- "All of Me" – Willie Nelson
- "Beyond Here Lies Nothing" – Bob Dylan
- "Tangled Up In Blue" – Bob Dylan
- "Simple Twist of Fate" – Bob Dylan
- "Shooting Star" – Bob Dylan
- "My Way" – Frank Sinatra
- "She Believes In Me" – Kenny Rogers
- "All I Want For Christmas" – Mariah Carey
- "Beautiful Boy" - John Lennon
- "The Best Is Yet to Come" – Frank Sinatra
- "Monday, Monday" – The Mamas & The Papas
- "Lets Talk About Sex" – Salt-N- Pepa
- "I'm So Tired" – The Beatles
- "Cruel Crazy Beautiful World" – Johnny Clegg and Savuka
- "Here Comes The Sun" – The Beatles
- "Nine Lives" – Aerosmith
- "Wagon Wheel" – Darius Rucker
- "Wagon Wheel" – Old Crow Medicine Show
- "Turn, Turn, Turn" – The Byrds
- "The Times They Are A-Changin" – Bob Dylan
- "King Creole" – Elvis Presley
- "Give Peace a Chance" – John Lennon
- "Love Me" – Elvis Presley
- "Here I Go Again" – Whitesnake
- "A Little Old Fashioned Karma" – Willie Nelson
- "Tax Man" – The Beatles
- "Stop Complaining" – Lyrics Born
- "Santa Claus is Coming to Town" – Alvin and The Chipmunks
- "I'm a Worried Man" – Willie Nelson
- "Promised Land" – Elvis Presley
- "Don't Think Twice, It's All Right" – Elvis Presley
- "I'm No Superman" – Lazlo Bane

- "WKRP in Cincinnati" – Steve Carlisle
- "Welcome To The Jungle" – Guns N' Roses
- "Time" – Pink Floyd
- "Uncloudy Day" - Willie Nelson
- "Long Haired Redneck" - David Allan Coe
- "Another Pretty Country Song" – David Allan Coe
- "I Feel Good" – James Brown
- "Alright Now" – Free
- "Riverbank" – Brad Paisley
- "Shake It Off" – Taylor Swift
- "Lately I've Been Thinking Too Much Lately" – David Allan Coe
- "Good Times" – Willie Nelson
- "If I Only Had a Brain" – The Wizard of Oz
- "Even a Miracle Needs a Hand" – 'Twas The Night Before Christmas
- "New Morning" – Bob Dylan
- "Chattanooga Choo Choo" – Glenn Miller and The Modernaires
- "When I Die You Better Second Line" – Kermit Ruffins
- "A Kiss to Build a Dream On" – Louis Armstrong
- "Cowboy" – Kid Rock
- "Joy To The World" – Three Dog Night
- "Whiskey River" – Willie Nelson
- "I Want You, I Need You, I Love You" – Elvis Presley
- "Master of the House" – Les Miserables
- "Season of the Witch" – Dovonan
- "Twist and Shout" – The Beatles
- "Jailhouse Rock" – Elvis Presley
- "I Got You Babe" – Sonny and Cher
- "Not Everybody Likes Us" – Hank Williams III
- "Doctor Love" – KISS
- "Suspicious Minds" –Elvis Presley
- "Holiday Road "– Lindsey Buckingham
- "Summer Nights" – John Travolta and Olivia Newton-John
- "Straight Outta Compton" - N.W.A.
- "There's Always Tomorrow" – *Rudolph The Red-Nosed Reindeer*
- "Ramblin' Man" – The Allman Brothers
- "Can You Feel The Love Tonight" – Elton John
- "Mammas Don't Let Your Babies Grow Up To Be Cowboys" – Willie Nelson
- "The Ride" – David Allan Coe

- “Paid The Cost To Be The Boss” – James Brown
- “All The Soft Places” – Willie Nelson
- “Devil In a Sleeping Bag” – Willie Nelson

ABOUT THE AUTHOR

Dustin Pari works too much and sleeps too little. Everything he does is to help others, especially his daughter who is known affectionately as "Beans". Dustin takes his work seriously but not himself. He often travels with a small rubber hippo named "Little Boobie" that he keeps in his pocket so that he is never alone. He is fond of the colors green and orange. Lucky number: 15